Homewords
A Book of Tennessee Writers

Homewords

A Book of Tennessee Writers

DOUGLAS PASCHALL
editor

ALICE SWANSON
associate editor

TENNESSEE ARTS COMMISSION AND
THE UNIVERSITY OF TENNESSEE PRESS/KNOXVILLE

Copyright © 1986 by The University of Tennessee Press/Knoxville.
All Rights Reserved.
Manufactured in the United States of America.
First Edition.

Publication of this anthology was made possible with assistance from the Tennessee Arts Commission.

The paper used in this book meets the minimum requirements of the American National Standard for Permanence of Paper for Printed Library Materials, Z39.48-1984.
Binding materials have been chosen for durability.

Library of Congress Cataloging-in-Publication Data
Main entry under title.
Homewords: a book of Tennessee writers.
    1. American literature—Tennessee. 2. American literature—20th century. 3.Tennessee—Literary collections. I. Paschall, Douglas, 1944-
II. Swanson, Alice.
PS558.T2H65 1986   810'.8'09768   85-26394
ISBN 0-87049-494-5 (alk. paper)
ISBN 0-87049-495-3 (pbk. : alk. paper)

TENNESSEE ARTS COMMISSION

Mrs. Robert Barger, Mrs. James Boswell, (Mrs.) Nina Brock, (Mrs.) Jimmie Farris, Natalie Haslam, Larry Haynes, Ms. Tish Hooker, Ms. Ruth Johnson, Walter G. Knestrick, Hubert McCullough, Ms. Nellie McNeil, James R. Martin, Dr. Allison Nelson, David W. Newell, Mrs. Etherage J. Parker, Jr., Mrs. Eugene Pearson, Mrs. R. J. Schroeder, Mrs. Roy A. Stone, Mrs. Carl Storey, Phil Whitaker, (Mrs.) Pat Wiley, (Mrs.) Annabel Woodall

LITERARY ADVISORY PANEL

F. Lynne Bachleda, Alan Cheuse, Joan C. Elliott, Dorothy Foltz-Gray, Dr. Richard Jackson, Ms. Nellie McNeil, Bob Millard, Dr. R. B. Miller, Dr. Douglas Paschall, Cynthia Pitcock, Charlotte Schultz, (Mrs.) Pat Wiley

TENNESSEE ARTS COMMISSION STAFF

Libby Adcock, Brenda Kay Andrews, Victoria Boone, Rich Boyd, Dr. Roby Cogswell, Doris Culver, Eddith Dashiell, Patti Jones, Trudy Koetzner, Jane Ann Lyall, Linda Nichols, Brenda Nunn, Rod Reiner, Alice Swanson, Bennett Tarleton, Molly Teague, Renda Williams, Fran Wilson

All of those listed have served during all or a portion of the three-year period from the inception of this anthology through its completion.

Contents

EDITOR'S PREFACE	XIII
ANDREW LYTLE: Jericho, Jericho, Jericho	3
ROBERT PENN WARREN: Boyhood in Tobacco Country; Mortal Limit	13
EVA TOUSTER: On the Bravery and Presumption of Old Women	15
GEORGE SCARBROUGH: Root Cellar; The Window	17
SHELBY FOOTE: The Battle of Franklin	21
PETER TAYLOR: The Hand of Emmagene	34
WILMA DYKEMAN: Lydia McQueen; Explorations	52
ALEX HALEY: Home to Henning	63
JACK FARRIS: Fire Enough For You	72
PAUL RAMSEY: The River; A Walk on All Saints' Day	81
MADISON JONES: A Beginning	83
JOHN BOWERS: Crackers	90
JESSE HILL FORD: Fishes, Birds and Sons of Men	98
ROBERT DRAKE: A Christmas Visit	105
ELEANOR GLAZE: Those Were the Afternoon Rooms	109
ETHERIDGE KNIGHT: The Bones of My Father; One Day We Shall All Go Back	113
DAVID MADDEN: A Fever of Dying	116
CORMAC MCCARTHY: Instruments of Liberation	128
PHYLLIS TICKLE: Of Bulls and Angels; Of A Remembered Quiet; The Holy Innocents	144
JOHN EGERTON: Visions of Utopia	154
CHARLES WRIGHT: Driving Through Tennessee; Two Stories	164
JEANNE MCDONALD: Settlement	168
TOM T. HALL: Wet Stump	178
MARILOU AWIAKTA: Motheroot; Baring the Atom's Mother Heart	182
H. T. KIRBY-SMITH: Highland Rim	189

GORDON OSING: Dauphin Island; Ostinato	191
ROBERT HERRING: Hub	194
MALCOLM GLASS: To the River	204
JOHN OSIER: Ritual	207
ISHMAEL REED: Chattanooga	214
ROY NEIL GRAVES: Buffet Night at the Pizza House	218
ALAN CHEUSE: The Tennessee Waltz	219
RICHARD TILLINGHAST: Lost Cove & The Rose of San Antone; Sewanee in Ruins, Part V	229
HENRY SAMPLES: Home Cooking	234
DON JOHNSON: Grabbling	240
JEFF DANIEL MARION: Touchstone; Ebbing & Flowing Spring	242
JUDY ODOM: Sole Owners of the Mountain	244
ELIZABETH COX: The Minister's Daughter; The Wish for Sea-Birds	253
NIKKI GIOVANNI: 400 Mulvaney Street; Her Cruising Car: A Portrait of Two Small Town Girls	255
ROBERT MICHIE: Naming the Trees; Sunset Rock (in White County, Tennessee)	266
LISA ALTHER: Termites	268
JEANNE GUERRERO GORE: Drowning at Radnor Lake	272
RICHARD JACKSON: Greenwood; Someone Is Always Saying Something	273
MELISSA CANNON: The Dark of Eyes	275
JEANETTE BLAIR: Child Abuse; Background	277
JAMES SUMMERVILLE: Paper Fires	280
WYATT PRUNTY: The Distance into Place	289
STEVE STERN: Shimmele Fly-By-Night	292
DAVID SPICER: The Back Row; Leaving Things Behind	308
DANIEL FOLTZ-GRAY: Departed Coming Back	312
DOROTHY FOLTZ-GRAY: The Lucky Roofers; The Chasing Heart	322
SANDRA MOORE: Dove Shooting	325
BOB MILLARD: Giles	334
LEVI FRAZIER, JR.: In the Presence of Mine Enemies	336
WENDELL CARL MURRAY: Desire, and Other Topics	340
DON KECK DUPREE: Gross Anatomy; Perspectives in the Dark	350
ALLISON T. REED: Red-Bellied Woodpecker	353
LEIGH ALLISON WILSON: The Snipe Hunters	356
DAVID DANIEL: December Portrait	367
KIERNAN DAVIS: Roach Bait	369
DAVID HUNTLEY: Gerald at the Fair; The Making of Voice	371
MADISON SMARTT BELL: The Day I Shot My Dog	373
CONTRIBUTORS	378

Authors
in Alphabetical Order

LISA ALTHER: Termites	268
MARILOU AWIAKTA: Motheroot (poem);	
Baring the Atom's Mother Heart	182
MADISON SMARTT BELL: The Day I Shot My Dog	373
JEANETTE BLAIR: Child Abuse; Background (poems)	277
JOHN BOWERS: Crackers	90
MELISSA CANNON: The Dark of Eyes (poem)	275
ALAN CHEUSE: The Tennessee Waltz	219
ELIZABETH COX: The Minister's Daughter;	
The Wish for Sea-Birds (poems)	253
DAVID DANIEL: December Portrait (poem)	367
KIERNAN DAVIS: Roach Bait	369
ROBERT DRAKE: A Christmas Visit	105
DON KECK DUPREE: Gross Anatomy;	
Perspectives in the Dark (poems)	350
WILMA DYKEMAN: Lydia McQueen; Explorations	52
JOHN EGERTON: Visions of Utopia	154
JACK FARRIS: Fire Enough for You	72
DANIEL FOLTZ-GRAY: Departed Coming Back	312
DOROTHY FOLTZ-GRAY: The Lucky Roofers;	
The Chasing Heart (poems)	322
SHELBY FOOTE: The Battle of Franklin	21
JESSE HILL FORD: Fishes, Birds and Sons of Men	98
LEVI FRAZIER, JR.: In the Presence of Mine Enemies	336
NIKKI GIOVANNI: 400 Mulvaney Street; Her Cruising Car:	
A Portrait of Two Small Town Girls (poem)	255
MALCOLM GLASS: To the River (poem)	204
ELEANOR GLAZE: Those Were the Afternoon Rooms	109
JEANNE GUERRERO GORE: Drowning at Radnor Lake (poem)	272

Roy Neil Graves: Buffet Night at the Pizza House (poem)	218
Alex Haley: Home to Henning	63
Tom T. Hall: Wet Stump	178
Robert Herring: Hub	194
David Huntley: Gerald at the Fair; The Making of Voice (poems)	371
Richard Jackson: Greenwood; Someone Is Always Saying Something (poems)	273
Don Johnson: Grabbling (poem)	240
Madison Jones: A Beginning	83
H. T. Kirby-Smith: Highland Rim (poem)	189
Etheridge Knight: The Bones of My Father; One Day We Shall All Go Back (poems)	113
Andrew Lytle: Jericho, Jericho, Jericho	3
Cormac McCarthy: Instruments of Liberation	128
Jeanne P. McDonald: Settlement	168
David Madden: A Fever of Dying	116
Jeff Daniel Marion: Touchstone; Ebbing & Flowing Spring (poems)	242
Robert Michie: Naming the Trees; Sunset Rock (poems)	266
Bob Millard: Giles (poem)	334
Sandra Moore: Dove Shooting	325
Wendell Carl Murray: Desire, and Other Topics	340
Judy Odom: Sole Owners of the Mountain	244
John Osier: The Ritual	207
Gordon Osing: Dauphin Island; Ostinato (poems)	191
Wyatt Prunty: The Distance into Place (poem)	289
Paul Ramsey: The River; A Walk on All Saints' Day (poems)	81
Alison T. Reed: Red-Bellied Woodpecker (poem)	353
Ishmael Reed: Chattanooga (poem)	214
Henry Samples: Home Cooking	234
George Scarbrough: Root Cellar; The Window (For My Father) (poems)	17
David Spicer: The Back Row; Leaving Things Behind (poems)	308
Steve Stern: Shimmele Fly-By-Night	292
James Summerville: Paper Fires	280
Peter Taylor: The Hand of Emmagene	34
Phyllis Tickle: Of Bulls and Angels; Of A Remembered Quiet; The Holy Innocents	144
Richard Tillinghast: Lost Cove & The Rose of San Antone; Sewanee in Ruins, Part V (poems)	229

EVA TOUSTER: On the Bravery and Presumption of Old Women (poem) 15
ROBERT PENN WARREN: Boyhood in Tobacco Country;
                Mortal Limit (poems)   13
LEIGH ALLISON WILSON: The Snipe Hunters   356
CHARLES WRIGHT: Driving Through Tennessee;
                Two Stories (poems)   164

Editor's Preface

Homewords: A Book of Tennessee Writers has come about through the conjunction of two originally discrete events: the decision, first of all, by the Tennessee Arts Commission to fund a major literary project during 1985, to be carried out by its Literary Advisory Panel; and the developing plans to celebrate the special qualities and achievements of Tennesseans during "Homecoming '86."

The panel canvassed many of the state's writers to find out what kinds of projects they might find useful to them as writers. Although the responses were far from unanimous, the greater number favored the idea of sponsoring a publication—some means by which to get the names and works of Tennessee's writers before a wider public, especially within the state itself.

Readings, workshops, and conferences, as productive as these may sometimes be, are unavoidably ephemeral; what was needed, as several writers said, was something more nearly permanent and more widely accessible, something capable of reaching many readers over a relatively long time. Simultaneously, members of the Commission, its executive committee, and the literary panel began to see the need to make the literature of Tennessee a significant part of whatever "Homecoming" observances might eventually occur. Out of these two happily conjoined motives, then, grew a plan for the present collection.

That plan took shape under the pressure of the question: Do Tennesseans really know in the mid-1980s who their own writers are? We concluded that while a certain few names had wide currency—James Agee and Donald Davidson among general readers, John Crowe Ransom and Allen Tate among the more academic—the names with the greatest currency were of men no longer living, or of a very few living writers (Robert Penn Warren, Alex Haley, Peter Taylor, Wilma Dykeman) who could not, for all their distinction, begin to represent or account for the enormous range and vitality of the literature by and about Tennesseans.

Thus, given that the primary and indispensable act of taking possession of anything is to be able to "name" it, we thought that any proposed collection of Tennessee writing should undertake at a minimum to "name" a substantial number of authors whom our state's citizens ought to know. Nor, of course, could mere naming suffice: such a collection would also need to convey an impression of the quality and distinctiveness and "voice" of writing by Tennesseans.

In our attempt to be comprehensive as well as central in selection, we determined on these basic points: that our collection should be limited to authors of whatever age who are still actively at work as writers, that it should include little-known and even previously unpublished writers of genuine distinction as well as those with established national and regional reputations, and that so far as possible the works chosen should bear closely on the actual lives and differing cultures of Tennesseans.

In addition to soliciting new work and obtaining permissions from established writers, the panel opened the opportunity of contributing work for possible inclusion to all Tennessee writers. Part of the purpose of allowing open submissions was to stir up interest among writers in the state, and, incidentally but not unimportantly, to enable the literary panel to determine more precisely who Tennessee's writers presently are, where they live and work, and what kinds of writing they are doing. If only as a "literary project" with these special goals, involving writers and perhaps sustaining them in a sense of literary community, it would have to be counted an emphatic success.

We received more than 600 individual submissions (some 1,730 separate items) from 400 different writers. From within Tennessee, work came from a hundred different localities, representing every nook and cranny of the state; among writers with Tennessee connections living elsewhere, 22 different states were represented. Writers submitting work for consideration include men and women born before 1900 and teenagers not yet out of high school. In styles, genres, subject matter, in breadth of reach in relation to Tennessee's geography and cultures, and of course in literary quality, the work submitted varied greatly. But quality was in general unusually impressive; on the whole, it was serious, professional, engaging work, rarely without some feature making it special and meritorious.

What has ultimately been chosen for the collection are some 85 pieces from 62 different writers, who range in ages from eldest to youngest by nearly sixty years, and who in the variety and distinctiveness of their contributions, range at least as far. The book opens with a fine and characteristic story by Andrew Lytle, first published, appropriately enough, in 1936, exactly fifty years ago. It closes with poems and stories by talented writers in their middle twenties. Between these extremes there come works that establish, whatever else, significant lines of continuity between the "then" and the "now" in the literature of Tennessee.

The emphasis, however, falls on the "now." With very few exceptions, the works chosen are new, either not previously published at all or published only in journals of more or less obscurity, and not yet collected. (In several instances, preferred examples of writers' newest work were unavailable because of publishers' refusals to grant permission to reprint.) In the instances where works are not new or quite recent, they have been picked because they are characteristic of a writer's attention specifically to Tennessee, or because of some distinctive element, whether of style or setting, or authorial provenance, not otherwise represented.

Deciding just who qualifies as a "Tennessee writer" proved easier than had been imagined. Simply put, what we wished to include were writers for whom Tennessee is avowedly and unmistakably "home," whether in physical fact or in the strength of emotional and imaginative ties. Almost 80 percent of the writers here actually live in Tennessee; the ones who reside mostly or entirely elsewhere are virtually without exception writers such as Robert Penn Warren, Peter Taylor, Madison Jones, Cormac McCarthy, David Madden, Charles Wright, Nikki Giovanni, who have made Tennessee an indelible feature of their imaginative worlds.

Even with the most careful effort to represent adequately the range, variety, and distinctive quality of literature in Tennessee today, inevitably, given the bounds of a single volume, significant and worthy writers are omitted. Almost every reader, in fact, can expect to look here for some particular favorite author and be disappointed not to find the name. Although such readers may not be consoled by even the most earnest expression of editorial regret, some hope remains that they may subdue their disappointments by discovering here, not merely one or two new favorites, but a host of them.

The temptation to offer a survey or commentary on the works chosen must be resisted: it will be up to the reader to judge, in any event, the true character and worth of the collection. However, I believe it worth emphasizing both how variously these pieces speak of Tennessee settings and subjects, and how well. The state's topography, its history, its levels and kinds and peculiarities of language, above all its people in their attitudes and feelings, habits and mores, so strongly bound by the pull they feel to the home place, the home community, the family, are all here; and here, moreover, in precisely the rich and inimitable fashion that bespeaks Tennessee.

This anthology, then, has not been given its title unadvisedly or lightly. With no pretense or expectation that this can be *the* book of Tennessee writers, what is to be found in these pages are at least some of Tennessee's best "home words"—words resonant and redolent of home, words too that (as we say) strike home; and words that are certain to move us as readers, as well as to move us specifically as Tennesseans, irresistibly homewards: in the direction, and more deeply into the consciousness, of those places of the heart we call our homes.

Sewanee, Tennessee   Douglas Paschall
August, 1985

Acknowledgments

The Editor must thank in particular Nellie McNeil, as chairman of the Literary Advisory Panel but more crucially as former chairman of the Tennessee Arts Commission when the literary arts needed a strong champion, without whose efforts and support this project could never have been undertaken. Similarly, Bennett Tarleton, executive director, has sustained the project with solid encouragement, good advice, and superhuman patience; Alice Swanson, who as staff member responsible for literature became saddled with this labor without choice in the matter, was heroically indispensable to its completion. I would also thank Thomas McConnell, who served as an editorial assistant, and the University of the South, which provided work space and logistical support as a gift to the project.

Homewords
A Book of Tennessee Writers

Andrew Lytle

Jericho, Jericho, Jericho

She opened her eyes. She must have been asleep for hours or months. She could not reckon; she could only feel the steady silence of time. She had been Joshua and made it swing suspended in her room. Forever she had floated above the counterpane; between the tester and the counterpane she had floated until her hand, long and bony, its speckled dried skin drawing away from the bulging blue veins, had reached and drawn her body under the covers. And now she was resting, clear-headed and quiet, her thoughts clicking like a new-greased mower. All creation could not make her lift her thumb or cross it over her finger. She looked at the bed, the bed her mother had died in, the bed her children had been born in, her marriage bed, the bed the General had drenched with his blood. Here it stood where it had stood for seventy years, square and firm on the floor, wide enough for three people to lie comfortable in, if they didn't sleep restless; but not wide enough for her nor long enough when her conscience scorched the cool wrinkles in the sheets. The two footposts, octagonal-shaped and mounted by carved pieces that looked like absurd flowers, stood up to comfort her when the world began to crumble. Her eyes followed down the posts and along the basket-quilt. She had made it before her marriage to the General, only he wasn't a general then. He was a slight, tall young man with a rolling mustache and perfume in his hair. A many a time she had seen her young love's locks dripping with scented oil, down upon his collar . . . She had cut the squares for the baskets in January, and for stuffing had used the letters of old lovers, fragments of passion cut to warm her of a winter's night. The General would have his fun. *Miss Kate, I didn't sleep well last night. I heard Sam Buchanan make love to you out of that farthest basket. If I*

"Jericho, Jericho, Jericho" from *Stories: Alchemy and Others*, by Andrew Lytle (Sewanee: The University of the South, *1984*). Copyright © *1984* by Andrew Lytle. Reprinted by permission of the publisher.

hear him again, I mean to toss this piece of quilt in the fire. Then he would chuckle in his round, soft voice; reach under the covers and pull her over to his side of the bed. On a cold and frosting night he would sleep with his nose against her neck. His nose was so quick to turn cold, he said, and her neck was so warm. Sometimes her hair, the loose unruly strands at the nape, would tickle his nostrils and he would wake up with a sneeze. This had been so long ago, and there had been so many years of trouble and worry. Her eyes, as apart from her as the mirror on the bureau, rested upon the half-tester, upon the enormous button that caught the rose-colored canopy and shot its folds out like the rays of the morning sun. She could not see but she could feel the heavy cluster of mahogany grapes that tumbled from the center of the headboard—out of its vines curling down the sides it tumbled. How much longer would these never-picked grapes hang above her head? How much longer would she, rather, hang to the vine of this world, she who lay beneath as dry as any raisin. Then she remembered. She looked at the blinds. They were closed.

"You, Ants, where's my stick? I'm a great mind to break it over your trifling back."

"Awake? What a nice long nap you've had," said Doctor Ed.

"The boy? Where's my grandson? Has he come?"

"I'll say he's come. What do you mean taking to your bed like this? Do you realize, beautiful lady, that this is the first time I ever saw you in bed in my whole life? I believe you've taken to bed on purpose. I don't believe you want to see me."

"Go long, boy, with your foolishness."

That's all she could say, and she blushed as she said it—she blushing at the words of a snip of a boy, whom she had diapered a hundred times and had washed as he stood before the fire in the round tin tub, his little back swayed and his little belly sticking out in front, rosy from the scrubbing he had gotten. *Mammy, what for I've got a hole in my stummick; what for, Mammy?* Now he was sitting on the edge of the bed calling her beautiful lady, an old hag like her, beautiful lady. A good-looker the girls would call him, with his bold, careless face and his hands with their fine, long fingers. Soft, how soft they were, running over her rough, skinny bones. He looked a little like his grandpa, but somehow there was something missing . . .

"Well, boy, it took you a time to come home to see me die."

"Nonsense. Cousin Edwin, I wouldn't wait on a woman who had so little faith in my healing powers."

"There an't nothing strange about dying. But I an't in such an all-fired hurry. I've got a heap to tell you about before I go."

The boy leaned over and touched her gently. "Not even death would dispute you here, on Long Gourd, Mammy."

He was trying to put her at her ease in his carefree way. It was so obvious a pretending, but she loved him for it. There was something nice in its awkwardness, the charm of the young's blundering and of their efforts to get along in the world. Their pretty arrogance, their patronizing airs, their colossal unknowing of what was to come. It was a quenching drink to a sin-thirsty old woman. Somehow his vitality had got crossed in her blood and made a dry heart leap, her blood that was almost water. Soon now she would be all water, water and dust, lying in the burying ground between the cedar—and fire. She could smell her soul burning and see it. What a fire it would make below, dripping with sin, like a rag soaked in kerosene. But she had known what she was doing. And here was Long Gourd, all its fields intact, ready to be handed on, in better shape than when she took it over. Yes, she had known what she was doing. How long, she wondered, would his spirit hold up under the trials of planting, of cultivating, and of the gathering time, year in and year out—how would he hold up before so many springs and so many autumns. The thought of him giving orders, riding over the place, or rocking on the piazza, and a great pain would pin her heart to her backbone. She wanted him by her to train—there was so much for him to know: how the creek field was cold and must be planted late, and where the orchards would best hold their fruit, and where the frosts crept soonest—that now could never be. She turned her head—who was that woman, that strange woman standing by the bed as if she owned it, as if . . .

"This is Eva, Mammy."

"Eva?"

"We are going to be married."

"I wanted to come and see— to meet Dick's grandmother . . ."

I wanted to come see her die. That's what she meant. Why didn't she finish and say it out. She had come to lick her chops and see what she would enjoy. That's what she had come for, the lying little slut. The richest acres in Long Gourd valley, so rich hit'd make yer feet greasy to walk over'm, Saul Oberly at the first tollgate had told the peddler once, and the peddler had told it to her, knowing it would please and make her trade. *Before you die.* Well, why didn't you finish it out? You might as well. You've given yourself away.

Her fierce thoughts dried up the water in her eyes, tired and resting far back in their sockets. They burned like a smothered fire stirred up by the wind as they traveled over the woman who would lie in her bed, eat with her silver, and caress her flesh and blood. The woman's body was soft enough to melt and pour about him. She could see that; and her firm, round breasts, too firm and round for any good to come from them. And her lips, full and red, her eyes bright and cunning. The heavy hair crawled about her head to tangle the poor, foolish boy in its ropes.

She might have known he would do something foolish like this. He had a foolish mother. There warn't any way to avoid it. But look at her belly, small and no-count. There wasn't a muscle the size of a worm as she could see. And those hips—

And then she heard her voice: "What did you say her name was, son? Eva? Eva Callahan, I'm glad to meet you, Eva. Where'd your folks come from, Eva? I knew some Callahans who lived in the Goosepad settlement. They couldn't be any of your kin, could they?"

"Oh, no, indeed. My people . . ."

"Right clever people they were. And good farmers, too. Worked hard. Honest—that is, most of 'em. As honest as that run of people go. We always gave them a good name."

"My father and mother live in Birmingham. Have always lived there."

"Birmingham," she heard herself say with contempt. They could have lived there all their lives and still come from somewhere. I've got a mule older'n Birmingham. "What's your pa's name?"

"Her father is Mister E. L. Callahan, Mammy."

"First name not Elijah by any chance? Lige they called him."

"No. Elmore, Mammy."

"Old Mason Callahan had a son they called Lige. Somebody told me he moved to Elyton. So you think you're going to live with the boy here."

"We're to be married . . . that is, if Eva doesn't change her mind."

And she saw his arm slip possessively about the woman's waist. "Well, take care of him, young woman, or I'll come back and ha'nt you. I'll come back and claw your eyes out."

"I'll take very good care of him, Mrs. McCowan."

"I can see that." She could hear the threat in her voice, and Eva heard it.

"Young man," spoke up Doctor Edwin, "you should feel powerful set up, two such women pestering each other about you."

The boy kept an embarrassed silence.

"All of you get out now. I want to talk to him by himself. I've got a lot to say and precious little time to say it in. And he's mighty young and helpless and ignorant."

"Why, Mammy, you forget I'm a man now. Twenty-six. All teeth cut. Long trousers."

"It takes a heap more than pants to make a man. Throw open them blinds, Ants."

"Yes'm."

"You don't have to close the door so all-fired soft. Close it naturally. And you can tip about all you want to—later. I won't be hurried to the burying ground. And keep your head away from that door. What I've got to say to your new master is private."

"Listen at you, mistiss."

6

"You listen to me. That's all. No, wait. I had something else on my mind—what is it? Yes. How many hens has Melissy set? You don't know. Find out. A few of the old hens ought to be setting. Tell her to be careful to turn the turkey eggs every day. No, you bring them and set them under my bed. I'll make sure. We got a mighty pore hatch last year. You may go now. I'm plumb worn out, boy, worn out thinking for these people. It's that that worries a body down. But you'll know all about it in good time. Stand out there and let me look at you good. You don't let me see enough of you, and I almost forget how you look. Not really, you understand. Just a little. It's your own fault. I've got so much to trouble me that you, when you're not here, naturally slip back in my mind. But that's all over now. You are here to stay, and I'm here to go. There will always be Long Gourd, and there must always be a McCowan on it. I had hoped to have you by me for several years, but you would have your fling in town. I thought it best to clear your blood of it, but as God is hard, I can't see what you find to do in town. And now you've gone and gotten you a woman. Well, they all have to do it. But do you reckon you've picked the right one—you must forgive the frankness of an old lady who can see the bottom of her grave—I had in mind one of the Carlisle girls. The Carlisle place lies so handy to Long Gourd and would give me a landing on the river. Have you seen Anna Belle since she's grown to be a woman? I'm told there's not a better housekeeper in the valley."

"I'm sure Anna Belle is a fine girl. But Mammy, I love Eva."

"She'll wrinkle up on you, Son; and the only wrinkles land gets can be smoothed out by the harrow. And she looks sort of puny to me, Son. She's powerful small in the waist and walks about like she had worms."

"Gee, Mammy, you're not jealous are you? That waist is in style."

"You want to look for the right kind of style in a woman. Old Mrs. Penter Matchem had two daughters with just such waists, but 'twarnt natural. She would tie their corset strings to the bed posts and whip'm out with a buggy whip. The poor girls never drew a hearty breath. Just to please that old woman's vanity. She got paid in kind. It did something to Eliza's bowels and she died before she was twenty. The other one never had any children. She used to whip'm out until they cried. I never liked that woman. She thought a whip could do anything."

"Well, anyway, Eva's small waist wasn't made by any corset strings. She doesn't wear any."

"How do you know, sir?"

"Well . . . I . . . What a question for a respectable woman to ask."

"I'm not a respectable woman. No woman can be respectable and run four thousand acres of land. Well, you'll have it your own way. I suppose the safest place for a man to take his folly is to bed."

"Mammy!"

"You must be lenient with your Cousin George. He wanders about night times talking about the War. I put him off in the west wing where he won't keep people awake, but sometimes he gets in the yard and gives orders to his troops. 'I will sweep that hill, General'—and many's the time he's done it when the battle was doubtful—'I'll sweep it with my iron brooms'; then he shouts out his orders, and pretty soon the dogs commence to barking. But he's been a heap of company for me. You must see that your wife humors him. It won't be for long. He's mighty feeble."

"Eva's not my wife yet, Mammy."

"You won't be free much longer—the way she looks at you, like a hungry hound."

"I was just wondering," he said hurriedly. "I hate to talk about anything like this . . . "

"Everybody has a time to die, and I'll have no maudlin nonsense about mine."

"I was wondering about Cousin George . . . If I could get somebody to keep him. You see, it will be difficult in the winters. Eva will want to spend the winters in town . . ."

He paused, startled, before the great bulk of his grandmother rising from her pillows, and in the silence that frightened the air, his unfinished words hung suspended about them.

After a moment he asked if he should call the doctor.

It was some time before she could find words to speak.

"Get out of the room."

"Forgive me, Mammy. You must be tired."

"I'll send for you," sounded the dead voice in the still room, "when I want to see you again. I'll send for you and—the woman."

She watched the door close quietly on his neat square back. Her head whirled and turned like a flying jennet. She lowered and steadied it on the pillows. Four thousand acres of the richest land in the valley he would sell and squander on that slut, and he didn't even know it and there was no way to warn him. This terrifying thought rushed through her mind, and she felt the bed shake with her pain, while before the footboard the specter of an old sin rose up to mock her. How she had struggled to get this land and keep it together—through the War, the pleasanter after days. For eighty-seven years she had suffered and slept and planned and rested and had pleasure in this valley, seventy of it, almost a turning century, on this place; and now that she must leave it . . .

The things she had done to keep it together. No. The one thing . . . From the dusty stacks the musty odor drifted through the room, met the tobacco smoke over the long table piled high with records, reports. Iva Louise stood at one end, her hat clinging perilously to the heavy auburn hair, the hard blue eyes and the voice:

You promised Pa to look after me"—she had waited for the voice to break and scream—"and you have stolen my land!"

"Now, Miss Iva Louise," the lawyer dropped his empty eyes along the floor, "you don't mean . . ."

"Yes. I do mean it."

Her own voice had restored calm to the room: "I promised your pa his land would not be squandered."

"My husband won't squander my property. You just want it for yourself."

She cut through the scream with the sharp edge of her scorn: "What about that weakling's farm in Madison? Who pays the taxes now?"

The girl had no answer to that. Desperate, she faced the lawyer: "Is there no way, sir, I can get my land from the clutches of this unnatural woman?"

The man coughed; the red rim of his eyes watered with embarrassment. "I'm afraid," he cleared his throat, "you say you can't raise the money . . . I'm afraid—"

That trapped look as the girl turned away. It had come back to her, now trapped in her bed. As a swoon spreads, she felt the desperate terror of weakness, more desperate where there has been strength. Did the girl see right? Had she stolen the land because she wanted it?

Suddenly, like the popping of a thread in a loom, the struggles of the flesh stopped, and the years backed up and covered her thoughts like the spring freshet she had seen so many times creep over the dark soil. Not in order, but as if they were stragglers trying to catch up, the events of her life passed before her sight that had never been so clear. Sweeping over the mounds of her body rising beneath the quilts came the old familiar odors—the damp, strong, penetrating smell of new-turned ground; the rank, clinging, resistless odor of green-picked feathers stuffed in a pillow by Guinea Nell, thirty-odd years ago; tobacco on the mantel, clean and sharp like smelling salts; her father's sweat, sweet like stale oil; the powerful ammonia of manure turned over in a stall; curing hay in the wind; the polecat's stink on the night air, almost pleasant, a sort of commingled scent of all the animals, man and beast; the dry smell of dust under a rug; the over-strong scent of too-sweet fruit trees blooming; the inhospitable wet ashes of a dead fire in a poor white's cabin; black Rebecca in the kitchen; a wet hound steaming before a fire. There were other odors she could not identify, overwhelming her, making her weak, taking her body and drawing out of it a choking longing to hover over all that she must leave, the animals, the fences, the crops growing in the fields, the houses, the people in them . . .

It was early summer, and she was standing in the garden after dark—she had heard something after the small chickens. Mericy and Yellow Jane passed beyond the paling fence. Dark shadows—gay full voices. *Where you gwine, gal? I dunno. Jest a-gwine. Where you? To the frolic, do I live. Well, stay off'n yoe back tonight.* Then out of the rich, gushing laughter: *All right, you stay off'n yourn. I done caught de stumbles.* More laughter.

The face of Uncle Ike, head man in slavery days, rose up. A tall Senegalese, he was standing in the crib of the barn unmoved before the bush-whackers. *Nigger, whar is that gold hid? You better tell us, nigger. Down in the well; in the far-place. By God, you black son of a bitch, we'll roast ye alive if you air too contrary to tell. Now listen, ole nigger, Miss McCowan ain't nothen to you no more. You been set free. We'll give ye some of it, a whole sack. Come on, now*—out of the dribbling, leering mouth—*whar air it?* Ike's tall form loomed towards the shadows. In the lamp flame his forehead shone like the point, the core of night. He stood there with no word for answer. As she saw the few white beads of sweat on his forehead, she spoke.

She heard her voice reach through the dark—*I know your kind. In better days you'd slip around and set people's barns afire. You shirked the War to live off the old and weak. You don't spare me because I'm a woman. You'd shoot a woman quicker because she has the name of being frail. Well, I'm not frail, and my Navy Six an't frail. Ike, take their guns.* Ike moved and one of them raised his pistol arm. He dropped it, and the acrid smoke stung her nostrils. *Now, Ike, get the rest of their weapons. Their knives, too. One of us might turn our backs.*

On top of the shot she heard the soft pat of her servants' feet. White eyeballs shining through the cracks in the barn. Then: *Caesar Al, Zebedee, step in here and lend a hand to Ike.* By sun the people had gathered in the yard. Uneasy, silent, they watched her on the porch. She gave the word, and the whips cracked. The mules strained, trotted off, skittish and afraid, dragging the white naked bodies bouncing and cursing over the sod: *Turn us loose. We'll not bother ye no more, lady. You ain't no woman, you're a devil.* She turned and went into the house. It is strange how a woman gets hard when trouble comes a-gobbling after her people.

Worn from memory, she closed her eyes to stop the whirl, but closing her eyes did no good. She released the lids and did not resist. Brother Jack stood before her, handsome and shy, but ruined from his cradle by a cleft palate, until he came to live only in the fire of spirits. And she understood, so clear was life, down to the smallest things. She had often heard tell of this clarity that took a body whose time was spending on the earth. Poor Brother Jack, the gentlest of men, but because of his mark, made the butt and wit of the valley. She saw him leave for school, where he was sent to separate him from his drinking companions, to a church school where the boys buried their liquor in the ground and sipped it up through straws. His letters: *Dear Ma, quit offering so much advice and send me more money. You send barely enough to keep me from stealing.* His buggy wheels scraping the gravel, driving up as the first roosters crowed. *Katharine, Malcolm, I thought you might want to have a little conversation.* Conversation two hours before sun! And down she would come and let him in, and the General would get up, stir the fire, and they would sit down and smoke. Jack would drink and sing, *If the Little Brown Jug was mine, I'd be drunk all the time and I'd never be sob-er a-gin*—or, *Hog drovers, hog drovers, hog drovers we air, a-courting your darter so sweet and so fair.* They would sit and smoke and drink until she got up to ring the bell.

He stayed as long as the whiskey held out, growing more violent towards the end. She watered his bottles; begged whiskey to make camphor—*Gre't God, Sis Kate, do you sell camphor? I gave you a pint this morning.* Poor Brother Jack, killed in Breckinridge's charge at Murfreesboro, cut in two by a chain shot from an enemy gun. All night long she had sat up after the message came. His body scattered about a splintered black gum tree. She had seen that night, as if she had been on the field, the parties moving over the dark field hunting the wounded and dead. Clyde Bascom had fallen near Jack with a bad hurt. They were messmates. He had to tell somebody; and somehow she was the one he must talk to. The spectral lanterns, swinging towards the dirge of pain and the monotonous cries of *Water,* caught by the river dew on the before-morning air and held suspended over the fields in its acrid quilt. There death dripped to mildew the noisy throats . . . and all the while relief parties, moving, blots of night, sullenly moving in the viscous blackness.

Her eyes widened, and she looked across the foot posts into the room. There was some mistake, some cruel blunder; for there now, tipping about the carpet, hunting in her wardrobe, under the bed, blowing down the fire to its ashes until they glowed in their dryness, stalked the burial parties. They stepped out of the ashes in twos and threes, hunting, hunting, and shaking their heads. Whom were they searching for? Jack had long been buried. They moved more rapidly; looked angry. They crowded the room until she gasped for breath. One, gaunt and haggard, jumped on the foot of her bed; rose to the ceiling; gesticulated, argued in animated silence. He leaned forward; pressed his hand upon her leg. She tried to tell him to take it off. Cold and crushing heavy, it pressed her down to the bowels of the earth. Her lips trembled, but no sound came forth. Now the hand moved up to her stomach; and the haggard eyes looked gravely at her, alert, as if they were waiting for something. Her head turned giddy. She called to Dick, to Ants, to Doctor Ed; but the words struck her teeth and fell back in her throat. She concentrated on lifting the words, and the burial parties sadly shook their heads. Always the cries struck her teeth and fell back down. She strained to hear the silence they made.

At last from a great distance she thought she heard . . . *too late* . . . *too late*. How exquisite the sound, like a bell swinging without ringing. Suddenly it came to her. She was dying.

How slyly death slipped up on a body, like sleep moving over the vague boundary. How many times she had laid awake to trick the unconscious there. At last she would know . . . But she wasn't ready. She must first do something about Long Gourd. That slut must not eat it up. She would give it to the hands first. He must be brought to understand this. But the specters shook their heads. Well let them shake. She'd be damned all right, and she smiled at the meaning the word took on now. She gathered together all the particles of her will; the specters faded; and there about her were the anxious faces of kin and servants. Edwin had his hands under the cover feeling her legs. She made to raise her own hand to the boy. It did not go up. Her eyes wanted to roll upward and look behind her forehead, but she pinched them down and looked at her grandson.

"You want to say something, Mammy?"—she saw his lips move.

She had a plenty to say, but her tongue had somehow got glued to her lips. Truly it was now too late. Her will left her. Life withdrawing gathered like a frosty dew on her skin. The last breath blew gently past her nose. The dusty nostrils tingled. She felt a great sneeze coming. There was a roaring; the wind blew through her head once, and a great cotton field bent before it, growing and spreading, the bolls swelling as big as cotton sacks and bursting white as thunder-heads. From a distance, out of the far end of the field, under a sky so blue that it was painful-bright, voices came singing, *Joshua fit the battle of Jericho, Jericho, Jericho—Joshua fit the battle of Jericho, and the walls come a-tumbling down.*

Robert Penn Warren

Boyhood In Tobacco Country

All I can dream tonight is an autumn sunset,
Red as a hayrick burning. The groves,
Not yet leafless, are black against red, as though,
Leaf by leaf, they were hammered of bronze blackened
To timelessness. Far off, from the curing barns of tobacco,
Blue smoke, in pale streaking, clings
To the world's dim, undefinable bulge.

Far past slashed stubs, homeward or homeless, a black
Voice, deeper and bluer than sea-heart, sweeter
Than sadness or sorghum, utters the namelessness
Of life to the birth of a first star,
And again, I am walking a dust-silent, dusky lane, and try
To forget my own name and be part of the world.

I move in its timelessness. From the deep and premature midnight
Of woodland, I hear the first whip-o-will's
Precious grief, and my young heart,
As darkling I stand, yearns for a grief
To be worthy of that sound. Ah, fool! Meanwhile,
Arrogant, eastward, lifts the slow dawn of the harvest moon.

Enormous, smoky, smoldering, it stirs.
First visibly, then paling in retardation, it begins
The long climb zenithward to preside

"Boyhood in Tobacco Country" from *Being Here: Poetry 1977-1980*, by Robert Penn Warren. Copyright © 1980 by Robert Penn Warren. Reprinted by permission of Random House, Inc.

There whitely on what the year has wrought.
What have the years wrought? I walk the house.
Oh, grief! Oh, joy! Tonight
The same season's moon holds sky-height.

The dark roof hides the sky.

Mortal Limit

I saw the hawk ride updraft in the sunset over Wyoming.
It rose from coniferous darkness, past gray jags
Of mercilessness, past whiteness, into the gloaming
Of dream-spectral light above the last purity of snow-snags.

There—west—were the Tetons. Snow-peaks would soon be
In dark profile to break constellations. Beyond what height
Hangs now the black speck? Beyond what range will gold eyes see
New ranges rise to mark a last scrawl of light?

Or, having tasted that atmosphere's thinness, does it
Hang motionless in dying vision before
It knows it will accept the mortal limit,
And swing into the great circular downwardness that will restore

The breath of earth? Of rock? Of rot? Of other such
Items, and the darkness of whatever dream we clutch?

"Mortal Limit" from *New and Selected Poems 1923-1985*, by Robert Penn Warren. Copyright © 1985 by Robert Penn Warren. Reprinted by permission of Random House, Inc.

Eva Touster

On The Bravery and Presumption of Old Women

There's an affecting heaviness of breath
In the bravery and presumption
Of old women long aware
Death is not optional. They surprise us
At the larger celebrations
Incredibly mobile, defying nature:

How one will dance at her grandson's
Wedding, barrel torso bobbing
On spindle legs,
Modish wig in place,
High color in her lips
And lifted face;

How another, faithful for fifty years,
In modest heels, mauve polyester
With pearls for the occasion,
Dips and turns and guides
Her husband's paralytic shuffle
On their own "golden anniversary";

And how the family friend surviving
All her kin is always there
At every ritual gathering
To tell her daughter had been "high
In Hadassah" and pass the snapshot round
And say "if only she had lived . . ."

So, too, the widows at their morning
Windows, tatting in the stronger
Light: Emma, arthritic,
Who can no longer finger
A fiddle string, and well-bred
Helen, who cannot hook a bra.

And passionate Claire Claremont
In her gentle eighties questioned
After half a century
On that notorious household
In Switzerland and poets dead,
On Byron's convent child (and hers)—
This Claire a kind old lady in laces
Smiling and remembering love:

"Ah, but it was Shelley—
Always Shelley!"

George Scarbrough

Root Cellar

Opening inward
the door makes an angle
with the wall.
It's the angle
that interests me.
More than the tooth-
marked potato
always lying just inside
on the dirt floor.

I have only
to close the door
to banish the angle
and disencumber myself
of the salient problem,
pocked potato included.
It's a short way out
to the tunnel's end
where night snow falls
and things die in the cold.

I know enough to know
a straight angle shuts in
more than it shuts out
when it appertains
to root cellar doors,

"Root Cellar" and "The Window," by George Scarbrough from *New and Selected Poems/1977*. Copyright © 1977 by George Scarbrough. Reprinted by permission of Iris Press.

and a right angle runs
quickest to distance.

But the peaches stand
on sagging shelves
at the very back
of the earthen hole.
In webbed and powdered
Mason glass
they shine in rows
like faint heat lightning
filtered through clouds
from below the rim
of a hot, black world.

But it isn't summer.
Not by a month and a half.
Not by a frost and a freeze.
I've told you that already.

So I go tiptoeing in.

God, don't let
the wind move the door,
if it is the wind!
Let it be steady.
Neither increase
nor decrease
the degree of my trouble!

O I act like a thief
with my own wealth
in the prowling dark
and, apprehended, flee,
hooking the door
shut behind me
with a flying foot.

I never reach for the knob.
It might shake hands.
Never disturb the potato.
It might, God grant, be
the same one next time!

George Scarbrough

The jars come clean
in the beautiful snow.
And, one in each hand,
I traverse the dark white yard
into the houseglow,
carrying sliced yellow quarts
of harvest moon.

The Window
For My Father

Yesterday, you scoffed when
I asked you to come and see.
Do not come now. There is,

however, the same strange bird
with all inverted plumes
wandering up and down the waves

of green water that once was
our dry backyard. O, look!
Preening, like you, he struts

into small waves himself,
is only a blackish shiver on
the running green, flaring and

diminishing, until I move my
eye to the white eyehole a bubble
makes in the crazed glass:

minor flaw in a major:
egg-shaped spot of correction
where the yard grows dry

and still again, and the fantastic,
offset cock (black as a tame gallinule,
purple as ripe elderberries,

his odd, dark head twisted on
his divided neck until it hinges only
in the light of pure imagination)

marches again into perspective,
at the oval edge of diffraction
becoming a real god's bird: two

somber refractive cocks in one.
His neck straightens to his head,
his tail remains a coiled

clutch of wry, unmeeting arches:
alphabetic, serpentine charade
of feathery hisses:

shattered cornucopia of sable
lights under the split blue cedars
shoring the yard's half-sea.

He is so medially mismatched, so
artfully indisposed, so halfway crafty
in his shifting bias, even you

would condone him. But do not come.
Stay smiling where you are. There is room
for only one before this beveled

glass in our cabin of love.
This morning I believe you most
when you are most disbelieving.

I would not estrange you into
belief. Until the bubble breaks,
I am, reluctant sir, at home.

Shelby Foote

The Battle of Franklin

[General Hood] said, years later, looking back. "I hereupon decided, before the enemy would be able to reach his stronghold at Nashville, to make that same afternoon another and final effort to overtake and rout him, and drive him into the Harpeth River at Franklin." . . . But when the Army of Tennessee set out from its camps around Spring Hill that morning—three fourths of it, at any rate; Stephen Lee was marching from Columbia, a dozen miles to the south, with his other two divisions and the artillery and trains—its commander, nearly beside himself with rage at last night's bungling, seemed "wrathy as a rattlesnake" to one of his subordinates who were themselves engaged in a hot-tempered flurry of charges and countercharges as a result of Schofield's escape from the trap so carefully laid for his destruction. Down in the ranks, where mutual recrimination afforded less relief, the soldiers "felt chagrined and mortified," one afterwards remarked, "at the occurrence of the preceding day."

Yet this soon passed, at least as the dominant reaction, partly because of the weather, which had faired. "The weather was clear and beautiful" another infantryman wrote; "the cool air was warmed by the bright sunshine, and our forces were in fine condition." By way of added encouragement, the band from a Louisiana brigade, reported to be the army's best, fell out beside the turnpike and cut loose with a few rollicking numbers to cheer the marchers tramping past. "Each man felt a pride in wiping out the stain," the first soldier would recall, while the second added: "Their spirits were animated by encouraging orders from General Hood, who held out to them the prospect that at any moment he might call on them to deal the enemy a decisive blow."

This was as he had done before, on the march north from Florence,

"The Battle of Franklin" from *The Civil War: A Narrative—Red River To Appomattox*, Volume III, by Shelby Foote. Copyright © 1974 by Shelby Foote. Reprinted by permission of Random House, Inc.

and the spirit now was much as it had been then, when the promise was that the Federals were about to be outflanked. For the Tennesseans the campaign was literally a homecoming, but for all the army's veterans it was a glad return to fields of anticipated glory, when they and the war were young and hopes were high. Once more patriot-volunteers of a Second American Revolution, many of them barefoot in the snow, as their forebears had been at Valley Forge, they were hailed along the way as returned deliverers, fulfillers of the faded dream that victory waited on the banks of the Ohio, which was once again their goal. Gladdest of all these scenes of welcome had been the march from Mount Pleasant to Columbia, a region of old families whose mansions lined the pike and whose place of worship—tiny, high-roofed St. John's Church, ivy-clad and Gothic, where Bishop-General Polk had preached and his Episcopal kinsmen had their graves amid flowers and shrubbery fresh and green in bleak November—had so impressed Pat Cleburne, for one, that he checked his horse in passing and remarked that it was "almost worth dying for, to be buried in such a beautiful spot." Impromptu receptions and serenades greeted the returning heroes, and prayers of thanksgiving were offered in this and other churches along the way, especially in Pulaski and Columbia, where the Yankees had been thrown into retreat by the gray army's passage round their flank. Spring Hill too had been delivered, though at a heavy cost in Confederate mortification, which soon was transmuted into determination that the bluecoats, having escaped their pursuers twice, would not manage it still a third time unscathed. Accordingly, the seven gray divisions stepped out smartly up the Franklin Turnpike, preceded by Forrest's troopers. Hood was pleased, he later said, to find his army "metamorphosed, as it were, in one night . . . The feeling existed which sometimes induces men who have long been wedded to but one policy to look beyond the sphere of their own convictions, and, at least, be willing to make trial of another course of action." In other words, they now seemed ready to charge breastworks, if need be, and he was prepared to take them up on that.

Stewart led the march today, having overshot the mark the night before, and Cheatham followed, accompanied by Johnson's division from Lee's corps, which was three hours in the rear. A dozen miles to the north by 2 o'clock, the vanguard approached Winstead Hill, three miles short of Franklin. On its crest, astride the turnpike, a Union brigade was posted with a battery, apparently under instructions to delay the gray pursuit; but Hood, unwilling to waste time on a preliminary skirmish—perhaps designed by Schofield to give the rest of his army a chance to get away unharmed—swung Stewart's three divisions to the right, along Henpeck Lane, and kept the other four marching straight on up the pike. To avoid being outflanked, the bluecoats limbered their guns and fell back out of sight beyond the rim of the slope up which the head of Cheatham's column now was toiling. When the Tennesseans topped the rise they gave a roaring cheer at the sight of the Harpeth Valley spread before them, with the town of Franklin nestled in a northeastward bend of the river and the Federals intrenched in a bulging curve along its southern and western outskirts. Beyond the crest, on the forward slope of Winstead Hill, Hood turned off to the left of the road, and while his staff got busy setting up a command post, the one-legged general dismounted—painfully, as always, with the help of an orderly who passed him his crutches once he was afoot—and there, in the shade of an isolated linn tree, removed his binoculars from their case for a careful study of the position his adversary had chosen for making a stand.

Schofield had been there since dawn, nine hours ago, and by now had completed the organization of an all-round defense of his Franklin bridgehead, on the off chance that the Confederates would attempt to interfere with the crossing or the follow-up sprint for the Tennessee capital, eighteen miles away. He would have been well on his way there already, safely over the river and hard on the march up the Nashville Pike, except that when he arrived with his two lead divisions, under Jacob Cox and Brigadier General Thomas Ruger, he found that the turnpike bridge had been wrecked by the rising Harpeth and Thomas had failed to send the pontoons he had so urgently requested, two days ago at Columbia, after burning his own for lack of transportation. Placing Cox in charge, he told him to have the two XXIII Corps divisions dig in astride the Columbia Pike, his own on the left and Ruger's on the right, half a mile south of the town in their rear, while awaiting the arrival of the three IV Corps divisions, still on the march from Rutherford Creek and Spring Hill. By the time Stanley got there with Thomas Wood's and Brigadier General Nathan Kimball's divisions, around midmorning, the engineers had floored the railroad bridge with planks ripped from nearby houses and the wagon train had started crossing. Schofield ordered Kimball to dig in on a line to the right of Ruger, extending the works northward so that they touched the river below as well as above the town, and passed Wood's division, along with most of Stanley's artillery, across the clattering, newly-planked railway span to take position on the high far bank of the Harpeth, overlooking Franklin and the fields lying south of the long curve of intrenchments thrown up by the other three division. That way, Wood could move fast to assist Wilson's horsemen in dealing with rebel flankers on that side of the river, upstream or down, and Cox was braced for confronting a headlong assault, if that was what developed.

This last seemed highly unlikely, however, since Hood—with two of his nine divisions far in the rear, together with all but eight of his guns—had fewer than 30,000 troops on hand, including cavalry, while Schofield had well above that number—34,000 of all arms—stoutly intrenched for the most part and supported by 60-odd guns, nearly all of them able to pound anything that tried to cross the two-mile-deep plain that lay between the bristling outskirts of Franklin and the foot of Winstead Hill. Moreover, that deadly stretch of ground was not only about as level as a tabletop, it was also unobstructed. Originally there had been a small grove of locusts in front of Ruger's part of the line, but these had been felled for use as headlogs and abatis. Similarly, on the left, a thick-set hedge of Osage orange had been thinned to clear a field of fire for Cox, leaving only enough of the growth to provide a thorny palisade. There was one obstacle out front: two brigades from Wagner's division, intrenched in an advance position, half a mile down and astride the Columbia Pike, with instructions to remain in observation there unless Hood, when he came up, "showed a disposition to advance in force," in which case they were to retire within the lines and serve as a reserve for the three divisions now in their rear. Otherwise, one defender said, there was "not so much as a mullein stalk" to obstruct the aim of the infantry in the trenches or the cannoneers in emplacements they had selected and dug at their leisure, not yet knowing there could be little or no counterbattery fire, even if the rebels were so foolish as to provoke battle on a field so disadvantageous to them.

Wagner had arrived at noon with the last of the five divisions, weary from yesterday's Spring Hill fight, the all-night vigil behind his fence-rail breastworks, and this morning's hurried march as rear guard of the army. Leaving one brigade on Winstead Hill to serve as a lookout force, he put the other two in position as instructed, half a mile in front of the main line, and set them digging. While they dug, the rest of the troops, snug in their completed works, did what they could to make up for their loss of sleep on last night's march. From across the river, at high-sited Fort Granger—a bastioned earthwork, constructed more than a year ago for the protection of the two critical bridges over the Harpeth—Schofield looked south, beyond the bulge of his semi-circular line, and saw the brigade Wagner had left on lookout withdraw in good order down the hill and up the turnpike. He knew from this that the rebels must be close behind, for the brigade commander was Colonel Emerson Opdycke, a thirty-four-year-old Ohioan with a fiery reputation earned in most of the theater's major battles, from Shiloh, where he had been a captain, to Resaca, where he had been badly wounded, back in May, but recovered in time to lead the charge up Kennesaw six weeks later. Sure enough, soon after Opdycke's displacement, the first graybacks appeared on Winstead Hill. They gathered faster and began to flow, rather like lava, in heavy columns down the forward slope and around the east flank of the hill. Schofield watched with mounting excitement. It was now about

3 o'clock; all but the last of his 700 wagons had clattered across the railroad bridge and he had just issued orders for the rest of his men and guns to follow at 6 o'clock, shortly after dark, unless Hood attacked before sunset; which Schofield did not believe he would do, once he had seen what lay before him there along the northern margin of that naked plain.

He was mistaken. Three miles away, under the linn tree on the hillside to the south, Hood completed his study of the Federal dispositions, lowered his glasses, and announced to the subordinates who by now had clustered round him: "We will make the fight."

When he explained what he meant by "make the fight"—an allout frontal assault, within the hour—consternation followed hard upon doubt by his lieutenants that they had heard aright. They too had looked out over the proposed arena, and could scarcely believe their ears. Attack? here? headlong and practically gunless, against a foe not only superior in numbers but also intrenched on chosen ground and backed by the frown of more than sixty pieces of artillery? . . . For a time, only too aware of their commander's repeated scornful charge that they invariably flinched at Yankee breastworks, they held their tongues. Then Ben Cheatham broke the silence. "I do not like the looks of this fight," he said. "The enemy has an excellent position and is well fortified." Leaning on his crutches, his blond beard glinting in the sunlight, Hood replied that he preferred to strike the Federals here, where they had had only a short time to organize their defenses, rather than at Nashville, "where they have been strengthening themselves for three years."

Cheatham protested no more, having been reproached quite enough for one day. But Bedford Forrest—who was familiar with the region, including the location of usable fords over the Harpeth well this side of the enemy position, and who moreover had Hood's respect for his aggressive instincts—spoke out in support of his fellow Tennessean's assessment of the situation, though with a different application. He favored an attack, yet not a frontal one. "Give me one strong division of infantry with my cavalry," he urged, "and within two hours I can flank the Federals from their works." Hood afterwards reported that "the nature of the position was such as to render it inexpedient to attempt any further flanking movement." Just now, however, he expressed doubt that, for all their apparent confidence, the bluecoats would "stand strong pressure from the front. The show of force they are making is a feint in order to hold me back from a more vigorous pursuit."

This put an end to such unasked-for opposition as had been voiced. Hood's fame had begun when he broke Fitz-John Porter's center at Gaines Mill, back in Virginia thirty months ago, and he intended to do the same to Schofield here today. His final order, dismissing the informal council of war, was explicit as to how this was to be accomplished: "Drive the enemy from his position into the river at all hazards."

Stewart, who had rounded Winstead Hill on the approach march, would attack on the right, up the railroad and the Lewisburg Pike, which ran northwest along the near bank of the Harpeth; Loring's division was on that flank of the corps front, French's on the other, over toward the Columbia Pike, and Major General Edward Walthall's was posted astride the railroad in the center. Cleburne and Brown, of Cheatham's corps, would advance due north up both sides of the Columbia Pike, Cleburne on the right, adjoining French, with Bate on Brown's left, extending the line westward to the Carter's Creek Pike, which ran northeast. All three turnpikes converged on the outskirts of Franklin, half a mile in rear of the southward bulge of the Union works; Hood assumed that this configuration would serve to compact the mass, like a hand clenched gradually into a fist, by the time the attackers reached and struck the main blue line. Johnson's division remained in reserve behind the center, for rapid exploitation of any breakthrough right or left, and Forrest's horsemen would go forward on the flanks, near the river in both directions. At 3:45, one hour before sundown, Stewart and Cheatham sent word that their lines were formed and they were ready.

Hood could see them in panorama from his command post, the two corps in an attack formation well over a mile in width, their starcrossed flags hanging limp in the windless air of this last day in November, which was also to be the last in the lives of many who were about to follow those tattered symbols across the fields now in their front: six divisions, twenty brigades, just over one hundred regiments, containing in all some 18,000 infantry, with another 3500 in the four reserve brigades. Promptly Hood's order came down from Winstead Hill for them to go forward, and they did, stepping out as smartly as if they were passing in review; "a grand sight, such as would make a lifelong impression on the mind of any man who could see such a resistless, well-conducted charge," a Federal officer discerned from his post near the blue center, just under two miles across the way. "For the moment we were spellbound with admiration, although we knew that in a few brief moments, as soon as they reached firing distance, all that orderly grandeur would be changed to bleeding, writhing confusion."

It did not work out quite that way just yet. Opdycke, when he retired from the crest of Winstead Hill, had not stopped alongside the other two brigades of Wagner's division, intrenched half a mile in front of the main works, but continued his withdrawal up the turnpike to the designated reserve position in rear of a one-story brick residence owned by a family named Carter, less than a hundred yards inside the lines. Wagner had set up headquarters in a grove of trees beside the pike and just beyond the house, anticipating the arrival of the rest of his troops as soon as the gray host, now gathering two miles to the south, showed what his orders termed "a disposition to advance." Apparently he doubted that Hood would do so at all, after studying the field, or else he believed the preparations would take a lot more time than they actually did. In any case, the mass advance was well under way before the Ohio-born former Hoosier politician, whose view in that direction was blocked by the house and trees, even knew that it had begun. As a result, the two colonels left in charge out front not only delayed their withdrawal, they also chose to stand fast in their shallow works long enough to get off a couple of short-range volleys before retiring. This was to cost Wagner his command within the week, but it cost the men of those two brigades a great deal more today.

The gray line advanced steadily, preceded by scampering rabbits and whirring coveys of quail, flushed from the brush by the approach of close to 20,000 pairs of tramping feet. When they got within range, the outpost Federals gave them a rattling fusillade that served to check them for a moment; but not for long. Absorbing the shock, the men under Cleburne and Brown—old rivals, from the days when the latter's division was under Cheatham—came on with a rush and a yell, directly against the front and around the flanks of the two unfortunate brigades, both of which gave way in a sudden bolt for the security of the intrenchments half a mile in their rear. Too late; "Let's go into the works with them!" the attackers cried, and pressed the pursuit up the turnpike, clubbing and shooting the terrified bluecoats as they fled. "It seemed bullets never before hissed with such diabolical venom," a Union captain was to say, recalling too that the cries of the wounded, left to the mercy of the screaming graybacks when they fell, "had a pathetic note of despair I had never heard before." More than 700 were captured, hurt or unhurt, and the main-line defenders, dead ahead, were kept from firing at the pursuers by fear of hitting their comrades in the lead. A staff colonel observed, however, that there was little time for thought at this critical juncture. "The triumphant Confederates, now more like a wild, howling mob than an organized army, swept on to the very works, with hardly a check from any quarter. So fierce was the rush that a number of the fleeing soldiers—officers and men—dropped exhausted into the ditch, and lay there while the terrific contest ranged over their heads." Of these, the captain who had outrun the hissing bullets noted, "some were found [afterwards] with their thumbs chewed to a pulp. Their agony had been so great that they had stuck their thumbs in their mouths and bit on them to keep from bleating like calves."

That was the kind of battle it was, first for one side, then the other, combining the grisliest features of Pickett's Charge and Spotsylvania's Bloody Angle. Because they had sprinted the last half mile, and had a shorter distance to cover in reaching the southward bulge of the enemy line, Cleburne's and Brown's divisions struck and penetrated the Federal works before the units on their left or right came up to add weight to the effort. In close pursuit of the two fugitive brigades, they not only broke through along the turnpike, they also widened the gap by knocking a regiment loose from the intrenchments on each side and seized four guns still loaded with canister, which they turned on the enemy but could not fire because the battery horses had bolted with the primers in the ammunition chests. Suddenly then it was too late; the blue reserves were upon them, advancing through the smoke with bayonets flashing, and they were too blown from their race up the pike, too confused by their abrupt success, to stand long under the pounding of most of the two dozen guns Cox and Ruger had posted along this part of the line. They yielded sullenly, under savage attack from Opdycke, who had brought his brigade on the run from north of the Carter house, and fell back to find cover in front of the works they had crossed when they broke through. There they stayed, exchanging point-blank fire with the bluecoats on the other side of the ditch.

Stewart by then had come up on the right, where French made contact with Cleburne, but the other two divisions were roughly handled in their attempt to get to grips with the Union left. Approaching a deep railroad cut near the northward bend of the Harpeth, they found it under plunging fire from the guns massed in Fort Granger, and when they changed front to move around this trap they were struck on the flank by other batteries masked on the east bank of the river. Forrest drove these last away by sending Jackson's division across a nearby ford, but Wilson met this threat to Schofield's rear by throwing the rebel troopers back on the crossing and holding them there, under pressure from three times their number. Walthall and Loring meantime had rounded the railway cut and clawed their way through the Osage hedge, only to find themselves confronting an intrenched brigade equipped with repeating rifles that seemed to one observer "to blaze out a continuous sheet of destruction." Here the attackers had all they could do to hang on where they were, though some among them continued to try for a breakthrough: Brigadier General John Adams, for example, who was killed while attempting a mounted leap over the enemy works and whose body was found next morning alongside his horse, dead too, with its forefeet over the Federal palisade. Another of Loring's three brigade commanders, Brigadier General T. M. Scott, was gravely wounded, as was Brigadier General William Quarles of Walthall's division; both were out of the war for good, and in Quarles's brigade, so heavy was the toll of successive commanders, there presently was no surviving officer above the rank of captain. French's division, fighting near the center, also lost two of its three brigade leaders—Colonel

William Witherspoon, killed outright, and Brigadier General Francis Cockrell, severely wounded—bringing Stewart's loss to five of the nine brigade commanders in his corps, along with more than half of the colonels and majors who began the attack at the head of his nearly fifty regiments.

Cheatham's losses were heavier still, though they were comparatively light in Bate's division, which only had one of its three brigades engaged when it struck the enemy trenches at an angle; the other two drifted northward to mingle with Chalmers' horsemen beyond the Carter's Creek Pike, where they remained in observation, dodging longrange shots from guns on the Union right. Cleburne and Brown, however, still holding the works astride the Columbia Turnpike in the center, more than made up for any shortage of bloodshed on the Confederate left. The sun by now was behind the rim of Winstead Hill, and in point of fact, so far as its outcome was concerned, the battle was over: had been over, at least in that respect, ever since Opdycke's furious counter-assault stopped and shattered the initial penetration. All that remained was additional killing and maiming, which continued well into the night. "I never saw the dead lay near so thick. I saw them upon each other, dead and ghastly in the powder-dimmed starlight." Opdycke would report. Brown himself was out of the action, badly crippled by a shell, and so were all four of his brigadiers, beginning with G. W. Gordon, who had been captured in the side yard of the Carter house just as the breakthrough was turned back. John C. Carter, who succeeded Brown in command of the division, was mortally wounded shortly afterwards (he would die within ten days) and States Rights Gist and Otho Strahl were killed in the close-quarters struggle that ensued. "Boys, this will be short but desperate," Strahl had told his Tennesseans as they prepared to charge; which was half right. After the repulse he stood in the Federal ditch, passing loaded rifles up to the men on top, and when one of them asked if it might not be wise to withdraw, he replied: "Keep on firing." Then he fell.

The resultant desperation, unrelieved by the saving grace of brevity, was quite as bad as he had predicted for Brown's division, but the strain was even worse for the Arkansans, Mississippians, Alabamians, and Texans next in line, heightened as it was by dread uncertainty as to the fate of their commander. "I never saw men put in such a terrible position as Cleburne's division was," an opposing bluecoat was to say. "The wonder is that any of them escaped death or capture." All too many of them did not; Hiram Granbury had been killed at the head of his Texas brigade in the first assault, and fourteen of the twenty regimental commanders were to fall before the conflict slacked and died away. Meantime a disheartening rumor spread through the ranks that Cleburne was missing—Irish Pat Cleburne, of whom it was said: "Men seemed to be afraid to *be* afraid where he was." He had last been seen going forward in the attack, dismounted because two horses had been shot from under him in the course of the advance. "If we are to die, let us die like men," he told a subordinate, speaking with the brogue that came on him at such times and thickened as the excitement rose. When his second horse was killed by a shot from a cannon, he went ahead on foot through the smoke and din, waving his cap. The hope of his veterans, who idolized him, was that he had been wounded for the third time in the war, or even captured; but this hope collapsed next morning, when his body was found beside the Columbia Pike just short of the enemy works. A single bullet had gone through his heart. His boots had been stolen, along with his sword and watch and everything else of value on him. He was buried first near Franklin, then in St. John's churchyard, whose beauty he had admired on the march to his last fight, and finally, years later, back in Arkansas on a ridge overlooking Helena, his home town. His epitaph, as well as that of his division, was pronounced by his old corps commander, William Hardee, who wrote when he learned of his death: "Where this division defended, no odds broke its line; where it attacked, no numbers resisted its onslaught, save only once; and there is the grave of Cleburne."

High on his hillside two miles to the south, Hood knew even less about the progress of the battle than did the troops involved in the moiling, flame-stabbed confusion down below; which was little indeed. He had seen Cleburne and Brown go storming into the Union center, hard on the heels of Wagner's unfortunates, but what happened next was blanketed in smoke that hung heavy in the windless air and thickened as the firing mounted to a sustained crescendo. At 7 o'clock, an hour after full darkness cloaked the field, he committed his reserve division, and though Old Clubby's men attacked with desperation, stumbling over Cheatham's dead and wounded in the gloom, they only succeeded in adding Brigadier General Arthur Manigault's name to the list of a dozen brigade and division commanders who had fallen in the past three hours, as well as nine more regimental commanders, bringing the total to fifty-four; roughly half the number present. Of the twelve generals lost to the army here today, six were dead or dying, one was captured, and three of the remaining five were out of the war for good, while the other two, Brown and Cockrell, would not return for months. Down in the ranks, moreover, this dreadful ratio was approximated; 6252 Confederate veterans were casualties, including 1750 killed in action—as many as had died on either side in the two days of Shiloh or under McClellan throughout the Seven Days: more than had died under Rosecrans at Stones River, under Burnside at Fredericksburg, or under Hood himself in any of his three Atlanta sorties: almost as many, indeed, as Grant had had killed outright when he assaulted at Cold Harbor with three times as many men. Hood had wrecked his army, top to bottom, and the army knew it; or soon would. In the judgement of a Tennessee private who survived the wrecking, he had done so in the manner of a clumsy blacksmith, thinking "he would strike while the iron was hot, and while it could be hammered into shape . . . But he was like the fellow who took a piece of iron to the shop, intending to make him an ax. After working for some time, and failing, he concluded he would make him a wedge, and, failing in this, said: 'I'll make a skeow.' So he heats the iron red-hot and drops it in the slack tub, and it went s-k-e-o-w, bubble, bubble, s-k-e-o-w, bust."

Hood did not know this yet, however—and would not have been likely to admit it if he had; Howard's word 'indomitable' still fit. He watched unseeing while the battle continued to rage with the same fury, even though all the combatants had to aim at now was the flesh of each other's weapons. "Time after time they came up to the very works," a Union colonel afterwards said of the attackers, "but they never crossed them except as prisoners." Around 9 o'clock the uproar slacked. "Don't shoot, Yanks; for God Amighty's sake, don't shoot!" defenders heard pinned-down rebels implore from the smoky darkness just beyond their parapets. Within two more hours the contest sputtered into silence. Stephen Lee was up by then with his other two divisions and the army's guns, and Hood ordered the attack renewed at daybreak, preceded this time by a hundred-round bombardment. The batteries opened at first light, as directed, then ceased fire when word came back that there was nothing in the works ahead but Federal dead and wounded. Schofield had departed in the night.

That was really all the northern commander had wanted from the outset: a chance to get away, if Hood would only let him. Soon after his arrival the previous morning, on finding the turnpike bridge washed out and no pontoons on hand, he wired Nashville for instructions, and was told to defend the Harpeth crossing unless such an effort would require him "to risk too much." He responded: "I am satisfied that I have heretofore run too much risk in trying to hold Hood in check . . . Possibly I may be able to hold him here, but do not expect to be able to do so long." Thomas, busy gathering troops to man the capital defenses, then put a limit to his request, in hope that this would serve to stiffen his lieutenant's resistance to the scarcely deterred advance of the rebel column up through Middle Tennessee. "Do you think you can hold Hood at Franklin for three days longer? Answer, giving your views," he wired, and Schofield replied: "I do not believe I can." In point of fact, both question and answer by then were academic. He had already ordered a nighttime withdrawal and Hood had just appeared on Winstead Hill. "I think he can effect a crossing tomorrow, in spite of all my efforts," Schofield added, "and probably tonight, if he attempts it. A worse position than this for an inferior force can hardly be found. . . . I have no doubt Forrest will be in my rear tomorrow, or doing some greater mischief. It appears to me that I ought to take position at Brentwood at once."

Nevertheless—having no choice—he stayed and fought, and won. His casualties totaled 2326, about one third the number he inflicted, and of these more than half were from Wagner's division: just under a thousand killed or captured in the two-brigade rearward sprint up the pike and just over two hundred killed and wounded in the other brigade, when Opdycke saved the day with a counterassault that cost him five of his seven regimental commanders but netted him 394 prisoners and nine Confederate flags. Except for David Stanley, who took a bullet through the nape of his neck and had to be lugged off the field at the height of the melee, no Federal above the rank of colonel was on the list of casualties when Schofield evacuated Franklin between 11 o'clock and midnight, leaving his dead and his nonwalking wounded behind as he crossed the river and set fire to the planked-over bridge in his rear. The blue column reached Brentwood by daylight, halfway to Nashville, and by noon all five divisions were safe in the capital works, alongside the others Thomas had been assembling all this time.

Hood sent Forrest to snap at the heels of the retreating victors, but deferred pursuit by his infantry now in occupation of the field. "Today spent in burying the dead, caring for the wounded, and reorganizing the remains of our corps," a diarist on Cheatham's staff recorded. Never before had even these veterans looked on horror so compacted. In places, hard against the abandoned works, the slain lay in windrows, seven deep; so thick, indeed, that often there was no room for those on top to touch the ground. One of Strahl's four successors was so tightly wedged by corpses, it was noted, that "when he at last received the fatal shot, he did not wholly fall, but was found stiffened in death and partly upright, seeming still to command the ghastly line of his comrades lying beneath the parapet." Blue and gray, in a ratio of about one to five, the wounded soon filled all the houses in the town, as well as every room in the courthouse, schools, and churches. Meantime the burial details were at work, digging long shallow ditches into which the perforated ragdoll shapes were tossed and covered over with the spoil. Federals and Confederates were lodged in separate trenches, and the even greater disparity in their numbers—roughly one to eight—imparted a hollow sound to Hood's congratulatory order, read at the head of what was left of each regiment that afternoon. "While we lament the fall of many gallant officers and brave men," its final sentence ran, "we have shown to our countrymen that we can carry any position occupied by our enemy."

Perhaps the battle did show that; perhaps it also settled in Hood's mind, at last, the question of whether the Army of Tennessee would charge breastworks. But, if so, the demonstration had been made at so high a cost that, when it was over, the army was in no condition, either in body or in spirit, to repeat it. Paradoxically, in refuting the disparagement, the troops who fell confirmed it for the future. Nor was the horror limited to those who had been actively involved; Franklin's citizens now knew, almost as well as did the few survivors among the men they had sent away three years ago, the suffering that ensued once the issue swung to war. This was especially true of the Carter family, an old man and his two daughters who took shelter in their cellar, just in rear of the initial breakthrough point, while the fighting raged outside and overhead. Emerging next morning from their night of terror, they found the body of their son and brother, Captain Tod Carter of Brown's division, Cheatham's corps, lying almost on the doorstep he had come home to when he died.

Peter Taylor

The Hand of Emmagene

    After high school she had come down from Hortonsburg
To find work in Nashville.
She stayed at our house.
And she began at once to take classes
In a secretarial school.
As a matter of fact, she wasn't *right* out of high school.
She had remained at home two years, I think it was,
To nurse her old grandmother
Who was dying of Bright's disease.
So she was not just some giddy young country girl
With her head full of nonsense
About running around to Nashville night spots
Or even about getting married
And who knew nothing about what it was to work.

    From the very beginning we had in mind
—My wife and I did—
That she ought to know some boys
Her own age. That was one of our first thoughts.
She was a cousin of ours, you see—or of Nancy's.
And she was from Hortonsburg,
Which is the little country place
Thirty miles north of Nashville
Where Nancy and I grew up.
That's why we felt responsible
For her social life

"The Hand of Emmagene" from *In the Miro District and Other Stories*, by Peter Taylor. Copyright © 1977 by Peter Taylor. Reprinted by permission of Random House, Inc.

As much as for her general welfare.
We always do what we can, of course,
For our kin when they come to town—
Especially when they're living under our roof.
But instead of trying to entertain Emmagene
At the Club
Or by having people in to meet her,
Nancy felt
We should first find out what the girl's interests were.
We would take our cue from that.

   Well, what seemed to interest her most in the world
Was work. I've never seen anything quite like it.
In some ways, this seemed the oddest thing about her.
When she first arrived, she would be up at dawn,
Before her "Cousin Nan" or I had stirred,
Cleaning the house—we would smell floor wax
Before we opened our bedroom door some mornings—
Or doing little repair jobs
On the table linen or bed linen
Or on my shirts or even Nancy's underwear.
Often as not she would have finished
The polishing or cleaning she had taken upon herself to do
Before we came down. But she would be in the living room
Or sun parlor or den or dining room
Examining the objects of her exertions, admiring them,
Caressing them even—Nancy's glass collection
Or the Canton china on the sideboard.
One morning we found her with pencil and paper
Copying the little geometrical animals
From one of the oriental rugs.

   Or some mornings she would be down in the kitchen cooking
Before the servants arrived
(And of course she'd have the dishes she'd dirtied
All washed and put away again before the cook
Came in to fix breakfast). What she was making
Down there in the pre-dawn hours
Would be a cake or a pie for Nancy and me.
(She didn't eat sweets, herself.)
Its aroma would reach us
Before we were out of bed or just as we started down the stairs.
But whether cleaning or cooking,
She was silent as a mouse those mornings.

We heard nothing. There were only the smells
Before we came down. And after we came down there'd be
Just the sense of her contentment.

   It was different at night. The washing machine
Would be going in the basement till the wee hours,
Or sometimes the vacuum cleaner
Would be running upstairs before we came up
Or running downstairs after we thought
We'd put the house to bed.
(We used to ask each other and even ask her
What she thought the cook and houseman
Were meant to do. Sometimes now we ask ourselves
What *did* they do during the time that Emmagene was here.)
And when she learned how much we liked to have fires
In the living room and den, she would lay them
In the morning, after cleaning out the old ashes.
But at night we'd hear her out in the back yard
Splitting a fireplace log, trying to get lightwood
Or wielding the ax to make kindling
Out of old crates or odd pieces of lumber.
More than once I saw her out there in the moonlight
Raising the ax high above her head
And coming down with perfect accuracy
Upon an up-ended log or a balanced two-by-four.

   There would be those noises at night
And then we noticed sometimes the phone would ring.
One of us would answer it from bed,
And there would be no one there.
Or there would be a click
And then another click which we knew in all likelihood
Was on the downstairs extension.
One night I called her name into the phone—"Emmagene?"—
Before the second click came, just to see if she were there.
But Emmagene said nothing.
There simply came the second click.

   There were other times, too, when the phone rang
And there would be dead silence when we answered.
"Who is it?" I would say. "Who are you calling?"
Or Nancy would say, "To whom do you wish to speak?"
Each of us, meanwhile, looking across the room at Emmagene.
For we already had ideas then, about it. We had already

Noticed cars that crept by the house
When we three sat on the porch in the late spring.
A car would mosey by, going so slow we thought surely it
   would stop.
But if Nancy or I stood up
And looked out over the shrubbery toward the street,
Suddenly there would be a burst of speed.
The driver would even turn on a cut-out as he roared away.

   More than once the phone rang while we were at the supper table
On Sunday night. Emmagene always prepared that meal
And did up the dishes afterward since the servants were off
On Sunday night. And ate with us too, of course.
I suppose it goes without saying
She always ate at the table with us.
She rather made a point of that from the start.
Though it never would have occurred to us
For it to be otherwise.
You see, up in Hortonsburg
Her family and my wife's had been kin, of course,
But quite different sorts of people really.
Her folks had belonged to a hard-bitten fundamentalist sect
And Nancy's tended to be Cumberland Presbyterians
Or Congregationalists or Methodists, at worse
(Or Episcopalians, I suppose I might say "at best").
The fact was, Nancy's family—like my own—
Went usually to the nearest church, whatever it was.
Whereas Emmagene's traveled thirteen miles each Sunday morning
To a church in the hilly north end of the County,
A church of a denomination that seemed always
To be *changing* its name by the addition of some qualifying adjective.
Either that or seceding from one synod or joining another.
Or deciding just to go it alone
Because of some disputed point of scripture.

   Religion aside, however, there were differences of style.
And Emmagene—very clearly—had resolved
Or been instructed before leaving home
To brook no condescension on our part.
"We're putting you in the guest room," Nancy said
Upon her arrival. And quick as a flash Emmagene added:
"And we'll take meals together?"
"Why of course, why of course," Nancy said,
Placing an arm about Emmagene's shoulder.

"You'll have the place of honored guest at our table."

   Well, on Sunday nights it was more like we
Were the honored guests,
With the servants off, of course,
And with Emmagene electing to prepare our favorite
Country dishes for us, and serving everything up
Out in the pantry, where we always take that meal.
It was as though we were all back home in Hortonsburg.
But if the phone rang,
Emmagene was up from the table in a split second
(It might have been her own house we were in)
And answered the call on the wall phone in the kitchen.
I can see her now, and hear her, too.
She would say "Hello," and then just stand there, listening,
The receiver pressed to her ear, and saying nothing more at all.
At first, we didn't even ask her who it was.
We would only look at each other
And go back to our food—
As I've said, we were more like guests at her house
On Sunday night. And so we'd wait till later
To speak about it to each other.
We both supposed from the start
It was some boy friend of hers she was too timid to talk with
Before us. You see, we kept worrying
About her not having any boy friends
Or any girl friends, either.
We asked ourselves again and again
Who in our acquaintance we could introduce her to,
What nice Nashville boy we knew who would not mind
Her plainness or her obvious puritanical nature—
She didn't wear make-up, not even lipstick or powder,
And didn't do anything with her hair.
She wore dresses that were like maid's uniforms except
Without any white collars and cuffs.
Nancy and I got so we hesitated to take a drink
Or even smoke a cigarette
When she was present.
I soon began watching my language.

   I don't know how many times we saw her
Answer the phone like that or heard the clickings
On the phone upstairs. At last I told Nancy
She ought to tell the girl she was free

To invite whatever friends she had to come to the house.
Nancy said she would have to wait for the opportunity;
You didn't just come out with suggestions like that
To Emmagene.

   One Sunday night the phone rang in the kitchen.
Emmagene answered it, of course, and stood listening for a time.
Finally, very deliberately, as always,
She returned the little wall phone to its hook.
I felt her looking at us very directly
As she always did when she put down the phone.
This time Nancy didn't pretend
To be busy with her food.
"Who *was* that, Emmagene?" she asked
In a very polite, indifferent tone.
"Well, I'll tell you," the girl began
As though she had been waiting forever to be asked.
"It's some boy or other I knew up home.
Or *didn't* know." She made an ugly mouth and shrugged.
"That's who it always is," she added, "in case you *care* to know."
There was a too obvious irony
In the way she said "*care* to know."
As though we ought to have asked her long before this.
"That's who it is in the cars, too," she informed us—
Again, as though she had been waiting only too long for us to ask.
"When they're off work and have nothing better to do
They ring up or drive by
Just to make a nuisance of themselves."
"How many of them are there?" Nancy asked.
"There's quite some few of them," Emmagene said with emphasis.
"Well, Emmagene," I suddenly joined in.
"You ought to make your choice
And maybe ask one or two of them to come to the house
   to see you."
She looked at me with something like rage.
"They are not a good sort," she said. "They're a bad lot.
You wouldn't want them to set foot on your front steps.
Much less your front porch or in your house."

   I was glad it was all coming out in the open and said,
"They can't all be all bad. A girl has to be selective."
She stood looking at me for a moment
In a kind of silence only she could keep.
Then she went into the kitchen and came back

Offering us second helpings from the pot of greens.
And before I could say more,
She had changed the subject and was talking about the sermon
She had heard that morning, quoting with evangelistic fervor,
Quoting the preacher and quoting the Bible.
It was as if she were herself hearing all over again
All she had heard that very morning
At that church of hers somewhere way over on the far side
Of East Nashville. It was while she was going on
About that sermon that I began to wonder for the first time
How long Emmagene was going to stay here with us.
I found myself reflecting:
She hasn't got a job yet and she hasn't got a beau.

   It wasn't that I hadn't welcomed Emmagene
     as much as Nancy
And hadn't really liked having her in the house.
We're always having relatives from the country
Stay with us this way. If we had children
It might be different. This big house wouldn't
Seem so empty then. (I often think we keep the servants
We have, at a time when so few people have any servants at all,
Just because the servants help fill the house.)
Sometimes it's the old folks from Hortonsburg we have
When they're taking treatments
At the hospital or at one of the clinics.
Or it may be a wife
Who has to leave some trifling husband for a while.
(Usually the couples in Hortonsburg go back together.)
More often than not it's one of the really close kin
Or a friend we were in school with or who was in our wedding.
We got Emmagene
Because Nancy heard she was all alone
Since her Grandma died
And because Emmagene's mother
Before *she* died
Had been a practical nurse and had looked after Nancy's mother
In her last days. It was that sort of thing.
And it was no more than that.
But we could see from the first how much she loved
Being here in this house and loved Nancy's nice things.
That's what they all love, of course.
That's what's so satisfying about having them here,

Peter Taylor

Seeing how they appreciate living for a while
In a house like ours. But I don't guess
Any of them ever liked it better than Emmagene
Or tried harder to please both Nancy and me
And the servants, too. Often we would notice her
Even after she had been here for months
Just wandering from room to room
Allowing her rather large but delicately made hands
To move lightly over every piece of furniture she passed.
One felt that in the houses she knew around Hortonsburg
—In her mother's and grandmother's houses—
There had not been pretty things—not things she loved to fondle.
It was heartbreaking to see her the day she broke
A pretty pink china vase that Nancy had set out in a new place
In the sun parlor. The girl hadn't seen it before.
She took it up in her strong right hand
To examine it. Something startled her—
A noise outside, I think. Maybe it was a car going by,
Maybe one of those boys . . . Suddenly the vase crashed to the floor.
Emmagene looked down at the pieces, literally wringing her hands
As if she would wring them off, like chickens' necks if she could.
I was not there. Nancy told me about it later.
She said that though there was not a sign of a tear in the girl's eyes,
She had never before seen such a look of regret and guilt
In a human face. And what the girl said
Was even stranger. Nancy and I
Have mentioned it to each other many times since.
"I despise my hand for doing that," she wailed.
"I wish—I do wish I could punish it in some way.
I ought to see it don't do anything useful for a week."

   One night on the porch
When one of those boys went by in his car
At a snail's pace
And kept tapping lightly on his horn,
I said to Emmagene, "Why don't you stand up and wave to him,
Just for fun, just to see what happens? I don't imagine
They mean any harm."
"Oh, you don't know!" she said.
"They're a mean lot.
They're not like some nice Nashville boy
That you and Cousin Nan might know."
Nancy and I sat quiet after that,

As if some home truth had been served up to us.
It wasn't just that she didn't want to know
Those Hortonsburg boys.
She *wanted* to know Nashville boys
Of a kind we might introduce her to and approve of.
I began to see—and so did Nancy, the same moment—
That Emmagene had got ideas about herself
Which it wouldn't be possible for her to realize.
She not only liked our things. She liked our life.
She meant somehow to stay. And of course
It would never do. The differences were too deep.
That is to say, she had no notion of changing herself.
She was just as sure now
About what one did and didn't do
As she had been when she came.
She still dressed herself without any ornamentation
Or any taste at all. And would have called it a sin to do so.
Levity of any kind seemed an offense to her.
There was only one Book anyone need read.
Dancing and drinking and all that
Was beyond even thinking about.
And yet the kind of luxury we had in our house
Had touched her. She felt perfectly safe, perfectly good
With it. It was a bad situation
And we felt ourselves somewhat to blame.
Yet what else could we do
But help her try to find a life of her own?
That had been our good intention from the outset.

   I investigated those boys who did the ringing up
And the horn blowing. In Nashville you have ways
Of finding out who's in town from your home town.
It's about like being in Paris or Rome
And wanting to know who's there from the U.S.A.
You ask around among those who speak the home tongue.
And so I asked about those boys.
They were, I had to acknowledge, an untamed breed.
But, still, I said to Nancy, "Who's to tame 'em
If not someone like Emmagene? It's been going on
Up there in Horton County for, I'd say—well,
For a good many generations anyway."

   I don't know what got into us, Nancy and me.
We set about it more seriously, more in earnest,

Trying to get her to see something of those boys.
I'm not sure what got into us. Maybe it was seeing Emmagene
Working her fingers to the bone
—For no reason at all. There was no necessity.—
And loving everything about it so.
Heading out to secretarial school each morning,
Beating the pavements in search of a job all afternoon,
Then coming home here and setting jobs for herself
That kept her up half the night.
Suddenly our house seemed crowded with her in it.
Not just to us, but to the servants, too.
I heard the cook talking to her one night in the kitchen.
"You ought to see some young folks your own age.
You ought to have yourself a nice fellow."
"What nice young fellow would I know?" Emmagene asked softly.
"I'm not sure there is such a fellow—not that I would know."
"Listen to her!" said the cook. "Do you think we don't see
Those fellows that go riding past here?"
"They're trash!" Emmagene said. "And not one of them
That knows what a decent girl is like!"
"Listen to her!" said the cook.
"I hear her," said the houseman, "and you hear her.
But she don't hear us. She don't hear nobody but herself."
"Ain't nobody good enough for you?" the cook said.
"I'd like to meet some boy
Who lives around here," the poor girl said.
And to this the cook said indignantly,
"Don't git above your raisin', honey."
Emmagene said no more. It was the most
Any of us would ever hear her say on that subject.
Presently she left the kitchen.
And went up the back stairs to her room.

   Yet during this time she seemed happier than ever
To be with us. She even took to singing
While she dusted and cleaned. We'd hear
Familiar old hymns above the washer and the vacuum cleaner.
And such suppers as we got on Sunday night!
Why, she came up with country ham and hot sausage
That was simply not to be had in stores where Nancy traded.
And then she *did* find a job!
She finished her secretarial training
And she came up with a job

Nowhere else but in the very building
Where my own office is.
There was nothing for it
But for me to take her to work in my car in the morning
And bring her home at night.

   But there was a stranger coincidence than where her job was.
One of those boys from Hortonsburg turned out to run the
    elevator
In our building. Another of them brought up my car each night
In the parking garage. I hadn't noticed before
Who those young fellows were that always called me by name.
But then I noticed them speaking to her too
And calling her "Emmagene." I teased her about them a little
But not too much, I think. I knew to take it easy
And not spoil everything.

   Then one night the boy in the garage
When he was opening the car door for Emmagene, said,
"George over there wants you to let him carry you home."
This George was still another boy from Hortonsburg
(Not one that worked in my building or in the garage)
And he saluted me across the ramp.
"Why don't you ride with him, Emmagene?" I said.
I said it rather urgently, I suppose.
Then without another word, before Emmagene could climb in
    beside me,
The garage boy had slammed my car door.
And I pulled off, down the ramp—
With my tires screeching.

   At home, Nancy said I ought to have been ashamed.
But she only said it after an hour had passed
And Emmagene had not come in.
At last she did arrive, though
Just as we were finishing dinner.
We heard a car door slam outside.
We looked at each other and waited.
Finally Emmagene appeared in the dining-room doorway.
She looked at us questioningly,
First at Nancy's face, then at mine.
When she saw how pleased we were
She came right on in to her place at the table
And she sat down, said her blessing,

And proceeded to eat her supper as though nothing unusual had
   happened.

   She never rode to or from work with me again.
There was always somebody out there
In the side driveway, blowing for her in the morning
And somebody letting her out in the driveway at night.
For some reason she always made them let her out
Near the back door, as though it would be wrong
For them to let her out at the front.
And then she would come on inside the house the back way.

   She went out evenings sometimes, too,
Though always in answer to a horn's blowing in the driveway
And never, it seemed, by appointment.
She would come to the living-room door
And say to us she was going out for a little ride.
When we answered with our smiling countenances
She would linger a moment, as if to be sure
About what she read in our eyes
Or perhaps to relish what she could so clearly read.
Then she would be off.
And she would be home again within an hour or two.

   It actually seemed as if she were still happier with us now
Than before. And yet something was different too.
We both noticed it. The hymn singing stopped.
And—almost incredible as it seemed to us—
She developed a clumsiness, began tripping over things
About the house, doing a little damage here and there
In the kitchen. The cook complained
That she'd all but ruined the meat grinder,
Dropping it twice when she was unfastening it from the table.
She sharpened the wood ax on the knife sharpener—or tried to—
And bent the thing so the houseman insisted
We'd have to have another.
What seemed more carelessness than clumsiness
Was that she accidentally threw away
One of Nancy's good spoons, which the cook retrieved
From the garbage can. Nancy got so she would glance at me
As if to ask, "What will it be next?—poor child."
We noticed how nervous she was at the table,
How she would drop her fork on her plate—
As if she intended to smash the Haviland—

Or spill something on a clean place mat.
Her hands would tremble, and she would look at us
As though she thought we were going to reprimand her,
Or as if she hoped we would.
One day when she broke off the head of a little figurine
While dusting, she came to Nancy with the head
In one hand and the body in the other.
Her two hands were held so tense,
Clasping so tightly the ceramic pieces,
That blue veins stood out where they were usually
All creamy whiteness. Nancy's heart went out to her.
She seized the two hands in her own
And commenced massaging them
As if they were a child's, in from the snow.
She told the girl that the broken shepherd
Didn't matter at all,
That there was nothing we owned
That mattered *that* much.

   Meanwhile, the girl continued to get calls at night
On the telephone. She would speak a few syllables
Into the telephone now. Usually we couldn't make out what
   she was saying
And we tried not to hear. All I ever managed
To hear her say—despite my wish not to hear—
Were things like "Hush, George," or "Don't say such things."
Finally one night Nancy heard her say:
"I haven't got the kind of dress to wear to such a thing."

   That was all Nancy needed. She got it out of the girl
What the event was to be. And next morning
Nancy was downtown by the time the stores opened,
Buying Emmagene a sleeveless, backless evening gown.
It seemed for a time Nancy had wasted her money.
The girl said she wasn't going to go out anywhere
Dressed like that. "You don't think I'd put you in a dress
That wasn't proper to wear," said Nancy, giving it to her very
   straight.
"It isn't a matter of what you think
Is proper," Emmagene replied. "It's what he would think it meant—
George, and maybe some of the others, too."
They were in the guest room, where Emmagene was staying,
And now Nancy sat down on the twin bed opposite
The one where Emmagene was sitting, and facing her.

"This boy George doesn't really misbehave with you,
Does he, Emmagene?" Nancy asked her. "Because if he does,
Then you mustn't, after all, go out with him—
With him or with the others."
"You know I wouldn't let him do that, Cousin Nan," she said.
"Not really. Not the real thing, Cousin Nan."
"What do you mean?" Nancy asked in genuine bewilderment.
The girl looked down at her hands, which were folded in her lap.
"I mean, it's my hands he likes," she said.
And she quickly put both her hands behind her, out of sight.
"It's what they all like if they can't have it any other way."
And then she looked at Nancy the way she had looked
At both of us when we finally asked her who it was on the
    telephone,
As though she'd only been waiting for such questions.
And then, as before, she gave more
Than she had been asked for.
"Right from the start, it was the most disgusting kind of things
They all said to me on the telephone. And the language, the words.
You wouldn't have known the meaning, Cousin Nan."
When she had said this the girl stood up
As if to tell Nancy it was time she leave her alone.
And with hardly another word Nancy come on to our room.
She was so stunned she was half the night
Putting it across to me just what the girl had told her
Or had tried to tell her.

    Naturally, we thought we'd hear no more about the dress.
But, no, it was the very next night, after dinner,
That she came down to us in the living room
And showed herself to us in that dress Nancy had bought.
It can't properly be said she was wearing it,
But she had it on her like a nightgown,
As if she didn't have anything on under it.
And her feet in a pair of black leather pumps—
No make-up, of course, her hair pulled back as usual into a knot.
There was something about her, though, as she stood there
With her clean scrubbed face and her freshly washed hair
And in that attire so strange and unfamiliar to her
That made one see the kind of beauty she had,
For the first time. And somehow one knew what she was going
    to say.
"I'll be going out," she said, searching our faces

As she had got so she was always doing when she spoke to us.
Nancy rose and threw her needlework on the chair arm
And didn't try to stop it when it fell onto the floor.
Clearly, she too had perceived suddenly a certain beauty about
    the girl.
She went over to her at once and said,
"Emmagene, don't go out with George again.
It isn't wise," They stepped into the hall
With Nancy's arm about the girl's waist.
"I've got to go," Emmagene said.
And as she spoke a horn sounded in the driveway.
"George is no worse than the rest," she said.
"He's *better*. I've come to like things about him now."
There was more tapping on the horn,
Not loud but insistent.
"He's not the kind of fellow I'd have liked to like.
But I can't stop now. And you've gone and bought this dress."

   Nancy didn't seem to hear her. "You mustn't go," she said.
"I couldn't live through this evening.
I'd never forgive myself." The horn kept it up outside,
And the girl drew herself away from Nancy.
Planting herself in the middle of the hall
She gave us the first line of preaching we'd ever heard from her:
"It is not for us to forgive ourselves. God forgives us."
Nancy turned and appealed to me. When I stood up
The girl said defiantly, "Oh, I'm going!"
She was speaking to both of us. "You can't stop me now!"
The car horn had begun a sort of rat-a-tat-tat.
"That's what he's like," she said, nodding her head
Toward the driveway where he was tapping the horn.
"You can't stop me now!
I'm free, white, and twenty-one.
That's what *he* says about me."
Still the horn kept on,
And there was nothing we could think to say or do.
Nancy did say, "Well, you'll have to have a wrap.
You can't go out like that in this weather."
She called to the cook, who came running
(She must have been waiting just beyond the hall door to the
    kitchen)
And Nancy sent her to the closet on the landing
To fetch her velvet evening cape.

Peter Taylor

There was such a commotion
With the girl running out through the kitchen,
The cape about her shoulders and billowing out behind,
Almost knocking over the brass umbrella stand,
I felt the best thing I could do was to sit down again.
Nancy and the cook were whispering to each other
In the hall. I could see their lips moving
And then suddenly I heard the groan or scream
That came from the kitchen and could be heard
    all over the house.

  I went out through the dining room and the pantry
But the cook got there first by way of the back hall door.
The cook said she heard the back door slam.
I didn't hear it. Nancy said afterward she heard
The car door slam. We all heard the car roar down the driveway
In reverse gear. We heard the tires whining
As the car backed into the street and swung around
Into forward motion. None of that matters,
But that's the kind of thing you tend to recall later.
What we saw in the kitchen was the blood everywhere.
And the ax lying in the middle of the linoleum floor
With the smeary trail of blood it left
When she sent it flying. The houseman
Came up from the servants' bathroom in the basement
Just when the cook and I got there.
He came in through the back porch.
He saw what we saw of course
Except he saw more. I followed his eyes
As he looked down into that trash can at the end of the counter
And just inside the porch door. But he turned away
And ran out onto the back porch without lifting his eyes again.
And I could hear him being sick out there.

  The cook and I looked at each other
To see who would go first.
I knew I had to do it, of course.
I said, "You keep Miss Nancy out of here,"
And saw her go back into the hall.
I went over to the trash can,
Stepping over the ax and with no thought in my head
But that I must look. When I did look,
My first thought was, "Why, that's a human hand."
I suppose it was ten seconds or so before I was enough myself

To own it was Emmagene's hand
She had cut off with the wood ax.
I did just what you would expect.
I ran out into the driveway, seeing the blood every step,
And then back inside, past the houseman still retching over the banister,
And telephoned the police on the kitchen telephone.
They were there in no time.

   The boy who had been waiting for Emmagene
In the car, and making the racket with his horn
Used better judgment than a lot of people might have.
When she drew back the velvet cape and showed him
What she had done to herself
And then passed out on the seat,
He didn't hesitate, didn't think of bringing her back inside the house,
He lit out for the emergency room at the hospital.
Though she was dead when he got her there,
It is probably true
That if anything at all could have saved her
It was his quiet thinking that would have done it.
Anyhow, everybody congratulated the boy—
The police, and the doctors as well.
The police arrested him in the emergency waiting room,
But I went down to the station that night
And we had him free by nine o'clock next morning.
He was just a big country boy, really,
Without any notion of what he was into.
We looked after arrangements for Emmagene, of course,
And took the body up to Hortonsburg for burial.
The pastor from her church came to the town cemetery
And held a graveside service for her.
He and everybody else said a lot of consoling things to us.
They were kind in a way that only country people
Of their sort can be,
Reminding us of how hospitable we'd always been
To our kinfolks from up there
And saying Emmagene had always been
A queer sort of a girl, even before she left home.
Even that boy George's parents were at the service.
Nancy and I did our best to make them see
George wasn't to be blamed too much.
After all, you could tell from looking at his parents

Peter Taylor

He hadn't had many advantages.
He was a country boy who grew up kind of wild no doubt.
He had come down to Nashville looking for a job
And didn't have any responsible relatives here
To put restraints upon him
Or to give him the kind of advice he needed.
That might have made all the difference for such a boy,
Though of course it wasn't something you could say
To George's parents—
Not there at Emmagene's funeral, anyway.

Wilma Dykeman

Lydia McQueen

The wind was a wild dark thing plucking at the trees outside, pushing at the door and chinks of the house, then dying down still as death before another rise and rush and plunge. Listening to it, Lydia McQueen waited and shrank deeper under the quilts, until the corn shucks in the mattress rustled and settled into new shapes.

She thought about the wind—like the great fine horse Papa had owned once, strong and willful with no bit or stirrup that could tame it. Quiet for a spell, it would break with a sudden burst of energy and, as Papa said, "No man who walked in shoe leather could hold it then." Yet her father, a gentle man, had controlled the wildness in the horse as surely and invisibly as the sun controlled the plants in her mother's garden.

The wind came again and she felt the pleasure of her own body-warmth. Like a seed, she felt, one of those sun-warmed seeds in the spring ground, growing, ready to give forth new life. She was aware of the dry smell of the corn shucks. Her mind went back to the day she had sorted them, pulling the leaves off the hard stalk ends, working toward a soft stuffing for the mattress. She was making ready to be Mark's wife, to take this and a wagonload of other furnishings to her own home. It was a day last spring.

Spring was chancy, but she liked it best of all the seasons. One day would be still and soft with the sun flowing like honey along the hillsides, over the brown winter leaves and the tender green things peeping through, with time slow and the bees buzzing somewhere in the sunshine—forever, forever—and the next day fierce, with the wind tearing through the woods in gusts, shaking the last dry oak leaves, bending treetops, piercing every crevice of house and clothing with a bitter chill, and time rushing with

"Lydia McQueen" from *The Tall Woman*, by Wilma Dykeman. Copyright © 1980 by Wilma Dykeman. New York: Holt, Rinehart and Winston, 1962. Reissued by Wakestone Books, 1980. Reprinted by permission of Wakestone Books.

it down the valley.

"It's a fair morning," she had said to her mother as they worked out in the yard beside the corncrib, where the shucks had been stored through the winter.

"Ah, fair enough today, but dogwood winter yet to come," her mother had answered.

And after the cold spell, when dogwoods bloomed, there would be whippoorwill winter and blackberry winter. The reminder cut through joy the way her father's knife cut through the living flesh of some animal on the farm, draining and deadening it. She set her mouth and determined to be stingy with her words the rest of the morning—until she spied the first flock of robins down in the new-cleared field. Then she cried out in pleasure again for her mother to come and see the plump, neat birds, for Lydia Moore was eighteen, and chancy too, like March. Anger would not hoard in her long.

But, "You're a girl turned woman now," her mother said. "No need for such wispy ways. Anyway, I'm of a mind they won't last long around Mark McQueen."

Lydia thrust a cornhusk into the sack so sharply that one dry blade cut her middle finger. She knew her mother had wanted her to marry Ham Nelson. "Ah, Hamilton's a well-turned boy, and the Nelsons are good livers," she had said when he brought Lydia home once from a sociable at the Burkes'. And Lydia had replied, remembering all that Ham had told her as they rode home that night, "Could he buy himself for what he's worth, and sell himself for what he thinks he's worth, he'd be princely rich overnight."

But Sarah Moore had not smiled. Neither had she smiled when her daughter came to ask her if Mark McQueen could speak to Jesse Moore about their wedding. "With all the boys in the valley, Lydia, you must choose him?"

"Mama, I didn't choose."

But she had felt helpless to explain how it was since that first day she'd seen Mark at the mill, big and dark with the strength of a mountain in him as he helped James Burke grind the corn. From that moment there had been no peace in her. Everything was changed; what she had thought fair now became fairer, and the homely grew ugly beyond endurance. She ran when walking would do as well, sang to herself as she worked in the field because she was full of a strange confidence and beauty, and wept to herself behind the barn because she had so little confidence and was so lacking in prettiness. It was a time of days like spring, changeable and quick with life. She had no words to fit such feelings. "I didn't choose, Mama. It's like I was chosen."

Her mother looked at her then, steadily. Lydia could close her eyes now, this bleak winter night as she lay in bed alone, with the cabin small and empty around her and the great bare mountains outside, and remember precisely how her mother stood in the door of the corncrib, small, grave, brown hair streaked with grey drawn tightly back from her forehead and temples into a firm knot. For that moment it was as if Lydia saw her mother for the first time in many years. Her brown eyes were small, even in the small face whose delicacy had been only partly erased by years of hard work, but they were bright as minnows flashing in the brook. Her mouth's softness had almost disappeared behind a thin set line of determination. A fine web of wrinkles had settled around her eyes, across her high white forehead, along the once-smooth skin of her throat. When Sarah Moore looked directly and thoughtfully at someone, as she looked at Lydia now, she seemed to be gazing from some height or depth familiar only to herself. She wiped her hands on her apron in unconscious movements of nervousness, and spoke slowly.

"I've never held with craving women. Your papa can tell you that I never asked for more than he could give. But I have craved one thing: for you children to see better times than ours. Could I a-brushed every tangle-bramble and stumble-stone out of your way, I'd have crawled to do it ere this. Wanting you to like Hamilton Nelson, I only wanted you to find the work of life a little easier."

She gestured to forestall any interruption from Lydia. "Your grandmother came from Virginia. She moved down from the Tidewater, through the Valley, into these mountains, after she was wedded. I was her eldest, born in the Valley. I was the only one remembered the softness and sweetness of her before the mountains wore it away. I learned the costs of new country to a woman—and to a girl-child. I'm not saying it's a cost beyond paying, Lydia, or beyond the worth. I'm a mind to set you a choice. Nothing's ever taken, or given, doesn't have its price."

Lydia nodded, suddenly shy, embarrassed by the intimate words passing between them, more than in any single day or year of all their lives before. And still her mother was not finished. Driving straight ahead, like a plowman behind oxen, she spoke again, fingers still busy with her apron.

"Living won't be easy with Mark McQueen. He's a proud man, with a restlessness on him that will be hard to still. Maybe he's not a body ever to find contentment this side the grave. I couldn't say. But such a man's life can hurt his wife, be he ever so in love with her or not."

For a moment she was quiet, looking no longer at her daughter but at the distant woods. Lydia heard the first spring insects humming out in the fields, heard their tiny rustling in the dry cornhusks around her where the warm sun was stirring them to life. But all she saw in her mind's eye was Mark McQueen's face and his stout sun-browned arms.

"It may not seem so to you now, being a girl only and a girl in love," her mother went on, "but there's something beyond even love, for a woman as well as a man. A body's personhood."

Her mother's gaze came back from the woods to the yard and the house and the garden patch beyond, and Lydia did not know how to answer all this strange talk. The insects ticked and droned even louder around them.

"Your papa has gentle ways not common to many men. Not many here in the back country look for what they're seeking in books. But when your papa came from the Low Country, up into these mountains, and the load in the wagon had to be lightened, he threw out the household plunder and kept his box of books. Oh, he's cleared and planted and prospered enough to own his own land and decent home, but half his world has always been in his mind. He's never been a driven man. A man who is driven is not easy to live with."

The silence between them was longer than the words before Lydia said softly, "I never asked for easy, Mama."

"I know, I know." Her mother turned suddenly back to the crib and an armful of shucks. Her voice was muffled. "I'm beseeching the Lord to hold you in the hollow of his hand."

Lydia had told Mark her family would not interfere with their marriage. If he noticed that she could not say they were rousing happy over it, he made no sign.

Mark had spoken to her father. The older man was troubled by something larger than either of them. He asked, "And what about this war? What do you aim to do about it?"

Mark McQueen answered slowly, "I've heard it named a rich man's war and a poor man's fight. I don't feel strong one way or the other. If it comes to choosing, I reckon I'd have to stand by union."

"Well, Mark," Jesse Moore said, walking the length of the room and pulling his beard as he spoke, "if it's not making any greater difference to you than that, couldn't you see fit to go with me in the North Carolina troops? Since they've come to the pinch and are calling up the seed-corn young'uns and the old ones, too, I don't doubt I'll be going. But I can't turn against my state. The Yankees, even the President, got no right to tell us down here what to do. I couldn't fight against Zeb Vance and all my neighbors, and still I'd hate to think I was fighting my own son by marriage."

Mark's quiet face and dark eyes did not change. "I don't reckon I could fight for slavery," he said.

Lydia, listening in the next room, felt her stomach tighten with the sudden emotion of love for this tall, strong man and fear of the unknown stranger in him that could be so unyielding.

After a short silence he offered one brief explanation, with difficulty, as though his own past was something to be buried without words. "I worked for too many men when I was a chap, and after I come to manhood, I said no man ever again would own the strength of my muscles. That's my way of thinking: every man's stoutness belongs to himself."

"But that's for white. You can't set white and black alongside each other in worth—"

"I couldn't say about all that. I know they're men, no matter the color of the hide covering their muscle." There was a note of finality in Marks' voice. "I won't go to war unless it's a have-to. I've rented some fields from old man Nelson and I aim to make a home for Lydia and me. We'll move on land of our own as soon as I save money enough. That's all I come to name to you."

"Maybe the war will be over before we have to go separate ways," Jesse Moore said. He extended his hand to Mark. "If Lydia's chosen you, and you her, you're welcome to our family." He swallowed, still gripping the younger man's hand. "There's a passage in the Bible, you know, sets the value of a good woman beyond rubies. My oldest girl has always seemed something special to me, Mark McQueen."

Explorations

It is difficult to remember that the land we "own" has been bought at many prices, not all recorded in registered deeds.

"Murder is murder, whether committed by the villain skulking in the dark or by uniformed men stepping to the strains of martial musick. Murder is murder, and somebody must answer. Somebody must explain the streams of blood that flowed in the Indian Country in the summer of 1838. Somebody must explain the four thousand silent graves that mark the trail of the Cherokee to their exile."

This angry plea for knowledge of a disgraceful event in America's past, this anguished cry for an awakened conscience, is contained in a remarkable memoir that might well be included in many of our history books. Ownership of land (do we ever really "own" earth?) is almost always won in blood and human sacrifice. Our corner of the Appalachians is no exception.

Excerpts from *Explorations*, by Wilma Dykeman. Copyright © 1984 by Wilma Dykeman. Reprinted by permission of Wakestone Books.

On a winter day in 1890 John G. Burnett felt the need to share some memories with his children. Here are a few of his thoughts:

"This is my birthday December the 11th 1890. I am eighty years old today. I was born in Sullivan County, Tennessee. I grew into manhood fishing in Beaver-Creek and roaming through the forest hunting the deer, the wild boar and the timber wolf . . . On these long hunting trips I met and became acquainted with many of the Cherokee Indians, hunting with them by day and sleeping 'round their camp fires by night . . .

"The removal of the Cherokee Indians from their life long homes in the year 1838 found me a young man in the prime of life and a private soldier in the American army, being acquainted with many of the Indians and able fluently to speak their language I was sent as interpreter into the Smoky Mountain Country in May 1838 and witnessed the execution of the most brutal order in the History of American Warfare. I saw the helpless Cherokees arrested, dragged from their homes and driven at the bayonet point into the stockades, and in the chill of a drizzleing rain on an October morning I saw them loaded like cattle or sheep into six hundred and forty five wagons and started toward the West.

"One can never forget the sadness and solemnity of that morning. Chief John Ross led in prayer, and when the bugle sounded and the wagons started rolling, many of the children rose to their feet and waved their little hands good-bye to their mountain homes knowing they were leaving them forever. Many of these helpless people did not have blankets, and many of them had been driven from home barefooted. On the morning of November the 17th we encountered a terrifick sleet and snow storm with freezing temperature, and from that day untill we reached the end of the fateful journey on March the 26th 1839, the sufferings of the Cherokees were awful. The trail of the exiles was a trail of death. They had to sleep in the wagons and on the ground without fire, and I have known as many as twenty-two of them to die in one night of pneumonia due to ill treatment, cold and exposure . . .

"The only trouble that I had with anybody on the entire journey to the West was with a brutal teamster by the name of Ben McDonal who was useing his whip on an old feeble Cherokee to hasten him into the wagon. The sight of that old and nearly blind creature quivering under the lashes of a bull whip was too much for me . . . The little hatchet that I had carried in my hunting days was in my belt and McDonal was carried unconscious from the scene . . .

"In May 1838 an army of four thousand regulars and three thousand volunteer soldiers under Command of General Winfield Scott marched into the Indian Country and wrote the blackest chapter on the pages of American History. Men working in the fields were arrested and driven to the stockades. Women were dragged from their homes by soldiers whose language they could not understand . . . "When Scott invaded the Indian Country, some of the Cherokees fled to caves and dens in the mountains and were never captured, and they are there today . . .

"I wish I could forget it all, but the picture of those six hundred and forty five wagons lumbering over the frozen ground with their cargo of suffering humanity still lingers in my memory. Let the Historian of a future day tell the sad story with its sighs, its tears, and dieing groans - let the Great Judge of all the Earth weigh our actions and reward us according to our works.

"Children, thus ends my promised birthday story."

Private Burnett could not forget. Neither must we.

Beneath a sheltering rhododendron bush, beside a clear spring-fed pool, near a winding stream—at three different places around my mother's home near Asheville—the shortia is in bloom once more.

Shortia is one of our mountain plants so delicate and rare that not many natives and few strangers in Southern Appalachia have ever seen it. Like many of our people, it does not adapt well to transplantation. Like much of our history, its story is little known. A few years ago I gathered details of its initial discovery and loss by a European botanist. This season of its bloom seems an appropriate time for calling attention to its discovery—and rediscovery—even as this region and its people are "rediscovered" from time to time.

Shortia is a small perennial that grows close to the ground in damp, rich earth. Its glossy leaves bespeak its kinship to the larger galax. Its pure white flowers have five fringed petals and their bell shape has given them their popular name, "oconee bells."

One of the rarest flowers in our mountains, shortia is found in only a few counties in North and South Carolina and Georgia. Indeed, it was so infrequently encountered that for several generations it was known as the lost plant of the Southern Appalachians.

The French botanist, Andre Michaux, discovered shortia during his travels in the Blue Ridge in the 1780s. The eminent naturalist, Donald Culross Peattie, has described Michaux as he must have looked when he returned to the port of Charleston after one of his long expeditions into the unmapped wilderness: "At the head of a pack train laden down with hundreds of plants—packets of seeds, frail flowers in moss, and shrubs and young trees balled in earth, swaying and joggling to the gate of the garden, looking bewildered and unnatural in this lowland heat and glare."

As he took his specimens back to Europe, Michaux's colleagues studied and named each one. With a single exception. One little leaf and pod—a mere fragment—had no notation except that it was found "in the high mountains of Carolina."

Half a century passed. Then Dr. Asa Gray and John Torrey were in Paris preparing the monumental work, *A Flora of North America*, and they discovered Michaux's little plant. Declaring it a new genus they named shortia in honor of Dr. Charles Wilkins Short, a pioneer botanist of Kentucky.

As soon as he returned to America, in summer of 1840, Dr. Gray began a search for "the little shrub with scalloped leaves." For years he hunted in vain. At last he wrote, "I grew sorrowful at having named after Dr. Short a plant that nobody could find."

It was Charles Sprague Sargent of Massachusetts, who finally turned back to Michaux's original diary and sought out the wild and beautiful country of the Toxaway River. In the autumn of 1886, almost a century after its first discovery, shortia was rediscovered—in a region of "steep gabled high ridges drenched much of the time in rains, its plunging stream valleys perpetually shaded by dense rhododendron thickets."

A century later Peattie wrote of his own first sight of shortia. Walking through the heavy forest under a veil of rain "suddenly, right under my feet, spreading far as I could see under the rhododendron, growing on the steep bank, I behold the long-sought-for little flower, its frail sweet bells swinging under the first pelting of rain."

No wonder my mother cherishes the plants brought to her years ago by a friend, plants that responded to her careful nurturing.

The young mountain man told me of his prize as matter-of-factly as early hunters must have told of bagging passenger pigeons, as triumphant seamen must have told of harpooning great whales.

"We were on our way home from town one Saturday afternoon. You see, I work in a plant that's a pretty far piece from our home way back here on the mountain and I have to leave before daylight and get back just about dark five days a week, so there's no chance for us to go to the grocery store or anything except on a Saturday.

"Well, we had the two young'uns in the back of our '69 Chevy and we were heading home that Saturday afternoon and just before we come into that big curve on the new highway down there alongside the national forest my wife let out a scream worse than an old she-pant'er. I was just hitting the brakes when she yelled, 'I saw it! Laying right there in the woods in plain sight. I saw it!'

"I didn't bother with the brakes then, just went on around the curve while I asked her what she saw back in the woods that would make her yell like that and she said, 'It was a deer—a white deer! Laying there in an open place among the big old trees with the sun flecking down on it through the limbs and leaves. A plumb white deer.'

"Now I'd heard tell of such a creature. I understand the Cherokee

Indians used to have a regular hymn or chant or whatever you call it to the spirit of the white deer. But till that afternoon I reckon I'd thought of it all more as a big tale than anything else. But when my wife hollered out that way and told me about seeing—what is it they call it? an albino deer—right then I said to myself, 'This is it. Here's something way out of the common run, something strange.'

"So I told her and the young'uns—they were all excited and jumping around on the back seat—to quieten down and I drove on home as fast as I could. I unloaded the family. I carried in the groceries. Then I went in the back room and got my rifle.

"I drove back up the highway till I come to the open place in the woods beyond the big curve. I slowed and I stretched my eyes a-looking. Then all at once I saw it. The white deer was still laying down. But its head was high, alert, not a muscle moving.

"I understood why my wife had cried out the way she did. That whiteness amongst all the green with the evening sun dappling down on it, and the stillness everywhere, it gave off a queer sort of feeling.

"A little farther on, along the shoulder of the highway, I parked my car. When I killed the motor I tell you everything was really quiet. There didn't seem to be the usual traffic along that way just then and there wasn't even any wind stirring in the mountains. I could fairly hear myself breathing. I reached to the back seat and picked up my rifle and made sure for the second time that it was loaded.

"There wasn't any trick a-tall to taking that deer. When I eased through the woods to where I could take aim it was laying just like I'd seen it. I'd say it was still as a statue—but that would be exactly wrong because that deer was alive. The eyes. The ears. Even that satin-white skin seemed like it was breathing. If I'd studied that creature half a minute longer I'm doubtful I could have squeezed the trigger.

"My shot was a good direct hit. The deer didn't hardly get afoot and running before it fell. The blood sure soaked red against that white skin.

"I felt downright queer when I come up to that carcass and stood there along with a prize no man I actually knowed had ever seen before. It was like looking at a ghost spirit. Or something—you know, pure.

"It dressed out nice. We gave a lot of the meat to folks around here. The hide is in yonder right now—in that big old freezer. I don't know exactly what to do with it. But there must be something real special to do with a white deer hide."

I return from China as I return from all explorations large and small, with a fresh awareness of home. And renewed perceptions of the traveler's lot.

"A traveler must have a falcon's eye, a donkey's ears, an ape's face, a merchant's words, a camel's back, a hog's mouth, and a stag's legs."

So says an old English proverb.

There are people who keep a coffee pot at a constant boil, ready for any unexpected visitor. There are those who keep the television turned on throughout the day and evening, ready for each immediate announcement of crisis or disaster. And there are individuals who keep a suitcase in constant state of preparedness, ready for any opportunity of exploration. I am one of the latter.

I find excitement and knowledge in visiting a mountain cove only a few hours' distant from my home; I relish the wonder of knowing a land and its people on the other side of the globe. Abroad in my own backyard or "across the waters" I try to remember wise old Samuel Johnson's remark: "The use of traveling is to regulate imagination by reality, and, instead of thinking how things may be, to see them as they are."

Whether or not I have the qualifications for travel that are listed above in the animals' characteristics, I have discovered that there are certain essentials for successful wayfarers. Not everyone possesses a measure of wanderlust. (Perhaps this is just as well; otherwise the world might resemble one immense beehive with drones and workers and an occasional queen swarming constantly to and fro.) If you do not yearn to seek out new paths and highways, listen to strange tongues, become familiar with different ways of thought and living, and if you are not prepared to pay a price in time and energy and resources for this exploration, then home is for you and you can bear witness to Shakespeare's sentiment, "When I was at home, I was in a better place."

But if there is a bit of the vagabond in you and you are going thirty or thirty thousand miles from home, there are choices to be made. They can determine the success or failure of your journey.

First, do you go alone or with others? It is true, as one English essayist has observed, that "Traveling in the company of those we love is home in motion." But if those we love are not available for the journey we might also reflect on astute Thoreau's counsel: "The man who goes alone can start today, but he who travels with another must wait til that other is ready." There seems to be a trade-off here between loneliness and freedom. The choice is yours.

Second, do we ramble to discover familiar comforts in new settings or to encounter the unfamiliar, receive the stimulation of difference? Two centuries ago Lord Chesterfield wrote in a letter to his son, "Those who travel heedlessly from place to place, observing only their distance from each other, and attending only to their accommodation at the inn at night, set out fools, and will certainly return so." To choose: why and how we travel.

And what luggage do we choose: stout hearts as well as stout shoes?

Curiosity as well as toothpaste? A sense of humor as well as traveler's checks? Acceptance of happiness which must be carried from within before it will be discovered abroad?

Then there is Rediscovery of Home. An Italian proverb says: "Dry bread at home is better than roast meat abroad."

Englishwoman Frances Burney described a household inhabitant of 1782 who seems familiar in many households today. In one of her novels she wrote, "He seemed to consider his own home merely as an hotel, where at any hour of the night he might disturb the family to claim admittance, where letters and messages might be left for him; where he dined when no other dinner was offered him, and where, when he made an appointment, he was to be met with." Such a person's dwelling is merely a way-station between trips. It is not a home.

People of all countries have recorded in their folk sayings the true sense of what home means. A West African proverb asserts, "There is no home that is not twice as beautiful as the most beautiful city." And for the Spanish, "The smoke of a man's own house is better than the fire of his neighbors." An American saying shuns sentimentality but carries sentiment: "Even when you're looking for trouble, there's no place like home."

Sometimes travel brings us to a new home, a place more compatible than we have known before. But whether root-bound or foot-loose, it is the capacity for enjoyment that will make us whole.

Alex Haley

Home to Henning

Pete Gause had been one more among Henning's annual young black men who decided that graduating from grammar school was enough of education, and then he went and hired himself out as a fieldworker. He chopped, plowed and picked cotton until he had saved up $9.65, with which he went downtown to the train depot where he bought, in advance, a one-way, coach-class ticket to Chicago on the Illinois Central. Then Pete kept right on farming for 5½ days every week, and even took other weekend jobs. Finally he had saved $50, which some Henning people living in Chicago, who were back home visiting, had assured him was enough to see him eat and sleep long enough to find himself a job that would put him on his feet. And so one Sunday afternoon, Pete Gause, 18, filled with his dreams, caught himself a train, like many another before him, to get Up North and do good.

As was always the case when anyone went Up North, the community expectantly waited to share the first report back to relatives. But quite a number of weeks went by and Pete's mama, good church Sister Fannie Gause, was only able to tell her closest friends that she had heard from her boy nary one word as yet. Her friends relayed this all along The Lane, where most of Henning's black people lived, and added that they could tell that she was worrying about her Pete pretty hard.

Then one day Sister Fannie went happily popping by to visit just about everybody. She let them read for themselves Pete's hand-printed letter saying he'd found a restaurant dishwashing job, and the beaming Sister Fannie also showed the five-dollar bill that Pete had enclosed for his mama. Up and down The Lane after she'd left, the people commented how nice that was, especially considering how plenty of others, Up North long

Condensed from "Home to Henning." Copyright © 1983 by Kinte Corporation. Reprinted with permission from the April 1983 issue of *Reader's Digest*. Copyright © 1983 by Reader's Digest Association, Inc.

before Pete, were still writing, begging their homefolks to send money.

Then a long time passed without any particular community mention of Pete Gause. But that wasn't unusual. No one expected a family to report every letter or penny postal card. Years could go by without Henning getting any specific news about certain homefolk Up North—which turned out to be the case with Pete Gause.

The next hearing that Henning finally did get about Pete was a little bit upsetting. Someone returning to visit told different people that, yes, they'd seen Pete, still working in that restaurant but no longer washing dishes; he now wore a black suit and black-leather bow tie and carried a tray, waiting on the customers out front. The upsetting part of the report was that an intent of having just a little friendly homefolks chat with Pete had been met with his acting pretty stuck-up, as if he wanted very little to do anymore with folks he knew from back yonder.

The folks living along The Lane expressed no particularly strong feelings about that report, though. Most agreed that even if it was really so, then Pete would have added only one more to an already mile-long list of those who had gone Up North and gotten afflicted with "the bighead"—airs of sudden importance, and talking *so* proper, like glancing at somebody's hogs and saying "haags," or dogs and saying "daags."

Some years passed before the Henning people's next Pete Gause news—and it was really important and exciting! Pete had been so lucky as to be signed on as a dining-car waiter on the Illinois Central Railroad's Seminole, which ran round-trips between Chicago and Florida. It was a sister train of the Panama Limited, which twice a day seemed to just fly through Henning, bound north for Chicago, or south for New Orleans.

What really excited the people was their automatic mental picture of homeboy Pete all dressed up to the nines and walking about seating and serving the rich people eating in another of the I. C. line's finest dining cars—which nearly everyone had quickly glimpsed within the windows of the speeding Panama Limited. The white-uniformed waiters were always stepping about so dignified amid white-clothed tables with the gleaming china and crystal and silver, and the long-stemmed roses within their heavy silver vases. In fact, a whole lot of the Henning people couldn't resist sending up a secret little prayer that at some time in the future, the Lord in his goodness might even see Pete Gause reassigned onto the Panama Limited. Then Henning people would only need to go and stand anywhere downtown, looking up at the I. C. railroad tracks, and maybe actually catch a glimpse of Pete, and wave, as he'd go *whooshing* through his own hometown—and, Lord have mercy, wouldn't that be something!

After a while, though, even such big news as that receded. Only now and then would some new item be heard about Pete, for instance that he had married some lady born and raised right up there in Chicago. Sister

Fannie confided among her closest friends that she really felt sort of pitiful about it that she hadn't even seen her new daughter-in-law.

Sister Fannie Gause would still share with close friends the occasional picture postal card from Pete, or sometimes his one-page letter in a Seminole envelope that also would contain another five- or even ten-dollar bill. Generally, the very next day, Sister Fannie would sit down in her living room and spend four or five hours making her answer to Pete. She would spell out the words for herself, one by one, until each one sounded right, before she'd then print a word on her lined writing tablet, such as "Dere son, I jes hope I liv to see fin grone man you mus got to be." Sister Fannie told her friends that every reply she got from Pete only told her once again how his running on the railroad kept him so busy he just never seemed off long enough for coming back to Henning.

Then one July Monday washday morning, Sister Fannie hurried all aflutter among different people's houses on The Lane, showing everyone she could the letter just received from Pete. He was coming home to visit "befor this sumer over," although he didn't say exactly when.

Down the shining tracks stretching alongside Henning's small, brown-and-tan I. C. lines depot, the daily local from Memphis steamed in and stopped at the usual 11:18 on that hot August Friday morning. The few people of both races who happened to be anywhere downtown within eyeshot saw a tall, solidly built, dark-suited, black-homburged, brownskinned man starting down that coach's steps, and the black people watching instantly knew that was Pete Gause. But none of them rushed to the depot waving to him and calling out his name, as they would have normally greeted any other such recognized surprise arrivals, because they had all heard that he no longer cared to mix with homepeople.

As he walked toward the depot, he was plainly dignified just from the way he carried his black-leather suitcase. He turned on to the graveled pathway leading to the wooden depot steps. He wasn't halfway down when Brother Mose's sort of "teched-in-the-head" boy of 12, "Juniebug," took off toward The Lane like a cottontail rabbit with the hot news he had for Sister Fannie.

By then, all of the storekeepers had ambled outside. They stood talking whatever came to mind with the few other white folks downtown. From the corners of their eyes all of them were watching Pete Gause, at the same time trying their best to seem as if they were paying him no attention at all. But the black people had been moving about, seeking positions along his most likely route, all of them in hopes to inspect him at a closer range.

But Pete didn't slacken his pace. Looking neither to right, nor to left, nor behind him, he didn't see some of the black folk trailing him, so that in later discussions they could declare he never got out of their sight. He passed right through town and finally stepped onto the wide dirt Lane. Making a right turn, he saw Sister Fannie just as she also saw him—and came running with her arms stretched wide, her apron flapping, and she was crying. Everybody else who Juniebug had found at home along that part of The Lane was watching them hug each other, before they went on into Sister Fannie's little old gray-planked, rundown, four-roomed house.

Sister Fannie later on told her close friends what happened inside, and they told everybody else. She said that from the second the door shut, for them both it felt so awkward. She was beyond being happy to see her boy again, of course, but she just didn't know what to say, or do. There was such a difference between the Pete she'd last seen and the man she stood looking at, holding his homburg in one hand as his other set down his fine black-leather bag against a worn-through in her linoleum floor. She reached and took the hat and said, "Let me rest your coat."

She stepped into the bedroom and put the coat on a wire hanger and hung it on the nail behind the door. Coming back out of the bedroom, she told Pete that would be his room. And then she said she couldn't believe her ears, hearing him tell her he really was sorry, but he was going to have to catch that afternoon's five-o'clock local to get back to Chicago in time for his regular Seminole job the next morning.

Sister Fannie said her knees and legs, both, suddenly felt weak. She could accept how busy he was and all, but it was just not having seen him for all *that* long, plus all of her friends whom she'd faithfully promised at least a chance to say hello to him. She said she collected her wits somehow and gestured him to a chair, and they both sat down. Pete asked how was she, and everybody? "All right," she said she told him, so confused and heartsick about him leaving that same *day*, that then in sudden embarrassment she realized she hadn't even asked about his wife. Then she did, and all he said was "Fine."

There had to be *something* they could talk about, Sister Fannie said she thought. And she just started making her head give her some names of people there in Henning whom Pete couldn't help but remember, and telling him such things as that they'd married, and how many children they had by now, and especially among the older people, how some had suffered sicknessess and most had gotten well, but a few had died. And Pete, sitting there, listened.

Sister Fannie said then she talked some about how hard the Depression had hit both black and white, had hit just everybody, and how the money Pete had sent had helped her out a lot, every time.

She was thinking about what to say next when, Sister Fannie said, somehow it popped into her mind to ask, "Son, maybe you'd care for a cup of coffee or tea?" And Pete even smiled a little when he nodded and said, "Yes ma'am, I'd love some tea."

Sister Fannie practically jumped up, having something she could do with herself, and she stepped through her doorway's bleached flour-sack curtains hanging from a wire tacked across the door frame between her living room and her kitchen. Pushing a few fatty pine kindling sticks over the old embers from her breakfast-cooking fire, she reached up after her dried green tea leaves in her cupboard. Then, she said, she kind of half-turned about, sensing that her Pete must have entered through the curtains.

She said that she hadn't realized what a really big man Pete was, that he filled the door frame entirely. And right then she noticed how strangely Pete was looking down upon her old cast-iron black cook-stove. She first hoped that maybe he was remembering that stove's thousands of breakfasts, dinners, and suppers eaten by him and his brothers. And then she felt embarrassed that her stove looked so bad, its slightly parted oven door hanging by one hinge, its missing right front leg substituted by some thickish hickory firewood sticks, and the baling wire she had nailed onto the ceiling looped down and around the rusting stovepipes to stop them from sagging further.

Sister Fannie said she saw such a frightening expression suddenly come over Pete's face that her own mouth just popped open to ask, "Is something the matter?"

Pete took one step and there he was half-crouched before that stove; suddenly his long-sleeved arms and thick hands were gripping the stove's underside.

Sister Fannie said she just jumped backward, her hands flying to her mouth, her eyes popping, as Pete with a great grunt wrenched up that whole heavy cast-iron stove from that floor, the kindling crackling inside, and her water kettle, breakfast-eggs skillet and tin biscuit pan all tumbling and clattering against the floor. With another two wrenchings, to the left, then to the right, like he used to wrestle cotton bales, Pete tore that cookstove's top loose from the overhead stovepipes.

She said with the stove held waist-high and a little stream of ashes sifting down from the firebox, Pete turned toward her kitchen's back door. Then, maneuvering that iron stove through that doorway, with another mighty grunt Pete just heaved it forward and outward, and it smashed down against her little grassy-patched dirt back yard, the sounds of the crash and the iron cracking open sending her little spotted feist dog and her few any-breed chickens all yelping and squawking and flying.

Pete's face was dripping sweat, said Sister Fannie, as he said between loud, hard breaths, "Be right back." And with long, dignified steps, he headed back downtown.

There in the Henning Hardware and Supply Company, which was owned by Mr. Jim Alston, the combined janitor-deliveryman was Spunk Johnson. How Spunk later told it along The Lane was that he was back in the store's rear, sort of shoving around some empty wooden boxes, for even without any business going on, Mr. Alston would get unhappy unless he could hear some noises sounding like Spunk was doing some kind of work. Spunk said that he liked being back in there because he could also hear everything that went on up front.

Spunk said that suddenly Mr. Alston's voice was strangely high-pitched, asking somebody, "What can I do for you?" Spunk said he quit shoving boxes, listening sharply to find out who it was that made Mr. Alston sound so uncertain. Then hearing, "I'm interested in a cookstove," Spunk said he nearly fell over, recognizing that the black man speaking so dignified could be nobody else but Pete Gause.

Spunk said he quickly moved between some tall cardboard cartons to where he could peep around them safely, and there sure enough stood Pete Gause.

Spunk said Mr. Jim Alston, pointing to a display model, spoke next in the same strained tone. "Your people buy that one. Fifteen dollars and ninety-five cents."

Then Spunk heard Pete Gause. "Which is the best stove you've got?"

Mr. Alston hesitated. "Well, this one. See, this side tank here keeps five gallons of water hot. And that thermometer right there measures what heat's in that oven. And this warming oven, up top here."

"How much? Cash." Spunk heard Pete Gause ask it, and he saw Mr. Alston react as if he didn't believe it. Even the richest of Henning's white folks wanting anything real big like that would very seldom pay full cash on the spot.

"Sixty dollars. Fifty-eight cash," Mr. Alston said.

Spunk Johnson said it was the first time his eyes ever beheld any black man just sliding his right hand into his pocket and drawing out his wallet and counting six green ten-dollar bills into Mr. Jim Alston's hand.

Spunk said Mr. Alston's face had begun turning that excited white folks' bright-pinkish color. And then Pete Gause said, "Can it be delivered to my mother's home, up on The Lane, right away?"

"Sure can, right away!" And Mr. Alston hollered, "Spunk!"

Spunk said he acted like he had no idea what was going on.

Mr. Alston pointed. "I want this man's stove delivered to his house, right now!"

"Yessir," said Spunk, and then he said he realized he was looking right at the Pete Gause he grew up with. So Spunk said, "Glad to see you back. Hear tell you workin' with the railroad up yonder roun' Chicago."

Pete Gause said, "Yes, I am, and I appreciate you taking this stove up to my mama."

Spunk said it sounded so weird considering how he and Pete went to Henning's Colored Grammar School together, so he tried again, being homefolksy. "Why, shore. Sister Fannie maybe's tol' you, ain't many weeks pass either Lucy Mae or me or both us don't jes' drop by an' say hi'dy—you know, jes' see how she doin'."

"I appreciate that, and know mama does, too," said Pete Gause. "If you set up her stove for her, I'd be glad to pay whatever you'd charge."

"Oh, ain't nothin', be glad to," said Spunk.

Then Spunk said he went on out to hitch up the store's big bay mare to pull the open-bed delivery wagon. Within only a little over an hour, he had set up Sister Fannie's brand-new, fine cookstove, all ready for starting a fire in it and cooking somebody a good supper.

But, instead, about when Sister Fannie would have been cooking a supper, as she would so much have loved to be doing for Pete on the stove he'd bought that she felt was too beautiful and wonderful to describe, she was down at the Henning I. C. railroad depot, keeping up her best efforts to hide her crying from Pete, as she had been trying to hide ever since he had told her he was leaving so soon.

Since Pete's arrival that morning, enough word had circulated that although by far most poeple were out working in the fields, still a good number, especially older people, had gathered in front of the stores across the highway from the depot. They wanted at least a peep, if nothing else, just to be able later to say they had really seen Pete Gause who, after 15 years, came home and then left the same day. The black people stood out in the open along the sidewalk, while the white people mostly looked out from behind different stores' windowpanes or closed screened doors, so nobody could say that they had showed enough concern to go outside.

At about 4:45 p.m., the I. C. local's first whistling was heard, and the people watching from downtown across the highway saw Pete Gause turn quickly and tightly hug Sister Fannie, who they could tell clear across the highway was now out-and-out crying. Lifting his real-leather bag, Pete walked onto the coach for black passengers. Everyone watching now strained their eyes, scanning the windows of the coach. That was because practically all black people, once on board, would rush to the nearest of the windows facing town, leaning over passengers already seated, if necessary, and just wave and wave through the window's double-paned plate glass at the homefolks they were leaving. But Pete Gause never showed up at all. He must have just taken a seat on the opposite side and stayed there.

The big locomotive whistled two little toots, its deep *chuff-chuff-chuffing* began moving the train ahead, and gradually it gathered speed, heading out of town.

Around that Friday's sundown, the news spread so fast among the arriving fieldworkers that by night the whole town's talk was of nothing but Pete Gause. By breakfasttime on Saturday morning, members of the Ladies' Aid Society who were living closest went to offer a morning prayer with Sister Fannie for the Lord's goodness just to have let her raise such a child. Of course afterward she showed them her new cookstove, which later some folk said had been their real purpose in the first place.

Then, as usual for a Saturday morning, downtown Henning began growing busier and busier as more and more wagons and buggies kept entering the town square. They were all filled with outlying country folk, who looked forward all through every week to spending Saturdays among the big crowds in town. And it was a peculiar thing that most people, town or country alike, after they had heard what had happened, showed no interest at all in Sister Fannie's new stove. Instead, starting around that Saturday's noontime, then increasing steadily during the afternoon, usually by twos and threes, both town and country people quietly began walking away from the crowded, busy downtown. They would keep on going until they'd reach and turn right into The Lane.

The people would sort of cater-corner in an angling toward Sister Fannie's small, partly grassed front yard decorated with big cantaloupe-size, white-painted rocks arranged in a circle around her two worn-out tin washtubs of dirt holding her flowering plants. And then passing her small, oblong house, the people would reach her back yard and see the broken old stove there, as they had heard.

The people generally wouldn't walk very close to the old cookstove—they'd stand a few yards back, as if to get a fuller look. It lay all crunched down on one side, even seeming to be dug-in a little into the disturbed hard surface of the yard. A gaping split about four or five inches wide had nearly left the stove in two halves.

After a while, some of the people would abruptly say something, almost to themselves, as one man marveled softly, "He sho' throwed it!" and the people close to him nodded. Other people seemed unable to believe buying anything so costly without a saved-up down payment, then fifty cents a month forever, which made another man kind of breathe, "He come at 'leven, he lef' at five—Lord have mercy!"

Somewhere between 200 and 300 people must have come and looked at Sister Fannie's old cookstove within the next few weeks. Different Henning people, in discussions, agreed what a beautiful thing it was that a hometown man had come back and done that for his mama. And it was the first time, it was further agreed, that anybody off The Lane ever was able to go downtown and order the very best of something costing really big money, and then peel off green bills until the white storeman didn't even know how to act.

Alex Haley

For years to come, in fact, black people kept on walking up to see Sister Fannie's broken old stove. And the reason was that just looking at it gave the black people of Henning a mighty big feeling of pride.

Jack Farris

Fire Enough for You

A public hanging is something you don't never want to see and if you do you won't never forget it. That night the vigilantes captured and brought back to Virginia City seven road agents not counting Plummer, and four was killed besides Ray and Stinson because they wouldn't be took and was shot dead out at the way stations.

We brought Plummer into town around ten o'clock and they'd done built a rough gallows down by Pfouts store. Word had got out about the vigilantes and by noon there was more people in town than I ever seen before, people from the ranches and miners from Alder Gulch, men women and children, and they was laughing and carrying on like they'd come to a picnic.

When we come over the rise at the end of town people seen we had Plummer and they stood along the street gaping as we rode in and things got quiet and once Plummer yelled out, you people know who I am, I'm sheriff of Beaverhead County, these men have broke the law and they'll be brought to justice. But the people just stared and didn't say nothing. Then Plummer seen the gallows in front of Pfouts store, and I reckon that's the first time he'd thought about being hung. He changed his tune then and started begging for his life, talking to Gallagher, but Gallagher didn't look at him or say nothing.

Colonel Thompson was waiting up at Pfouts store and he said, what about Ray and Stinson? Gallagher said, dead. Then some men took Plummer to a feed room out back where a watch was being kept over the road agents and Plummer was yelling at the crowd, saying how he had kept peace in the territory for two years and done only what was right and how he was a god fearing man.

"Fire Enough for You," excerpt from *Me and Gallagher*, by Jack Farris. Copyright © 1982 by Jack Farris. Reprinted by permission of Simon & Schuster, Inc.

Then me and Gallagher went to the Stockade Cafe and eat the first meal we'd eat in awhile and after that we went back to the Grayland House to catch up on our sleep because Colonel Thompson said he'd send somebody to wake us before the hanging. I couldn't sleep so many things was going around in my head, the day we went out to Hanley's Creek and how Gallagher shot and killed Coyle and we brought Helm in, and the shooting over at Bannack and the ride back. Also maybe I was thinking about the hanging, and after awhile I said, you ever see a hanging before? But Gallagher was done asleep, so I laid there wide eyed till Litner came a little before sundown to wake us.

The people was gathered in the streets and on the tops of buildings and in the trees by the blacksmith shop, but there wasn't no laughing or yelling now.

The gallows was blood red in the sunset, and they led in the road agents single file, first Plummer then Bill Buntyn and Johnny Cooper and Frank Parish and Al Allen and three more whose names I don't remember. When the crowd seen them coming there wasn't a sound anywhere. The vigilantes was in charge and four or five stood facing the crowd, keeping them back aways, and there was a vigilante guarding each one of the agents.

The gallows was built simple. There was a platform and on it was eight empty crates and hanging from a beam above was eight hangman's nooses, with another beam behind to tie off the ropes. The road agents was led up on the platform and there was a noose hanging over each one of them and the vigilante guards stood behind, and the agents hands was tied behind their backs.

The crowd was still quiet, then I seen Colonel Thompson coming out of Pfouts store and behind him was Gallagher, and they went up on the platform and Colonel Thompson come forward and made it quick. He said, these men are being hung for the evil they done, it is right and proper that they pay for their crimes. It was Gallagher that went and put the nooses around the necks of the agents, and about then Plummer and Parish started yelling at the same time, Plummer was begging for his life in a pitiful voice, asking the crowd to have mercy on his soul, and Parish was saying things not fit for the women and children to hear, calling the vigilantes goddam murderers and sonsabitches and things worse than that. Allen stood looking out at the people with a smile on his face and died brave.

Gallagher was standing at one end of the platform with his hand up and the guards told the agents to stand on the crates and they done it. All except Parish who was still screaming, so Gallagher went over and him and the guard forced Parish to stand on the crate. Then Gallagher held up his hand again and when he brought it down the guards tightened the hanging ropes till the agents was stretched out, and their eyes was bugged out and Parish was still trying to yell but couldn't, and the guards went and kicked the crates out from under the agents and they was all hanging there twitching and jerking. Then somehow Bill Buntyn got one hand loose and got hold of the noose and took the pressure off the hanging rope, and Gallagher went over and pried his fingers from the rope and held his hand still till Buntyn hung limp in the last rays of the sun.

The last agent to die was Plummer. Then they was all hanging there not moving, swaying a little in the wind, their heads twisted to one side and their tongues hanging out of their mouths. It was the awfulist sight I ever seen or hope to see, and the crowd was quiet as the dead agents.

I looked over at Gallagher and his face under his black beaver hat was hard as granite stone and I don't know how he felt or what he was thinking.

The road agents was left hanging there with dusk coming in for all to see, and sometime during the night they was took down and put on a wagon and carried up the hill west of town to Boot Hill a quarter mile away.

Without a word being said over them they was put in the ground and left to rot for their crimes.

After the hanging me and Gallagher went up to Colonel Thompson's house and Mr. Pfouts was there and Judge Miller and eight or ten of the vigilantes. Colonel Thompson said word moved fast in the Territory, that we had to move in a hurry if we wanted to round up the other agents, but some was bound to get away. He had talked to Dick who was still being held out at his cabin, and had some idea where the other agents might be holed up. Two of them was named Pressly and Donahue who had been living at a shack out at Ruby River, and Gallagher said, me and the boy will ride out there, and Colonel Thompson said, all right, take Litner and Daniels with you, then he told the others where they would go and who to be looking for.

After a little Colonel Thompson said, there is still the problem of Bob Dick, and nobody said nothing for a minute. They was all watching Gallagher, and Gallagher said, hold him forty eight hours then let him go. It was quiet again, and Judge Miller said, it was Dick and Coyle that killed them people out at Deer Lodge, Dick ought to die for his crimes same as the others.

Gallagher give Judge Miller a straight look, and he said, no, I give him my word, forty eight hours we turn him loose, and Judge Miller said, we're dealing with a murderer, there ain't no question of honor with a man like that.

Gallagher said, it's my honor we're talking about.

So it was decided to wait forty eight hours when the other road agents would be captured or gone out of the Territory then let Dick ride.

Then me and Gallagher left and when we got to the porch somebody was standing in the shadows. It was Miss Sarah, and she said, is it over, Mr. Gallagher, is the killing and the hanging and the violence over?

Gallagher looked at her and didn't for a minute say nothing, then he said, no, there are others. Miss Sarah came across to where Gallagher was standing and she said, what happens to men who take the law in their own hands, men who kill in the name of righteousness, what happens to men like my brother, what goes on in the mind of a fifteen year old boy, what goes on in your mind, Mr. Gallagher?

Then Gallagher said, it's a dirty business, we all know that, the night in the back room of Kinna's store, after we took the oath, your brother said, we won't make no friends by what we're doing, however right our cause, even decent folks will turn against us before we're done, a home truth, lady, violence bitters the heart and blinds the judgment, turn a pack of hounds loose on a sheep-killing wolf there's folks will end up rooting for the wolf, there's some will say the vigilantes ain't no better than the road agents, worse maybe because they kill self-righteously and without no guilt, so much for human nature take it as it is. He was quiet a little, then he said, self-righteous, that's another man's word, maybe true because I don't feel no guilt and nothing troubles my sleep, I don't look on the movement as a cause, its something has to be done that's all, either vigilante law or no law atall, it comes to that, you don't reason with a clutch of rattlesnakes.

The longest speech I ever heard Gallagher make, and Miss Sarah said, I pity you all. Which I didn't know what she meant by that and maybe Gallagher didn't know either because he stood a minute not saying nothing then he turned and walked off in the dark. Then Miss Sarah said a strange thing to me, she said, when its all over will you come and talk to me? and I said, yes mam, and there wasn't nothing more to say so I left.

The shack out on Ruby River was about four miles out of town and it was around ten o'clock when me and Gallagher and Litner and Daniels got there. Me and Daniels stayed outside with our guns ready and Gallagher and Litner went to the door and Gallagher kicked it so hard it tore off its hinges, but nobody was there and hadn't been for two or three days, so we rode back to town without nothing to show for our trouble and Pressly and Donahue was never seen in the Territory again that I know of.

That night the vigilantes captured two more road agents named George Ives and Bill Tollet, and three more was shot dead, one at the Stinkingwater and two more out on Deadwood Creek. Ives and Tollet wasn't never hung, anyways not in Virginia City, because three of the vigilantes was told to take them to Denver and later it was said they was shot down on the trail. Which I can't say if that's true or not.

Two days later Bob Dick was turned loose and left the Territory and the rest of the road agents maybe six or seven high tailed it and the Vigilance Committee disbanded and began looking for a new sheriff of Beaverhead County. It didn't surprise me none that the man they wanted was Gallagher.

A week after the vigilantes disbanded me and Gallagher was still hanging around Virginia City. I didn't see nothing to keep us but Gallagher hadn't said nothing about moving on. Truth is I didn't see much of him those days. We was still staying at the Grayland House but he come and went at odd times and any talking we done wasn't about where we was going or when. Then I heard the talk, that they wanted him to be sheriff of Beaverhead County, and that caused me to be uneasy because I'd done had enough of that town to last me the rest of my days. Anyhow who the hell ever heard of a fifteen year old deputy.

Then something happened which is maybe why I'm writing this down. I was having a bite at the Blue Ox and Miss Sarah come by and seen me through the window, so she come in and come over and sat down and for a minute didn't say nothing, then she said, I thought you was coming to see me. I said, well I'd been pretty busy the last few days, and she said, will you come this afternoon? I couldn't think of nothing else to say so I said, yes mam.

So after I got done I went up to Colonel Thompson's house and Miss Sarah was waiting for me and we sit in the living room and I wished the hell I hadn't come because I didn't feel easy answering all them questions. She asked me where I come from and did I have any people and how I got hooked up with Gallagher. Then she talked about the vigilante movement and how there hadn't never been nothing like it before and maybe wouldn't never be again and how somebody would someday write about it and it would be a part of history. And I thought, it won't be nothing but words wrote on a piece of paper because you would a had to been there, then later after I left the Territory I would sometimes lay awake nights and I'd get to thinking about what Miss Sarah said, and I'd think, I seen it, seen it and lived it too, maybe it'll be me that writes it down.

Nothing was said for a little and I could hear the fire crackling. Then Miss Sarah got up and come over and sit beside me on the divan and she said it had troubled her me riding with the vigilantes, that violence done something to you that you didn't even know was happening, said I was too young to live that way and what I ought to do was settle down and finish my schooling, which I remembered Gallagher had said the same thing. It looked like I was getting more advice than I asked for. Anyhow I didn't say nothing because I didn't have my mind on no more schooling or settling down neither.

It was quiet again and it looked like we'd about run out of conversation. I could feel her watching me, and finally Miss Sarah said her and Colonel Thompson had been talking about it and they wanted me to come and live with them, and I thought, damn you, Gallagher, this is some of your doing.

I couldn't right off think of nothing to say, then I said, well, I'm obliged to you and Colonel Thompson but me and Gallagher will be riding out in a day or two.

She was quiet again, then she said, Wilbur and some of the others want Mr. Gallagher to be the sheriff, and I said, well he ain't said nothing to me about it. I felt her watching me but she didn't say nothing, so I said, I been with Gallagher seems like since long as I can remember, I learnt things from him I couldn't a learnt from nobody else, things about living and dying too. There was some other things I wanted to say but didn't know how to say them, maybe I'd done said too much, so I said, I reckon if Gallagher has in mind to take the sheriff's job, he would a said something to me about it.

After a little she said, well, you think about it, I just want you to be happy.

Sometimes I get to thinking about Miss Sarah and that talk we had at her house that day and what happened later on, and when I get this all wrote down and take care of one or two other things maybe I'll go back to Virginia City and look her up.

When it come time to decide what he aimed to do Gallagher and me talked about it like I knew we would.

The morning after I had the talk with Miss Sarah I woken early and Gallagher was standing at the basin on the table in the corner shaving and I laid there awhile watching him, bared to the waist his skin dark as a ripe buckeye, and after a little without looking at me he said, you awake? I said I was, and he said, I reckon you and me better have a talk. I said, that's fine with me.

So we got dressed and went down to the Miners Cafe and ordered some breakfast and didn't say nothing for awhile, then he said, they asked me to be sheriff of Beaverhead. I thought, here it comes, and I said, yeah, that's what I hear. He give me a level look and said, Colonel Thompson says him and his sister want you to live with them. I said, she said I could if I wanted to. He said, do you want to? and I said, no. He said, they're good people, and I said, I know, it ain't that, there's other things I want to do. He was still watching me and didn't say nothing, so I said, you aim to take that job? and he said, no.

He was quiet awhile looking out the front window, then talking slow he said, I reckon I've had enough playing lawman, after awhile it gets to you, turns you into something you don't want to be, you start out doing what has to be done and end up liking it, end up with a taste for violence you don't understand yourself. He didn't say nothing for a minute, then he said, man has to work things out piece by piece, about the worst enemy he's got is hisself.

Nothing was said for awhile and I wanted to ask him what he aimed to do but wanted him to say it first. After a little he said, remember the talk you and me had on the trail, about going back to California, maybe buying us some land? Something inside me come alive and I said, I remember, and he give me a slant look and said, you got any better ideas? I said, I reckon not, that's what I been thinking about ever since you brought it up, and he said, one thing we get straight now, we get settled out there you're going back to school. I said, you think I need more schooling I'm willing to give it a try, and he said, we'll look around, maybe hire on with a train heading that way.

So that's what we decided to do and if we had a left town that day I don't know where we'd be or what we'd be doing but we'd still be together. There ain't no way you can know what will happen and you have to take things the way they are and go on living which is something that's hard to understand.

But I'm still trying because like Gallagher once said, if you ain't learnt that you ain't learnt nothing.

The rest ain't something I want to remember but it also ain't something I can forget. It was a Sunday, a gray day with heavy overcast. Gallagher had signed us on with a train of miners leaving two days later, so after we'd eat breakfast we went to the livery stable and saddled our horses and rode down Alder Gulch a mile or so because Gallagher wanted to talk to a man named Halstead who was wagon master of the train we'd signed on with.

Except for the gray skies it started out to be the best day I'd seen since we come to that town. I said to Gallagher, we aim to run cattle when we get to California? Which is something I'd thought about since we joined that drive to Kansas. He said, cattle, sheep, whatever we can make a living at, and I said, well, it don't make me no difference, and he didn't say nothing so I said, one thing I know, I won't miss this town none. He give me a look and said, I reckon it ain't one we'll forget.

There was a few miners working Alder for gold but not many and after awhile we come to a wagon sit back a little ways from the creek and a big man with a long beard was standing at the back of the wagon hammering the tailgate together. He seen us riding up and put down his hammer and come over and Gallagher said, got troubles? Mr. Halstead said, just some patching up, and Gallagher said, this here is Grubber Graves, the boy I told you about. Mr. Halstead said, I seen him around, and he give me a long look and said, kind of young to be riding scout ain't he? and Gallagher said, old enough. Mr. Halstead said, well, if you say so, and he come over and held out his hand and we shook.

Then Gallagher asked how many wagons and people would be in the train and Mr. Halstead said six wagons and twenty five people, and Gallagher said, carrying gold? Mr. Halstead said none to speak of, they all come late and got poor claims, hadn't much more than made their keep. Then him and Gallagher talked about supplies they'd need and Mr. Halstead said some of the women was worried about Indians and Gallagher said the weather was more to worry about than Indians. Gallagher got back on his horse and said we'd be there Tuesday at daybreak, and Mr. Halstead said a strange thing, he said, all of us know you rode with the vigilantes, some seen you at the hanging. He didn't say nothing for a little then he said, I don't want you to take it personal but it come up at a meeting we had, I reckon there's a question I've got to ask you. For a minute he couldn't think how to ask it, then he said, Mr. Gallagher, are you a god fearing man? Gallagher thought about that for a little, then he said, I can't say as I am. Mr. Halstead said, well, it don't matter, it was just something come up when the women was talking.

We got back to town around eleven because the church bells was ringing up on Kimble Hill, which always made me think of granny and was she all right, not knowing she had died in her sleep the summer before.

Gallagher said he had some things to do so I stopped at the Blue Ox and got a cup of coffee and sit over by the window where I could see across the street Toby's Saloon and next to it the livery stable and farther down Mrs. Petrie's dress shop. After awhile I seen Gallagher ride over to the livery stable and take his mare inside and a little later he come out and walked across the street towards the Blue Ox, and I seen he had left his shotgun somewheres, after all the talking he done.

Then it happened and I seen it and there wasn't nothing I could do to stop it. First I seen the woman out the corner of my eye, standing in the alleyway between the porch of Toby's Saloon and the dress shop, a tall, stringy haired woman in a black coat. She was watching Gallagher and when he was in the middle of the street she took a step forward and yelled something and was raising the rifle to her shoulder. Gallagher turned towards her and the crack of the rifle rattled the window where I was sitting and Gallagher's hands went up to his face and I seen the slug had struck him in the head. He fell forward with one arm twisted under him, and the woman was still standing there with the rifle to her shoulder and she fired again and Gallagher's body twitched when the bullet hit him, then he was still.

I run out to the street and over to where he was laying face down and

I knew before I touched him he was dead. I turned him over on his back but it wasn't Gallagher I seen. Half his face was shot away and I kept saying to myself, that ain't Gallagher, it ain't him.

So that's how Gallagher died, on a cold gray Sunday morning, shot down in broad daylight by a half crazed woman.

Some people come running up and a woman somewheres behind me was yelling, oh my god, over and over, then somebody said, go get Colonel Thompson.

I put my coat over Gallagher's face, then I walked over to Toby's Saloon where they had the woman that killed him. She just stood there, being held by two men, a gaunt purse-mouthed woman with humped shoulders and mean snake eyes full of hate and damnation. And I didn't feel nothing or say nothing either, because there wasn't nothing to say.

Her name was Bessie Tuggle and she'd been living with one of the road agents named Pardee out at Bitter Creek. She later said she was out there the night the vigilantes came and seen through a window when they drug him from the house and led him over to a watering trough and shot him dead.

Maybe what she told was the truth, she didn't have no reason to lie, but I didn't hang around to find out what they done with her because I didn't care. Whatever they done wasn't going to bring Gallagher back, so why not let it go. Which is something else I learnt from him.

Some men took Gallagher's body over to Toby's and laid it out on the porch and after a little Dr. Booth come and felt for a pulse and said he was dead, which anybody could a told him.

Then Colonel Thompson come down from the church and he stood about five minutes looking down at Gallagher and he never said a word, just shook his head and walked away.

After a little Colonel Thompson took me off to one side and asked did Gallagher have any people and I said just me. He didn't say nothing and I said I wanted him buried right away, and he said he understood. Then he went and talked to some men at the other end of the porch and he come back and told me we would bury Gallagher that afternoon. And in a way I knew Gallagher was dead and in another way I didn't.

I think about it sometimes and it still ain't easy for me to believe, after all me and him had been through together, out at the Stinkingwater and after we joined up with the vigilantes and the night over in Bannack when he took Plummer in his sleep, and all them road agents out gunning for him, then he walks out of that livery stable without his shotgun and gets hisself shot dead in the street by Pardee's woman.

I remember Gallagher once saying it don't do no good to brood over what you can't change, but that's one thing I ain't yet learnt from him.

Paul Ramsey

The River

At the edge of the river, stone.
Cold astute glances of the rivermen.

The boat, marble of keel, floats none.

Grey web and talon. Misplanted seeds. A dour silence.

The tribute of snow to flame.

A cold flame sown
On a wide water's passage, and we turn
In the eye of justice's unfamiliar storm
And cry for shelter.

Sleep pervades
The root-keep and the bells' spent clamor.

White eyes becalm us in the white restlessness of water,
The bell buoys' sounding,
The river speaking, the lost voices gaining
On the closing tumult of our ears' retreat.

The sounds of harvest.

It is winter wheat.

"The River" and "A Walk on All Saints' Day," from *The Keepers*. Copyright © 1984 by Paul Ramsey. Reprinted by permission of Irvington Publishers.

A Walk on All Saints' Day

Men carefully set markers here.
To read them all would take a while.
Walking along a row I look,
Lazy and intent, at cut stone,
Names without memory to me
Until I remember the cut
On a distant stone, and I bleed
Quietly within me and take thought
Softly and with no tears, and so
Accept the fellowship of death
And walk in company a while.
The dead live in us, we in them,
Members of one another, long
Seeking and finding the great weight
Of a stone, of a taken cross.
Later shall be the proclaiming,
The heavens opening, the vision,
The illimitable host gathered
That at the last day shall be seen.
Now but an hour's slow partaking
And the near sharing of a pain
That Christ's blood softens and garners.
I leave the graveyard, walk glad in
The tumultuous brilliance of fall.

Madison Jones

A Beginning

Wendell Corbin's mother had used to tell him that he was born not just to make trouble but to be hanged. This could have been prophesied even when he was still in his cradle, she said, because he yelled and kicked and generally fidgeted ten times as much as his five brothers and sisters all put together had. And for no reason, because he was never sick. Just born that way, she said, and added that he took after a brother of hers that he had never laid eyes on in his life. That would make it a genetic inheritance, he guessed, because he could not in his infancy have been rebelling against what he was born into—such as the orange or other kind of crate that no doubt had been his cradle.

Whether or not Wendell's meanness was inborn there were, after he had had time to develop human good sense, more than enough possible reasons for its origin. As he saw it the first reason was his parents, the second was his brothers and sisters and the third was all the kinfolks with whom he had ever had any acquaintance. Their brains poured together in a tablespoon would not have made a heap. In a few of them, like his mother, there was a certain canniness, but nothing that anybody above the category of moron would call intelligence. Therein was the real puzzle. How did he, with his shining intelligence, ever get born into such a clan? Jumping genes had to have been the answer, the same kind of genes that presumably explained why he had never laid eyes on his mother's brother. He could only conclude that he and his maternal uncle had been awfully lucky, because it was a long jump for those genes. In all the family talk he had ever heard there was never once mention of a deceased family member who appeared to have had even so much as a knee up on the present generations.

"A Beginning," by Madison Jones appeared in *The Chattahoochee Review*, Vol. V, no. 3, Spring 1985. Copyright © 1985 by *The Chattahoochee Review*. Reprinted by permission of the publisher.

Intelligence and backbone went together, he thought, but there was such a thing as the latter without the former. Except for his mother a little bit, his family did not have the backbone either. Every male he was kin to—including the three brothers as long as they were still around—barely hung on to jobs as farm laborers or handymen at stores in and around Bison Springs and Turnbull. He had never known one of them to get a promotion, to clerk or anything else. The females, including his two sisters, all got married to men about like his brothers and his father and settled down or moved away to repeat the same dismal process of generation over again.

The father was if anything a cut beneath the least of his children. There was a time Wendell barely remembered when his father owned some property, thirty-eight acres with a house, sort of, two miles out of Bison Springs. He had got hold of it through the only stroke of luck ever to befall any of his family or kin: his wife won an automobile in a lottery and sold it and had enough money to buy the place. The result was four or five years of scrounging to keep off the tax collector and then the quite predictable occurred. After that it was Mr. Haney Cartwright's big farm where the family lived in a house that must have cost seventy-five dollars brand new and where every family member was supposed to be farm help. There, on that farm and in that house, was where Wendell spent all but the first few years of his happy youth.

It was not very happy, though the place did have a few advantages. The house sat on a knoll with a nice view of a big green pasture in front and nearby there was a creek to swim and fish in. But the walls of that house did not do a thing except shred the winter wind and when there was not any wind, smoke from the two fireplaces was so thick that they had to keep the windows open, or choke to death. Besides this, the place was too little for them. Wendell, the youngest, and his three brothers slept in a room that would have crowded one pair of midgets and his sisters and his parents were not much better off in their own rooms. Of course there was never enough money. The family diet (Wendell remembered best a pot of white beans heated over and over again and added to every few days) should have given them all permanent cases of the rickets, and the only clothes any of them ever had came from some such place as the Good Will store.

Wendell could have put up with these things, though, if it had not been for the character of his family. By the time he was eight he had already begun to look at them with a cold eye, and it got colder. The first thing he could remember being embarrassed about was the names of his brothers. By God knew what freakish inspiration of his parents the boys were named Majer, Miner, and Fawbus, in that order. Wendell (he had later added the second 'l' to his name) felt that he himself had somehow come off much better, though in that house he was never called anything but Bubba. His sisters' names, Ramona and Ronda, seemed, if only by contrast with his brothers', also not too bad. Majer, Miner, and Fawbus Corbin. He tried to forget they even had names.

But this little embarrassment was only the beginning. Before long, at least at school, he was also trying to forget that he had any brothers. This was impossible. Their stupidity alone was enough to guarantee that they would be always on display. Although Wendell was by three years the younger he caught up with Fawbus in the fifth grade. He caught up with Miner in the seventh and was saved from catching Majer only by the fact that Majer turned sixteen, the age at which he was legally permitted to quit school. But they were on display also by reason of their incorrigible rowdiness. Spit-balls, stink-bombs, snakes turned loose, thumb tacks planted in the seat of desks: whatever the uproar the principal went looking first for Wendell's brothers—while Wendell, humped over his own desk, labored to be oblivious to it all. It was no use. If nothing else the brothers themselves kept him reminded of their bond. They were always hailing him in the hall or on the playground, or from inside the principal's office where they spent half their time, or on the way out as they headed home on another three-day suspension. Hate might have been too strong a word for what Wendell felt, but outrage was not—an outrage that at one intensity or another was always there inside him.

At home where there was no rational eye but his own to observe them it was less bad for Wendell, if bad enough. Majer and Miner, who were barely a year apart, were always getting into fistfights, usually because one of them had lost something and accused the other of having taken it. Their mother would stand there screaming at them and Fawbus and the girls would cry and their father, without even getting up from the decomposing cane rocker he always sat in, would lift his voice in a stream of loud steady cussing. If there had been anybody within a quarter of a mile he would have had to call the sheriff, but there was nobody. Wendell always took off for the creek bank and stayed fifteen minutes and when he came back everything would be not only over with but forgotten. It would be really forgotten—no red faces or sniping or any signs of disgruntlement. That fight might just as well have happened a week before.

This forgetting, Wendell saw, had nothing whatever to do with goodness of heart. It was simply a spectacular lack of attention span that the whole family except him shared, if not in quite equal parts. He was sure that his father had the largest share. The old boy (Hap, people called him) was just barely capable of forming habits. One of his chores was to milk Mr. Cartwright's cows morning and evening seven days a week, yet every so often for no reason he would just forget to. "Plumb slipped my mind," he would say. He would forget to close gates and have to spend hours driving the cows back in, and he would walk away and leave a tractor motor idling all night. "A man can't think of ev'ything." Wendell was always worried about his losing his job until he realized the cause and extent of Mr. Cartwright's tolerance. Where else could Mr. Cartwright find a hand who was big enough fool to do even the kind of work that Wendell's father did for beggar's wages and use of a shack that never had to be repaired.

In a family like that Wendell was naturally looked on as downright weird. The lesser reason was his relentless and often raging pursuit of privacy: after his early years he had practically stopped talking to members of the family except when compelled to. The greater reason was his strange love of reading. He was not only constantly reading, he even owned some books, which he kept like treasure, under wraps, in a corner of his bedroom. With no other escape in that house he submerged himself in the world those books gave him, where people, however curious or depraved, had more sense in a minute than his whole family did in a year. He got so good at submerging himself that he did not even hear what passed for conversation around him. Sometimes he did not even hear the fights. To bring him out they usually had to shake him and when he looked up there would be one or another of them watching him the way you would have watched Lazarus emerging from the tomb. He was something for them to roll their heads about, and he did not know how many times he had heard his father say, "That there boy's the first un ever knowed in my whole connection to read aer book." And he might add, though not directly in Wendell's presence, "Them books is what makes him so funny."

Wendell's weirdness made them uneasy and also angry sometimes, but it was not hard to detect a half-buried measure of respect among their feelings: he was, after all, a prodigy among them. His father, though he did well to spell out the words on a road sign, for some reason especially felt this way. He had used to tell Wendell that once upon a time he had known how to read real good too but that over the years he had just forgot. And then, maybe, he would ask Wendell to read him something from one of the books. The result was always the same. Wendell would read a paragraph or two and suddenly the old boy would lift his long burnt-red hand and tell him to stop, that was enough. All them words: he didn't understand none of them. But he would be looking at Wendell in a certain way, blinking as at a mystery enacted there before him. This was the closest any family member ever came to open acknowledgment of Wendell's gifts, and it was the basis for the only bond he ever felt with any of them.

This was the basis but it was a change of circumstances that allowed the bond to grow as strong as it did—(which was not really very strong, or durable). At fourteen Wendell was the only child left at home, and that was one thing. Another was that by this time his father had developed rheumatism and instead of out at work he spent most of his days sitting or lying around the house groaning. Mr. Cartwright let him stay on: the house was in such a shape that nobody else would have been willing to live in it. So Wendell not only saw more of his father than in the past, he also had to listen to his groans. These groans got seriously on Wendell's nerves and finally drove him to a step that turned out to be a very important, in fact a crucial one—and not only for his relationship with his father.

Wendell's brothers were—he supposed *still* were—always smoking pot. For the simple reason that *they* did he had never even tried it, but he had heard them talk enough to know where the stuff was to be acquired. One day, a day when his father was groaning even more than usual, he happened to read in a magazine that pot was good for such as rheumatism. He went in to Bison Springs and located an older boy he had heard his brothers name and, with money he had been hoarding, bought a nickel bag. That started it. Once he had got the old boy to take and hold a few drags off the cigarette he had rolled for him with one of his father's own cigarette papers their little bond was sealed. It was a mutual dependency as strong on his part as on his father's, curiously, and it lasted a couple of years. That was the nearest Wendell had ever come to participating in a friendship. If his father had had anything at all in his head their relationship might possibly have blossomed into something that would have endured.

But this was to exaggerate a little. The old boy did have *something* in his head, some old dusty and fragmented memories which were almost the only subject of the conversation Wendell had with him. These were conversations that Wendell remembered pleasantly, especially the ones on that front porch from which certain floorboards were perilously missing, in mild weather when they sat looking out over the green pasture where whiteface cows were grazing in the sun. If it was early spring the thicket of plum bushes that was closing in on the house would be white with bloom, and so with the two dogwoods in the fencerow just out front. Occasionally Wendell's mother would, in a way of speaking, join them, sitting on what was left of the steps to shell a bucket of peas. But she never said anything much except to correct in an irritable voice slips in her husband's recollections. Physically she was almost his exact opposite, a low fat woman with no neck at all. Leaning back in that unraveling cane rocker Wendell's father looked like a just-living body loosely held together by hooks at all its joints. His neck was extraordinarily long and on top of it was a little ball of a head from which all but a little rim of gray hair had vanished. There was nearly as much hair in his big flaplike ears, but this was yellow from all the wax he never thought to remove.

His skin, of course, face and crown and neck and hands, was a permanent burnt-red. He was essence of Redneck.

From these conversations Wendell learned all he was ever to know about his ancestors—which was not much and hardly worth knowing. As best he could tell, not one of them had ever amounted to anything. Most of them seemed to have spent their misbegotten lives losing things and almost getting things they did not get and having children and accidents and violent encounters. "My uncle Floyd," Wendell's father said, "didn't have no right arm atall. Lost hit in old Mr. Buck Rainer's cotton gin. Tore hit plumb right off at the shoulder. Biggest mess I ever seen."

This was only one of what must have been a dozen uncles. Another one called Wedge was even more unlucky. "Taken out after that nigger, gonna kill him. Nigger shot him in the foot. Wedge drug hisself back home till he got well, and took out after that nigger agin. Nigger shot him in the head. They ain't ketched that nigger yet."

Another uncle, though, had come very close to being actually lucky. He had almost inherited a hundred acres, from an old widow who took a shine to him and aimed to put him down in her will. Shirt-tail close, he come. That widow dropped dead on the way to the bank to put her name on that paper. Wendell's father would shake his round little head. His only memory of an encounter with luck in the family was when a now-dead sister of his on top of eight other children, had triplets and got a picture of herself and the babies on page 2 of the *Bliss County Weekly News*.

Wendell's father's memories, such as they were, ranged back through two generations of his family and stopped right there as if against a blank wall that was where human history had had its beginning—nothing on the other side. It was if his grandfather's generation had been set down there like Adam and Eve already full grown and shaped the way they were and the way they always would be. Around about through the county there were a few of the old ante-bellum houses still surviving, standing there like reminders. They did not remind Wendell's father of anything. His memories, though ranging over the same stretch of countryside that contained those houses, afforded hardly a glimpse of them. That the houses were supposed to remind people of a vanished and different way of life was something Wendell had to learn from books, because nothing he heard his father recall suggested that this was true. Instead of an Eden to start with, there was nothing but a dark backward and abysm of time.

The old boy did not seem to regard his haphazard portrait as especially bleak: the bleakness was just life. Sometimes, as when he told about a particularly heartbreaking failure of luck or a gruesome accident, he would even show a certain zest for that life. His voice would break out of its monotone and rise a little and he might bob his head and clench his knees with his loose boney fingers. Such an outburst was usually followed by an extended period of reverie and after that he would want a few more drags off the now-dead reefer he probably had dropped onto the floor.

The pot did him good and, Wendell was sure, had nothing to do with causing the stroke that finally hit him. One day Wendell tried it himself and shared with his father that little interval of silly laughter and after that the stopping of time and the comical way that words and meanings kept escaping from his grasp. It was like a little holiday. People, especially people like his father, needed such holidays and he began to reflect on what a shame and more than a shame it was that the law pursued and put people in jail because of pot. Stupid. Mainly because his brothers had such a hatred of the law, being always just barely out of trouble with it, Wendell had never had any such feelings. He began to now, and his hostility grew stronger. Partly in defiance he started taking these little holidays pretty often himself and finally he even got some seed and grew a few plants in the woods behind the house. This gave him a good deal of satisfaction. It was also the real beginning of his rebellion—his usually discreet and prudent rebelling—against established things.

John Bowers

Crackers

Young Tex fries baloney. He cuts four symmetrical lines to a slice, so the baloney will lay flat in the skillet and cook in its own grease. The two-burner gas stove rests on a table in his "light-housekeeping" room on the second story. Tex lights it with a wooden kitchen match, after first trying for fire on the seat of his pants, then successfully on the side of the gunk-encrusted stove. He keeps his stock of baloney as well as his souring milk and tart butter and browning head of iceberg lettuce in the communal hall refrigerator. In a bag with "Tex" scrawled on. Someone has been stealing a slice or two of his meat as well as swigs of his milk, but he has never apprehended that person. He suspects, but he doesn't name. Even if he caught the bandit he probably wouldn't cause a fuss. Tex is too unsure of himself at this stage of his life to ever cause a fuss.

The scent of frying baloney, like nothing else on earth, permeates his once-white, now axle-grease stained britches—his upper torso bare and sweat cooled—goes into the rumpled debris on his narrow bed, into the rug of undetermined original color, under the door, out into the hall and still doing ninety. Mr. Bruno in 2-B catches a whiff. Mr. Bruno sits on the edge of his bed. His room is as neat as that of a West Point cadet. Mr. Bruno is bald, slim, and has his hands pressed tightly against his skull. He has not eaten in three days. And he will not, by God, steal any more! Help me, oh my Lord! The dishonor! Think of the meals he used to provide for. He had once stood before the carving board on Thanksgiving in Minneapolis, Minnesota. The thin crackling skin of a game bird, steamy, nut-rich stuffing up the rear end, hot rolls and butter and asparagus in hand-whipped hollandaise. Pie a la mode and strong black coffee afterwards, all thanks to Karl T. Bruno, man of the house.

He was turned down for a filling station job yesterday because he was 55 years old and couldn't keep from smiling when there was nothing to smile about. His bladder is acting up. His car won't start because of the dead battery. He hasn't paid his weekly room rent in a month. But he won't cause problems. No blood. He takes off his belt. He puts the end through the buckle, making a large bow. He tightens it around his neck, while walking around and lifting the end towards the ceiling. He pauses to draw the window shade. A brown person is looking up from the street with his mouth open. Mr. Bruno selects a hook used for suspending laundry on the sly, and ties the loose end around. Crouching on a chair, weak and weaving, he jumps, keeping his arms around his bent knees so his feet won't touch the floor, swinging out sideways.

"What's that?' says Birdie, down below, in her wheelchair. She owns the rooming house, and is more conscious than others of the least out of ordinary noise. She can identify a wide variety of sounds peculiar to rooming houses. She says, "Sounds like somebody hit the deck. Go check, will you, Bob?"

"What for? Let it allllll hang out!" Bob says, putting a splash more Seven Crown in his Seven-and-Seven. He fills Birdie's and Myrna's glasses, too, feeling good because day is done. Day consists of overhauling motors, in a narrow blackened workspace with light from a fly-specked fluorescent bulb. "Let 'em all hit the deck! I say, let's all have another drink." Pause. "Pardon the glove."

Bob has his eye on Myrna. Myrna has rouged cheeks and a ruby-red mouth. Her large eyes roam, as if amused. She does not have much to say, letting Birdie do most of the talking. Birdie is the business woman, the one with the hard head for unpleasant facts, who'll kick you out if it comes to it. Fair, though. Myrna is drunk on Bob's whiskey. She supports herself by hanging on to the back of Birdie's wheelchair. She has not had intercourse in 15 years. She does not know what to do with Bob's attention, except to be pleased. There are pictures on the wall of Myrna and Birdie in days past. Myrna tap danced at one time on the stage and Birdie walked around and managed a show business troop. Myrna beams in the early photographs and Birdie's face is serious and aloof, her clothing ritzy. Their present living quarters, in which Bob now sits after handing over his weekly rent, smells. It smells of sachet and powder, dust and tea, and a unique aroma that one hesitates to analyze. The light is never bright, even at high noon.

After the pint of Seven Crown is drained, Bob leaves. He does not like to stay around women if he is not drinking. And he never buys whiskey by the fifth, always the pint and one bottle at a time. That's just how he likes to do it. A pint you can squirrel away in the glove compartment and the hip pocket, being able to offer friends a little swig and take one yourself anytime you feel like it. A fifth is thinking too big. You set a fifth down and you're liable to be corralled all evening. No, thanks. Keep moving!

Bob goes to see Tex. While Mr. Bruno, behind closed door, tries to rise from the floor. He thinks, on top of everything else, he may have broken his hip. He landed sideways after the belt snapped on the first swing. He crawls to the window but can't open the screen because Birdie has had the screens nailed shut from the outside. He goes to sleep with his mouth on the rug.

Birdie wishes she had one more drink. She curses the fact, tells Myrna that they should always ask Bob to go to the market and get them a bottle when they suspect they might be needing another snort. That boy is a sweet old thing and wouldn't have minded doing it a bit. All she can think about is getting drunk. Myrna's big eyes roam. She is thinking about 15 years ago. It was a Mexican-American named Juan, who later went up on a phony 10-to-20 rap because he resembled the actual gunman a little too closely. Mexican-Americans tend to resemble one another in L.A. to people who aren't Mexican-Americans. He had pleaded and pleaded with Myrna to have intercourse with him. Finally she could not stop him. She had tried to make her tongue work to tell him that she was getting past all that, that she had never been much of a success at it in the best of times, that the doctors had fooled around with her insides in an operation and done God knows what. Why not just one drink and look at each other? You'll be sorry, Juan. He was sorry. Or she thought he was sorry because after he went up to San Quentin she never once heard from him.

Bob and Tex do not exchange ideas but lines, and both like it that way. Bob has incorporated a few standard lines in his speech over the years and they come out of him like a song. A buddy back in Tennessee used to say, "Let it allll hang out." And a character in a movie he once viewed said, "Pardon the glove," shaking hands with a glove on his mitt. Bob really likes that one. Pardon the glove. Tex eats his fried baloney sandwich, which is coated with mustard and a slab of lettuce, sitting on what he takes to be the edge of his cot-like bed. There is so much piled there he can't be sure. His chair he cannot sit in because his filling station uniforms for the past week rise from it, plus an assortment of underwear and socks and a month's editions of the *Los Angeles Times*. He drinks from a fresh cold can of Lucky Lager. Bob will not accept a Lucky out of Tex's six-pack. He does not like to barge in on a man and take anything from his six-pack. But he is very generous himself. All of his money is gone by Wednesday after he gets paid on Friday.

"Pardon the glove,"

"Whoopie!" Tex says it like Joe E. Brown.

Bob would like to incorporate "Whoopie!" in his repertoire but can't because Tex owns the rights. He pulls a smudged letter from his grimy windbreaker. His face is indented with permanent, tiny, almost indistinguishable, black dots that are caused by the whirling soot where he works. The letter, Tex notes, is from Tennessee and it includes snapshots. It reads:

Dear Bob,
I'em awefully sorry I turned you down when you asked me for a little back here. Put hit down to a olde married woman that don't know her mind. But, I garantee ya that if we see each other agin I'm agoint to do anything you want. Do you know what I mean??? I garentee you. Just send me bus fare out and I'll stay with you in L.A. as long as you like. Buster has hitten me once too often.

X X X June

The snapshots are of a saucy-looking brunette in a motel room. She is dressed in panties and bra—sitting on a bed in profile with one knee drawn up, leaning back on her elbows full face, knees spread. Tex wonders who might have been in position to take the pictures but thinks it best not to ask. He hopes that Bob sends the money and that this woman comes to L.A. "Hey, how about that? Whoopie! Are you going to send her the dough?"

"I ain't sure. But listen to this." Pause. "I'm . . . going . . . to . . . do . . . anything . . . you . . . want. Let it allll hang out!"

Bob will send the money. Twice. The woman will claim the first time that she has had to pay some debts. He will not hear from her after the second installment. He decides now to get some beer of his own since he cannot stand to be around Tex and not have one. The Chinaman who runs the hole-in-the-wall on Alvarado accepts his money for a six-pack and says, "Who got big pecker?" And laughs. Bob pretends to laugh. He thinks the Chinaman is making a fool of him. It is not that. The Chinaman has three English phrases he's playing around with: "It's late I got no money." "Man in back hold cleaver." And, "Don't worry I got no big pecker." Later he will be shot for remark number three. A Negro with a woman's silk stocking squashing his face into a brown sausage will pull a nickel-plated .38 on him, demand money, and hear talk about a big pecker. He will fire. The place will be closed for a month. The Chinaman will return to the cash register, bent a little to the side, still playing with the three phrases.

Bob can't sit still. He jiggles his foot over his leg in Tex's room, in the easy chair, Tex having cradled the mess from it and dropped it on the floor, to keep company with cardboard from laundry shirts, empty milk cartons, and many other newspapers. Bob crooks his little finger as he holds a can of Brew 102, a further touch from his repertoire. He saw a bar-fly do it once, the bar-fly himself having seen it done by an American actor in an American movie about Englishmen. "I say," says Bob, "are we going to get with it this evening or are we not? I'm just asking. Are we going to get this thing together or are we not? I'm asking."

"You mean, are we going to go out and search for a little pungtange tonight or are we not? Is that what you're asking?"

"I mean, are we going to let some girl go without it tonight just because we didn't go out and get with it? I'm asking you. Just asking you."

"You've asked the right man."

It's a little chant they go through. Tex had wanted to stay in tonight. He is keeping a log of money he spends: Dinner, 99¢; paper, 7¢; two cups of coffee, 20¢." For today he will have to add "Good times, $5.00." He has a savings account at the Bank of America, using it the way others use a checking account. His holdings have never gone over $200, but he has gone through a bank book or two because of all the necessary notations. He sort of likes walking in the place on Vermont and doing business.

Actually, Tex is not from Texas. His first day at the filling station a man from Boston thought he identified his accent as one from Texas and called him Tex. Up until then he had been someone else. Now he is Tex. He liked the ring of the new name. And he had never met Bob until he came to L.A. and walked up to the door at Birdie's rooming house on Elden Avenue. They had grown up 35 miles from each other in Tennessee, but hadn't met until L.A. They were overjoyed to meet.

Bob combs his hair after rubbing in Vitalis, his only preparation. But Tex takes a bath. It's his training from other days. He will even squirt on an underarm deodorant, something his ex-wife delicately pointed out he should do. At Birdie's you take a bath down the hall, dry off on a towel, and shave and deodorize, put on fresh underwear, ball up old underwear in hand, gather toilet articles under arm, and sail back to room in loosely-buttoned clothes. Mr. Bruno in 2-B is the only one who wears a robe to the bath. His robe shows wear and the sense of comfort.

Bob and Tex drive. They only have four blocks to go, but they drive. It's L.A. And, who knows, they might strike out at the Red Rooster and want to travel to Hollywood or Santa Monica. L.A., its freeways, its possibilities! Everything looks promising when you have a buzz on. They go in Bob's Chevy because he insists. He feels uncomfortable being someone's passenger. Inside the Red Rooster they take seats at the bar and order beer. The bartender is a man and the other customers are female. Bob and Tex never saw anything like this in Tennessee; they like it. The women wear slacks, dresses, some with hair short like a boy's, others girlishly perfumed and lacquered. It is not a large bar and it smells like a brewery. It is also lit as if for an aquarium. A very pretty and large blonds sits beside Tex. "Hiya."

"Hiya, yourself," she says.

Tex keeps his change on the bar, trusting-like, and not in his pocket. That's how they do it in California. He likes that. But he is careful to keep his hands hidden as much as possible. His hands are blackened from filling station work and no amount of scrubbing and kinds of soap can remove it. A lead-like rim lies beneath each nail, impervious to any file made. Dark whorls stand embossed on finger tips, and fingers once long and almost elegant are starting to become puffy. He strikes a match beneath the bar counter and swiftly waves it across the cigarette jutting from the blondes's pucker. "Thanks, I'm Ruth. I'll have another beer."

Tex pushes his change forward toward the bartender. The bartender gently extracts the price of the blonde's beer as if plucking a flower. Tex is wondering where he might take the blonde. Already, in his mind, he is outside the bar. He has only been here a minute, but already he is outside. "What do you do?" he says.

"I am currently unemployed. I am seeking employment. What's your line?"

"I'm in the oil business."

His room is definitely out. How could any sane person take a woman to his room on Elden? The woman must have her own apartment. She must invite him there. He buys the blonde another beer, and she asks him additionally for a quarter to play the juke-box. That's all right, but must he listen to stuff with xylophones and a harp? You call that music? What about some Hank Williams? On the third beer, Ruth, so sparkling before, suddenly rests an elbow on the bar, her hand flopping down with a cigarette lazily stuck between two fingers. She is unconcerned that her legs splay apart. "You know something, Ted?"

"Tex."

"You know something, Tex? I gotta confess to you. I really came in with a girl. I'm going out with that girl."

"Yeah? Who's that?"

"Over there."

It's a woman built like a tank. She has slick wet hair combed in a ducktail and she wears tight pants that allow no room for doubt that her ass is a yard wide. She also has large arms. Tex is taught the same lesson time after time in the Red Rooster. Still, he can never quite come to terms with it. "Gee—you look so . . ."

"Regular. Yeah, I know."

Ruth smiles kindly. She relates the trials of growing up in Southeast Virginia, the tingle of a female's touch, the shiver from a man's. Oh, she had tried to fit in! She tells of proms and going steady and then of being pressed to the mat by a rampaging gym teacher in bloomers. She had had to come to California to breathe! Freedom to be! She lights up, takes a sip. Tex is fascinated. He'll never learn. She plays both butch and femme, depending. With Frankie over there one must naturally gear up femme. Tex suggests that Ruth and Frankie might possibly like to take a spin with him and Bob. (Bob would get Frankie.) Ruth immediately douses that idea with cold water. "Frankie is too jealous. Look at the way she's looking over here. I don't want to get killed."

Tex turns his attention to the front door. It's standard procedure these days after being turned down. He imagines his ex walking in. To create verisimilitude he designs the circumstances. She has become fed up with the hometown. She can't stop loving him. She buys a bus ticket and comes right out, not stopping anyplace en route until she walks through that Red Rooster door with her cute little bags. No, there's not enough pain in that; too many loopholes. Try this out for size. She comes West with her new man. Both are walking down Vermont and decide to have a quick one. Why not? Why can't that new man of hers show some spunk and come West? Tex sees her at the far end of the bar. They eye one another. Tex tells her about his new life, all the adventures he is having.

Is there anything in life, Tex thinks, designed to interrupt the flow of human happiness like the institution of marriage? Tex had worn a suit and tie to his measly job in Tennessee. He had walked home for lunch—leftovers—to save money. Strange pussy dried up. At nights he never got a crack at the taverns. He had to be home, had to listen to a recounting of her day, had to do chores, had to exercise the dog, deal with relatives, wait for bedtime. He knew every pair of panties she owned. There was no dish that ever came to the table that he hadn't seen before. Whenever he shot the bull with anyone, he didn't care who, it was always as a married man. I am a married man talking to you about marriage kind of things. He had had to go to church. God damn, he had had to sit there and listen to some asshole tell him about spiritual life. He was drowning in marriage kind of things. He had to have freedom or perish! Abandon ship!

And then around Albuquerque, at three in the morning, driving all night to avoid a motel and save money, a strange thing happened. She magically fell beside him in the car, just the way she used to before taking his dick out on occasion. He smelled her, observed the tiny beauty mark on her left cheek, listened to her distinct girlish trill. They carried on a little conversation and he played with her leg. He had just broken free, but would anyone ever again do with him what she had done? She never left him from that moment, tagging along wherever he went in L.A., available as a wisp of smoke the moment he beckoned. As he took trips through the city, he pointed out the movie studios, the Brown Derby, Forest Lawn, places she would have been interested in. During spaghetti meals he was careful to keep his head raised above his plate; she had once complained that he ate like a hog. He was much more considerate of her as smoke than when she had been present in the flesh.

And Bob? Bob ends up with a serious-talking, baggy-eyed woman and her short female sidekick. The women cannot be separated outside of pulling a gun on them and they do not want Tex along. No reason given, they just aren't overjoyed when his name crops up in their plans. They know a bar way out in Venice that keeps jumping all night. Why doesn't Bob come out there with them. It's a dyke bar, too. But Bob is given the distinct impression that if he hauls ass out there he might be in line for some action. Not in so many words is this told him, but the serious-talking, baggy-eyed woman tells him that she's sick of being frigid. She wants to open up with someone, and it could be Bob. Bob is too thoughtful to tell them that he has to rise at 7:30 tomorrow. He is also too thoughtful to disregard the bar tab the girls have accumulated. Instead of being dead broke by next Wednesday, he will be dead broke in three hours. He will drive to work after a little shut-eye by some beach, with a dim memory of clutching tight flesh and pressing against tight lips. He will not remember much else except the rapidity with which he had to keep reaching for his billfold. And the girls will vanish into the fog the moment his last bill goes down the drain. Driving in early morning, raw in the throat, he will compose a fresh narrative for Tex. After all, he is the one who left with two females, arm in arm, not seen until the next day. He has won the contest, for that's how they keep score in Tennessee, the prize going to the man who waltzes off with the woman (women). It is a way of keeping your self-respect.

Tex buys a sixpack on the way back by foot. All those books he has read about L.A., those that are supposed to paint it as so tawdry and depressing, the ass-end of America, strike him as inspiring. Heroes stay in bungalows while next door are girls who want to be in the movies. None of the books he has ever read ever comes up with the crazy and unobtainable females he actually meets. No way of life he ever encounters is anywhere near the plan of a seedy private eye or a failed producer or scriptwriter. It was actually a motion picture show that tipped the scales and made Tex light out for L.A. He couldn't get over the image of William Holden sitting before a typewriter, in a sunny room, a pencil stuck between his teeth. William Holden drove a convertible in the hot sunshine. He knew girls and had girls. Was it any tragedy that he took up with Gloria Swanson in a Beverly Hills mansion? What if William Holden had had to trot out to waiting autos in a black bow tie and white ice cream cap and flute, "Fill 'er up?"

Jesse Hill Ford

Fishes, Birds and Sons of Men

Until he was eighteen Mr. Tommy Hassell ran all over the river bottoms. There was never such a boy to hunt the way he did, running, always running, and the sound of his gun roaring over the Tennessee River, the sound of it *pang-pang* in the cornfields, like a hammer striking the end of a long iron pipe, and the flat pop of sound when he fired into the air above a tobacco patch, or the booming echo rolling out of the hillsides when he hunted squirrels deep in the woods.

The gun went silent when Mr. Tommy was eighteen. The doctor told him he had a bad heart and advised him to take it easy. Mr. Tommy, who wanted to live as long as any other man, went back home and lay upon the bed and had his food brought to him by his father, Mr. Ed, who was lame in one knee, and his mama, Miss Hanna, who was deaf and blind in her right eye. These three were all that remained of the Hassell family. Mr. Tommy's older sisters had long since married; his older brothers had long since gone north into Illinois, seeking work.

After two months on the bed Mr. Tommy found courage to be up, and though he felt faint he walked far down the hill by easy stages and watched the work going on there. Government workers were felling trees and rolling up barbed-wire fences as far as the eye could reach, not only along Bear Creek nearby but for miles on either side of the Tennessee River. Mr. Tommy walked back home by easy stages and again lay on the bed.

Autumn came, and he lay listening to his heart by day and at night listened to fox hounds trailing along the creek bank and circling back over the ridge. Night after night they ran, nearly till dawn. Then winter, spring, summer, and autumn again. It frightened him sometimes to lift a spoon.

From *Fishes, Birds and Sons of Men*, by Jesse Hill Ford. Boston: Little, Brown and Company, 1967. Copyright © 1967 by Jesse Hill Ford; and Sarah David Ford and Katherine Kieffer Musgrove, Trustees. Reprinted by permission of Harold Ober Associates.

He was almost twenty when he left his bed again and, though very weak, walked down the long hill but could not reach the creek bank. Even the foot of the hill lay drowned in backwater, and the government lake stretched for miles about, covering the ground he had hunted over.

That winter his father, Mr. Ed, fell through the ice in the backwater cove while shooting ducks. After his death poor old Miss Hanna lost her mind and very often wandered outdoors, raving and mourning, so that in the spring she too died, and was buried beside the old man in the family graveyard, a grove of cedars overlooking the cove where the old man had gone through the ice.

With the family so scattered only three of the Hassell sisters could be found, and only one brother besides Mr. Tommy himself.

There was a sister who wanted to take Mr. Tommy to Nashville to live with her, but Mr. Tommy wouldn't go. The brother offered to take him to Hammond, Indiana, to live with him, but again Mr. Tommy refused. He seemed to feel death pounding inside his chest. He only wanted to be left where he was, to die in familiar surroundings.

So the sisters took the bedding, the china, the skillets, the iron pots, and almost all the furniture. The brother took the guns, the new ax, the Victrola, fifty feet of new rope, the hams and the bacon and shoulders from the smokehouse, old Mr. Ed's almost new boots, and the family Bible.

Mr. Tommy ended up with the conch shell, the old music box which had been broken for as long as he could remember, and the mantel clock.

Save for the house lot and the barn, which nobody wanted anyway, the farm was sold. The brother and sisters divided this cash money and gave Mr. Tommy, as his share, the house and the unsold ground, the well, the empty smokehouse, and the falling-down barn where the mule and the cow had stayed. Everything else—plows, rakes, tools, chains, harness, and the old ax—was sold at auction along with the mule and the cow. Out of this the lawyer was paid and Mr. Tommy was allowed ten dollars cash money, "to tide him over," as they said. He never asked what they meant by that. Finally one of the sisters left him an old quilt and a pillow, and when the last car had passed from sight, rocking and groaning under its load of plunder tied to the roof, Mr. Tommy went inside the house and lay down on his bed to die.

The dog, old Hoover, as though he too sensed what was coming, followed Mr. Tommy inside and lay down by the bed, resting his muzzle on his paws. Night fell, and with it a late frost came, and both Mr. Tommy and Hoover shivered with cold. The dog heaved himself up on the bed, and Mr. Tommy, who was already wearing all the clothes he had, got up and fetched Mr. Ed's old army overcoat. Between the coat and the quilt and the dog he managed to keep warm, and morning found him no nearer to dying, it seemed, than he had been the night before. Something clearly had to be done.

When the sun was high Mr. Tommy went outside and sat down in the yard to warm up. He spent all morning there, wrapped in his thoughts while jaybirds called and whistled and crows signaled each other from afar off, lighting now and again in the top snag of a chestnut tree and cawing. Everywhere the woods were turning green, and redbud trees shone pink as lungs against the side of the ridge. Think as he might, Mr. Tommy saw only one way out of his predicament, and with the sun at last slanting down into the west and cold night threatening again, he set off walking fast as he dared, warning Hoover not to follow. He set off and reached the preacher's house by suppertime, a small, neat, painted place near the highway, by a yellow chert road.

The preacher asked him inside and insisted he break bread with the family, after which Mr. Tommy told him just what it was he had in mind.

The preacher, a young man himself, served three churches in the Bear Creek neighborhood, and in one there was a widow, older than Mr. Tommy by two or three years, it was true, but a strong industrious woman who didn't mind hard work and was well broken in to hard times.

She had some insurance money inherited from her first husband, who had been killed, the preacher said, but he didn't say *how* the husband died; no, he skirted that, and Mr. Tommy was in no bargaining position to ask about it a second time. Her name, said the preacher, was Miss Margaret, and before her first marriage she had been a Kenny. Her people were fishermen and trappers, and like Mr. Tommy himself they lived upon poor ground nobody wanted to buy. A marriage such as this one might be arranged rather quickly, the preacher said.

"Well, fine," said Mr. Tommy, and in less than a week he found himself married. Miss Margaret moved into Mr. Tommy's house with her featherbed mattresses, her bird of paradise quilts, her china, kettles, skillets, rolling pins, and biscuit boards. She also brought her guns, including her dead husband's pistol, and a practically brand-new ax.

When Mr. Tommy asked, she told him her first husband had been killed almost two years before while shooting it out with revenue agents. This had been about the same time, Mr. Tommy calculated, that the doctor had told him about his heart.

"Never you mind," said Miss Margaret, shifting the pillows behind him, making him comfortable on their well-furnished bed. She had a heavy solemn face and fat strong arms, and she wore her brown hair rolled in a knot at the back of her head. "We'll make out just fine. I don't want you to worry about *nothing*, understand?"

Mr. Tommy nodded. She went right to work. She cleaned the house inside and painted it gray outside. She repaired the dogtrot porch. She laid down new linoleum. She papered their bedroom a design of red roses. She put up yellow calico curtains. When the house was fixed she fenced in a chicken yard and built a laying house. She repaired the barn, mended the fences, and seemed always moving—feeding the chickens, milking the new cow, hoeing the garden, fixing Mr. Tommy's meals.

Miss Margaret worked like a machine that never runs down, never stops. At night while Mr. Tommy slept she sewed shirts for him and tied fishnets and trotlines. Soon Mr. Tommy found himself getting fat. It seemed strange, because he had been warned that a bad heart kept any man thin as a rail.

Presently, when cold weather came, he took up Miss Margaret's shotgun and all her shells and walked carefully down to the cove and hid in the grass beside the water's edge. With Hoover at his side he killed twenty-five mallard ducks. The old dog patiently swam out after each one and dragged it back ashore. The ducks were so heavy that when Mr. Tommy ran out of shells it was all he could do to carry them back to the house. Miss Margaret said nothing. She plucked the feathers and saved them for pillows. She cooked six of the ducks and hung the rest outside in a meal sack, to freeze.

They ate some of the ducks that evening, and after dinner Mr. Tommy went to bed wearing his long underwear and his socks for warmth. While he lay under the quilts waiting to get warm he listened to his heart and remembered the biscuits and the rice and the ducks and the brown gravy.

For remembering the food and listening to his heart Mr. Tommy couldn't sleep, so he got up and put on the old man's army overcoat and took the conch shell from the mantelpiece beside the clock. He sat down before the fire on the bench by Miss Margaret, who was still sewing, and turned the pink shell in the firelight, marveling at the beauty of it. The conch shell was smooth from having been handled by so many generations of hands. It had been in the Hassell family longer than anyone could remember, and no one of them knew for sure where it had come from, except that they thought it had been a wedding gift back long ago. Put it to your ear and hear the ocean.

"I think my heart's beating a little better tonight," Mr. Tommy said. "I think maybe it's stronger today than it was yesterday or even Thursday."

"I expect it's the duck meat," Miss Margaret said. "I always did hear that duck meat made the heart strong. Duck meat is heart food. A duck has about the biggest heart of any bird."

"That must be," said Mr. Tommy, stroking the shell in his pale hands.

"Ducks have to fly such a great distance," Miss Margaret said.

"I never thought about that," Mr. Tommy said.

"Fish is brain food," Miss Margaret continued. "I once knew of an idiot, and they fed him nothing but pure fish a whole year and his head got big as a pumpkin. His brain grew and grew that way, and he got to be so smart people come from all over everywhere to ask his advice. His family made a regular business out of him. They charged a dollar for his advice."

"Well, I'll say," said Mr. Tommy. "What ever become of him?"

"Oh, he finally commenced to having fits," Miss Margaret said. "And finally he had this one real terrible fit and he turned blue and died."

"Oh," said Mr. Tommy.

"We all thought they fed him *too much* fish," Miss Margaret said. "Once they got his brain built up to normal it wasn't no use to keep on and on fattening it up that way."

"Well," said Mr. Tommy.

"They had their eye on them dollar bills," Miss Margaret said. "Their own greed killed him when they could have had a fortune off of him if they had of just been patient. His head got so big it looked like a washtub."

Mr. Tommy pulled the army overcoat closer about his shoulders and stretched out one of his sock feet to stroke Hoover's neck. The dog was dreaming beside the hearth, kicking in his sleep. He didn't stop kicking even when Mr. Tommy's foot touched his neck. His eyes only opened a slit, but he kept on as he was, carried away in his old hound's dream. Maybe he was retrieving the ducks again, Mr. Tommy thought, and remembered the whisper sound of wings as the ducks slanted low over the cove and pitched toward him into the wind, reaching down their little orange feet to light on the water.

"I think I'll lay back down and listen to my heart a while," Mr. Tommy said. He stood up and kissed Miss Margaret timidly on her broad cheek.

"Good night, sweetie," Miss Margaret said after him. He put the overcoat aside and stretched out again under the covers listening to the steady thumps inside his chest. This time he was soon warm.

He felt sleep drifting in after him, and then he saw it, a long drifting cloud stealing over the ground like mist, so that he hardly knew when it overtook him and rolled over him, so quietly, so stealthily had it come. He woke only when Miss Margaret came in from milking the next morning. He raised up and saw the sky was still dark. Then he lay back warm in bed, dozing while Miss Margaret began frying bacon and sausage and making biscuits. When she set the molasses on the table he got up and put on the overcoat and sat down before the fire.

"Had a queer dream last night," said Miss Margaret. She dreamed often.

"What was that?"

"I don't know. Like I say, I never *remember* my dreams after they're over. But it was a queer dream. Something good. That's all I know," Miss

Margaret said.

"Well, the only dream I ever dream is about flying through the air," said Mr. Tommy. "I dream it every now and again, and it's always the same thing. I take a running jump. All of a sudden I'm flying through the air and something's chasing me, but I always manage to fly faster than it can run."

"If you dream about water, it's a sign of death," Miss Margaret said.

"Well, I never dream about water, only flying."

"Before my first husband died his mama dreamed about water. She dreamed the river rose up and flooded its banks," Miss Margaret said. "And my husband's mama was on the roof out of the water's reach, and what do you think came drifting by holding to a tree limb?"

"I wouldn't know," said Mr. Tommy.

"It was my first husband," Miss Marrgaret said. "His mama tried to catch him, but he drifted off beyond her reach and was lost from sight. That very next day friends sent word the law was coming after him. I begged him to hide in the woods."

"You did?" said Mr. Tommy.

"Oh, yes, I begged him, and all he would say was the law didn't have nothing on him, only somebody else's word for it. That night they come up to the house and hollered for him to come out, and all he would say was they better not try to take him."

"Was he really making whiskey?"

"I reckon he was. Every closet we had was full of gallon jugs. Like another man would keep well water, he kept a churn full of whiskey in the corner with a gourd dipper on the wall over it. Him and his whole entire family drank it that way, but they were Scottish-blooded people, McNeillys. Whiskey was bred in their bones, just as fishing is bred in my people."

"Well," said Mr. Tommy. "Bred right in his bones."

"Oh, yes," said Miss Margaret. "He had me lie down on the floor by the chimney before he opened fire on them with that pistol yonder." Miss Margaret smiled. "Them revenue agents skimmed off into the corn like deer, and my husband laughed and swore a curse and grabbed a box of pistol shells off the mantel and run after them."

"Chased the rascals, did he?" Mr. Tommy made a face at the idea of such a fool thing.

"But he wasn't halfway across the yard till they shot him down. I knew it because a pain cut me right across here," Miss Margaret said, moving her hand across her stomach. "I heard *them* shoot, and this pain run through me like a charge of electricity, and I knew Mr. McNeilly was dead. Afterwards I brought him indoors all by myself and undressed him and washed him, all myself. Couldn't nobody else touch him but me—I wouldn't have it. He weighed two hundred and seventeen pounds and wasn't a spare ounce of fat on him, and his monkey hair grew clean up his back, thick as grass, black as night. I always said there never was such a hairy man as my first husband, as Mr. McNeilly, before or since. The saying is a hairy man will be rich someday. Monkey hair draws money like a magnet draws iron."

"So I've heard," said Mr. Tommy. "Flying," he said. "You might say that's about the only thing I ever dream about."

Miss Margaret was busy about her work. She went out the door with her buckets. He heard the well windlass squeaking. She returned with water and set out dishes on the table.

Mr. Tommy got up and slipped on his trousers and shoes and went outside. The ground under him was frozen hard as bone, and over him, though the sun was not yet up, there was light enough in the sky to see the ducks swiftly stringing through the pale clean air, going east to the grainfields where they would feed all the morning before they returned to rest in the coves that afternoon.

Mr. Tommy wiped the sleep from his eyes. He looked about at the gray painted house and the clutter of barrel nets and fish baskets beside it. He looked at the cedars rising above the little family cemetery, and beyond them saw the flooded cove itself, rimmed white about its edges with ice.

Holding his breath an instant, he listened for his heart and felt it, steady, and steady as wings and strong as the hundreds of wild hearts beating so high above him; patient, and patient as the very fish themselves, these too, these unblinking, these staring thousands waiting deep in the icy waters.

He caught his breath as the pinching cold came sharp into his nostrils and brought him wide awake. He turned and going back into the house slammed the door hard behind him. Miss Margaret looked around from the stove.

"What is it?" she said.

"Ain't you seen a man before?" Mr. Tommy yelled in a new loud voice.

"What?"

"I'd of chased them rascals myself—*the same as him*," he said.

"I never said different, did I? Look, you can't no more help it if you—"

He didn't let her finish. "You better believe it!" he yelled, breathing hard, looking squarely at her gray eyes, gray as water, still as a pane of glass.

Robert Drake

A Christmas Visit

I think of King Lear and the color white—the color of age and winter, the color of despair. I sit in the waiting room after the receptionist has telephoned the "senile ward" that my patient has visitors, and I watch them drift by, the men in rumpled work clothes, the women in untidy cotton house dresses. More often than not, they are without their teeth, their chins and noses sometimes almost meeting, looking something like caricatures of their former selves, back when they were well, back when they were young. Their eyes often have a faraway look in them, sometimes bleared, as though they are trying to look beyond me, to see through me, into the future or, more probably, the past. The blues and the browns of the irises are faded now and the sparkle gone. Indeed, their eyes are almost lusterless, even opaque, sometimes even downright milky, especially when they seem to have lost all interest in looking outward and concentrate only on whatever vision can be discovered within. These are the ones whose worlds now are very private indeed.

They make little noise; they are well cared for, and they are clean. I can see that right off. ("O, there is a world of difference in things over there these days from what they used to be! Then they were just given food and a place to sleep. It's not an 'asylum' anymore, but a real hospital where people go—nobody is 'put' there these days—to get well and then come back home.") It is true that a meekness surrounds the ones there now—nothing really erratic or peculiar and certainly nothing violent or dangerous. ("Why, they don't have to use any kind of restraints on them now: the new drugs have made all the difference in the world! You won't see a thing to upset you over there—no more than you would out at the regular hospital here at home. It's just real nice over there: everybody ought

---

"A Christmas Visit" appeared in *The Christian Century*, 22 December 1976, and in *The Home Place*, by Robert Drake. Copyright © 1980 by Robert Drake. Reprinted by permission of Memphis State University Press.

to go over and see for himself.") These patients, the ones there now, are soft-spoken, sometimes even silent, but when they do turn their gaze toward me, I often notice something wistful about them, as though they are looking for something or someone but are afraid to ask for fear of being denied or rebuffed. What are they looking for; whom do they seek?

Is it some son or daughter out of the present, some friend or relative out of the past? Occasionally, one of them will stop and ask me whether I have come to see him; perhaps I will go along with him and say I have, which seems to satisfy him, for the moment, and he wanders off again. Or else he will stop and ask me when I last saw his family and when are they going to come and get him and take him home. I reply that I do not know but that I imagine it will be soon. What else can I say? Not the truth, certainly—that no one these days can handle such cases at home, that no one has the space or the servants to take care of them there, that no one has the time, for these days, life is definitely for the living—preferably the young. The dead must bury the dead, but I cannot tell them that. It is all I can do to tell myself that and make myself believe it.

There is a stir out front as new patients arrive: it is that time of day, the afternoon. A white man and a Negro woman are escorted in by a couple of deputy sheriffs, one of whom is a woman, and I wonder idly whether a troubled mind is still a crime. These two are not oldsters and therefore must be classified not as "senile" but as "insane." Did the deputies have to go out and "catch" this pair, maybe even arrest them and tell them to come along peaceably? The Negro woman, particularly, with her hair in wild disorder, looks agitated, and the woman deputy asks her to sit on a bench separate from the white man, who looks merely silent and subdued. Does that mean that racial segregation is preserved even into and beyond mental darkness, that there is no end to it anywhere, even in the grave? Or are they afraid that the woman will become violent at any minute and attack the man or someone else?

Again, the soft voices rise as the old people duck their heads in bashfulness and talk among themselves or to the nurses and their visitors if they have any. I look down at the legs of the women and they are often without stockings; all of a sudden, I think of all the naked legs outside the Nazi gas chambers, stacked row on row, the bodies of the victims arranged in orderly piles for *Life* magazine. What do they talk about? They hardly ever talk loud enough for me to hear. Is it just the minutiae of their daily lives, what they had for breakfast, what they want for supper, or are there complaints, misgivings, forlorn hopes, idle tears? Perhaps they discuss all of these. Now and then one of them will announce, as though no one else in the world cares (and who does?), "I've got to go to the bathroom," and then will wander off.

I notice the other visitors, too. They seem, on the whole, much like me, but we are reluctant to enter into conversation with one another. Indeed, we even avoid one another's eyes, as though sharing some secret shame. (A common sorrow, pure and simple, would bring us together.)

Finally, my patient comes, shuffling down the hall, holding onto a nurse's arm, taking the dance-like steps of the elderly arthritic, quick and short, as though anything else would be overly ambitious. As always, she is dressed in a clean print dress, her white hair beautifully combed and brushed. She is surprised all over again to see me, as though I am the last person in the world she had expected to see. Perhaps it is better than in the old days, when she first was a patient here, the times when she used to hug me and cry and beg to go home. She never talks about home now except to ask about various relatives and friends. Sometimes I have to tell her they are dead; at other times, I have to acknowledge that they just have not written.

She gets the home town newspaper, and I write to her once a week. So she knows all the news there is of a general nature. But she forgets: nothing stays long with her now, not even her surroundings. That is not to say of course that she does not know where she is, but where she lives is immaterial now; one place is as good as another. She has made a few friends among the nursing staff and with the other patients, but on the whole she holds herself aloof from them, perhaps seeing them as potential invaders of her private world. The old smile, somewhat puzzled now, is still there at times, and she still has the most gracious manners in the world—the courtesy that was grace itself and the tact that was famous. But all of this is somewhat perfunctory now, worn like a mask which has been on so long that there is no face behind it—automatic, ritualistic, dead.

The eyes are still blue. ("Blue is my color," she always said, just as she assumed an almost proprietary interest in arithmetic and algebra: "Mathematics was always my long suit.") But the vitality is gone from them: more and more, they seem to exist in repose—indifferent, uncaring, if not absolutely turned inward. They no longer are seeking, I feel; they no longer are waiting for anybody, anything. There is no outright retreat into the past, but a wall of impassivity seems to surround her, almost like a shelter, an impenetrable bulwark. Her peace with the world—at least with the present—seems made. O, there are flashes of the old wit from time to time. (She: "I never heard such cursing as there is over here, from the other patients." I: "Well, you haven't heard any words that you didn't know, have you?" She: "No, but some of the combinations have been unusual.") But more and more nothing is in evidence except a quiet politeness and a docility, a willingness to be noticed by anybody at all, but no great craving for attention. Because she is growing deaf, her voice, always kind and soft before, has begun to sound harsh and strident. Thus she may seem unhappy or petulant when really she is neither.

She shows me a little package of Christmas goodies some church group has brought her, along with all the other patients in her ward; it contains a wash rag and a bar of soap, a small box of talcum powder, and a little container of chocolate-covered cherries. She used to love those, and she could eat them now even with no teeth (perhaps that is why they were chosen), but she is indifferent about all the gifts, caring only enough to show them to me. I think: my mother is the object of charity, of philanthropy, however well meant; and I find that almost unbearable. Who would ever have thought it would come to this? But then what are the alternatives? There are none and I know it, for I have been through all that before.

I sit there a little while longer, with the poinsettia and some new print dresses I have brought her for Christmas. (My aunt: "They never seem to put the dresses on her that we bring; they're all just some sort of community property, I guess." I: "Well, they do the best they can, all things considered. She's certainly receiving better care than we could provide for her at home.") After a while, I get up and go into the Canteen and get some Coca-Colas for us both and also stop to ask there whether she still has money on deposit to use when she wants a snack. (She hardly ever does.) Soon the time arrives for me to go. And I have run out of anything else to say. What else can the two of us talk about anyway? More and more she has withdrawn into her own world, the world of the institution. She is not unhappy, nor is she really happy. She simply is. She no longer cries when I get up to go. I say, "I'll see you soon," and she says, "Come back real soon now." But does either of us really mean it or believe it?

The nurse comes back for her now, and she kisses me goodbye with some tenderness but no real sorrow and begins her shuffle back down the corridor. All of a sudden I feel inexpressibly sad though, again, it no longer tears me all to pieces to go over there as it used to. This is not a knife-edged sorrow now, rather more like a puzzled, reflective sadness as I watch her disappearing back into her ward. And I find myself wondering whether *she* has given all to her daughters—or to her son. Some lines of poetry, too, unbidden and unsought, begin to revolve in my head:

> For I could tell you a story which is true;
> I know a lady with a terrible tongue,
> Blear eyes fallen from blue,
> All her perfections tarnished—yet it is not long
> Since she was lovelier than any of you.

Outside the winter sky looms cold and bleak. It may snow before night.

Eleanor Glaze

Those Were the Afternoon Rooms

. . . of an old house, spacious, open high-ceilinged rooms of soft faded hues; forms remorseless and fixed. Often, as from within, the rooms were gently sunlit, more often settled in shadow, clouded and damp. Conjuring shadows, cognizant, would shyly advance a step or so from their corners, then recede, draw back unsure, retreat, again draw back to the safe walls. There before fading the shadows would linger. Deepening, guarding, they would hold as they lingered to their own corners, to their own places.

Being a child in those rooms, the only child, made me envy shadows for their quiet appearances and escapes, made me identify with shadows, made me believe that I would be a child always and like the shadows always . . . causeless, changeless, choiceless.

There was an evening room of dim yellow light, mellow substance, all covering of comfort unmeasurable, manifesting objects trustworthy and large. Evening was most often in the second room, the room after the parlor, evening came only to that second room with the touch-home center, the huge wooden table, a solid heavy circle. Of such solemnness was that circle that it supported light, of such solidness as to allow light to cover it as a rich textured cloth. In the same room stood a dresser thick-slabbed with cool marble where there was nothing else cool to touch. Framed in wood above it hung a narrow mirror six feet tall. Grandmother lifted me to the dresser to stand before the mirror so that I could see for myself that I was only a child. In the second room, the room after the parlor, the only room where evening was allowed, invited, lived out, great-grandmother sat on a brown leather sofa, her hands locked behind her head, her elbows jutting out at a winged angle. She sat silent and motionless in evening as a carving from pale grey wood.

Wide as an avenue down the center of the house ran a long hallway. At the end of the hallway, off to the side, rose curving stairs, an ascending spiral of banister glossy slick, of dark wood which gave subtle gleamings. Within the rooms I thought and counted on orange Tiger Lilies, there always, outside against the left wall, on slender stems holding their heads high, eager, inquisitive; the rash, defiant Tiger Lilies dipping in and out of sun/shade cycles.

In the front yard on either side of the walk two squat, funny umbrella tress grew. They protected nothing. Across the entire front of the house ran a wide front porch. Heavy round columns were at each end of the porch and on either side of the steps. At each end of the porch hung a wooden swing. Great-grandmother sat in the swing with the rose lattice behind it where she was protected from being seen. Great-grandmother was very thin, her hands and wrist covered with splotches, her lap too small for anything but a grey cat, the cat the exact color of her knotted hair. Because there were no roses behind it, the other swing could go higher. I could push that swing to motion and before it ceased swaying, fall asleep in it.

At the window seat in the second room a snowball tree outside nestled close to the wall. Across the cinder driveway was a house with a window seat facing the one I sat in. When I climbed into the window seat, I expected to see myself in the one facing me, the duplicate. I waited.

There were many rooms to the house, many levels. There was a cellar. There was an attic.

A musky ether was in the cellar, intoxicating: hearing, touch, sight, on first entering, overwhelmed. It made me inhale deeply. The furnace loomed up as though from deep within the earth, centered in the cellar, its pipe arms thrust upward through the house, a monster metal spider, holding the house up. It was evil, yet supportive, martyred. When it burned within, its square eyes glowed brilliant flickering blue and yellow-orange. Heavy clouds of dark dust arose when coal thundered down the chute to feed it. The dust would choke you, grandmother said. Don't go in the cellar when the coal comes down.

Thin ropes were nailed to the rafter for hanging wash when it rained. Inverted criss-crossed arcs at the corners formed interlaced patterns. Insects traveled those limp highways and they swung and hung daringly down, the insects, the crazy acrobats. From enormous tin tubs and scrub boards and cakes of brick-sized brown soap came sounds of sloshings and scrubbings. When I sat at the top of the cellar stairs hot steam would rise, a mist on my bare arms and knees and face, making my dress and my hair limp. Then the acrid lye smell, warm and moist, would come in alternating waves with the cool musky ether, competing, but never merging.

Up the stairs . . . up the long spiral at the end of the hallway on the way to the attic, a long trek which made grandmother pant as I followed past rented rooms on the second floor where the doors were closed tight and perhaps locked, and grandmother called me away from the doors and told me not to bother them, as if those who lived behind those doors were unnecessary, beneath her, and to be deliberately avoided. But on the way to the attic those doors and rooms of intermediate and unknowable people were passed where I tarried and had to be urged forward, those doors so precariously connected and carefully hidden from the dominant personality of the house.

The attic was warm. It made me think of Heaven. But in a few minutes it was hot and close and stifling. That passed, also. Shafted sunlight in the attic, straight pure shafts wider at the bottom, at a holy angle slanted from right to left. Closed off, not often visited, never available to renters, attic secrets were stored in piled boxes and trunks, treasures gathering sun motes and dust. It was as if the sun had poured into the attic for countless ages, raising the value of every secret. Grandmother was busy sorting or looking for something, or putting something else away to be saved, but I stood still until my vision cleared and focused, beginning as it cleared to reach, to touch.

In the corner near the slanted window, the dressmaker's manikin, with ribs of a desert skeleton picked clean, stood firm. Carcass and sovereign, she presided over all debris, over the paradox: neglect and treasure, treasure and neglect. Chipped mirrors so caked with grime as to give distorted reflections or none at all. Dolls sprawled, with their heads off, or their hair matted and awry, bald in spots, or their heads turned all the way backward, eyeless faces pressed down into chaos, their legs flung apart. Gifts new from the red clown came to this? In an arranged, but never the same, disorder lay small useless parts of so many things separated from what they once belonged to, or were a part of, torn apart, pulled apart, fallen apart. The mechanics or grace of wholes was absent in these separations which were somehow a part of one and the same overwhelming accident. Each separate piece was thus entirely object.

Especially forlorn were old books in piles, how they hugged to themselves their own fragile dry pages, or all that was left of them. Photographs in dust-filmed frames were of people who no longer existed, no longer mattered, no longer related to anything except perhaps to other useless scattered pieces and parts. In such golden warmth, these things were abandoned, yet saved and stored. And by not only the sun. The attic was warmed by a spread, collective slight smile of ghosts, lying low, close to the floor, hiding in the piles. O the forgotten dust dreams of forgotten people in picture frames. Even in profile their eyes looked bravely straight into the border of white nothingness within the frame. Bland, tight-lipped, haughty or compliant, male or female, child or adult, their eyes look unflinchingly into whatever had captured them, past to present, past to now, their eyes looked straight into whatever had led them, guilty of time, away.

On the middle shelf of an empty bookcase of darkest blue there was a white glass horse with a broken leg. Pale lines and cracks netted his arched sensuous body. With three legs he galloped, forever in motion, forever still, at breakneck speed.

And a light green mold outlined and lifted many edges of many pieces of separate things, a light green mold was entrusted with the keeping of tattered books and tokens and dry dead flowers and withered letters. And the golden keeping of the dust did not resist the ageless filtered sun.

Great-grandmother was very old then. And then she died. Then grandmother grew old and died. Then my mother was not so very old but she died anyway.

It is afternoon. I am a Tiger Lily. I am a shadow.

But those were the morning and evening and afternoon rooms of old houses . . . through which moved moist rich airs . . . through which moved echoes faintly, and shadows more strongly than echoes, and through which moved as though from far, far away, lost and unfinished voices.

Etheridge Knight

The Bones of My Father

There are no dry bones
here in this valley. The skull
of my father grins
at the Mississippi moon
from the bottom
of the Tallahatchie,
the bones of my father
are buried in the mud
of these creeks and brooks that twist
and flow their secrets to the sea.
But the wind sings to me
here the sun speaks to me
of the dry bones of my father.

  2

There are no dry bones
in the northern valley, in the Harlem alleys
young/black/men with knees bent
nod on the stoops of the tenements
and dream
of the dry bones of my father.

"The Bones of My Father" and "One Day We Shall All Go Back" from *Belly Songs and Other Poems*, by Etheridge Knight. Copyright © 1973 by Etheridge Knight. Reprinted by permission of Broadside Press.

And young white longhairs who flee
their homes, and bend their minds
and sing their songs of brotherhood
and no more wars are searching for
my father's bones

   3

There are no dry bones
here, my brothers. We hide from the sun.
No more do we take the long straight strides.
Our steps have been shaped by the cages
that kept us. We glide sideways
like crabs across the sand.
We perch on green lilies, we search
beneath white rocks . . . .
THERE ARE NO DRY BONES HERE

The skull of my father
grins at the Mississippi moon
from the bottom
of the Tallahatchie.

One Day We Shall All Go Back

(For Jake & Margaret Milliones, and Nicky & Curtis)

One day we shall all go back—
we shall all go back (down home
to the brown hills and red gullies (down home
where the blood of our fathers
has fed the black earth (down home
where the slow/flowing rivers, dark and silent,
sing to the bones of our brothers (down home
wrapped forever in black wetness (down home . . . .

One day we shall all go back (down home
we shall leave the cold northlands
of icy stares, frozen hearts, stiff snot, cold flats,
racking coughs, hard cash, and go back (down home
to be kissed by sweet rain and warm sun on black backs.

Etheridge Knight

We shall all go back (down home
to avenge Medgar, and Martin, and lil Emmett Till,
and all the others who died the good death (down home—
back—back to avenge our fathers and mothers killed and raped
in Natchez, Memphis, Montgomery, Mobile, Lake Charles,
New Orleans, Baton Rouge, Macon, Waycross, Charleston,
Jackson, Savannah, Tougoloosa . . . .

One day we shall all go back—
We shall surely all go back (down home
and the southland will tremble to our marching feet (down home
where our freedom cries will shake the southern skies (down home
and the shame will leave our children's eyes (down home . . . .

David Madden

A Fever of Dying

April 14, 1884
(Three days after Doctor Ramsey died)
Written on Holston Mountain

In the Beginning was the Word. Parson Brownlow's words in the North, sparked by what he envisioned—a Federal force penetrating East Tennessee—lent motive power, in a sense, even to General William Price Sanders' raid. General Sanders came down from Eastern Kentucky (before he became a General) to burn bridges, tear up railroads, and draw Confederate troops back to Knoxville, in preparation for Burnside's invasion, his mission not to take and hold, but to destroy.

A battle, even a raid, is so confusing to the ordinary soldier who is a living part of it and often to the commander who leads it that writing about a battle is even harder than fighting in it. I hear that Thomas William Humes, William Rule, and Oliver Temple down in Knoxville are writing books about Loyal Mountaineers of Tennessee. And it is known at Knoxville that before Doctor Ramsey left Charlotte and returned to Knoxville in 1872 he had finished his autobiography. I have not read it, of course, nor met anyone who has, for he intends it for his children and grandchildren, but I suppose he devotes space to Sanders' raid, and I often imagine how he, a historian, who did not witness it, for he was a fugitive from it, would write of it.

Here are the facts, as Parson Brownlow would say, and I give them as *he* would give them in *The Whig*, not unmixed with rhetoric and folklore, for I have read, I have listened, and I have meditated. I have heard eyewitnesses recount their experiences, laced with statistics, I have witnessed re-enactments by remnants of the old forces and their young relatives. Why did I feel nothing? Why did my imagination remain inert, my intellect stagnant? Something ought to be done. I will start with you and me. I hope I haven't missed anything. If this gets confusing, pay better attention.

Let me get my bearings: "Ever-before" I spied General Sanders from the tower in Bleak House, many others got him in their sights. Through their eyes, I see him coming. Daily we see and are seen; we know that we see, but seldom know that we are seen. Sometimes we arrange *what we see*; seldom do we arrange *the ways we are seen*. To see, we must see ourselves as others see us, combine those images with the images of others that *we* see into a conception. Then as we *are* seen, we see; and all ambiguities are a natural part of a conception that we control.

I am always aware of the one *I* do not see seeing me.

On the evening of the seventeenth of June, some rebel farmers saw General Sanders leading 1500 mounted men into the vicinity of Montgomery, Tennessee, near Big Emory River.

Then a small party of rebel soldiers stationed a mile east of Montgomery at Wartburg saw 400 of him, in the vital sense that a commander's men are, through his commands, an extension of himself. The 400 men he detached to surprise and capture them were successful, except for several who escaped to transmit their vision of him to rebels in Kingston, Loudon, Knoxville, and other places, so that he was imagined lucidly by more people than actually ever saw him on this raid. Thus are we all seen, and never imagine that we are. As we pass, we are sketched, photographed.

At daylight of the 19th, three miles equidistant between Loudon and Lenoir's, a captured courier, carrying orders from the commanding officer at Loudon, saw him, watched him read the order directing forces from Kingston to combine with men from Lenoir already called to Loudon, where the most important bridge in the area was heavily fortified, in expectation of a raid by this expedition. The courier was taken with Sanders in the direction of the now unprotected Lenoir's.

I once heard how Doctor James Gettys McGready Ramsey's great-grandmother missed America. Imagining that he lay dreaming again of her, that morning in June in his daughter's house at Lenoir's, helps me somehow really to *see* Doctor Ramsey for the first time. In 1730, his Scotch-Irish Presbyterian great-grandparents, with their son, Reynolds Ramsey, set out from Ireland for New Castle, Delaware (where William Penn, not "by the way," first set foot on this soil). She fell into the Atlantic. The quilted dress that was the fashion in the high latitude they were leaving buoyed her above the waves, so that her husband and her son (and now her great-grandson, dream) watched her body float a long time, until she sank over the horizon. The sight young Reynolds witnessed in broad daylight on the Atlantic became, I would suppose, a nightmare image that he passed on in story to his son Francis Alexander who passed it on to his children.

Knocking at the door woke Doctor Ramsey, and he heard his son-in-law, Doctor Lenoir, calling to him. "Wake up, Doctor, I must tell you something urgent."

"What is it. B. B.?"

"A neighbor has come to tell us that the Yankees were at Kingston last night."

"Thank you, B. B. I am getting up."

Seeing a Yankee officer leading his men in a violation of Tennessee soil, Doctor Ramsey's mind leapt up more quickly than his body.

He was daily more aware that two separate sources of energy resided in him. The terror of the lifelong nightmare and the humidity of June in an upstairs bedroom had made his body moist. An effort of will shook off the effects of the dream, allowing the images of his daytime preoccupation for the past month to hover for attention: John Sevier and Andrew Jackson meet (as might Doctor Ramsey and Parson Brownlow) on Gay Street, Jackson saying again, "In view of my services to my country, I wonder at your criticisms of me," Sevier replying, "Services? I know of no great service you have rendered the country except taking a trip to Natchez with another man's wife." Buttoning his trousers, the historian smiled, even though the scene sometimes gave him pain, for John Sevier was the leathershirt hero of his *Annals of Tennessee* to 1800 and General Andrew Jackson was taking shape as the hero of the sequel. He was glad Tennessee was spared the death that day on Gay Street in Knoxville of either man, or both men, for Jackson carried only his sword cane and Sevier his cutlass. (I see editor Brownlow and editor Landon Haynes in Jonesboro fighting in the street May 14, 1840.) The figure of the Yankee officer advancing toward Lenoir reminded Dr. Ramsey of his duties as State Director of the East Tennessee and Georgia Railroad and Confederate treasury agent for Tennessee.

Henrietta stood at the bottom of the stairs, setting her bonnet straight on her head. "What are you about, daughter?" he asked, descending toward her.

I'm going on the cars with you as far as Concord."

"Even if I were indeed senile, I wouldn't permit it. I should stay and aid your husband in watching over *you* and the boys. But they won't linger here. Knoxville is their point of attack. And I must move the Confederate depository to Greeneville."

"Do you think I can let my father leave my house alone at a time like this? Father, the Yankees are finally *here*."

"Let *me* go with grandfather," said William.

"You and your brother are dearer to your mother than a legion of fathers," said Ramsey, smiling.

"Don't talk so," said Henrietta.

"Anyway, I can't wait for the passenger train. I must flag down the freight. It's due in a few minutes."

"I'll put my ear on the track," said William, "and tell you when I hear it."

"Who taught you that one?"

"James."

Ramsey imagined William's cheek on one rail, James's on the opposite rail, the engine named after himself bearing down on them. "William, did grandfather ever tell you about your great-great-great-grandmother who sailed from Ireland more than a century ago?"

"Father, must you?" asked Henrietta, shivering.

"No, tell me," said William.

"Good. I'll tell you a *better* story next time I come."

"I think I hear the train, father," said Henrietta.

"It's late. My watch is never tardy."

Doctor Ramsey bade Henrietta and Doctor Lenoir and his three grandchildren goodbye, walked down the short slope to the tracks and flagged down the freight train. As it chugged to a crawl, the engineer pulled him up into the cab. "You're not late are you, Fred?"

As the train pulled out of Lenoir's, Ramsey looked back at the Lenoirs standing on the long porch as they had done many times before, when Yankee raiders were *not* twelve miles north, heading South along the Great Truck Lines up The Valley of East Tennessee.

"The track and the rolling stock has deteriorated, Doctor Ramsey. Yes, I am late. I reckon, I'll *be* late on the *next* run, too. Don't reckon you could scare up some Richmond money for the road, they way you done when it first got built? Didn't you even go up to New York and help sell some bonds?"

"Your information has some semblance of accuracy." 'If there is any merit in having equipped so many miles with so little money,' Doctor Ramsey thought, 'I claim it as my own. I, *egome*—my very self, did it all.'

"And now," Doctor Ramsey said, reaching for a chunk of wood as the engineer jerked open the fire door for him, "if overused equipment may be urged a little more forcibly, I must get to Knoxville." 'And rescue my Confederate depository from the invading enemy.'

So the first time I *see* Doctor Ramsey, he, like Brownlow when I first conjured him, is on the run, *in medias res*.

From the porch, Henrietta watched the train until the caboose made the curve past the salt works and she could not see it any longer except in her head as she turned to go into the house. The rooms through which she passed were cool and dark in the early morning and she listened to her dress move as she walked, and a pot clatter in the basement where the Negroes were getting up breakfast.

At 8:30, she opened the back porch door to see if the image of Confederate cavalry in her head was actually coming down the Kingston road yet. She saw a cavalry force riding rapidly towards her gate in an escort of dust, still dense with night moisture.

She went out to the gate and called to one of the riders. "Are you escaping from the Yankees?"

"We *are* the Yankees." She searched for the face of the man who spoke and recognized Colonel R. K. Byrd.

"We haven't seen you in several years, Mr. Byrd. We figured you were at the North."

"I have come home, Mrs. Lenoir. Let me put your mind at ease. You have no more to fear from me, and my comrades, today than you did before this revolution. I think I speak for my commander."

A tall officer of about 29 or 30 beside Colonel Byrd nodded politely and smiled. How did Sanders look to her? Handsome? Ugly? She didn't notice how he looked.

They rode on a little piece opposite the house, dismounted and went inside the store and post office building.

Henrietta remembered that B. B. had opened the safe that morning—the key was still in its door. Without hesitation, she walked across the road to the store. She avoided Colonel Byrd and his commanding officer, and trusted her bonnet to conceal her face from my other soldiers native to this area who might recognize her.

Unrecognized, unmolested, she moved among the enemy, the first she had ever seen, and went directly to the safe, removed large parcels of money from the open shelves, tucked them in the bend of her thin arm, and in one motion as she rose, slipped two hanks of yarn from an open bale that set beside the safe over her arm. Passing out of the store, she was a quiet, contained storm of emotional energy. She crossed the great road faintly aware of Confederate soldiers under guard around a tree, passed through her back gate, passed some cavalry men decorously sprawled on her lawn, strode through the house out onto the front porch and down into the garden by the railroad tracks, where she deposited the money under the flowering rhododendron hedge. I impute to her my own reflection that even before Doctor Ramsey could get to Knoxville and transport the assets of the Bank of Tennessee and the Confederate Treasury beyond Yankee capture, even before his train reached Concord, his daughter had rescued the proceeds of her own family business.

As she walked up to the front porch (the front of the house faced the railroad, but long before the railroad came four years ago, the house was built to face Lenoir, North Carolina, where her husband's father, William Ballard Lenoir, the first, had built the first version of this house) she realized that not only had she not been the victim of monstrous Yankee atrocities, such as her men had long taught her to expect, no one had said a single word to her. Though she knew some had looked at her, covertly, it was as if she had been invisible, or they had been shadows of the imagination.

Looking out her parlor window, she saw that they were as real as the silver.

David Madden

The small Confederate force that had left Lenoir to meet the Yankees on the Kingston Road last night was now captive there under her trees, some of them wounded, but being attended to by her husband and others.

The young Yankee commander of the cavalry raiders stood in the road absently brushing dust from his sleeves, looking at her. A thrill rushed over her as the certainty that he knew what she had done struck her.

So General Sanders is real to her. But why is *she* more real to me than *he* is? Knowing from examining my own experience that the reader's imagination is not obliged to hew to the writing, I wonder if he is more real to *you*, reading, than he is now as I write. For me, he is a being struggling to get born.

I know that he made a terse, one-sentence report on his mission, when he got back into Kentucky; maybe, as is also the general procedure, a second brief report to Burnside. A few weeks later would have to come a fuller report, an actual copy of which is now being processed in Washington as part of a project that began in 1864, the first volumes of which will be published, we are told, in about 1888. Until then . . . I imagine . . .

Lexington, Ky.
July 26, 1863

General: I have the honor to report that, in obedience to special instructions from the General, I left Mount Vernon, Kentucky, June 14, 1863, with a force of 1,500 mounted men, composed of detachments of different regiments, for the East Tennessee and Virginia railroad. From Mount Vernon to Williamsburg, on the Cumberland River, a distance of 60 miles, a train of wagons containing forage and subsistence stores, accompanied the expedition.

From this point, I followed the Marsh Creek road to near Huntsville, Tennessee, leaving that place a few miles to my left. On the evening of the 17th, we reached the vicinity of Montgomery, Tennessee (Morgan Court House on some maps). When I learned that a small party of rebels were stationed one mile from Montgomery at Wartburg, I sent 400 men from the First East Tennessee to surprise and capture them.

An hour later, I followed with the remainder of the command. The surprise was complete, except for a small portion of this command, who were with their horses some distance from camp; they escaped and gave the first notice of our approach at Knoxville, Kingston, Loudon, and other places. We captured at Wartburg 102 enlisted men and 2 officers (one of them an aide to General Pegram), together with a large number of horses, 60 boxes of artillery ammunition, several thousand pounds of salt, meal, flour, bacon, some corn, 500 spades, 100 picks, besides a large quantity of other public stores, and 6 wagons with mule teams. I paroled the prisoners and destroyed the property.

From this point, I marched toward Kingston. When within 8 miles of that place, I learned that Scott's brigade and one battery guarded the ford of Clinch River there. For this reason, leaving Kingston to my right, I crossed the river at Waller's Ford eight miles above, which is on the direct road to Loudon.

At daylight on the 19th, I was three miles equidistant between Loudon and Lenoir's. Here I learned that a force of three regiments was at the Loudon Bridge, with eight pieces of artillery, and that the rebels had been digging rifle-pits, ditches, etc., at that place for two weeks. A captured courier of the commanding officer carried dispatches ordering the forces from Kingston to follow in my rear; the order states that the troops from Lenoir's had already been ordered to join them. I determined on this intelligence to avoid Loudon, and started immediately for Lenoir's Station, which place I reached about 8 a.m., some thirty minutes after the rebel troops had departed. (Does the fact he makes no mention of Henrietta make this a false report?) At this station I captured a detachment of artillerymen, with 3 six-pounder iron guns, 8 officers, and 57 enlisted men. Burned the depot, a large brick building, which contained five pieces of artillery, harness and saddles, 2500 stand of small arms, large amount of artillery and musket ammunition, artillery and cavalry equipments. We also captured some 75 Confederate States' mules and horses.

There was a large cotton factory owned by Dr. Lenoir and a large amount of cotton at this place, but I ordered that it should not be burned, as it furnished the Union citizens of the surrounding country with their only material for making cloth, but have since learned that it was burned by mistake or accidentally.

From Lenoir Station to Knoxville, 24 miles east, I had the telegraph wire cut and the railroad destroyed at points about 1 mile apart. (He comes in from the West along Kingston Road. Through the scope of my sharpshooter's rifle, I look down on him from the tower, even though on that occasion I was far from the tower, with no conception of it or of him. That evening at dusk, the Confederate pickets were waiting for him on the hill down from Bleak House, across the road.) At about 7 p.m. we met the enemy's pickets at Knoxville and drove them to within a mile of the city.

As soon as it was full dark, I left a portion of the First Kentucky Cavalry on this side of town and moved the rest of the command by another road entirely around to the other side, driving in the pickets at several places. To prevent the sending of troops to the bridges above, I cut the railroad. At daylight, on the Tazewell road, I moved up to the city. I found the enemy well-posted on the heights and in the adjacent buildings, with eight or nine pieces of artillery. The enemy had protected the batteries and barricaded the streets with cotton bales. Their force was estimated at 3,000, including citizens who were impressed into service. After about one hour's skirmishing, I withdrew. Just east of the city, I captured two pieces of artillery and all the camp equipage of a regiment of conscripts who had joined the defending force in the city, and about 80 horses and 31 prisoners.

I then started for Strawberry Plains, following the railroad. I destroyed all the small bridges and depots to within 4 miles. At Flat Creek I burned a finely built covered bridge and also a county bridge. The guard had retreated. Three miles below Strawberry Plains, I left the railroad and crossed the Holston River, so as to attack the bridge on the same side the enemy were.

As soon as we came in sight, they opened on the advance with four pieces of artillery. I dismounted the infantry and sent the Forty-fourth Ohio, under Major Moore, up the river, and the rest, under Colonel Byrd and Major Dow, to get in their rear. After about an hour's skirmishing, the enemy were driven off, and having a train and locomotive, with steam up, in waiting, a portion of them escaped, leaving all their guns (five), 137 enlisted men and 2 officers as prisoners, a vast amount of stores, equipage and ammunition, in our possession. I remained at this place all night, and destroyed the splendid bridge over the Holston River, over 1,600 feet long, built on eleven piers. The trestle-work included, this bridge was 2,100 feet in length, the most important on the East Tennessee and Virginia line.

At daylight on the 21st of June I started up the railroad for Mossy Creek, New Market, and vicinity. I captured 120 prisoners and destroyed several cars and a large quantity of stores, and I burned the fine bridge at Mossy Creek, over 300 feet long. Near this place I also destroyed the machinery of a gun factory and a saltpeter factory.

As I knew the enemy was making every effort to capture my command, I determined to leave the railroad here and endeavor to cross the mountains at Rogers' Gap. Fording the Holston at Hayworth's Bend, I started for the Powder Springs Gap of Clinch Mountain. Here a large force opposed me directly in my front, and another strong force overtook and commenced skirmishing with my rear guard. But with all this force in my rear, I took country roads and got into the gap. A mile and half from Rogers' Gap, I found that it was blockaded by fallen timber and strongly guarded by artillery and infantry. All the other practical Gaps were obstructed and guarded in a similar manner.

I determined to destroy and abandon my artillery and move by a wood path to Smith's Gap, 3 miles from Rogers' Gap. I now opposed a large force both in front and rear and could avoid capture only by getting into the mountains, placing all of them in my rear. After driving a regiment of cavalry from Smith's Gap, I was able to execute my plan. The road through this pass is only a bridle path, and very rough. I did not get up the mountain until after night. About 170 of my men and officers got on the wrong road and did not join the command until we reached Kentucky.

Owing to the continued march, many horses gave out and were left, and although we captured several hundred on the march, there were not enough to supply all the men. We reached Boston, Kentucky, on the 24th. Our loss was 2 killed, 4 wounded, 13 missing, and several drowned. I enclose an abstract of these. I also enclose the parole of 461 prisoners.

Colonel William Price Sanders

Missing from the report would be the fact that he sent to Major Haynes, commanding at Knoxville in the absence of General Buckner, by a Lieutenant Luttrell, a paroled prisoner, this note: "I send you my compliments, and say that but for the admirable manner with which you managed your artillery I would have taken Knoxville today."

For Colonel Sanders, soon promoted to General, was a southerner, born in Frankfort, Kentucky, raised in Natchez, Mississippi, a cousin of Jefferson Davis, who had interceded when Cadet Sanders was about to be dismissed in 1853 from West Point for deficiency in language. Had it not been for his cousin's devotion, he would not have graduated and gone on the Utah expedition, defended Washington against his own people, served on the Peninsula at Yorktown and Williamsburg, and at Mechanicsville and Hanover Courthouse—putting his cousin's capital in jeopardy, made a raid into Knoxville and invaded East Tennessee with Burnside, and ridden a white horse on the Kingston Road within view of the windows of Bleak House's tower.

Autumn 1863

Mrs. Lenoir's face was not at the window, but that made General Sanders see all the more lucidly, made him feel her presence fill the house, giving him a sense of all its rooms simultaneously.

Most of the trees within sight were stumps now, cut down, and buildings dismantled for firewood and to erect villas of cabins in the fertile fields. He had been the first to use her property, but only for resting his men. Other officers, General Shackleford most recently, had come after him, had established headquarters in Doctor Lenoir's office. Two brigades, usually, at a given time, were camped on the place. The officers' tents were pitched in the yard and gardens around the house.

As he instructed his officers, he placed himself in view of the windows that faced the road, hoping she would see him.

Finally, he sent Captain Brill to ask Dr. Lenoir to prepare a room for him in the house. The Captain returned fifteen minutes later to inform him that the Lenoirs were ready to receive him, that supper was on the table.

Doctor Lenoir greeted him at the door and showed him into the dining room, and introduced him to Mrs. J. G. M. Ramsey, wife of the historian of Tennessee, to Elizabeth Breck, his widowed daughter, to Susan Ramsey, to young Arthur Ramsey, to his two boys, saying that the babe in Mrs. Breck's arms was his youngest child. One chair was empty. "Is Mrs. Lenoir not joining us?"

"She is ill. She hasn't come to the table in several weeks. We lost two of our boys in a single night to fever."

"I am very sorry to hear that, sir."

"Is there anything I can do for you, Mrs. Ramsey?" he asked.

"Mother, why don't you ask General Sanders," said Susan "if he would rebuild our house at Mecklenburg and restore from the ashes father's books and research material for his sequel to THE ANNALS OF TENNESSEE?" Susan turned as much of her back toward him as she could.

"Forgive my daughter, General, for reasons that should be obvious to a cousin of *our* President."

He nodded, and moved his gaze a little over the heads of the family, falling upon the doors as a Negress very gently slid them open, and Henrietta walked very slowly into the room.

General Sanders rose and held her chair. She smelled of crushed lavender and musk, like something put away in an armoir for weeks. He sat down again and looked into her face. Her eyes were full of death-before-death.

The food sickened him, but not because it was bad.

Throughout the meal, he knew that she had come to the table just to sit with him. They were alone together. She hardly *looked* at the others, and she *spoke* to no one.

But young Arthur had looked at her from the moment she came in and he was aware that it was obvious to everyone that he was staring at her, to everyone but Henrietta.

"I miss Sister Charlotte," Arthur murmured, still gazing at Henrietta.

"Charlotte," explained Dr. Lenoir, realizing that all the others were too moved to explain to him, "died early in the war of typhus fever."

"A dutiful daughter," said Mrs. Ramsey, "an affectionate sister, a patriotic and humane girl, a humble Christian."

"Doctor Curry said, 'She bade adieu to Earth's transience, and went to Heaven.'"

"Don't you know," his mother said to Arthur, "it's no more complicated than that?"

Arthur seemed to have caught a glimpse of God's design, how things only *appear* without connection. His brothers were all in the Confederate army, he was not yet seventeen, and had an irrepressible desire to join them and share their fate even though looking at Henrietta, remembering Charlotte, he had sensed for the first time what life came to. He was clearly affectionate and devoted to his mother and sisters. It would be hard to leave them and go into the camps.

"Doctor Curry wrote a beautiful tribute to her memory," said Mrs. Breck, " 'No one of her age was more highly esteemed, none more cordially loved.' "

"It's made an irreparable chasm in our family," said Mrs. Ramsey, "which amid war is otherwise whole. Henrietta . . . She does not hear me," she said, to *the family*. Henrietta seemed more of Charlotte's company than theirs. "Henrietta." she looked up. "Mind your duty to God to mind your health. You must eat."

Henrietta's faint nod of filial obedience was reassuring to no one.

As each person left the room, General Sanders dreaded the moment when Arthur would rise to go, and he would have to look and speak directly to him. He remembered the story he had heard of General Sherman saying goodbye to his cadets in Alexandria, Louisiana, when word came of Fort Sumter. With tears in his eyes, he had said to them, "I may have to meet you again on the battlefield." He imagined himself on a horse somewhere, caught in this boy's sights, the boy himself fixed in the sights of one of the sharpshooters under his own command—all these assembled here mourning the death of the boy, celebrating his own death. Either was always both victory and defeat, a Janus-faced event.

After a while, after several had excused themselves from the table, he saw that deep inside, beneath the look of death in Mrs. Lenoir's eyes, something came alive and glowed.

Finally, even Doctor Lenoir left the room, and they were literally alone.

"I knew you hid the silver from me that first time we camped here."

She nodded. "I saw in your face, as you looked up at me when I stood at the window, that you knew."

He shared with her the sense of certainty that there was no need to explain why he didn't confiscate the silver, and that both knew it was still there under the rhododendron hedge.

Watching her grow weaker, he said, "I must go to my room, so you can rest."

"Have they told you? That my two boys—"

"Yes. You have surrendered, Mrs. Lenoir," he said, trying to soften the tone of admonishment.

"I am lingering, I am only lingering."

"No one can help you. I see that. And I am very sad."

"I want you to be sad."

"Because I am the enemy?"

"You are not the enemy. There *is* no enemy."
"I must continue to pretend that there is."
"I am sorry that you must."
"How did you and I come to be sitting here like this?"
"For me, there is only the *question*. Do you have an *answer?*"
"No."
General Sanders rose.
Henrietta looked up at him. "Goodbye, General Sanders."
"Goodbye, Mrs. Lenoir."
Lying on the bed that had belonged, Doctor Lenoir had told him, to his grandfather, the bed that the Negress, who seemed paralyzed between devotion to the family to which she was enslaved and devotion to an abstract ideal of freedom that her own grandfather had perhaps known but that she had perhaps not known, told him Doctor Ramsey always slept in when he stayed at Lenoir's, he imagined how the old historian must have felt lying here the night his daughter had told him about how the raiders had passed her house on the morning of 19th of June, how she had concealed the silver from the store safe under her shawl. His daughter had acted the lady and the heroine, and Doctor Ramsey had gone to sleep here very proud of her. The old historian had lain here again in fitful sleep, he imagined, when he visited more recently, more in danger of capture by his enemies, and seen her contrasting mood all the more vividly: sad, disconsolate, uneasy about the situation, anxious about the exposure of the family at Mecklenburg, about the exposure of her own family here at Lenoir's. Dejected, she must have conveyed a sense of how she felt, an ominous presentiment of future disaster and of cause for overwhelming bereavement. Voicing none of it. The old historian being able plainly to discern what she apprehended and felt. So that he had lingered with her until the hour grew late, then gotten up the next morning to ride across his favorite bridge with his son, the last to cross before they had to burn it. Not knowing how efficiently Orlando Poe could on that site put out his pontoon bridge.

The General became aware of his own heavy breathing, and gradually of the breathing of all those asleep in the house, except Henrietta's, for the house itself seemed only an *image* in *her* mind, transfixed but palpitating in a prolonged fever of dying.

Cormac McCarthy

Instruments of Liberation

He was lying naked under the trees with his rags spread across the limbs above him when another rider going down the river reined up and stopped.

He turned his head. Through the willows he could see the legs of the horse. He rolled over on his stomach.

The man got down and stood beside the horse.

He reached and got his twinehanded knife.

Howdy there, said the rider.

He didnt answer. He moved to the side to see better through the branches.

Howdy there. Where ye at?

Wanted to talk to ye.

What about?

Hell fire, come on out. I'm white and christian.

The kid was reaching up through the willows trying to get his breeches. The belt was hanging down and he tugged at it but the breeches were hung on limb.

Goddamn, said the man. You aint up in the tree are ye?

Why dont you go and leave me the hell alone.

Just wanted to talk to ye. Didnt intend to get ye all riled up.

You done got me riled.

Was you the feller knocked in that Mexer's head yesterday evenin? I aint the law.

Who wants to know?

Captain White. He wants to sign that feller up to join the army.

The army?

Yessir.

"Instruments of Liberation" from *Blood Meridian*, by Cormac McCarthy. Copyright © 1984 by Cormac McCarthy. Reprinted by permission of Random House, Inc.

What army?

Company under Captain White. We goin to whip up on the Mexicans.

The war's over.

He says it aint over. Where are you at?

He rose and hauled the breeches down from where he'd hung them and pulled them on. He pulled on his boots and put the knife in the right bootleg and came out from the willows pulling on his shirt.

The man was sitting in the grass with his legs crossed. He was dressed in buckskin and he wore a plug hat of dusty black silk and he had a small Mexican cigar in the corner of his teeth. When he saw what clawed its way out through the willows he shook his head.

Kindly fell on hard times aint ye son? he said.

I just aint fell on no good ones.

You ready to go to Mexico.

I aint lost nothin down there.

It's a chance for ye to raise ye self in the world. You best make a move someway or another fore ye go plumb in under.

What do they give ye?

Ever man gets a horse and his ammunition. I reckon we might find some clothes in your case.

I aint go no rifle.

We'll find ye one.

What about wages?

Hell fire son, you wont need no wages. You get to keep everthing you can raise. We goin to Mexico. Spoils of war. Aint a man in the company wont come out a big landowner. How much land you own now?

I dont know nothin about soldierin.

The man eyed him. He took the unlit cigar from his teeth and turned his head and spat and put it back again. Where ye from? he said.

Tennessee.

Tennessee. Well I dont misdoubt but what you can shoot a rifle.

The kid squatted in the grass. He looked at the man's horse. The horse was fitted out in tooled leather with worked silver trim. It had a white blaze on its face and four white stockings and it was cropping up great teethfuls of the rich grass. Where you from, said the kid.

I been in Texas since thirty-eight. If I'd not run up on Captain White I dont know where I'd be this day. I was a sorrier sight even than what you are and he come along and raise me up like Lazurus. Set my feet in the path of righteousness. I'd done took to drinkin and whorin till hell wouldnt have me. He seen somethin in me worth savin and I see it in you. What do ye say?

I dont know.

Just come with me and meet the captain.

The boy pulled at the halms of grass. He looked at the horse again. Well, he said. Dont reckon it'd hurt nothin.

They rode through the town with the recruiter splendid on the stockingfooted horse and the kid behind him on the mule like something he'd captured. They rode through narrow lanes where the wattled huts steamed in the heat. Grass and prickly pear grew on the roofs and goats walked about on them and somewhere off in that squalid kingdom of mud the sound of the little deathbells tolled thinly. They turned up Commerce Street through the Main Plaza among rafts of wagons and they crossed another plaza where boys were selling grapes and figs from little trundlecarts. A few bony dogs slank off before them. They rode through the Military Plaza and they passed the little street where the boy and the mule had drunk the night before and there were clusters of women and girls at the well and many shapes of wickercovered clay jars standing about. They passed a little house where women inside were wailing and the little hearsecart stood at the door with the horses patient and motionless in the heat and the flies.

The captain kept quarters in a hotel on a plaza where there were trees and a small green gazebo with benches. An iron gate at the hotel front opened into a passageway with a courtyard at the rear. The walls were whitewashed and set with little ornate colored tiles. The captain's man wore carved boots with tall heels that rang smartly on the tiles and on the stairs ascending from the courtyard to the rooms above. In the courtyard there were green plants growing and they were freshly watered and steaming. The captain's man strode down the long balcony and rapped sharply at the door at the end. A voice said for them to come in.

He sat a wickerwork desk writing letters, the captain. They stood attending, the captain's man with his black hat in his hands. The captain wrote on nor did he look up. Outside the kid could hear a woman speaking in spanish. Other than that there was just the scratching of the captain's pen.

When he had done he laid down the pen and looked up. He looked at his man and then he looked at the kid and then he bent his head to read what he'd written. He nodded to himself and dusted the letter with sand from a little onyx box and folded it. Taking a match from a box of them on the desk he lit it up and held it to a stick of sealing wax until a small red medallion had pooled onto the paper and knuckled the seal with his ring. Then he stood the letter between two books on his desk and leaned back in his chair and looked at the kid again. He nodded gravely. Take seats, he said.

They eased themselves into a kind of settle made from some dark wood. The captain's man had a large revolver at his belt and as he sat he hitched the belt around so that the piece lay cradled between his thighs. He put his hat over it and leaned back. The kid folded his busted boots one behind the other and sat upright.

The captain pushed his chair back and rose and came around to the front of the desk. He stood there for a measured minute and then he hitched himself up on the desk and sat with his boots dangling. He had gray in his hair and in the sweeping moustaches that he wore but he was not old. So you're the man, he said.

What man? said the kid.

What man sir, said the captain's man.

How old are you, son?

Nineteen.

The captain nodded his head. He was looking the kid over. What happened to you?

What?

Say sir, said the recruiter.

Sir?

I said what happened to you.

The kid looked at the man sitting next to him. He looked down at himself and he looked at the captain again. I was fell on by robbers, he said.

Robbers, said the captain.

Took everthing I had. Took my watch and everthing.

Have you got a rifle?

Not no more I aint.

Where was it you were robbed.

I dont know. They wasnt no name to it. It was just a wilderness.

Where were you coming from?

I was coming from Naca, Naca . . .

Nacogdoches?

Yeah.

Yessir.

Yessir.

How many were there?

The kid stared at him.

Robbers. How many robbers.

Seven or eight, I reckon. I got busted in the head with a scantlin.

The captain squinted one eye at him. Were they Mexicans?

Some. Mexicans and niggers. They was a white or two with em. They had a bunch of cattle they'd stole. Only thing they left me with was a old piece of knife I had in my boot.

The captain nodded. He folded his hands between his knees. What do you think of the treaty? he said.

The kid looked at the man on the settle next to him. He had his eyes shut. He looked down at his thumbs. I dont know nothin about it, he said.

I'm afraid that's the case with a lot of Americans, said the captain. Where are you from, son?

Tennessee.

You werent with the Volunteers at Monterrey were you?

No sir.

Bravest bunch of men under fire I believe I ever saw. I suppose more men from Tennessee bled and died on the field in northern Mexico than from any other state. Did you know that?

No sir.

They were sold out. Fought and died down there in that desert and then they were sold out by their own country.

The kid sat silent.

The captain leaned forward. We fought for it. Lost friends and brothers down there. And then by God if we didnt give it back. Back to a bunch of barbarians that even the most biased in their favor will admit have no least notion in God's earth of honor or justice or the meaning of republican government. A people so cowardly they've paid tribute a hundred years to tribes of naked savages. Given up their crops and livestock. Mines shut down. Whole villages abandoned. While a heathen horde rides over the land looting and killing with total impunity. Not a hand raised against them. What kind of people are these? The Apaches wont even shoot them. Did you know that? They kill them with rocks. The captain shook his head. He seemed made sad by what he had to tell.

Did you know that when Colonel Doniphan took Chihuahua City he inflicted over a thousand casualties on the enemy and lost only one man and him all but a suicide? With an army of unpaid irregulars that called him Bill, were half naked, and had walked to the battlefield from Missouri?

No sir.

The captain leaned back and folded his arms. What we are dealing with, he said, is a race of degenerates. A mongrel race, little better than niggers. And maybe no better. There is no government in Mexico. Hell, there's no God in Mexico. Never will be. We are dealing with a people manifestly incapable of governing themselves. And do you know what happens with people who cannot govern themselves? That's right. Others come in to govern for them.

There are already some fourteen thousand French colonists in the state of Sonora. They're being given free land to settle. They're being given tools and livestock. Enlightened Mexicans encourage this. Paredes is already calling for secession from the Mexican government. They'd rather be ruled by toadeaters than thieves and imbeciles. Colonel Carrasco is asking for American intervention. And he's going to get it.

Right now they are forming in Washington a commission to come out here and draw up the boundary lines between our country and Mexico. I dont think there's any question that ultimately Sonora will become a United States territory. Guaymas a U S port. Americans will be able to get to California without having to pass through our benighted sister republic and our citizens will be protected at last from the notorious packs of cutthroats presently infesting the routes which they are obliged to travel.

The captain was watching the kid. The kid looked uneasy. Son, said the captain. We are to be the instruments of liberation in a dark and troubled land. That's right. We are to spearhead the drive. We have the tacit support of Governor Burnett of California.

He leaned forward and placed his hands on his knees. And we will be the ones who will divide the spoils. There will be a section of land for every man in my company. Fine grassland. Some of the finest in the world. A land rich in minerals, in gold and silver I would say beyond the wildest speculation. You're young. But I dont misread you. I'm seldom mistaken in a man. I think you mean to make your mark in this world. Am I wrong?

No sir.

No. And I don't think you're the sort of chap to abandon a land that Americans fought and died for to a foreign power. And mark my word. Unless Americans act, people like you and me who take their country seriously while those mollycoddles in Washington sit on their hindsides, unless we act, Mexico—and I mean the whole of the country—will one day fly a European flag. Monroe Doctrine or no.

The captain's voice had become soft and intense. He tilted his head to one side and regarded the kid with a sort of benevolence. The kid rubbed the palms of his hands on the knees of his filthy jeans. He glanced at the man beside him but he seemed to be asleep.

What about a saddle? he said.

Saddle?

Yessir.

You dont have a saddle?

No sir.

I thought you had a horse.

A mule.

I see.

I got a old hull on the mule but they aint much left of it. Aint a whole lot left of the mule. He said I was to get a horse and a rifle.

Sergeant Trammel did?

I never promised him no saddle, said the sergeant.

We'll get you a saddle.

I did tell him we might find him some clothes, Captain.

Right. We may be irregulars but we dont want to look like bobtails, do we?

No sir.
We aint got no more broke horses neither, said the sergeant.
Well break one.
That old boy that was so good about breakin em is out of commission.
I know that. Get somebody else.
Yessir. Maybe this man can break horses. You ever break horses?
No sir.
Aint no need to sir me.
Yessir.
Sergeant, said the captain, easing himself down from the desk.
Yessir.
Sign this man up.

Five days later on the dead man's horse he followed the riders and wagons through the plaza and out of the town on the road downcountry. They rode through Castroville where coyotes had dug up the dead and scattered their bones and they crossed the Frio River and they crossed the Nueces and they left the Presidio road and turned north with scouts posted ahead and to the rear. They crossed the del Norte by night and waded up out of the shallow sandy ford into a howling wilderness.

Dawn saw them deployed in long file over the plain, the dry wood wagons already moaning, horses snuffling. A dull thump of hooves and clank of gear and the constant light chink of harness. Save for scattered clumps of buckbrush and pricklypear and the little patches of twisted grass the ground was bare and there were low mountains to the south and they were bare too. Westward the horizon lay flat and true as a spirit level.

Those first days they saw no game, no birds save buzzards. They saw in the distance herds of sheep or goats moving along the skyline in scarves of dust and they ate the meat of wild asses shot on the plain. The sergeant carried in his saddle scabbard a heavy Wesson rifle that used a false muzzle and paper patch and fired a coneshaped ball. With it he killed the little wild pigs of the desert and later when they began to see herds of antelope he would halt in the dusk with the sun off the land and screwing a bipod into the threaded boss on the underside of the barrel would kill these animals where they stood grazing at distances of half a mile. The rifle carried a vernier sight on the tang and he would eye the distance and gauge the wind and set the sight like a man using micrometer. The second corporal would lie at his elbow with a glass and call the shots high or low should he miss and the wagon would wait by until he had shot a stand of three or four and then rumble across the cooling land with the skinners jostling and grinning in the bed. The sergeant never put the rifle up but what he wiped and greased the bore.

The rode well armed, each man with a rifle and many with the smallbore fiveshot Colt's revolvers. The captain carried a pair of dragoon pistols in scabbards that mounted across the pommel of the saddle so that they rode at each knee. These guns were United States issue, Colt's patent, and he had bought them from a deserter in a Soledad livery stable and paid eighty dollars in gold for them and the scabbards and the mold and flask they came with.

The rifle the kid carried had been sawed down and rebored till it weighed very light indeed and the mold for it was so small he had to patch the balls with buckskin. He had fired it a few times and it carried much where it chose. It rode before him on the saddlebow, he having no scabbard. It had been carried so before, God's years of it, and the forestock was much worn beneath.

In the early dark the wagon came back with the meat. The skinners had piled the wagonbed with mesquite brush and stumps they'd drug out of the ground with the horses and they unloaded the firewood and commenced cutting up the gutted antelopes in the floor of the wagon with bowieknives and handaxes, laughing and hacking in a welter of gore, a reeking scene in the light of the handheld lanterns. By full dark the blackened ribracks leaned steaming at the fires and there was a jousting over the coals with shaven sticks whereon were skewered gobs of meat and a clank of canteens and endless raillery. And sleep that night on the cold plains of a foreign land, forty-six men wrapped in their blankets under the selfsame stars, the prairie wolves so like in their yammering, yet all about so changed and strange.

They caught up and set out each day in the dark before the day yet was and they ate cold meat and biscuit and made no fire. The sun rose on a column already ragged these six days out. Among their clothes there was small agreement and among their hats less. The little painted horses stepped shifty and truculent and a vicious snarl of flies fought constantly in the bed of the gamewagon. The dust the party raised was quickly dispersed and lost in the immensity of that landscape and there was no dust other for the pale sutler who pursued them drives unseen and his lean horse and his lean cart leave no track upon such ground or any ground. By a thousand fires in the iron blue dusk he keeps his commissary and he's a wry and grinning tradesman good to follow every campaign or hound men from their holes in just those whited regions where they've gone to hide from God. On this day two men fell sick and one died before dark. In the morning there was another ill to take his place. The two of them were laid among sacks of beans and rice and coffee in the supplywagon with blankets over them to keep them from the sun and they rode with slamming and jarring of the wagon half shirring the meat from their bones so that they cried out to be left and then they died. The men turned out in the early morning darkness to dig their graves with the bladebones of antelope and they covered them with stones and rode on again.

They rode on and the sun in the east flushed pale streaks of light and then a deeper run of color like blood seeping up in sudden reaches flaring planewise and where the earth drained up into the sky at the edge of creation the top of the sun rose out of nothing like the head of a great red phallus until it cleared the unseen rim and sat squat and pulsing and malevolent behind them. The shadows of the smallest stones lay like pencil lines across the sand and the shapes of the men and their mounts advanced elongate before them like strands of the night from which they'd ridden, like tentacles to bind them to the darkness yet to come. They rode with their heads down, faceless under their hats, like an army asleep on the march. By midmorning another man had died and they lifted him from the wagon where he'd stained the sacks he'd lain among and buried him also and rode on.

Now wolves had come to follow them, great pale lobos with yellow eyes that trotted neat of foot or squatted in the shimmering heat to watch them where they made their noon halt. Moving on again. Loping, sidling, ambling with their long noses to the ground. In the evening their eyes shifted and winked out there on the edge of the firelight and in the morning when the riders rode out in the cool dark they could hear the snarling and the pop of their mouths behind them as they sacked the camp for meatscraps.

The wagons drew so dry they slouched from side to side like dogs and the sand was grinding them away. The wheels shrank and the poles reeled in their hubs and clattered like loomshafts and at night they'd drive false spokes into the mortices and tie them down with strips of green hide and they'd drive wedges between the iron of the tires and the suncracked felloes. They wobbled on, the trace of their untrue labors like sidewinder tracks in the sand. The duledge pegs worked loose and dropped behind. Wheels began to break up.

Ten days out with four men dead they started across a plain of pure pumice where there grew no shrub, no weed, far as the eye could see. The captain called a halt and he called up the Mexican who served as guide. They talked and the Mexican gestured and the captain gestured and after a while they moved on again.

This looks like the high road to hell to me, said a man from the ranks.

What does he reckon for the horses to eat?

I believe they're supposed to just grit up on this sand like chickens and be ready for the shelled corn when it does come.

In two days they began to come upon bones and cast-off apparel. They saw halfburied skeletons of mules with the bones so white and polished they seemed incandescent even in that blazing heat and they saw panniers and packsaddles and the bones of men and they saw a mule entire, the dried and blackened carcass hard as iron. The rode on. The white noon saw them through the waste like a ghost army, so pale they were with dust, like shades of figures erased upon a board. The wolves loped paler yet and grouped and skittered and lifted their lean snouts on the air. At night the horses were fed by hand from sacks of meal and watered from buckets. There was no more sickness. The survivors lay quietly in that cratered void and watched the whitehot stars go rifling down the dark. Or slept with their alien hearts beating in the sand like pilgrims exhausted upon the face of the plant Anareta, clutched to a namelessness wheeling in the night. They moved on and the iron of the wagontires grew polished bright as chrome in the pumice. To the south the blue cordilleras stood footed in their paler image on the sand like reflections in a lake and there were no wolves now.

They took to riding by night, silent jornadas save for the trundling of the wagons and the wheeze of the animals. Under the moonlight a strange party of elders with the white dust thick on their moustaches and their eyebrows. They moved on and the stars jostled and arced across the firmament and died beyond the inkblack mountains. They came to know the nightskies well. Western eyes that read more geometric constructions than those names given by the ancients. Tethered to the polestar they rode the Dipper round while Orion rose in the southwest like a great electric kite. The sand lay blue in the moonlight and the iron tires of the wagons rolled among the shapes of the riders in gleaming hoops that veered and wheeled woundedly and vaguely navigational like slender astrolabes and the polished shoes of the horses kept hasping up like a myriad of eyes winking across the desert floor. They watched storms out there so distant they could not be heard, the silent lightning flaring sheetwise and the thin black spine of the mountain chain fluttering and sucked away again in the dark. They saw wild horses racing on the plain, pounding their shadows down the night and leaving in the moonlight a vaporous dust like the palest stain of their passing.

All night the wind blew and the fine dust set their teeth on edge. Sand in everything, grit in all they ate. In the morning a urinecolored sun rose blearily through panes of dust on a dim world and without feature. The animals were failing. They halted and made a dry camp without wood or water and the wretched ponies huddled and whimpered like dogs.

That night they rode through a region electric and wild where strange shapes of soft blue fire ran over the metal of the horses' trappings and the wagonwheels rolled in hoops of fire and little shapes of pale blue light came to perch in the ears of the horses and in the beards of the men. All night sheetlightning quaked sourceless to the west beyond the midnight thunderheads, making a bluish day of the distant desert, the mountains on the sudden skyline stark and black and livid like a land of some other order out there whose true geology was not stone but fear. The thunder moved up from the southwest and lightning lit the desert all about them, blue and barren, great clanging reaches ordered out of the absolute night like some demon kingdom summoned up or changeling land that come the day would leave them neither trace nor smoke nor ruin nor more than any troubling dream.

They halted in the dark to recruit the animals and some of the men stowed their arms in the wagons for fear of drawing the lightning and a man named Hayward prayed for rain.

He prayed: Almighty God, if it aint too far out of the way of things in your eternal plan do you reckon we could have a little rain down here.

Pray it up, some called, and kneeling he cried out among the thunder and the wind: Lord we are dried to jerky down here. Just a few drops for some old boys out here on the prairie and a long ways from home.

Amen, they said, and catching up their mounts they rode on. Within the hour the wind cooled and drops of rain the size of grapeshot fell upon them out of that wild darkness. They could smell wet stone and the sweet smell of the wet horses and wet leather. They rode on.

They rode through the heat of the day following with the waterkegs empty and the horses perishing and in the evening these elect, shabby and white with dust like a company of armed and mounted millers wandering in dementia, rode up off the desert through a gap in the low stone hills and down upon a solitary jacal, crude hut of mud and wattles and a rudimentary stable and corrals.

Bone palings ruled the small and dusty purlieus here and death seemed the most prevalent feature of the landscape. Strange fences that the sand and wind had scoured and the sun bleached and cracked like old porcelain with dry brown weather cracks and where no life moved. The corrugated forms of the riders passed jingling across the dry bistre land and across the mud facade of the jacal, the horses trembling, smelling water. The captain raised his hand and the sergeant spoke and two men dismounted and advanced upon the hut with rifles. They pushed open a door made of rawhide and entered. In a few minutes they reappeared.

Somebody's here somewheres. They's hot coals.

The captain surveyed the distance with an air of vigilance. He dismounted with the patience of one used to dealing with incompetence and crossed to the jacal. When he came out he surveyed the terrain again. The horses shifted and clinked and stamped and the men pulled their jaws down and spoke roughly to them.

Sergeant.

Yessir.

These people cant be far. See if you can find them. And see if there's any forage here for the animals.

Forage?

Forage.

The sergeant placed a hand on the cattle and looked down at the place they were in and shook his head and dismounted.

They went through the jacal and into the enclosure behind and out to the stable. There were no animals and nothing but a stall half filled with dry sotols in the way of feed. They walked out the back to a sink among the stones where water stood and a thin stream flowed away over the sand. There were hoofprints about the tank and dry manure and some small birds ran mindlessly along the rim of the little creek.

The sergeant had been squatting on his heels and now he rose and spat. Well, he said. Is there any direction you caint see twenty mile in?

The recruits studied the emptiness about.

I dont believe the folks here is gone that long.

They drank and walked back toward the jacal. Horses were being led along the narrow path.

The captain was standing with his thumbs in his belt.

I caint see where they've got to, said the sergeant.

What's in the shed.

Some old dry fodder.

The captain frowned. They ought to have a goat or a hog. Something. Chickens.

In a few minutes two men came dragging an old man from the stable. He was covered with dust and dry chaff and he held one arm across his eyes. He was dragged moaning to the captain's feet where he lay prostrate in what looked like windings of white cotton. He put his hands over his ears and his elbows before his eyes like one called upon to witness some appalling thing. The captain turned away in disgust. The sergeant toed him with his boot. What's wrong with him? he said.

He's pissing himself, Sergeant. He's pissing himself. The captain gestured at the man with his gloves.

Yessir.

Well get him the hell out of here.

You want Candelario to talk to him?

He's a halfwit. Get him away from me.

They dragged the old man away. He had begun to babble but no one listened and in the morning he was gone.

They bivouacked by the tank and the farrier saw to the mules and ponies that had thrown shoes and they worked on the wagons by firelight far into the night. They set forth in a crimson dawn where sky and earth closed in a razorous plane. Out there dark little archipelagos of cloud and the vast world of sand and scrub shearing upward into the shoreless void where those blue islands trembled and the earth grew uncertain, gravely canted and veering out through tinctures of rose and the dark beyond the dawn to the uttermost rebate of space.

They rode through regions of particolored stone upthrust in ragged kerfs and shelves of traprock reared in faults and anticlines curved back upon themselves and broken off like stumps of great stone treeboles and stones the lightning had clove open, seeps exploding in steam in some old storm. They rode past trapdykes of brown rock running down the narrow chines of the ridges and onto the plain like the ruins of old walls, such auguries everywhere of the hand of man before man was or any living thing.

They passed through a village then and now in ruins and they camped in the walls of a tall mud church and burned the fallen timbers of the roof for their fire while owls cried from the arches in the dark.

The following day on the skyline to the south they saw clouds of dust that lay across the earth for miles. They rode on, watching the dust until it began to near and the captain raised his hand for a halt and took from his saddlebag his old brass cavalry telescope and uncoupled it and swept it slowly over the land. The sergeant sat his horse beside him and after a while the captain handed him the glass.

Hell of a herd of something.

I believe it's horses.

How far off do you make them?

Hard to tell.

Call Candelario up here.

The sergeant turned and motioned for the Mexican. When he rode up he handed him the glass and the Mexican raised it to his eye and squinted. Then he lowered the glass and watched it with his naked eyes and then he raised it and looked again. Then he sat his horse with the glass at his chest like a crucifix.

Well? said the captain.

He shook his head.

What the hell does that mean? They're not buffalo are they?

No. I think maybe horses.

Let me have the glass.

The Mexican handed him the telescope and he glassed the horizon again and collapsed the tube shut with the heel of his hand and replaced it in his bag and raised his hand and they went on.

They were cattle, mules, horses. There were several thousand head and they were moving quarterwise toward the company. By late afternoon riders were visible to the bare eye, a handful of ragged indians mending the outer flanks of the herd with their nimble ponies. Others in hats, perhaps Mexicans. The sergeant dropped back to where the captain was riding.

What do you make of that, Captain?

I make it a parcel of heathen stockthieves is what I make it. What do you?

Looks like it to me.

The captain watched through the glass. I suppose they've seen us, he said.

They've seen us.

How many riders do you make it?

A dozen maybe.

The captain tapped the instrument in his gloved hand. They dont seem concerned do they.

No sir. They dont.

The captain smiled grimly. We may see a little sport here before the day is out.

The first of the herd began to swing past them in a pall of yellow dust, rangy slatribbed cattle with horns that grew agoggle and no two alike and small thin mules coalblack that shouldered one another and reared their malletshaped heads above the backs of the others and then more cattle and finally the first of the herders riding up the outer side and keeping the stock between themselves and the mounted company. Behind them came a herd of several hundred ponies. The sergeant looked for Candelario. He kept backing along the ranks but he could not find him. He nudged his horse through the column and moved up the far side. The lattermost of the drovers were now coming through the dust and the captain was gesturing and shouting. The ponies had begun to veer off from the herd and the drovers were beating their way toward this armed company met with on the plain. Already you could see through the dust on the ponies' hides the painted chevrons and the hands and rising suns and birds and fish of every device like the shade of old work through sizing on a canvas and now too you could hear above the pounding of the unshod hooves the piping of the quena, flutes made from human bones and some among the company had begun to saw back on their mounts and some to mill in confusion when up from the offside of those ponies there rose a fabled horde of mounted lancers and archers bearing shields bedight with bits of broken mirrorglass that cast a thousand unpieced suns against the eyes of their enemies. A legion of horribles, hundreds in number, half naked or clad in costumes attic or biblical or wardrobed out of a fevered dream with the skins of animals and silk finery and pieces of uniform still tracked with the blood of prior owners, coats of slain dragoons, frogged and braided calvary jackets, one in a stovepipe hat and one with an umbrella and one in white stockings and a bloodstained weddingveil and some in headgear of cranefeathers or rawhide helmets that bore the horns of bull or buffalo and one in a pigeontailed coat worn backwards and otherwise naked and one in the armour of a spanish conquistador, the breastplate and pauldrons deeply dented with old blows of mace or sabre done in another country by men whose very bones were dust and many with their braids spliced up with the hair of other beasts until they trailed upon the ground and their horses' ears and tails worked with bits of brightly colored cloth and one whose horse's whole head was painted crimson red and all the horsemen's faces gaudy and grotesque with daubings like a company of mounted clowns, death hilarious, all howling in a barbarous tongue and riding down upon them like a horde from a hell more horrible yet than the brimstone land of christian reckoning, screeching and yammering and clothed in smoke like those vaporous beings in regions beyond right knowing where the eye wanders and the lip jerks and drools.

Oh my god, said the sergeant.

A rattling drove of arrows passed through the company and men tottered and dropped from their mounts. Horses were rearing and plunging and the mongol hordes swung up along their flanks and turned and rode full upon them with lances.

The company was now come to a halt and the first shots were fired and the gray riflesmoke rolled through the dust as the lancers breached their ranks. The kid's horse sank beneath him with a long pneumatic sigh. He had already fired his rifle and now he sat on the ground and fumbled with his shotpouch. A man near him sat with an arrow hanging out of his neck. He was bent slightly as if in prayer. The kid would have reached for the bloody hoop-iron point but then he saw that the man wore another arrow in his breast to the fletching and he was dead. Everywhere there were horses down and men scrambling and he saw a man who sat charging his rifle while blood ran from his ears and he saw men with their revolvers disassembled trying to fit the spare loaded cylinders they carried and he saw men kneeling who tilted and clasped their shadows on the ground and he saw men lanced and caught up by the hair and scalped standing and he saw the horses of war trample down the fallen and a little whitefaced pony with one clouded eye leaned out of the murk and snapped at him like a dog and was gone. Among the wounded some seemed dumb and without understanding and some were pale through the masks of dust and some had fouled themselves or tottered brokenly onto the spears of the savages. Now driving in a wild frieze of headlong horses with eyes walled and teeth cropped and naked riders with clusters of arrows clenched in their jaws and their shields winking in the dust and up the far side of the ruined ranks in a piping of boneflutes and dropping down off the sides of their mounts with one heel hung in the withers strap and their short bows flexing beneath the outstretched necks of the ponies until they had circled the company and cut their ranks in two and then rising up again like funhouse figures, some with nightmare faces painted on their breasts, riding down the unhorsed Saxons and spearing and clubbing them and leaping from their mounts with knives and running about on the ground with a peculiar bandylegged trot like creatures driven to alien forms of locomotion and stripping the clothes from the dead and seizing them up by the hair and passing their blades about the skulls of the living and the dead alike and snatching aloft the bloody wigs and hacking and chopping at the naked bodies, ripping off limbs, heads, gutting the strange white torsos and holding up great handfuls of viscera, genitals, some of the savages so slathered up with gore they might have rolled in it like dogs and some who fell upon the dying and sodomized them with loud cries to their fellows. And now the horses of the dead came pounding out of the smoke and dust and circled with flapping leather and wild manes and eyes whited with fear like the eyes of the blind and some were feathered with arrows and some lanced through and stumbling and vomiting blood as they wheeled across the killing ground and clattered from sight again. Dust stanched the wet and naked heads of the scalped who with the fringe of hair below their wounds and tonsured to the bone now lay like maimed and naked monks in the bloodslaked dust and everywhere the dying groaned and gibbered and horses lay screaming.

Phyllis Tickle

Of Bulls and Angels

The late September sunshine, benign and dry, glowed quietly over the yard and the meadows beyond as we drove into the drive and parked. Like the children, I was looking forward to this week of interrupted routine, of holiday from all the schedules and chores that one should follow—but doesn't, whenever escape is possible.

We had just put Sam on the airplane for a week of meetings in Boston. For me that meant supper would be sandwiches, not entree and vegetables—fifteen minutes not ninety, in other words. Time to read. Tomorrow night, frozen dinners. Monday night? We would see how we all felt by then.

For the two boys it meant a definite laxity about the grass. Wait until Friday to cut it again; it doesn't grow all that fast in September. A certain casualness about the hens' nests; they can run a week without new pine needles. A tendency to let the last of the okra get too large to be worth picking, the peppers too red, the eggplants too wormy. A lot of fishing down at the pond, however. Now there was the crop that needed to be garnered while there was still time!

For Rebecca, the youngest and age nine, the prospect was less heady. She alone faced the next six days with hesitation. Our chores and routines were not yet her burdens; rather they were her days' definition. Daddy's big hands and hearty hugs, like his long talks with her while they planted and pruned and harvested, were the mirrors in which she saw herself as engaging, accomplished, precious beyond all other things in life. And I, remembering from past experience, knew that after the sandwiches were eaten and the book enjoyed for an hour or two, those intimate hours of the night would come and I too would be as morose as she and for much the same reasons.

So we parked the car and, ideal day or not, we went into the house. I to wash up the breakfast mess we had left in order to get to the airport on time, the boys to fall dead in sleeping bags in front of the Saturday morning TV. Only Rebecca veered off to the fields. "Like Electra mourning," I thought to myself as I watched her through the kitchen window. She wandered aimlessly along the fence line, crawled through finally and started toward the pond. I finished the dishes and was thinking sinfully of jumping the laundry in favor of a manuscript I was working on, when I saw Rebecca come back up over the hillock from the pond. "Something's wrong with Saint's calf," she said as she came in the back door. "It's just standing at the pond bawling."

"Oh, I wouldn't worry about it," I answered. "She's just looking for her mama to feed her."

"I don't think so," she said, with the kind of calm that I have long since learned to believe instantly when it occurs in children. I looked at her and then looked out toward the pasture. As I watched, I saw cow after cow move laboriously over the crest of the hillock and come to stand at the fence, looking toward the house. That also is a gesture that years of living with them has made me respect in animals. There was something wrong or they would not have come for us.

I called for the boys, both of whom protested viciously that this was supposed to be their free Saturday. "Give us a break, Ma," was the chorus, but there was to be no break.

The cows parted as the four of us climbed back through the fence, following the bawling of the calf as it led us toward the pond. Halfway down the sloping pasture stood the calf. Two weeks old and a beauty. Much too old and pretty, I suddenly realized, to look wobbly and weak. Something was wrong. What Rebecca had sensed intuitively I could give adult reason to: that calf had not been fed in at least twelve hours. Beside me I heard fourteen year old John mutter, "Oh, boy," and I knew that he had reached the same conclusion. Behind us the herd had reassembled, waiting for something. The calf began to move and Rebecca started after her. "Wait!," I grabbed her arm. "Let the calf go." We watched her as she wobbled off toward the east meadow below the barn. Slowly the herd began to break and follow. We did likewise. And there, on the rise just beyond the cow path to the feeding racks, lay Saint on her side; legs stuck stiffly out in front of her; eyes open; flies already eating around her face. As we watched the calf walked over and tried once more to nurse the stiffened udder. The herd moved off, as if totally uninterested now that we had been led to the spot. "Like gossipy old women who just love a tragedy!" I thought bitterly to myself as I began to figure dully what all of this meant to our intended holiday.

The first necessity obviously was to get some milk into the calf. I sent John back to get some rope, and Sam, Jr. and Rebecca to open up the smallest stall in the barn and get some hay spread out. It had been three or four years since I had tried to manhandle a calf, and I had forgotten how hard they can kick and how tough a ride it can be to hold one. This one might be weak and young, but she had no intention of being caught, much less hauled away from her mother. We finally got her down, her legs lashed somewhat inexpertly, and the whole thrashing mass back to the barn. For two hours we struggled, as one always must, with a calf who did not—most definitely did not, in fact—like the feel of the rubber nipple or the taste of the milk replacement that we were forcing on her. Finally she ate enough to allow us to go back in for the sandwiches that did not seem nearly so attractive after all.

As lunch ended, John asked the question we had been trying to avoid all morning. What about Saint? Saturday and no one to call for extra help. To leave her where she was would bring the coyotes and wild dogs up from the Loosahatchie Bottoms and into the pasture. Once there, they would kill the calves as soon as they had finished the carcass. To bury her would be impossible without the backhoe which none of us could operate. I thought of Boston and meetings and wondered how we could have been so foolish as to look forward to this week without structure. Well, obviously we had to move her. I remembered that once Sam had disposed of a yearling by taking the body down to a natural depression at the foot of the meadow where the close began, setting it in the little eroded valley just at the edge of the uncleared bog. We still wouldn't be strong enough to dig sufficient earth to bury her, but we could at least get her half buried and away from the vulnerable younger cattle, assuming we could contrive a way to move her there.

Back to the field we went, John driving the pick-up ahead of the rest of us. He negotiated the terracing and hills with a skill far beyond that of most boys his age, and I felt not only that swell of pride that comes to women who have produced good male children, but also that sense of wonder that recognizes—abruptly and humbly—that these skills were not self-taught. They were learned, acquired, taught by the man who, absent in Boston, was still working the pasture with us at this very moment. The eternal line of maleness, unbroken and unbreakable, I thought to myself, as I watched him back the truck up and begin to maneuver it into alignment, back bumper even with the outstretched legs of the carcass.

Suddenly over the rise I saw the bull move heavily and forcefully up the slope and toward the truck. Long since turned into a useful pet, loved on, stroked, scratched upon every occasion, the bull was certainly nothing to be concerned about. John continued to move the truck as the bull moved deliberately toward us. A little uneasy somehow, I picked Rebecca up and told Sam, Jr. to go jump into the bed of the truck. Still the bull came on toward us. I called to John to pull away—"Give him room!" John pulled the truck down twenty feet or so from the cow, parked it and crawled into the truck bed with his brother. I slid Rebecca back down to ground beside me. Whatever this was all about, there was no danger to us if we were still.

Solemnly over the hill came the rest of the herd. I backed off farther, holding Rebecca's hand as we watched. The herd stopped at the top of the ridge, watching the scene below them. The bull approached Saint, running his nose along her now distended underside. He snorted the flies off her head, walked around her full circle once and then began ritually to mount the carcass. She was too long dead, of course, to admit of penetration and the effort was not that which usually accompanies mating. It was, ultimately, ritualistic.

Farm children learn early the purposes of sex; they also learn early to reverence the emotions of it. All three of ours watched with quietness—not a word said in the whole meadow—while the bull dismounted and stood to one side. As we watched, he raised his head and looked across the fields with a magnificence that becomes a king. Coal black and polished by the fall sun, he uttered a sound which I had never before heard from a bull, a kind of call to the herd that was summons, explanation, and completion. Then, as simply as he had began, he lowered his head and moved on toward the close.

For whatever reasons—and I shall never know what they were or what set of peculiar circumstances had contrived to permit it—for whatever reasons, we had been witness to something that, I have since learned, few farmers are ever allowed to see. Like Jacob on the fields of Luz, we had watched the customs and conventions of a life as complete as our own; one with which for years we had shared daily space and purpose, but one which we had, until that afternoon, never seen. Like Jacob, too, we knew we were on holy ground; we had been in Bethel and seen the mysteries of another order of life. Through the tears in my own eyes, I looked down and saw Rebecca swipe at hers with her forearm.

The herd began slowly to come down the rise toward us. Most of them paused to smell the carcass with their lowered noses; they all moved toward the bull, still waiting for them in the shade of the close. Once there, they followed the way of cows and settled down to doze in the fading sun as if nothing had happened. The bull alone stood watching us.

Without asking, John swung back over into the cab and cranked the motor. Adroitly he put the truck back into position and lifted out the lengths of rope he had brought from the barn. Together, with Rebecca and Sam, Jr. watching, we lashed the stiffened legs together and then to the hitch on the back of the truck and began the tedious process of inch by inch dragging the body down the edge of the bog. With nothing said, Sam, Jr. picked up a pole and the three of us, once the body was unlashed, rolled the last of Saint down into the gully below.

Rebecca and I walked back to the house while the boys finished and parked the truck. Without thinking, I began to chop salad and season a quart of beans. There would be left-over fried chicken and I could throw some biscuits in the oven . . . an entree and vegetables, I thought to myself. Sam, Jr. came in and silently picked up the garden basket. I saw him a few minutes later picking the okra in the garden. Far to the front I heard John turn over the motor on the lawn tractor. We would have a trim yard for Sunday after all. Supper would be ready in a little while, then early to bed. Tomorrow was Michaelmas—the Feast of St. Michael and All Angels—and we must be ready.

Of A Remembered Quiet

(Notes From The Hill Country)

It was not, I think, that I grew up assuming that it was impossible to be free in a world controlled by the fundamentalists. It was rather that in the dark mountain days of my early years sheer isolation forced conformity. We all became identical by default, and there was no blame of any kind to be placed for our condition.

There was in those still days between the Great Depression and the outbreak of World War II a bleakness, a coal-sooted sombreness dusting the faces and the lives of those of us growing up in my part of Appalachia. Except for the Teachers' College where my father (with his Ph.D. and his years of study abroad) was a leader of men, the life of the inquiring mind was homeless in our part of the hill country. Few ideas beyond the immediacy of the seasons moved our lives. Those few artists, teachers, and actors who came in to us from the outside and who held some magic in their hands soon left, taking with them the glitter of what the community had but briefly seen and for which it had developed little taste.

I remember those transient thinkers now as the enchanted ones who, like consummate Merlins, came with the secrets of Excalibur and who were, almost as quickly, driven away either by direct order or by social pressure. As a child, I was too naive to perceive that either process was operating. It was only in early adulthood that I came to realize—painfully, but accurately—that at least several of those with the ideas had retreated into our hills because they were outcasts in their own worlds . . . many of them homosexuals, I suspect, in a society that could not yet tolerate even artistic and academic homosexuals. So they came to us and were as quickly driven away by a microcosm that refused their ideas while being itself too naive to even begin to suspect their deviations.

For me there was in that early experience and its later understanding a primer of instruction in irony. That true uniformity can not perceive deviation beyond the limits of its own experience had to mean that the ability to recognize and catalog any given evil presupposes some prior contact with that evil. And there was the corollary—even more amazing—that if a society can restrict freedom, it does not save its young; it merely keeps them shackled to the sins it itself knows and understands.

Thus the lesbian who took me into her office shortly after I had turned thirteen and who read me Eliot's "Love Song of J. Alfred Prufrock" tore my head open. Suddenly I, who had long since scorned "Hiawatha" as a bunch of unbelieveable pap and had to heart only "Abou Ben Adhem" and some Kipling, was hearing the cascading sounds and breathtaking distortions of language which my soul somehow knew must lie beyond the mountains and beyond the confining wall of their worn peaks. She was removed at the end of term—not for making passes at young girls (which she may or may not have been attempting with me), but for her refusal to give up the contemporary poets in her classroom. Their deliberate violations of syntax and their abandonment of end rhyme constituted a breach of propriety which was moral in its overtones and deemed to be fundamentally dangerous to young minds.

So variety was limited in the moralism of East Tennessee and so was spirituality. There was no indigenous religion which had preceded the white man save only the animism of the Cherokee whose nation had once flourished on the same earth. His had been a gentle union with the forces of nature. During his years of supremacy in the hills, he had kept absolute faith with the doctrine of balance between man and life, and had made of life itself the concept of the Great Spirit. But the Cherokee had been driven so violently from the land that he left little impression on the interior lives of those of us who followed him into the hills. Even the old granny women practiced only a crude folk medicine based more on reasonably adept herbal lore than on any spiritual hocus-pocus.

There were almost no blacks in the mountain country, then or now, and those who were there showed, as I remember them, a remarkable lack of separateness. Their homes were poorer than ours sometimes, but not always. Their music was as anemic as ours always. And their sense of rhythm was, like ours, four-beat European mixed with the high wail of the mountains. How they came to be so devoid of their rich African heritage has always remained a mystery to me. I have always felt that had they managed to retain at least some small portion of that heritage, my childhood and that of most of us in upper East Tennessee would have been spared much of its somber silence and puritanical barrenness.

Certainly where there is no variety of experience, the people grow as docile and as gray as the winter landscape around them.

My paternal grandmother had been of Jewish descent. Unlike most parts of the country, however, among mountain Protestants, Jewishness was not regarded either as a source of concern or as an anomaly. The Jews were simply the first ones to get to the truth. The fact that not all of them had arrived at a full understanding of truth did not mean that they would not ultimately do so—or that they should be cast aside individually just because they had not corporately changed their ways. The intermarriage of Jew and Gentile was not uncommon in the South before the turn of the century. It often, as in my family, was simply the bald-faced wedding of mercantile interests to landed interests and assured the perpetuation of both; so anti-semitism was not upon us until well into the Second World War, at least not in the hills. But because there was no anti-semitism there was also little recognition of religious alternatives and options.

The result of all of this was a fundamentalist's delight. There was little or no prejudice for we lacked variation; little or no integration for we lacked segregation; little or no sinning for we lacked opportunity; and little or no celebration for we lacked ourselves. It was as if the hills had washed us down into one sameness, had eroded us as steadily and insidiously as they themselves had been eroded. So there was no blaming because there was no basis for blaming. No question had been asked and no answers could be offered in that pervasive quietness.

It was, of course, a quietness which I learned to fear and which I remembered with bitterness long after I had escaped the isolation of those years; a quietness which can only be interrupted by the human voice singing of itself; a quietness that can stifle a whole nation almost as easily as it stifled the mountains, especially a nation which can not say "Pharisee" to its professional moralists and "Fascist" to its expedient reformers.

The Holy Innocents

December 28, 1959. Six forty-five on a Thursday morning and the weather as cold as the old stoker furnace in the basement could pull against. Too cold to get out of the covers. Too cold to answer the door . . . the persistent, deadly beating on the door downstairs, the insistent faintness of, "Doc! Doc!" coming up the stairwell. Sam rolled out and into his robe from one side of the bed and I out from the other. Through the ice coating on the window sashes, the mill village below our bedroom was a postcard etching in desperation gray. Beyond the village and the mill, the rolling land of the South Carolina Piedmont churned silently in the low cold of coming snow.

It was our second year of general practice in this remote rural area of textile mills and nothingness, our second winter among the silent serfs whose lives a mill steals. "Doc! Doc!" Too quiet, much too quiet a voice. Even the hand beating on the front door was too steady. Why wasn't he using the doorbell? Or better yet, why hadn't he gone around to the clinic building and rung the emergency call bell? Sam headed down the steps while I slipped in to cover the new baby and close her door against the muffled beating . . . more like the rhythm of a man's heartbeat than like an earnest caller in the morning twilight.

I was halfway down the stairs when Sam opened the front door. Jeb Martin stood there, his hand still raised against the memory of the door. No more than nineteen, he worked in the carding room where the cotton was processed for its trip through the machines and looms that would turn it into cloth. Woolies the other mill hands called the carders, and Jeb still had on his black hair the dusting of white lint from yesterday's shift. Otherwise there was no expression in his face, no tone to his body or his voice. "You gotta help her, Doc." No other sounds rose from the outside cold. No cars passed on the street below us. No sparrows moved in the warm leaves around the house. Even the soft cushion of insect noises had been folded away into paper-walled nests and fragile egg-sacks until spring. Everywhere around us the earth was winter quiet.

Behind Jeb and two feet back stood Tina, older than Jeb, twenty two or three perhaps, and drab. She had delivered their second child only some six or seven weeks earlier, but she was already back at work in the weaving room. Hard work, too hard for her kind of thinness, her kind of blond pallor. She had thrown an old army blanket around herself and I could see that she was holding the baby against herself under its warmth. Jeb stepped sideways and nodded to her. She walked into the square front room which served all the millhouses as a kind of parlor/entrance hall/coatroom. While we watched in silence, she went past Sam to the wooden long bench beneath the stairwell, sat down, shrugged off the blanket and began to cuddle the baby. From my place halfway up the staircase I looked down on her and the child. It was rigid, fingers crooked and skin waxy like a plastic doll that had gotten too hot in shipping and run a bit. Sam looked at Jeb. "It were like that when we got up this morning. She didn't hear it cry and I knowed afore she went and looked."

Jeb turned and closed the door between himself and us. We watched through the glass as he went to stand soundless and motionless, leaning against the support railing of the front stoop, waiting for her as if in all of time only his waiting mattered.

She kissed the child and began to rock it. A tuneless, primal hum like the soft wind under the eaves in November came up from the bench below me. I started down the steps when Sam motioned me to stay where I was. I slipped quietly down onto the stair tread to wait. He disappeared into the kitchen and I could hear him moving on back through the house to the enclosed back porch where we had the washing machine and where I stored the linens. In a few minutes he came back. He had found my vegetable basket with the bailing wire handle and had padded it with some clean rags from the closet. Over the rags he had spread a freshly washed baby blanket. The little blue and yellow rocking horses that rode across it were faded but still baby pretty. Tina looked up from her rocking only once as he sat the basket down on the bench beside her. The crooning sound began again, deeper in her throat now, less soft, more craggy.

For an hour we watched, I on the stairs and Sam from the next room. The crooning broke, ceased, died as effortlessly as it had begun. She rocked on without sound or weariness until, mid-way of her arc, she abruptly stopped. She lifted the baby into the basket, covered it, face as well as body. Saying nothing to either of us, she stood up, wrapped the old blanket around herself, opened the front door and walked out. Jeb trailed quietly behind her down the front walkway to the street and then left up the hill toward their house.

Sam set the basket on top of the old washing machine on the back porch. In a little while the gray panel truck from the mortuary drove into the driveway. Joe White knocked as he came through the back door. Stepping in, he picked up the basket and called in to the kitchen, "This it, Doc?" Sam nodded. "We'll send you the paper work as soon as we get it," and he was gone, as simply as he had come, back into the hush of the beginning snow.

Because there was no way to know yet what had happened and because we had two small children of our own, we began the long process of washing down the front room and the furniture, our bodies and our clothes. Whether contagion or poverty or sleep apnea, it would be days before we would know and much too dangerous to wait. A neighbor woman come in and took our children while we disinfected and scrubbed and disinfected again. Three days later the Methodist sexton spent most of his New Year's morning digging through the winter ground to make the grave for a funeral to which no one came.

Nothing was ever said about that frozen morning in late December. I saw Tina from time to time during the next two years that we stayed on in South Carolina and we saw Jeb frequently as he walked to and from the grocery store below our house. But no words ever passed between us beyond the obvious and the necessary. They had another child the next year and Tina named him Timothy George for no reason anyone could ever figure out. She went back to work in the mill three weeks later, as thin and as washed as always

It has been almost thirty years now for her and Jeb, if they are still alive. For me it has been three decades of wanting to at last hold their grief out from me, to turn it in my hand, to consider it in my ear, to finally give it some body which I can bury. For almost thirty winters I have searched the wordless snow and the muffling clouds, but they were right, Tina and Jeb. Whether in the mill towns of our deep South or in those of Poland, whether in the jungles of Central America or the hovels of Lebanon, there are no words for mourning the holy innocents who pass through the year's door into unrelieved memory. They are the naive ghosts who already haunt the coming year.

John Egerton

Visions of Utopia

Athens . . . Rome . . . Carthage . . . Sparta . . . Troy . . . Sardis . . . Alexandria . . . Memphis . . . Milan . . . Como . . . Paris . . . Bordeaux . . . Moscow . . .Dresden . . . Dover . . . Belfast . . . Bogata. Cities of the world, ancient and modern—and also place names on the contemporary map of Tennessee.

Every state has its "far-away places with strange-sounding names," and Tennessee is no exception. You can go to Egypt and Persia, to India, to Denmark, to Cuba and Brazil, and never leave the Volunteer State. The founders of those towns and villages probably never saw Rome or Moscow or Bogota or any of the other exotic places whose names they chose, but there are some Tennessee communities with names that do have a direct connection with the past. Alamo, the county seat of Crockett County, recalls the heroism of Tennessee frontiersman David Crockett and the Texas fortress he and others died defending. Santa Fe, in Maury County, may owe its name to the same period of nineteenth-century warfare in the West. It is popularly believed that the Tennessee men who went in such great numbers to fight in the war with Mexico inspired the state's nickname—Volunteer—and veterans returning from that campaign brought back stories of the battles at Tampico, Saltillo, and Buena Vista, giving those Spanish names to three new communities in the state. There is also a Montezuma, Tennessee.

Long before the nineteenth century, the land that is now Tennessee belonged to its original natives—the Indians—and dozens of cities, towns, and rivers in the state (indeed, the name Tennessee itself) are reminiscent of those first Americans. Chattanooga, Tullahoma, Etowah, Sequatchie, Chewalla, Pocahontas, Culleoka: in bustling metropolises and quiet

From *Visions of Utopia*, by John Egerton. Copyright © 1977 by John Egerton. Reprinted by permission of the University of Tennessee Press.

hamlets alike, the Indian heritage lives on, at least in name.

Another group of Tennessee towns is distinguished by colorful and descriptive names that stimulate the imagination. Nankipoo, near the Mississippi River, was inspired by a character in the nineteenth-century Gilbert and Sullivan comic opera, *The Mikado*. There is a Liberty and a Reverie, a Static and a Dull, a Harmony and a Prosperity, an Only and a Nameless, a Difficult and a Defeated. There is Hanging Limb, and Peeled Chestnut, and Finger, and Frog Jump, and Tiger Tail. There is Nosey Valley ("Population Varies," says the road sign outside it); and there is Stupidville ("Population 187—Unincorporated As Of Now"), so named by a village storekeeper, allegedly in protest against what he considered the low caliber of local officeholders.

Discovering what's in a name is one way of gaining a better understanding of who we are and how we got here. It is instructive to learn that when the Spanish explorer Hernando DeSoto led the first party of white men into the Tennessee country in about 1540, there was a large Indian village called Chiaha on an island in the Tennessee River a few miles north of the present location of Chattanooga, and the place where DeSoto is believed to have crossed the Mississippi River—identified then as the fourth Chickasaw Bluff—is now the site of Memphis. French and English explorers who came into the territory in the 1600s found the Chickasaws and the Cherokees already here in great numbers, and the Cherokees in particular had a highly organized society. Their seven "mother towns" in the eastern mountains included Tanasi (Tennessee) and Great Tellico (on the site of what is now Tellico Plains), and those towns (also including Toskegee, birthplace of the great inventor of the Cherokee alphabet, Sequoyah) were highly developed and thriving when whites began to arrive in greater numbers in the eighteenth century. A site on the Cumberland River known as the Big Salt Lick or the French Lick was a busy French and Indian trading post almost a hundred years before James Robertson and John Donelson began the Nashborough settlement (now Nashville) on the site during the Revolutionary War.

The first white people to settle permanently in what is now the state of Tennessee were probably William Bean of Virginia in 1769 and James Robertson of North Carolina in 1770. They, and others who joined them in what became known as the Watauga Settlements, later formed an association and adopted the first written constitution among European settlers in America. During and after the Revolutionary War, the Watauga territory was the subject of claims and counterclaims involving its white settlers, the Cherokees, the British, the state governments of Virginia and North Carolina, and the government of the United States. In 1977, the Wataugans asked North Carolina to make them part of that state; the following year, all of Tennessee became Washington County, North

Carolina, and Jonesboro, now known as Tennessee's "first town," was established as the county seat.

But the problems of frontier warfare and disputed land claims continued, and the people of the Watauga region became increasingly dissatisfied with their North Carolina connection. In 1784, they held a convention in Jonesboro and voted to form a separate state, to be called Franklin (in honor of Benjamin Franklin). A year later, Franklin's elected legislature met, and under the leadership of John Sevier (later to become the first governor of the state of Tennessee), counties were created, a militia and a court system were set up, a taxing mechanism was established, and Congress was asked to formally recognize the new government. North Carolina's strenuous opposition to the separation was decisive, however, and Congress refused to recognize the new state; by 1788, the government of Franklin had collapsed, and a year later, North Carolina ceded the entire Tennessee territory to the United States. Seven years after that, in 1796, Tennessee became the sixteenth state of the Union.

The leaders of Franklin had wanted to include in it all of what is now known as Southern Appalachia—the mountain counties of eastern Tennessee and Kentucky, southern West Virginia, western Virginia, and northern Georgia. More than fifty years after Franklin failed, another East Tennessean resurrected the idea of mountain unity, and once again came close to forming a new state.

Ezekiel Birdseye, a transplanted Connecticut Yankee who had become a successful businessman in the Tennessee town of Newport, collaborated in 1840 with Jacob Peck, a one-time Tennessee state senator and Supreme Court justice, in an attempt to form a free labor colony in East Tennessee. Their long-range plan was to join together the mountain counties of five states to create the new state of Frankland, a sovereign entity pledged to industry, free labor, and the abolition of slavery. According to an article by Henry Lee Swint in a 1944 issue of the *Tennessee Historical Quarterly*, Birdseye and Peck sought to merge two reformist sentiments then present in East Tennessee: abolition and secession. The former drew upon small but influential groups of whites who opposed slavery; the latter was a result of pervasive sectional hostility to the political and economic power that had shifted from the mountains to the western two-thirds of the state. The abolitionists and those who felt alienated from the state's power base were not necessarily allies, but Birdseye and Peck adroitly drew upon both groups to form their "free state" movement.

They came surprisingly close to success. A resolution calling for a study of "the expediency and constitutionality" of East Tennessee's secession from the state—and requiring the governor to open discussions on the subject with governors in the adjacent mountain states—was introduced in both houses of the Tennessee General Assembly in 1841. The sponsor of the measure in the Senate was Andrew Johnson, an East Tennessean who later became President of the United States. The Senate passed the resolution by a vote of 17 to 6, but it failed in the House, and the dream of a free Frankland faded and finally died.

Some of the names on the present map of Tennessee can be traced to the arrival of European immigrants in the nineteenth century; other communities established in that same period have since disappeared. One of the latter was a Welsh setlement in Scott County known as Brynyffynon ("the hill with a spring"). A Welshman named Samuel Roberts, seeking relief from hard times in his native country, purchased a large tract of land in East Tennessee and prepared a brochure to advertise it as a new frontier calling to his fellow countrymen. About forty people bought land from him at the equivalent of approximately fifty cents an acre, and in 1856 the first small group of them arrived and began clearing land for a settlement. But only a few families ever came, and only Roberts and his brother stayed. "The courage and tenacity of the Robertses kept alive the dream of a truly Welsh settlement in Tennessee for another decade," wrote Wilbur Shepperson in the *Tennessee Historical Quarterly* in 1959; but when they left, Brynyffynon "was deserted and quickly dissolved into the forests from which the cabins had been hewn." Welsh immigrants came again to Tennessee after the days of Samuel Roberts—as we shall see later. There is also an ancient legend alive in Wales today of Welshmen building smelting furnaces in the Tennessee mountains in the twelfth century.

More successful than Brynyffynon—if no less arduous—was a Swiss colonization venture in Grundy County after the Civil War. E. H. Plumacher, a Swiss government official, was sent to the United States in 1867 to seek settlement sites as a partial answer to overpopulation and economic depression in his native country. President Andrew Johnson, himself an East Tennessean, referred Plumacher to friends of his in the mountains; and a private company from Switzerland headed by Peter Staub subsequently bought up a twenty-square-mile tract of land in Grundy County and promoted it for sale at about fifty cents an acre to Swiss citizens eager to leave their homeland.

The first party of settlers arrived in 1869, and in time more than seventy-five families emigrated to the colony, which was named Gruetli ("a clearing, a meadow"), after a place by that name in Switzerland. The colonists suffered great hardships in the beginning, and the primitive conditions they found there contrasted so sharply with the picture of paradise Peter Staub had painted for them that the angry settlers felt misled and abandoned. But they were determined to succeed, and they built a community that at its peak numbered close to 300 Swiss, a tight-knit and homogeneous group with a strong sense of cultural identity. For nearly thirty years they managed to preserve their German language, their school and church

(Protestant), their music and dance, their woodcarving and winemaking skills, and their agricultural way of life. But many of those qualities succumbed to the influences of assimilation and mobility and the changing times, and Gruetli today bears little resemblance to the authentic Swiss village it once was. The original settlers never lost their contempt for Peter Staub, however. One of them told Frances Helen Jackson, a Vanderbilt University graduate student doing research at Gruetli for a master's thesis in 1933, that Staub was, in the opinion of the colony's survivors, "a first-class swindler."

European promoters of land sales in Tennessee and other American states in the middle of the nineteenth century apparently included more than one "first-class swindler." In a brochure called "East Tennessee U. S. A.," published in London in 1842, depressed and oppressed Europeans were invited to buy "fertile meadows, bold limpid streams, evergreen pastures . . . every requisite for comfort, convenience, and pleasure"—in the rugged and formidable mountains of Tennessee.

German-Swiss emigration to the United States between 1840 and 1860 was substantial, and although the foreign-born proportion of Tennessee's population was only 1 percent as late as 1880 (compared to 15 percent nationwide), several communities in the state originated in the nineteenth century as German or Swiss settlements. More than half a dozen of them still exist, among them Gruetli, Germantown, Mosheim, Hohenwald, Belvidere, Allardt, and Wartburg. Wartburg was a substantial land development enterprise that began in 1844 and in ten years attracted close to 1,000 immigrants. Now Morgan County's seat of government, Wartburg has a population of approximately that same figure, but few traces of its German heritage remain.

An altogether different kind of new community in Tennessee in the nineteenth century was the health spa. Middle Tennessee abounds with mineral springs, and more than thirty of them were developed into health and recreation resorts attracting affluent Tennesseans to spend their summers there. One of the first, and by some accounts the finest, was Beersheba Springs in Grundy County. Incorporated in 1839, its first hotel opened that year, and the resort had its heyday in about 1859, before declining during the Civil War. Perhaps the best-known spa was Red Boiling Springs in Macon County. It had several boarding houses and hotels in the 1880s, and both before and after World War I it was a thriving and prosperous summer community. Before a series of disastrous fires, the Great Depression, and the advent of the automobile signaled the end of its good times, Red Boiling Springs had nine hotels, a rich variety of cuisine and entertainment, and its famous mineral waters, reputed to be a cure for almost any ailment from diarrhea to gonorrhea. Among the other watering spas that are still on the map are Hermitage Springs, Eldorado Springs,

Castalian Springs, and Bon Aqua; the latter, in Hickman County, was a health resort as early as the 1820s, a decade or more before Beersheba Springs began to attract visitors. Charles B. Thorne, writing about the watering spas in the *Tennessee Historical Quarterly* in 1970, noted that one or two of them still have limited facilities in operation during the summer months, but for the most part, the small, quiet villages have been bypassed by a new generation of vacationers bound for Gatlinburg and Opryland and the bright lights of modern diversions elsewhere.

The contemporary version of the resort community can be seen in the proliferation of heavily promoted land development projects, particularly in the eastern half of the state, that cater to the recreation, retirement, and second-home dreams of the American middle and upper classes. The largest of them has more than 15,000 homesites, and the promotional literature extolling their assets is reminiscent of the "fertile meadows—limpid streams—evergreen pastures" language in that 1842 brochure from London. On the Cumberland Plateau alone, more than a dozen major speculative land developments have sprung up on the mountainsides and in the forestlands of a people who have never known great economic prosperity, and the contrast between the indigenous residents and the affluent newcomers is stark and pervasive. A number of apparent or potential problems related to these developments—problems of environmental impact, water supply, sewage treatment, solid waste disposal, police and fire protection, medical services, and property valuation—are cited in a 1974 report issued by the Upper Cumberland Development District, a regional planning and development agency. The report also describes an adverse social consequence of the new communities:

> The large developments themselves are highly self-sufficient in terms of the particular needs of the residents of the development. One of their selling points is that an almost total play and relaxation environment is provided within the confines of the development (there are some exceptions, notably potable water and health care) . . . Seemingly, the developments are assuming the character of super "country clubs" or resorts for metropolitan residents [and] retirees . . . The new community residents [come] to relax and play while the established residents carry on working and day-to-day living. The differences in life-style contrasted in affluence and marginal subsistence . . . portray the likely divergence of the communities . . . There will probably be a high degree of social isolation unless there is ample opportunity to break the barriers.

The Tennessee General Assembly, in an attempt to reduce the problems caused by the creation of these new communities, enacted in 1974 the New Community Development Act; the law provides for a Tennessee

Community Development Board to regulate and oversee the establishment of new communities in the state. As the phenomenon of land speculation and promotion continues, the quality, stability, and permanence of Tennessee's new communities of the present period cannot yet be adequately assessed. Whether they will be the Nashvilles and Knoxvilles of the future—or the Brynyffynons, the Bon Aquas, and the Beershebas—will remain for a later generation of Tennesseans to say.

Not many new communities have come and gone in Tennessee since the beginning of the present century, but there have been a few. For example, there was a Bohemian (Czechoslovakian) settlement on the Cumberland Plateau near Mayland in 1913. Its residents, most of them immigrants who had been struggling to survive in the cities of the North, attempted to farm collectively and to recapture the agricultural way of life they had known in their homeland. Internal dissension quickly shattered their agrarian dream, however, and most of them returned to the cities.

During the administration of Franklin D. Roosevelt, a rural resettlement program brought poverty-stricken coal miners and others into the Cumberland Homesteads near Crossville. The community did not become an incorporated town with an official name, but it was successful nonetheless; several of the original families still live there. Two other unincorporated but distinct communities that have existed in Tennessee for more than twenty-five years are the Amish and Mennonite settlements in Lawrence and Overton counties.

There are older cities, such as Kingsport and Oak Ridge, which have been made over, so to speak, by industrialization and by the massive intervention of the federal government. Kingsport, which was an unnamed settlement when the Declaration of Independence was written, began its "reconstruction" during World War I, and blossomed, ironically, during the Great Depression, when the Eastman Kodak Company initiated expansion of its industrial complex there. Kingsport grew from 12,000 people in 1930 to more than 50,000 by the end of World War II. The renaissance of Oak Ridge resulted from creation of the Tennessee Valley Authority and the Atomic Energy Commission.

Only a handful of place names on the contemporary map of Tennessee have been added in this century. One of those is Norris, a town that was built by the Tennessee Valley Authority in 1933 for construction workers at Norris Dam, the hydroelectric facility named for Senator George Norris of Nebraska, who introduced the legislation creating TVA. Norris, now a town of about 2,000 people, was owned by TVA until 1948, when it was sold at public auction for $2.1 million to a group of Philadelphia businessmen who in turn sold individual properties to occupants as their leases expired. (More recently, TVA has talked of developing a new city, a planned community to be named Timberlake—for Henry Timberlake, a British emissary among the Cherokees in the eighteenth century—but so far, the idea has not materialized because of litigation.) Another twentieth-century name on the Tennessee map is Pressman's Home (identified on some maps as Camelot) in Hawkins County. Developed as the headquarters of the International Printing Pressmen's and Assistants' Union of North America, it once boasted a large hospital, printing facilities, a training school, and housing for several hundred residents; now, it is all but deserted. The name Camelot was given to the community by real estate developers who bought the property from the union.

There is in all of these ventures, spanning more than four centuries on the land of Tennessee, a common element of exploration and enterprise. The motivating forces behind them have varied greatly from each to the next. Some were nationalistic in nature, some ethnic, some cultural; others were political, or social, or religious, or ideological; still others have been economic or commercial. The history of every state and every country is, at least in part, a running account of the endless succession of individuals who have merged their common interests and objectives in order to start anew, to form new alliances and build new communities. Human nature being what it is, the impulses have not always been pure; the desire to exploit and control and gain advantage has dominated almost as often as the desire to find liberty and equality and peace. Yet for good and ill, these new communities have added much to the total character and the history of Tennessee. Each has attempted in its own way to preserve a familiar way of life, to extend it from one setting to another, and, overall, the contribution they have made to the state's heritage has been positive and substantial.

There has been another group of new communities in Tennessee history that can be considered in a class apart from the ones already mentioned here. Rather than attempting to preserve and extend an accepted pattern of living, they were consciously founded on one theory or another of social reorganization, and their intent was not to recreate an image of the past but to give substance to an idealistic vision of the future. In a book he wrote in 1516, Thomas More described an imaginary island that had a perfect political and social system. He called the island—and his book—Utopia, and the word has survived as a descriptive term for the still-sought and still-imaginary social order that can justly be called ideal and perfect. A few of Tennessee's new communities seem legitimately to belong to the mixture of myth and reality and idealism that sets apart the utopias of history.

The most recent Tennessee utopian venture, and the only one currently in existence, is The Farm, a self-styled "family monastery" near

Summertown in Lewis County. Established in 1970 by a former California college instructor named Stephen Gaskin, The Farm is a spiritual and agricultural commune embracing more than 1,500 acres of woods and fields and more than 800 people, most of them young adults and children. Having overcome the initial suspicions of their neighbors in the surrounding countryside, Gaskin and his followers have established themselves as a respected fixture on the local scene, even though their way of living differs greatly in many respects from that of the indigenous people. (Gaskin, with three of his disciples, served a prison sentence in 1974 for growing marijuana.) His spiritual teachings to his flock are a cosmopolitan blend of Eastern and Western religious thought, often couched in the contemporary vernacular of the American youth culture. The residents of The Farm hold all their property in common, eat no meat or dairy products, practice neither birth control nor abortion, and apparently regard Gaskin as a sort of messiah whose wisdom and leadership approach infallibility. That such beliefs and practices can coexist peacefully with the conservative traditions of people in rural Middle Tennessee seems surprising. On the other hand, the young residents of the commune are themselves conservative in many ways. In appearance, they resemble nineteenth-century country folks: they wear beards, long hair, bib overalls, full-length dresses and bonnets. They are industrious, hard-working, law-abiding, and—in their own fashion—pious, moralistic, and orthodox. And, in a county that had only 6,761 people in the 1970 census, The Farm represents a bloc vote that compels local politicians and officeholders to regard the colony with seriousness and respect.

One of the common characteristics of utopias is their impermanence. If The Farm follows the pattern of history, one of two things can be expected eventually to happen to it: it will become more and more like its surroundings (and thus no longer a utopia, a "perfect social order"), or it will break up and disappear. It is the faith of Gaskin and the people of The Farm that they have found the formula for a perfect social system, and that with it they can save the world. Such has been the faith of all utopians.

Gaskin's spiritual ancestor in Tennessee could be said to be Christian Gottlieb Priber, a German socialist and utopian who joined the Cherokee Nation in 1736 and for seven years labored to create what he called the "Kingdom of Paradise." Verner W. Crane wrote about him in a 1919 article in the *Sewanee Review*.

Priber was known as a polite, refined, well-educated, and intelligent man who believed deeply in equalitarianism and an open society. Such views were incompatible with the political and social thought of the times, and the price he paid for holding them was repeated exile, first from Germany, then from England, and finally, in 1735, from South Carolina.

At Great Tellico, the principal town of the Overhill Cherokees, Priber became a willing and welcome convert among the Indian people, and there he lived until 1743, when he was captured and imprisoned by the British.

East Tennessee in those years was Cherokee land coveted by both the British and the French—those two forces of imperialism were soon to engage in a war for supremacy in the American wilderness—and each side suspected that Priber was an agent of the other. In fact, his loyalty was to neither, but to the Cherokees, whom he sought to protect from exploitation, and who in turn protected him from the Europeans who wanted him removed. Priber's idealistic conception of a Kingdom of Paradise envisioned a society in which "all colours and complexions" of people would live in friendship as equals, holding all things—including their children—in common. He also hoped to unite all Southern Indians into a single political body, and the French and English viewed such a "red empire" with alarm. The English, who were eventually to win the wilderness war, were particularly distrustful of Priber, and James Adair, one of the few Englishmen to see and talk to the elusive utopian during his years at Great Tellico, reported that Priber "impressed them [the Cherokees] with a very ill opinion of the English, representing them as a fraudulent, avaritious [sic], and encroaching people."

The Kingdom of Paradise apparently was well received by the Cherokees, who regarded Priber as an honored brother, but it had not reached an advanced state when he was finally seized and imprisoned for life. Priber was known to have in his possession when he was captured a dictionary of the Cherokee language and a manuscript describing his life among the Indians and his visionary plan for the Kingdom of Paradise. Both apparently were destroyed. The backwoods utopian died a few years later in a South Carolina prison. The Cherokees suffered under successive assaults from smallpox, from the British, and finally from the U. S. Government, which forced their removal to Oklahoma in 1838 on the infamous "Trail of Tears." The Kingdom of Paradise, and the Cherokee Nation itself, succumbed to what Christian Priber had called "an encroaching people."

Between the Kingdom of Paradise in the eighteenth century and The Farm in the twentieth, three fascinating and extraordinary utopian colonies came and went in Tennessee: Nashoba, in Shelby County, in the 1820s; Rugby, in Morgan County, in the 1880s; and Ruskin, in Dickson County, in the 1890s. Each of them was widely known in its time, and each merits a contemporary recounting.

Charles Wright

Driving Through Tennessee

It's strange what the past brings back.
Our parents, for instance, how ardently they still loom
In the brief and flushed
Fleshtones of memory, one foot in front of the next
Even in retrospect, and so unimpeachable.

And towns that we lived in once,
And who we were then, the roads we went back and forth on
Returning ahead of us like rime
In the moonlight's fall, and Jesus returning, and Stephen Martyr
And St. Paul of the Sword . . .

—I am their music,
Mothers and fathers and places we hurried through in the night:
I put my mouth to the dust and sing their song.
Remember us, Galeoto, and whistle our tune, when the time comes,
For charity's sake.

"Driving Through Tennessee" from *The Southern Cross*, by Charles Wright. Copyright © 1981 by Charles Wright. Reprinted by permission of Random House, Inc.

Charles Wright

Two Stories

Tonight, on the deck, the lights
Semaphore up at me through the atmosphere,
Town lights, familiar lights
                        pulsing and slacking off
The way they used to back on the ridge outside of Kingsport
35 years ago,
The moonlight sitting inside my head
Like knives,
          the cold like a drug I knew I'd settle down with.
I used to imagine them shore lights, as these are, then,
As something inside me listened with all its weight
For the sea-surge and the sea-change.

———————

There's a soft spot in everything
Our fingers touch,
                 the one place where everything breaks
When we press it just right.
The past is like that with its arduous edges and blind sides,
The whorls of our fingerprints
                      embedded along its walls
Like fossils the sea has left behind.

———————

"Two Stories" from *The Other Side Of the River*, by Charles Wright. Copyright © 1984 by Charles Wright. Reprinted by permission of Random House, Inc.

This is a story I swear is true.

I used to sleepwalk, But only
On camping trips,
                or whenever I slept outside.
One August, when I was 11, on Mount LeConte in Tennessee,
Campfire over, and ghost story over,
Everyone still asleep, apparently I arose
From my sleeping bag,
                opened the tent flap, and started out on the trail
That led to the drop-off, where the mountainside
Went straight down for almost a thousand feet.
Half-moon and cloud cover, so some light
As I went on up the path through the rhododendron,
The small pebbles and split roots
                like nothing under my feet.
The cliff-side was half-a-mile from the campsite.
As I got closer,
        moving blindly, unerringly,
Deeper in sleep than the shrubs,
I stepped out, it appears,
Onto the smooth lip of the rock cape of the cliff,
When my left hand, and then my right hand,
Stopped me as they were stopped
By the breathing side of a bear which woke me
And there we were,
              the child and the black bear and the cliff-drop,
And this is the way it went—
                I stepped back, and I turned around,
And I walked down through the rhododendron
And never looked back,
            truly awake in the throbbing world,
And I ducked through the low flap
Of the tent, so quietly, and I went to sleep
And never told anyone
Till years later when I thought I knew what it meant,
                which now I've forgot.

Charles Wright

And this one is questionable,

Though sworn to me by an old friend
Who'd killed a six-foot diamondback about seven o'clock in the morning
(He'd found it coiled in a sunny place),
And threw it into a croker sack with its head chopped off,
       and threw the sack in the back of a jeep,
Then left for his day's work
On the farm.
    That evening he started to show the snake
To someone, and put his hand in the sack to pull it out.
As he reached in, the snake's stump struck him.
His wrist was bruised for a week.

———————

It's not age,
    nor time with its gold eyelid and blink,
Nor dissolution in all its mimicry
That lifts us and sorts us out.
It's discontinuity
    and all its spangled coming between
That sends us apart and keeps us there in a dread.
It's what's in the rearview mirror,
      smaller and out of sight.

———————

What do you do when the words don't come to you any more,
And all the embolisms fade in the dirt?
And the ocean sings in its hammock,
      rocking itself back and forth?
And you live at the end of the road where the sky starts its dark decline?
The barking goes on and on
    from the far hill, constantly
Sticking its noise in my good ear.

Goodbye, Miss Sweeney, goodbye.
I'm starting to think about the psychotransference of all things.
It's small bones in the next life.
It's small bones,
    and heel and toe forever and ever.

Jeanne McDonald

Settlement

Becker opened the screen and passed from the bright light of the porch into the dim interior of the house. The door slapped softly behind him, propelled by a sudden gust from the ocean, then made an ominous, scraping sound. Becker remembered the loose stress bar that had fallen away the summer before, the one he had been meaning to fix and had never gotten around to. He pushed it to the back of his mind, to the nether region where he stored all his guilts, like the big one that stabbed him only yesterday, when he had met Michael in the city for lunch.

He had noticed, when Michael laughed, how uneven his front teeth were, one leaning crookedly left and making a gap beside the eye tooth. Too bad. It was Becker who reminded himself (and not Michael, who had never even put two and two together) that the money that should have gone for the braces had been spent instead for a Caribbean cruise for him and Rose.

The thing was, it hadn't worked. No romance was rekindled; there was no second honeymoon. They had argued instead about whether to go snorkeling or sailing and whether the seafood was really imported or local, and, of all things, what baskets to bring back to his mother. And here was Michael, a grown man now who could worry about his own teeth— why couldn't Becker give him that legacy at least?—but who was instead concerned only about Becker's role in the upcoming divorce and why Becker hadn't done more to prevent it.

Christ, he had done everything in his power to prevent it, but Rose wouldn't listen. And Becker hadn't had the heart to tell Michael that it was all Rose's fault. She was the guilty party, but suddenly she was accusing Becker. And of what? Disinterest. He had never really *looked* at her, she said. He had never seen her as a *person*. So here and now he was, it was true, looking at her as a *person*, and he saw, yes, how she could attract a younger man who had, from the *beginning*, seen her as a person. And he saw too how she would want finally to leave him. Him—Nathan Becker—tired, paunchy, ready to settle down into the twilight of his life and now about to lose the only woman he had ever wanted to settle down *with*.

He tossed his bag next to the door and heard the gritty scrape of sand on the floor. Ever since Michael had left home for college, five years before, Rose had been spending summers in the beach house. She swept the floors maybe once a month, so that the sand carried in on bare feet, or by the wind, maybe, gathered in miniature drifts, in corners and along the risers on the steps and even on the kitchen counter. Becker, coming out only on the weekends, was not allowed to complain, because this was Rose's domain, her place, left to her by her father, to do with as she wished. And by God she would not be governed by his inflexible rules, his anal old-maidishness, she called it, in her own house, because that was at least one part of her life, she kept reminding Becker, that had nothing to do with him.

Ah, but there she was wrong. Becker had, through the years, managed to leave his imprint on the place. A clever detective or historian could come back years later and find evidence of his presence, his character. Now that his eyes had become accustomed to the dimness, he looked around. It was his first visit this summer, and that was only to go over the property settlement with Rose. Outside, the sun had been so bright, colors lost their edge. The heat had brushed a blinding glaze over everything. But now, with pleasure, Becker noticed his shells on the mantelpiece. Those were exclusively his. Rose had been derisive about his collection, said the shells belonged in the ocean, where their colors were brightest. She had let the dust coat them, not so much out of spite as from her casual approach to housekeeping.

Becker picked one up, found it so thick with dust and salt and film that it felt greasy. He wanted to cry. He loved his shells, loved their loops and swirls and trumpeting mouths, their graceful necks. He loved their names, too. Sometimes at the gift shop in the cove he had bought, for their names alone, shells from other, more exotic beaches: White Miniature Ark, Warty Cone, Trivia, Precious Wentletrap, Bleeding Tooth, Leafy Jewel Box, Bittersweets, Netted Olive. He laughed at some of the names, they made him happy: Common Baby's Ear, Little Corrugated J. Box.

Throw them back, Rose would say. Leave them for glass boxes or people with servants who don't have to worry about dust as you do.

Was that the prize for being wealthy? Not having to worry about dust? What about wives? Did the wealthy worry as much after their wives? Out of nowhere, like an old toothache, his pain surfaced, and Becker plunged his hand deep into the pocket of his seersucker jacket and felt the cuff link that had stayed there for weeks, gathered in a flimsy nest of threads and lint. Suddenly, with one open-handed thrust, he swept his arm across the mantel and sent the shells crashing to the floor. They hit in bright, hollow explosions, making quick, brittle protests. Becker, shaken, stood for a moment surveying the striped and freckled splinters, the rosy gleaming shards of conches and cones.

Then his sense of order took over. He shuffled into the kitchen and found the broom in its customary place beside the refrigerator. At first he meant only to sweep up the shells, but then he took off his jacket—after the air-conditioned vault of his car, he was beginning to sweat—and pushed the worn angles of the broom into corners, under the furniture, swept the bare floor until he had accumulated in the center of the room a small dune colored with bits of paper and crumbs and a single dead swamp roach. On the lamp table he found a magazine three years old, folded it, and used it for his dust pan.

Returning the broom to the kitchen, Becker picked up two coffee cups that had been left on the living room table and carried them into the sink. Why two? One for Rose and the other, perhaps, for David, owner of the cuff link. Surely, knowing Becker was coming, Rose would not have allowed David here today. Considering her housekeeping faults, she had probably left the cups there for days. It might have been funny, though. Becker could have handed David the cuff link and said, "I believe this is yours. I found it in my bed."

Why carry it around? What was the point? Only Becker knew it was there. Sometimes he even forgot it, then out of habit he would put his hand in his pocket and feel the curved ridge, the raised "D W," and the long, smooth shank. Having that solid reminder seemed easier to deal with than a nebulous list of accusations.

Rose knew of its discovery, of course. The subsequent confrontation had prompted her departure. At last, after all the threats over the years, after all the arguments, she was really and truly gone. She had moved into the beach house for the summer, but after that, colder weather would force her to make more permanent decisions. It was the first summer in years that had seemed too long to Becker. Since his fortieth birthday he had watched the time whistle by him, stopping only to bump him occasionally with discovery that his hair had moved even farther back on his forehead, that his limbs were a bit less flexible, that Michael was growing up, had left home, married. Before this summer, there had always been too many concerts in the park to choose from, too few weekends at the beach before the hurricane season lumbered in. Now he had to stay at home in the big, echoing house, or go out alone. He knew no women, at least no suitable women. His male friends were all tied to women of their own, so beyond a Saturday golf game or a drink after work, he could not count on them for company. He sat at the window in the evenings and listened to the voices of the last children playing in the neighborhood. He watched the soft darkness descend and fill up the corners of the yard. He sat in the blue light of the television set and switched to channel after channel, watched shows he had never watched before and cried at the most ridiculous things. Then he would go to bed, his head aching from crying and too much whiskey, and lie on the wrinkled sheets, longing for Rose and nursing incongruous memories of Michael as a baby, his fly-away hair and sweet, milky skin, his dimpled, clinging hands. He would remember, too, how, when Michael was old enough to drive, Becker had lain in that same bed and worried every night, waiting for him to come home. When he heard sirens miles away on the highway, he would have visions of Michael crushed under twisted metal. He could even see his face, distorted in pain, hear the screams that he remembered from the time the boy had fallen from the tree house and broken his leg. When at last he heard the whisper of the tires at the curb and the soft slam of the car door, he would turn over and immediately fall asleep. Back when the world was flat, did people worry about their children falling off the edge?

Now Michael seldom came to the house. His young wife was shy and awkward, uncertain whether to call Nathan "Mr. Becker" or "Dad" or "Nathan," so she avoided calling him by any name at all. No, it was easier to meet Michael alone at a fancy restaurant, treat him to an expensive lunch at a place which harbored memories for neither of them.

Becker rinsed the cups and put them on the dish rack to dry. The rack was coated with a rubber finish, red, but the corners were chipped off, and rust and the salt air had begun their slow devastation.

Becker heard footsteps on the deck outside and looked up to see Rose coming toward the house. She was just out of the water, hadn't even bothered to dry off. She never carried a towel to the beach. Her long hair, which she usually wore twisted and off her neck, clung to her shoulders like dark epaulettes. Becker breathed deeply. It had been weeks since he had seen her. He had forgotten how good she looked in her bathing suit, gleaming like that, her square shoulders outlined in the sun, the long legs still slender and firm. At the top of the steps she stopped, flung her hair forward, and pulling her hands down its length, wrung it like a towel. When she straightened up, she looked toward the house, as if she had sensed him there. "Nathan?"

He pushed open the kitchen door and stepped outside. The sun was behind him now, and Rose was shading her eyes. "It's me," he said, feeling guilty somehow. She came forward, dripping. It annoyed him that when she absently kissed his cheek, she put her wet hand on his shirt. "Aren't you even going to dry off before you go inside?" he asked.

"This is a beach house, Nathan," she said over her shoulder, and from inside, after the slam of the screen, he heard, "and it's remarks like that have brought us to this point."

Becker followed her inside. She was pulling off her suit in the middle of the living room, where anyone passing on the beach road could have seen. She scowled at his disapproving face and started for the upstairs shower. "Fix me a drink," she said.

Becker followed her to the foot of the stairs and watched the lift of her buttocks as she took each step. There was a line across her lower back where the suit had left its mark. "Still a gin and tonic?"

Rose leaned over the banister and grinned. Her breasts swung forward. "It hasn't been *that* long, Nathan."

"Right. It just *seems* that long," Nathan muttered as he heard the shower come on. He shuffled back to the kitchen, past the old victrola, broken for years, and the mounted head of an elk that Rose's father had shot years before. The yellow glass eyes, dust-covered, stared balefully out at the sea. Rose's red bathing suit, crumpled and sandy, seemed like a gauntlet thrown down in the middle of the living room floor. Becker picked it up and carried it to the kitchen sink, where he rinsed it under the pitted faucet. Hanging it on the outside line, he heard Rose moving around the front upstairs bedroom, his favorite room in the house, a room where they had lain in each other's arms and listened together to the liquid roll of the sea. For a minute he closed his eyes and was lost in a reverie that was all mouths and breasts and long, slender legs. Where would he sleep tonight—in the marsh-side bedroom, where the breeze was scarce? Or would Rose ask him to leave when their business was finished?

Back in the kitchen, he opened the cabinet doors. Inside were the dishes and glasses Rose had brought from her father's house when he died, a strange collection of left-over lives, old pieces of gold-colored carnival glass, a set of Shirley Temple bowls, a Blue Willow platter, and various chipped and crazed ironstone plates and serving pieces. Most of the glasses were jelly jars, and over the years Becker had grown used to fitting his lip over their thick, cloudy rims.

By the time he had mixed the drinks, Rose appeared in a loose white shift, her cheeks burnished by the sun. She had made up her eyes in that smoky way she knew, and her hair, still damp, was pulled up on top of her head. Becker wanted to tell her how beautiful she looked, but it seemed somehow inappropriate, as if she were already somebody else's wife. He handed her the gin and tonic and watched carefully as she took the first sip. Maybe she had been right: maybe he never *had* seen her as a person, only a wife. For instance, he had never noticed that flat mole on the back of her left hand, or that just at the edge of her eyes her skin was a translucent green. He stood and watched her as closely as if he were memorizing that moment for a future and lonelier day.

Rose eyed him obliquely. "Should we start now, Nathan?" Not waiting for his answer, she walked into the living room, put down her drink, and started gathering pencils and tablets from a bookshelf. "I've made a few notes," she said, "but now it doesn't seem fair, really. Or have you been thinking about what you want, too?"

"There's only one thing I want," Nathan said pointedly.

"No, Nathan, it'll be fifty-fifty. You'd regret it later, otherwise."

He stepped forward and took her arm. "Don't you want to know what that one thing is, Rose?"

Her face came up as young and beautiful as he'd ever remembered it, but hard. Not angry, but hard. "It's me, isn't it? You want me." Her fingers were prying at his hand on her arm.

"I'm willing to forget," Nathan said.

"Not me," Rose said flatly, laying the tablets and pencils out on the table. "I'm not willing to forget anything. And I'm not willing to turn back."

"But why, Rose? It couldn't have been that bad. David can't be that good."

"Nobody has said that David cancels out the past. But he's good for right now. He *is* that good. He makes you feel alive." She held up her hand, palm out, as if to ward off whatever defense Becker had ready to throw at her. "Oh, we got by, Nathan, we got by, but I'm forty-six years old. I want more than that." She stepped back, surveyed her table as if it had been set for a dinner party, then picked up her drink again. "Let's get started."

"Already? Can't we at least wait until dinner? Maybe I'd like a swim."

"Nathan, you *hate* the beach. Stop being a baby."

Becker swallowed the rest of his martini and went in to mix himself another. "And don't get drunk," Rose warned. "You know I hate it when you drink too much. Please, Nathan."

Becker ignored her, filled his glass, then sat down across from her. Rose had laid two pencils beside his tablet. That they were new and freshly sharpened seemed somehow cruel.

When he leaned toward her, a little wave of dizziness pulled at him, then subsided. He remembered that he hadn't eaten anything at all that day. "Have you ever noticed," he asked, "how crooked Michael's front teeth are?"

"Of course I've noticed. I nagged you about it for years, and you kept saying they'd straighten themselves out, only of course they didn't. It's a little late now to be noticing, isn't it?"

"Well, we did talk about it," Becker said, reaching back in his memory, "but we *both* agreed—remember? to go to the Caribbean. And then the money was all used up. And later, when your father left you everything, Michael was already in college."

Rose looked at him squarely. "We muffed it, Nathan. Now Michael will have to take care of it."

"Won't he look funny with braces, at his age?"

Rose tapped a pencil sharply against the table. "For God's sake, Nathan, let's get down to business."

"I *love* Michael," Becker insisted.

"Of course you do. So do I. But he has nothing to do with what we're here for."

Becker sipped his drink and stared glumly out the window. On the other side of the road, the marsh grass stood in brilliant sun-painted clumps along the flat white ribbon of the creek. Becker turned back to Rose. "How does one go about dividing up property?"

She shrugged, and he thought her shoulders to be singularly sensuous. "I'm not sure, really. I suppose you start with one room at a time and divide everything in it, then go on to the next."

"We ought to be there, then."

"Where, Nathan?"

"At the house. Otherwise, how else can we remember everything?"

"Nathan, we lived there for twenty-six years. We can remember. Start with the living room." Somewhere down the shore, thunder rumbled.

"The Aubusson," Becker said. "I'd like that."

"Don't be difficult," Rose said. "That rug belonged to my mother."

"Well, so did most of the furniture. All the antiques, certainly," Becker said. "We gave all our old stuff to Michael when you got your inheritance. Does that mean none of it is mine?"

"No, Nathan, but the Aubusson is special to me. I insist on that. Take the sofa. It's a Chippendale, it's worth a lot of money."

"And damned uncomfortable. I've always hated it. It's yours, and welcome to it."

"Well, tell me what you want, then. The Klee painting?"

"You'd give me that? I'm surprised."

"I'm not a complete bitch, Nathan."

He couldn't help it. A sound came from his throat, nearly a laugh, but closer to a sob.

"Nathan, please." For a minute her eyes softened, and her hand came up to his face, but she pulled it away just as quickly.

Becker laid his head on the table. The dizziness had come back, and he was dangerously close to tears. Without looking, he could sense Rose's resolve, feel the stiffness in her shoulders. When at last he sat up and looked at her, she seemed like no one he had ever known. "Keep the Klee," he said, choking back tears. "Give me the Webster's."

"The Webster's?"

"Yes, the unabridged dictionary." He had suddenly remembered that for several summers, early in their marriage, he had used that book as a flower press. In the s's he had carefully laid blue statice, white Star of Bethlehem, and silvery Stardrift. Among the a's he had pressed lavender azalea blooms and red anemones; in the r's, pink rose petals, white ranunculus; and in the b's, shiny buttercups with curved, downy stems. Somehow having that book seemed important now to help him gather up the pieces of his life.

"And the encyclopedias," he went on, downing the last of his drink, "and Michael's shoes."

"Michael's shoes?"

"The baby shoes, the bronzed ones."

"I wanted those," Rose said.

"We'll split them. You take one, I'll take the other."

"Nathan, they're bookends."

"So were we."

He held up his empty glass and stared at her through it. Her distorted face seemed to him a truer vision. "Do you remember how we used to sleep, back to back, our rears always in contact?"

"Nathan . . ."

"And then one of us would turn over and we'd sleep like spoons. Remember the way we fit?"

Rose looked away. The room was dim now, and the breeze was picking up. The curtains flapped. Becker smelled rain coming. He reached for his coat, slid his arms into it and at once felt for the cuff link, the physical manifestation of his irrefutable pain. "I'm having another drink. What about you?"

"You've had enough, Nathan. Please, let's finish this, and I'll fix dinner."

Becker started for the kitchen, stumbled over the door jamb.

"Nathan!"

"No, it's all right," he said. On the darkening beach he saw a sharp javelin of lightning hit the shore. He mixed his martini and leaned against the frame of the doorway, looking at Rose. The shutters in the upstairs windows were rattling. "What about with David?" he asked.

Rose looked up at him. "What do you mean?"

"I mean, how do you sleep with him? Face to face? Back to back? How? I want to know."

Rose stood up, "I need to close the windows. A storm's blowing up."

Becker grabbed her arm. "I want to know, Rose."

He could feel the gooseflesh on her arm. "Don't do this, Nathan. Let me go."

"Tell me. Hurt me so I'll hate you. Then you can have everything."

They both jumped with a bolt of lightning that came down close to the house. Rose screamed and Nathan gathered her into his arms. Though her skin was cool, he could still smell the sun on her flesh. But she suddenly cried out and pushed away from him, and he saw that in reaching for her he had spilled his drink on the back of her dress. "Damn you, Nathan," she spit out. "Look what you've done. You're drunk. Damn you!"

They heard the rain then, hard, relentless, slamming against the east side of the house. "Get the windows down here, Nathan," Rose cried. "I'll check upstairs." She disappeared into the darkness of the hallway.

Nathan put down his drink and started pulling down windows. Everything was soaked through already, and the old leak in the ceiling, where the upstairs porch joined the house, had begun to drip. He tried the lamps, but nothing happened. Looking out, he saw the curve of the beach, dark for miles up the coast. The power had failed. He rummaged in drawers for candles, found a few stubs in the kitchen, and lit one on the gas burner. Then he dripped wax onto a saucer, secured the candles and carried them into the living room.

Rose came down in her robe, pulled tight over her breasts. With the windows closed, the air was thick, but Nathan shivered in his damp jacket. The candlelight deepened Rose's eyes, lifted the planes of her face.

Becker sat on the sofa, his head against the window pane. "Remember how we used to love a storm at the beach, Rose? We used to sit here by the window and watch the lightning dance along the shore. You would sit on my lap, with your arm around my neck, and sometimes I'd put my hand on your breast. I remember that. It was exciting, wasn't it?"

Rose stood in the shadows, silent.

Becker persisted. "Wasn't that exciting, Rose? One night we made love, right here on this sofa, during a storm."

"I don't remember that, Nathan," Rose said. "I can't remember your ever being that spontaneous."

Becker laughed. "How quickly we forget." He pressed his face against the glass of the window. The rain hit in sharp needles outside, playing a cool staccato against his cheek. "I remember, Rose. Does that make it true if only one of us remembers?"

"You're drunk," she said. "I asked you not to get drunk. You never listen to me."

Becker felt faint again. He let his weight fall against the windowsill. Suddenly lightning flashed and in that blinding moment he saw her face as ghostly, as if she were dead, and somehow in that moment he realized that he had finally, truly lost her. But he would not make it easy. "I insist, Rose," he said, his words blurring at the edges, "I insist on getting the Aubusson."

In the dark corner of the room she was crying softly. "You drunk, you rotten drunk."

They were both silent then, listening to the storm move down the beach.

The wind was letting up. When the lamps suddenly came on, Becker saw that Rose's cheeks were wet. Her eyes came up to meet his with a coldness he had never seen before. She hissed at him. "You never really loved me."

Becker stood up to look out the window, and with his back to her, gave her the answer that was easiest for them both. "Guilty as charged." Then he stumbled up the stairs and fell onto the bed in the marsh-side bedroom. He was too tired to open the windows and shutters again. The bed smelled musty and damp. Outside it was very dark.

At dawn he woke to the rhythm of the blood surging painfully in his temples. His mouth was cottony, and everything was stifling. He stumbled downstairs, where the rooms were still quiet and closed. Then he stepped out onto the deck, breathed deeply, saw the damp drifts of sand, pock-marked from the rain. A crane flew up abruptly from the swamp behind him like a ragged white kite. The beach houses sat sleepily, shouldering off the mist the way a man shakes off sleep. A thin breeze blew the salt air cleanly across the dunes. It reminded Becker of something. It reminded him of Rose's smell, the night they had made love in the storm. Redolent of sea shells.

He walked across the deck, passed over the laurel thicket and stepped down between the dunes that were crested with sea oats, damp now, and drooping. On the beach he saw everything as though magnified—each immeasurably tiny grain of sand—brown, cream, blue. He saw silvery slivers of bleached wood, pale, broken shells, conches, clams, and stretched, dried seaweed.

At the lip of the ocean, Becker stopped to pull off his shoes and socks. The icy splash of the water at his ankles made him forget, for a moment, his aching head. He looked into the rising sun and saw its reflection, a hard white span, on the waves. He kept his eye on a single glimmering swell and reached into his pocket for the cuff link. He grasped it tightly and swung back his arm, bringing it forward again in an arc. Then he opened his hand and let the cuff link sail. It was surprising how far it went, a weightless thing like that. His muscles ached from the effort. Yet, with the glare of the sun and the ripples on the water, he had not seen it break the surface.

Slowly he turned and started walking down the beach, wondering whether he should insist on the Aubusson or settle for the Chippendale sofa. This happened the summer he was fifty years old.

Tom T. Hall

Wet Stump

Now this is hard to explain. You take a four pound test monofilament fishing line and thread it through a #4 short shank fishing hook, double the line back three inches parallel, turn the loose end around the long portion of the line an odd number of times (more than three), and then place the loose end of the line through the small opening at the end of the loop and pull the whole of the thing together to form a perfect fishing hook tie.

A man by the name of Wet Stump taught me to do that. He was superstitious about the odd number of times. If you only turned the line four, six, or any even number of times, the fish would get away. I had respect for the man.

We fished out of James Parson's boat dock on Grover Lake. It was a pretty good-sized lake. There were two hundred miles of shoreline and the water got as deep as two hundred feet.

Wet Stump got his name by believing that fish had an attraction to any stump of a tree that was surrounded by water. He hunted out the stumps in winter when the water was low and would fish them in the spring when the rains came and the Corps of Engineers would let the water level rise above them.

Wet Stump had been raised in South Africa by his missionary parents. We never could talk about politics or religion. He had the darndest notion about such things. That's why I was not surprised when he told me he wanted to be cremated when he died, and he wanted me to spread his ashes on Grover Lake. He asked me to do that one morning when the sun was shining and the fish were biting. I didn't expect him to die anyway, so I said I would do it. Besides that, I didn't want to hear any long speeches about cremation and the hereafter.

Wet Stump died all right. He was a retired school teacher, and he was bringing a big box of books out of the attic of his house and had a heart attack.

I learned about his death at the boat dock. I was washing my boat when one of the guys came along the boardwalk and said, "Old Wet Stump died last night. Heart attack."

The guy who told me that was a cheater. Wet Stump and I had caught him borrowing fish in a bass tournament one time and he didn't like either one of us. He stood there looking at me. He knew I didn't like what he was telling me. I started to say something like, "Well, we all gotta go sometime," or "Well, it's a quick way to go," but I didn't say anything. I sat there on my boat and looked at him. He said, "How old was he?"

I said I didn't know. The guy stood there another minute looking at me, and he said, "Well, we all gotta go sometime." He walked away.

I can't honestly say I had forgotten what I had promised Wet Stump about throwing his ashes in the lake, but I convinced myself I had.

The phone rang three days later and it was Wet Stump's widow on the line. She got right to the point of the thing. She asked me if Tuesday morning at nine would be all right with me. I got right up front trying to get out of it. I said, "Ma'am, I don't know if I can do it or not."

She said, "Well, how about Wednesday?"

I said, "It's not that I'm busy, I just never did anything like that before."

She turned real huffy. "Well, mister, my husband has never done anything like this before either."

I backed off. "Well, how we gonna go about it?"

She said, "Call the Corps of Engineers and ask them if there are any particular regulations."

I said, "You want me to do that?"

She said, "I got these ashes here. Are you in or out?" I could see her standing there with the ashes in an urn or something. I wanted off the phone so I said, "I'll call you back."

The first person I talked to at the Engineers' office was very nice about it, but she put me through to a man who was very blunt. "Look," he said, "you can't throw anything in that lake. Nothing! The only thing I can let you throw in that lake is a fishhook and it better have a line on it."

I couldn't get any further with the story I wanted to tell him. He said, "Now listen, this is me talkin' personal. But I don't think anybody wants to fish in a graveyard." There was another pause, and then he said, "I can give you a Washington address where you can write to if you want to get more information." I told him I would call him back.

I worried about it a lot. I tried to take a nap and not think about it for a while. It became real important. After an hour or so, I called Wet Stump's widow. I said, "Ma'am, they're not gonna let us do it." I told her an exaggerated version of the phone conversation with the engineer. She sat quiet on the phone for a minute. "Well, you be out there Tuesday morning at nine o'clock and we'll do it anyway." She hung up the phone.

Now here's what goes through a man's mind when he has to do something he never expected he would have to do. Don't show up. What do we owe these people? How did we get involved in this? What if we get arrested? What if we get sick? We editorialize.

Tuesday morning was a nice morning. The day was perfect for fishing. When I got down to the ramp that led out to the boat dock I was a little bit late. There were seven boats gathered around the gas pumps. Widow Wet Stump was dressed in a black outfit that was tight around her throat. I wore my jeans and sneakers and a t-shirt and was surprised to see the other members of the party dressed in suits and ties.

It was the first time I felt sorry for Wet Stump. He would not have imagined a scene like this. It was eerie looking. I nodded as I went by them to my boat. It started easily and I maneuvered it out into the group. The cheater and Wet Stump's widow led the procession down past the "no wake" sign. We continued on past the sign at idle speed. I followed along at the rear of the procession. I was either being punished for being late, for not being dressed properly, or for having a dirty boat. I didn't know which, but I was guilty of all three.

We more or less circled the boats when we got to what we all called Stump Row. It was a line of hardwood stumps that rose about two feet above the water level in normal season. Wet Stump's widow pulled a sheet of yellowed paper from her purse and said, "You won't understand this, it's in African." She began to read what sounded like The Lord's Prayer. You could kind of tell by the cadence of the thing.

When she finished the reading she reached into the bottom of the boat she was in and lifted a clear pastic bag. It looked like a bag for leftovers. She handed the bag across to a guy who handed it to me. I sat there staring at the bag; the widow said, "Proceed, please."

I pulled one of the corners of the bag loose and sort of unzipped it. I stood in my boat and sprinkled the ashes of my friend along side in the water. I felt a sudden sense of elation to be doing such an honorable thing, keeping a promise of such magnitude.

The widow said, "Thank you all for honoring my husband in a way he thought appropriate."

I sat with my head down as the other boats moved away. A minnow came to the surface and nibbled at the ashes of my friend.

The great and noble deeds of man are probably stories. It completely ruins a good fishing day to dispose of the remains of a pal. It does me no good to see a stern widow in a severe black dress. It is of no value to be reminded of mortality on playgrounds. We drink beer on such days and are acutely aware of the insult.

It was not many days later that I traded my boat for a fourwheel drive vehicle and turned to hunting.

It's like the man said, "Nobody likes to fish in a graveyard."

Marilou Awiakta

Motheroot

Creation often
needs two hearts
one to root
and one to flower
One to sustain
in time of drought
and hold fast
against winds of pain
the fragile bloom
that in the glory
of its hour
affirms a heart
unsung, unseen.

"Motheroot" appeared untitled in *Abiding Appalachia: Where Mountain and Atom Meet*, by Marilou Awiakta. Copyright © 1977 by Marilou Awiakta. Reprinted by permission of St. Luke's Press.

Marilou Awiakta

Baring the Atom's Mother Heart

"What is the atom, Mother? Will it hurt us?"

I was nine years old. It was December, 1945. Four months earlier, in the heat of an August morning—Hiroshima. Destruction. Death. Power beyond belief, released from something invisible. Without knowing its name, I'd already felt the atom's power in another form. Since 1943, my father commuted the 18 miles from our apartment in Knoxville to the plant in Oak Ridge—the atomic frontier where the atom had been split, where it still was splitting. He left before dawn and came home long after dark. "What do you do, Daddy?"—"I can't tell you, Marilou. It's part of something for the war. I don't know what they're making out there or how my job fits into it."

He did tell me what it was like "out there"—swarms of people . . . 82,000 of them . . . and a fence around it all, with armed guards, patrols, watch towers. He showed me his badge with his picture and number on it. "I have to show this to get in the main gate, but I can only go to my plant. I don't have clearance to go to the most secret part. You have to pass through a maze of fences to get to it."

"What's inside the maze?"

"Something important . . . and strange. I see long, heavy trucks coming in. What they're bringing just seems to disappear. Somebody must know what happens to it, but nobody ever talks about it. One thing for sure—the government doesn't spend millions of dollars for nothing. It's something big. I can't imagine what."

I couldn't either. But I could feel its energy like a great hum.

Then, suddenly, it had an image: the mushroom cloud. It had a name: the atom. And our family was living in Oak Ridge. My father had given

"Baring the Atom's Mother Heart," by Marilou Awiakta. Copyright © 1983 by Marilou Awiakta. Reprinted by permission of the author. A condensed version of this was published in *Ms. Magazine*, July 1983.

me the facts. I also needed an interpreter.

"*What is the atom, Mother? Will it hurt us?*"

"It can be used to hurt everybody, Marilou. It killed thousands of people in Hiroshima and Nagasaki. But the atom itself . . . ? It's invisible, the smallest bit of matter. And it's in everything. Your hand, my dress, the milk you're drinking—all of it is made with millions and millions of atoms and they're all moving. But what the atom means . . . ? I don't think anyone knows yet. We have to have reverence for its nature and learn to live in harmony with it. Remember the burning man."

"I remember." When I was six years old, his screams had brought my mother and me running to our front porch. Mother was eight months pregnant. What we saw made her hold me tight against her side. Across the street, in the small parking lot of the dry cleaner's, a man in flames ran, waving his arms. Another man chased him, carrying a garden hose turned on full force, and shouting, "Stop, stop!" The burning man stumbled and sank to his knees, shrieking, clawing the air, trying to climb out of his pain. When water hit his arms, flesh fell off in fiery chunks. As the flames went out his cries ceased. He collapsed slowly into a charred and steaming heap.

Silence. Burned flesh. Water trickling into the gutter . . .

The memory flowed between Mother and me, and she said, as she had that day, "Never tempt nature, Marilou. It's the nature of fire to burn. And of cleaning fluid to flame near heat. The man had been warned over and over not to work with the fluid, then stoke the furnace. But he kept doing it. Nothing happened. He thought he was in control. Then one day a spark . . . The atom is like the fire."

"So it *will* hurt us."

"That depends on us, Marilou."

I understood. Mother already had taught me that beyond surface differences, everything is in physical and spiritual connection—God, nature, humanity. All are one, a circle. It seemed natural for the atom to be part of this connection. At school, when I was introduced to Eistein's Theory of Relativity—that energy and matter are one—I accepted the concept easily.

Peacetime brought relaxation of some restrictions in Oak Ridge. I learned that my father was an accountant. The "long, heavy trucks" brought uranium ore to the Graphite Reactor, which was still guarded by a maze of fences. The reactor reduced the ore to a small amount of radioactive material. Safety required care and caution. Scientists called the reactor "The lady" and, in moments of high emotion, referred to her as "our beloved reactor."

"What does she look like, Daddy?"

"They tell me she has a seven foot shield of concrete around a graphite core, where the atom is split." I asked the color of graphite. "Black," he said. And I imagined a great, black queen, standing behind her shield, holding the splitting atom in the shelter of her arms.

I also saw the immense nurturing potential of the atom. There was intensive research into fuels, fertilizers, mechanical and interpretative tools. Crops and animals were studied for the effects of radiation. Terminal cancer patients came from everywhere to the research hospital. I especially remember one newspaper picture of a man with incredibly thin hands reaching for the "atomic cocktail" (a container of radioactive isotopes). His face was lighted with hope.

At school we had "disaster drills," in case of nuclear attack (or in case someone got careless around the reactor). Scientists explained the effects of an explosion—from "death light" to fallout. They also emphasized the peaceful potential of the atom and the importance of personal commitment in using it. Essentially, their message was the same as my mother's. "If we treat the atom with reverence, all will be well."

But all is not well now with the atom. The arms race, the entry of Big Business into the nuclear industry, and accidents like Three Mile Island cause alarm. Along with men, women protest, organize anti-nuclear groups, speak out. But we must also take time to ponder woman's affinities with the atom and to consider that our responsibilities for its use are more profound than we may have imagined.

We should begin with the atom itself, which is approximately two trillion times smaller than the point of a pin. We will focus on the nature and movement of the atom, not on the intricacies of nuclear physics. To understand the atom, we must flow with its pattern, which is circular.

During the 19th and early 20th centuries, scientists theorized about the atom, isolated it, discovered the nucleus, with its neutrons, protons, electrons. The atom appeared to resemble a Chinese nesting ball—a particle within a particle. Scientists believed the descending order would lead to the ultimate particle—the final, tiny bead. Man would penetrate the secret of matter and dominate it. All life could then be controlled, like a machine.

Around the turn of the century, however, a few scientists began to observe the atom asserting its nature, which was more flexible and unpredictable than had been thought. To explain it required a new logic and, in 1905, Einstein published his Theory of Relativity. To describe the atom also required new use of language in science because our senses cannot experience the nuclear world except by analogy. The great Danish physicist, Neils Bohr said, "When it comes to atoms, language can be used only as in poetry. The poet, too, is not nearly so concerned with describing facts as with creating images and mental connections."

As research progressed the word "mystery" began to appear in scientific writing, along with theories that matter might not end in a particle after all. Perhaps the universe resembled a great thought more than a great machine. The linear path was bending . . . and in the mid-1970's the path ended in an infinitesimal circle: the quark. A particle so small that even with the help of huge machines, humans can see only its trace, as we see the vapor trail of an airplane in the stratosphere. A particle 10 to 100 million times smaller than the atom. Within the quark scientists now perceive matter refining beyond space-time into a kind of mathematical operation, as nebulous and real as an unspoken thought. It is a mystery that no conceivable research is likely to dispell, the life force in process—nurturing, enabling, enduring, fierce.

I call it the atom's mother heart.

Nuclear energy is the nurturing energy of the universe. Except for stellar explosions, this energy works not by fission (splitting) but by fusion—attraction and melding. With this relational process, the atom creates and transforms life. Women are part of this life force. One of our natural and chosen purposes is to create and sustain life—biological, mental and/or spiritual. Women nurture and enable. Our "process" is to perceive relationships among elements, draw their energies to the center and fuse them into a whole. Thought is our essence; it is intrinsic for us, not an aberration of our nature as tradition often asserts.

Another commonality with the atom's mother heart is ferocity. When the atom is split—when her whole is disturbed—a chain reaction begins that will end in an explosion unless the reaction is contained, usually by a nuclear reactor. To be productive and safe, the atom must be restored to its harmonic, natural pattern. Similarly, to split woman from her thought, sexuality, and spirit is unnatural. Explosions are inevitable, unless wholeness is restored.

In theory, nature has been linked to woman for centuries—from the cosmic principle of the Great Mother-Goddess to the familiar metaphors of Mother Nature and Mother Earth. But to connect the life force with *living* woman is something only some ancient or so-called "primitive" cultures have been wise enough to do. The linear, Western, masculine mode of thought has been too intent on conquering nature to learn from her a basic truth: *to separate the gender that bears life from the power to sustain it is as destructive as to tempt nature itself.*

This obvious truth is ignored because to accept it would acknowledge woman's power, upset the concept of woman as sentiment—passive, all-giving, all-suffering—and disturb public and private patterns. But the atom's mother heart makes it impossible to ignore this truth any longer. She is the interpreter not only of new images and mental connections for humanity, but also, most particularly for women, who have profound responsibilities in solving the nuclear dilemma. We can do much to restore harmony. But time is running out . . .

Shortly after Hiroshima Albert Einstein said, "The unleashed power of the atom has changed everything save our modes of thought, and thus we drift toward unparalledled catastrophe." Now, deployment of nuclear missiles is increasing. A going phrase in Washington is, "When the war starts . . . " Many nuclear power plants are being built and operated with money, not safety, as the bottom line. In spite of repeated warnings from scientists and protests from the public, the linear-thinking people continue to ignore the nature of the atom. They act irreverently. They think they're in control. One day a spark . . .

I look beyond the spectres of the mushroom cloud and the burning man to the time 200 years ago, when destruction was bearing down on the Cherokee nation. My foremothers took their places in the circles of power along with the men. Out-numbered and out-gunned, the nation could not be saved. But the Cherokee and their culture survived—and women played a strong part in that survival.

Although the American culture is making only slow progress toward empowering women, there is much we can do to restore productive harmony with the atom. Protest and litigation are important in stopping nuclear abuse, but total polarization between pro- and anti-nuclear people is simplistic and dangerous. It is not true that all who believe in nuclear energy are bent on destruction. Neither is it true that all who oppose it are "kooks" or "against progress." Such linear, polar thinking generates so much anger on both sides that there is no consensual climate where reasonable solutions can be found. The center cannot hold. We need a network of the committed. Women can use our traditional intercessory skills to create this network through organizations, through education and through weaving together conscientious protagonists in industry, science and government.

Our energies may fuse with energies of others in ways we cannot foresee. I think of two groups of protestors who came to Diablo Canyon (CA) in the fall of 1981. Women and men protested the activation of a nuclear power plant so near an earthquake fault. The first group numbered nearly 3000. The protest was effective, but it says much about the dominant, *non*-holistic mode of American thought that an article about the second group was buried in the middle of a San Francisco newspaper.

After the 3000 had left Diablo Canyon to wind and silence, a band of about 80 Chumash Indians came to the site of the power plant. They raised a wood-sculpted totem and sat in a circle around it for a day-long prayer vigil. Jonathan Swift Turtle, a Mewok medicine man, said that the Indians did not oppose nuclear technology but objected to the plant's being built atop a sacred Chumash burial site, as well as near an earthquake fault. He said he hoped the vigil would bring about "a moment of harmony between the pro- and anti-nuclear factions."

The Chumash understand that to split the atom from the sacred is a deadly fission that will ultimately destroy nature and humanity. I join this circle of belief with an emblem I created for my life and work—the sacred white deer of the Cherokee, leaping in the heart of the atom. My ancestors believed that if a hunter took the life of a deer without asking its spirit for pardon, the immortal Little Deer would track the hunter to his home and cripple him. The reverent hunter evoked the white deer's blessing and guidance.

For me, Little Deer is a symbol of reverence. Of hope. Of belief that if we humans relent our anger and create a listening space, we may attain harmony with the atom in time. If we do not, our world will become a charred and steaming heap. Burned flesh. Silence . . .

There will be no sign of hope except deep in the invisible, where the atom's mother heart—slowly and patiently—bears new life.

H. T. Kirby-Smith

Highland Rim

This air is a close shave,
slicing across the frozen ponds, scraping chins raw,
icicle-edged and keen as stars. Wind meets
small resistance, skimming the spiky sedge
when such cold hills etch their bulk on polished sky
and the men come stamping after the beagles—
rabbit-hunters—across the slopes as the sun sets.

Configuration of land and purpose: too steep
for farms—though corn does as well
on the slopes as the bottom land
if you still have a mule to plow with.
Flint and chert skreek under a boot heel and clatter
or, if it's wet, grind down into the clay
—all of it weathered out of rotted limestone.

What are they doing here, those hunters—
a thousand feet up from the sea, five hundred miles
    inland?
Underfoot those blocky fragments—a silica jelly
that set four hundred million years ago in the limy ooze
silting a sea-bottom far from shore—
what do they have to do with men whose breath the sunset
stains with the faintest roseate hue as it vanishes?

"Highland Rim," by H. T. Kirby-Smith appeared in *Ploughshares*, Vol. 9, no. 2 & 3. Copyright © 1983 by H. T. Kirby-Smith. Reprinted by permission of the publisher and the author.

One of the beagles catches a scent and yelps.
The pack takes it up. Half-moons of sound collide
belled out of their throats. They are their own echoes.
And then the abrupt thrust of blue vapor from a gun
and a half-second later the punched air recoils.
Reverberations die away and the pack quietens
and mills while the man slits out the rabbit guts.

Distance shrinks them, but they, preoccupied,
go on in their ways. Now the sky—
black porcelain overhead, curving to a luminous edge—
releases stars: one, two, a dozen. Lights come on
in distant farmhouses. With little fuss or commotion
the men get the dogs in the truck, start up
the engine, switch on headlights, drive away.

A thousand stars prick designs on the night.
Orion spraddles the sky over the eastern hills;
Aldebaran glares redly, not far from the Pleiades.
So quiet that the air carries the susurration of distant river
    rapids,
the faintest last tremble of wind in the sage grass.
The hills are invisible as dreams,
the stones impalpable as starlight.

Gordon Osing

Dauphin Island

No sun today; everything lighted from within
instead. Fine sands running in the incandescences.
Naturally all this emptiness fills with what one brings,
stories originally without the grace of endings,
landlocked, the locals say thinking of home-states inland
and those who drive-up storms to crash here at land's end.

Off shore the famed saviors are wont to play.
A colony of balconies along the broken and continually
revised line of the shore are lifted up to squint outward,
quotidian heavens for their unchangeable reward,
the glimmerings and whispers of an essentially thoughtless sea
that throws out its diamonds and emeralds in waves,

and, Mon Dieu!, the fabulous undressing of the weather.
If a self seethes in all this it needs only to remember
at the last dark the neck can yet relish the chill
of what is meant in the rising-up of these watery fields,
which, in the first dawn, will bloom and tremble
like the savanna, when the mist and failing dark, together

with that nameless letter the moon in daylight conspire
to distance breathing. White-haired waves won't cease
coming in. It's that ancient deal between Gulf waters and
      veins.
They rhythm the ground right to the feet, their relentless
      claims

"Dauphin Island" appeared in *The Southern Review*, Vol. 20, no. 1, Winter 1984 and in *Town Down River*, by Gordon T. Osing, St. Luke's Press, 1985. Copyright © 1985 by Gordon T. Osing. Reprinted by permission of St. Luke's Press.

undermining continually one's self, too, to always another
          place.
Thirty yards in past dangers lick easily around the pilings

and every remaining house marks the famous names that
          stormed
the times booze ran fast as the citizens. They saw Camille
put barges in the trees. Now all their escapes have turned
          comedies;
they have a great drink for the occasions. Near misses parties,
One hits, they get out there in the green sun and rebuild.
No doubt about it, some can stick it out till God comes.

Hot middays give the mind back to the skin,
the same skin that right now can browse distances
(pity the poor gator caged in the Civil War Fort)
for sea-oats crowning the dunes, the blue sky orange
twice a day. Here there are purity of touching, sea-lit glances
that live in a lunar comment, and in the stars' sly grin,

whole days fading white past a certain point,
each night the chill that takes everybody's sins away
but they don't know it, knife-eyes silvering the land
that rises only a little from the briny breathing, dark winds
and the moon quivering, a thing at the right ear, allayed
times, stolen and buried, and maps to bloodied coins.

However long ago this strand moved flickerings
out in the mapless dark, a center park of tangled oaks
still holds these waters together, and an absent palace.
True saints find God's voice only in things is the madness
cultivated here. Carib demons turn everything into jokes,
they who discovered the tie between the shout and whispering.

Alas, the salty jungle abides only luck's cruelties,
for there are still buried treasures. Bogey-land? Maybe.
The senses dreamt? Think what you will with a good
          fishmarket eye
besides. Crackling songs of a nearby Mexican night
are perfect, too, in this a last garden of the mind's playing,
where there is after a while nothing to see, until one sees

a girl singing along a beach, the tune immaterial, offhand.
A girl not in the least different from all she shadows.
Or, if not, maties, then it's the patched eye catches it all

Gordon Osing

while the live one laughs into the stretched optical
and Wallace Beery's good eye is the olive in the gin, gravelly
liar that he was, and a wily beggar, and a Prince of Sand.

Ostinato

> "The bones! The bones!"
> —Frost

No question the soul lives right in the bones,
as every comic knows, and because nobody knows
the soul's name haunting the glass case in the lab
sans more than everything and deader than a desert.
The more thanks thereunto the lust that teacheth:
(Oh tend the great spangled tree of the night,
my bones!) It's the bones move in a song
as in her sweet moral racket walking to the bath.
The way she walks tells all about the bones
in a tune, even as all her smiles are in the keys
plus the dumb blood tune of the baseman's thumb.
A nasty holiness this life, these masks with skin.
We know and choose knowing, as the wild ones do,
as in the magic counting seizing the drummer in his
hands.

"Ostinato" appeared in *The Southern Review*, Vol. 18, no. 3, Summer 1982, and in *From the Boundary Waters*, by Gordon T. Osing, Memphis State University Press, 1981. Copyright © 1981 by Gordon T. Osing. Reprinted by permission of Memphis State University Press.

Robert Herring

HUB

"Uncle Ethel," Hub said. The old man looked at him. "He'll be coming again, won't he?"

"He'd be comin' again," the old man said quietly.

An ambient restlessness touched the island, worrying the willow forest, turning up the silver underbellies of its leaf and thicket tangle.

"Wind's blowin' in," the old man continued. "Be up a right smart more too. Likely be rain."

The boy listened to the wind. It shifted east to west bringing the sound and warm smell of the flooded river, then wheeled abruptly, passing up the island and bringing with it the massed sound of slapping leaves, of limbs rubbing, scuffing, of troubled birds catching at their willow roosts. Then it was past and the boy looked at the old man once again—

"Why? Why's he after us? Why?" he said.

"Heubert," Uncle Ethel said, "it's some as jest goes sour. Like foxes. Some's borned that way. You cain't never tell and it ain't no why to it. This here Freeman likely has it in his mind we'll tell where he's at when this old river drops. He's done killed twicet. He'd be comin." The old man paused a moment, glanced at the dark thicket about them, then continued—"We'll jest have t'make do."

"The arrow trap didn't stop him, did it?" the boy said.

"Nosir," the old man said. "Jest slowed him some."

Hub considered this before speaking. Then—"You've got the gun!"

"Yessir," the old man said.

"And I'll help too this time."

The old man was still watching him. "I jest might have some need fer a extry pair of ears," he said. "You reckon you could help me thataway?"

From *HUB*, by Robert Herring. Copyright © 1981 by Robert Herring. Reprinted by permission of Viking Penguin Inc.

"Shoot yeah. I mean, yessir. And I got my spear, too." But something moved deep within him, something quavering against the darkness beyond the cover, beyond the glow of the dwindling coals.

"That's fine," the old man said.

Hub fought that which stirred within him. "Anyway, you said we'd have to do for ourselves." Then he added, his voice vaguely hesitant, "And it might somebody come, too."

"Heubert."

"Yessir," Hub said.

"You be afeared?"

"Nosir!"

"Heubert?"

Silence again. Hub looked away, then back. The old man's flinty eyes burned into him. "Yessir," he said. "I guess some."

"Good. Did you believe I was some too."

"Sir?" Hub said. *Afraid! Uncle Ethel?*

The old man glanced off toward the fire. "Man's not some afeared sometimes is a fool. You'n me ain't got no room fer fools this night."

"Yessir," Hub said, wondering at the old man's words.

"He'll be comin', yessir. Got his blood up. He'll be coming'," Uncle Ethel added at large.

Hub was quietly watching the old man. Then he too turned his eyes toward the glow. Across the cove the strung bottles and cans rattled lightly and Hub started at the sound.

"It's some cans I put there to let us know. But that weren't him. I'll know when it is. Likely jest that old chukkerwill."

"Oh," Hub said.

"Don't get worrisome. I'll be needin' a steady hand to help me."

"Yessir," Hub said. "Yessir," he repeated.

The old man glanced toward the woods, then back to the boy—"Now you see, Heubert," he said, his voice low and steady and firm, "they ain't no fools on this here island." His powerful hand grasped the boy's shoulder.

Again the wound had begun to hurt, throbbing. He had washed it clean in his flight down the chute, numbing the punctured flesh in the cool water, then scraped it again and again in his movement into the woods. He had turned up the island and for nearly an hour he had waited, crouched in the spurred and wrinkled thicket along the southern edge of the cove. The fog thinned briefly and a faint moonlit path fell like a fairy's walkway across the water, nebulous and trembling. The only other movement was the steady stropping of the knife down the sleeve of his shirt. Then he ceased even this. Motionless, cataleptic in the darkness, Lute stared across the cove. Beyond lay the cabin fortress.

And his quarry.

Above him a river bird passed, wind-tossed in the lowering cloud quilts about the moon, calling its anonymity like a sibyl, and the walkway faded. From its place in the shed the mule watched the closing night, shuffling nervously, its spavined legs worrying the earth, and another hour passed. Fog-shapes formed and dissipated as the river brushed them past and pulled them after the wide vortex of its passage.

At the fallen sycamore Hub waited, listening, remembering. Uncle Ethel had said *You jest set'n listen behind that buttonball tree that's all*, and when he had turned on the stoop to ask what he should listen for, the old man was no longer there.

All about him tree frogs and crickets sang the coming rain. Shadows moved, shaping threatfully, then falling away. Hub wanted to run, to strike blindly off through the dark for the cabin—but he could not, remembering the old man's words on the stoop, remembering too a day long past, a trapped crow, and the old man's admonition, *You'll have got to decide*. So.

He nestled against the root wall, tightening his grip on the willow spear. A few feet away the river tugged gently at the trunk of the tree and it shifted, rolling slightly, then settled again and held its place across the mouth of the cove. Once Hub thought he heard a fish tremble the water's surface but he could not be sure.

Silence.

Along the bank the old man moved stump to stump, grasping the shotgun by the barrels. Fireflies like will-o'-the-wisps trailed his passage, then settled in the grass. Here and there he stopped, listening, searching the darkness. His eyes never left the opposite bank.

There, hidden among the elms, Lute too searched for movement. He had heard voices. *But where? Where was the old man? The shotgun?* He drew one hand down the festering wound in his thigh. His blunt fingers found little lumps just beneath the flesh where the shot had not penetrated the muscle. Then his hand moved up, gently touching the torn flesh beneath his arm. In his other hand the knife turned over and over and over and— "You over there, old man?" he called—*Where's he at? Dammit, where's he at?*—abruptly, shattering the stillness. "I know you're there. You'n the gun. But I'm coming' on anyway, y'hear?" He moved quickly.

Silence. An easy rain had begun.

"Y'ain't got some more of them traps laid out, do you?" His voice, like the river's, was low and wet. "Took a plug out'n my side with that last one. My turn now. I was thinkin' t'visit that garden agin. Maybe have me some of them veg'tables." *Find him, make him speak.* Again he moved but still there was only silence from the other side of the cove. The glow of coals. Stump-shapes along the bank. Nothing more. "I been thinkin' you prob'ly ain't too good a shot in the dark. Kinda puts us up even," Lute continued.

Hub turned his face toward the voice, listening to it, listening too for some reply, expecting one yet knowing there would be none, knowing there must be silence. *Be still, be still, still*—the words drummed through his mind—*You just set'n listen, listen,* a pulsing injunction. But the willow spear trembled.

Lute called again. This time his voice issued from somewhere closer to the bluff, cat-soft through the darkness, jockeying for position—"That fancy arrow trap near 'bout fixed me. Didn't though."

Silence.

"I tell you what—" Lute continued, languid, cajoling.

Hub peeped around the edge of the root wall and searched the thicket, trying to follow the voice. *How can he move so quiet?*

"—ain't got no fuss with you. No real fuss anyhows. River'll be droppin' maybe tomorrer. You could see your way t'givin' me some of them veg'tables I'd be obliged. And I'll be on my way you's to swear not t'tell nobody—*You're gonna die, old man, you'n them smartass kids*—y'hear?" There was no reply and a moment later something rushed through the air and thudded, crumbling, just over the stumps and down into the garden.

He's throwing dirt-clods! Hub realized, astonished. *Dirt-clods!* A second followed the first, crashing dryly.

"I git you, old man?" Lute called, farther away. He might have been two people, his voice here and there along the cove like the indifferent and sourceless cry of a toad.

And still Uncle Ethel was silent. *Where's he at?* Hub, too, wondered, glancing toward the garden and the dimly contoured scarecrow. *Where's he at?*

The old man knelt motionless in the thicket at the shallows, where he had planned it, prepared for it—*He'll have to come across it right here. I got to see he does.* The cane he had wedged horizontally between the saplings was still drawn tautly back, lashed and covered with loose brush. Beneath the cove bank the bound cane pole with its row of sharpened stakes was secure. The trip wire, looped across the water and tied down the opposite bank, was still fixed to the toggle there. It was the last trap. The last defense.

Still, he had his knife—and something else. In his overalls he carried a short dry stick he had shaped with his pocketknife, so that at one end thin shavings splintered loosely away like bristles. And his coat bulged with a mason jar filled with kerosene.

"You bastard," Lute called from the opposite bank. "I believe I'll just gut them kids too when I'm through with you. Huh? What you say? Say somethin', damn you!" Lute was closer to the shallows and the old man.

That's right, Uncle Ethel thought. Keep on thisaway.

Wide-eyed, standing now and leaning against the upturned root base, Hub listened. Then suddenly it shifted beneath his hand and a cascade of loosed mud-chunks fell into the water. He cried out and thrust his hands forward as if to stop the noise. Then he slumped to his knees again. *I'm sorry . . . I'm sorry, Uncle Ethel . . . I'm sorry* once again.

At the sound Lute wheeled about. So they were *there*. He dropped to his hands and knees. The knife was between his teeth and he pushed back through the thicket. This time his hand caught against the alarm cord and a medley of cans and bottles rang thinly. Lute lunged forward and down, waiting the blast from the shotgun—*Heard me sure*—but there was none. He turned, withdrawing deeper into the thicket. When he stopped he crouched, confused, thinking about it—How come he never took a shot? Knowed where I was, him'n his little tricks. How come? He thought about it and thought about it, then let it go, thinking of something else now—Won't figure me t'come no way but across where it's shallow. His hands knotted to fists. The tree. The tree!

The old man too had moved at the sound. There was no choice. Lute would have heard the boy. The mason jar in his pocket sloshed wetly as he passed along the bank, slipping easily between the stumps as if somehow he could see each one in the darkness. Then he was no longer moving. Hub had not heard his approach.

"Heubert," Uncle Ethel said softly. Hub twisted about, lost his balance, and sat back heavily.

"Heubert!" the old man repeated firmly.

"Yessir," Hub said.

"That's a boy," Uncle Ethel said and knelt beside him. "You'll have to more'n listen now," he added. "You'll still help me?"

"Yessir."

"Take a 'holt of this," the old man said, and drew the whittled stick from his overalls.

Hub reached for it—"By the smooth end."

"Yessir."

—and held it as the old man had instructed.

Uncle Ethel pulled the jar from his coat and unscrewed the cap. Coal oil, Hub thought as the odor took away his breath. He turned his head.

"I kindly think I got him ciphered," Uncle Ethel said. "We'll wait here."

And they had not waited long when movement at the other end of the sycamore sent a tremor through its leaves. Then the tree was still again.

"Hold it straight out," the old man whispered steadily, and when Hub extended the stick Uncle Ethel poured a small amount of the kerosene on the shavings, then placed the open jar close by on the ground. "Now be real stilly."

"Yessir."

Again there was hesitant movement in the fallen tree and the old man eased to his feet.

"He's coming across the tree," Hub wispered.

"Yessir." The old man grasped the shotgun with both hands. *He's got to know the gun's empty but he ain't fer sure.* He held the gun a moment longer, touched the stock slowly, drawing his fingers down its textured surface—*He's got to know*—and stepped from behind the root wall. He raised the gun over his head and sent it wagon-wheeling through the air.

It struck the limbs, rattled down, and sank into the water.

Silence. Stillness.

Then—"Hey, old man, that your gun you throwed, wasn't it? That's how come you never took a shot, ain't it?"

"Uncle Ethel—"

"Sh-h," the old man said. He was fumbling for something else in the pocket. Then he withdrew a small box.

"Was you thinkin' to hit me with it, you ain't even come close."

"It's matches," Uncle Ethel whispered, handing the box to Hub, "You take out three or four."

Hub took the matches from the box. Then the tree shuddered gently as Lute tested its strength, moving slowly out upon it.

"You'll fall in," the old man called over his shoulder.

"I ain't gonna fall in, old man. I'm just comin' straight on over. I ain't wastin' no more time."

Uncle Ethel dropped to his knees. "Now you could hand me back the stick," he whispered, taking it with one hand and with the other lifting the mason jar from the ground.

The tree sagged deeply. Lute was halfway across.

"When I tell you, strike a match'n set it to the stick," the old man continued.

The tree rolled, then righted itself as Lute moved through its branches feeling his way cautiously.

"Now?" Hub whispered.

"Not jest yet," Uncle Ethel said. Then the limbs dipped beneath the surface and the root wall tilted outward as the trunk bowed downward beneath Lute's weight.

"Now," the old man whispered sharply, and even as he spoke the word he stepped to one side of the uprooted trunk. Hub drew a match frantically down the rasped edge of the box and it snapped, falling from his fingers.

"Agin!" Uncle Ethel said steadily.

And carefully this time the boy shielded and drew a second match along the edge—it struck, briefly flaring, and the old man thrust the first stick into it. With his other hand he tossed the mason jar like a grenade, waited a split second, and sent the torch sailing after it. Lute, intent upon his passage across the trunk, recoiled at the sharp odor of kerosene. Droplets had spattered him, but no more. And he had begun his forward progress once more when the fire stick dropped loosely into the branches. For a moment it hung suspended, wobbling, caught in a dry fork inches above the first wet leaves. Lute was reaching for it when it tilted, then fell dusting down through the tree. The leaves ignited slowly at first, a cantabile of diminutive tambourines spitting and popping, mounting along the thinner branches, little fiery vagaries of red heat crackling limb to limb as if the leaf mass were a woman's worn and crinkled crinoline.

Lute recoiled, retreating back along the trunk, slipping, flailing wildly. His face contorted as the flames raced hungrily through the foliage. Each limb caught and pushed at him, slapping at his face like talons and slashing across his neck and hands as if the sycamore like the river consciously sought to hold him. Then his wounded leg buckled beneath him and he tumbled back and to one side, found the sand beneath him, and rolled out of reach of the blaze. The tree before him was a riotous wall of heat now, impenetrable.

"Did you still want yourself a bait?" the old man shouted above the roar of the fire. Beside him Hub leaped up and down, something old and deep within him finding its voice, up and down brandishing the sharpened willow spear like a savage and chanting, "We ain't scared, we ain't scared, we ain't scared," over and over, the pitched apotheosis of a child's fear and anger.

Lute didn't move. He was facing them, still lying where he had fallen. Something burned in his ankle, as if a single tongue of the fire had embedded itself there. He tried to move his leg and pain shot through his calf like a charred shaft. Across the cove the old man and the boy danced, or seemed to dance, as the light flared and ebbed, then flared again and they were equally shadow puppets cavorting in the night.

So he did not move. For some time he simply continued to watch them, his eyes red and feverish, unblinking. The first thin rain had begun, but the tree crackled its defiance and burned on. Then he pulled himself up to one elbow. "Ain't goin' burn all night, old man," he called. "Be dark agin before long. You done just put it off a little is all."

Uncle Ethel said nothing. *That's so, it ain't,* he thought. And he was pleased. He shouted back, "Well, I don't s'pose it makes no never mind unlessen you could get at us. You comin' across that tree when she's thew?"

Lute rolled his eyes toward the flames, then away. "Old man, you tryin' to git me out on some burnt-out log? You think I'm stupid like all them bastards up to the courthouse does? Nosir. I'll just come around t'other end for them veg'tables."

Yessir.

So the final siege—the final test.

The old man turned to the boy. "Heubert, you got to hide now. Go git Hitesy and hide down along the point. They's somebody likely could of seen that fire." And abruptly he turned and started off along the bank.

"Uncle Ethel—"

"Hide, boy, like I done told you. Help your buddy," the old man called over his shoulder as he disappeared into the darkness of the garden.

Hub backed away toward the cabin.

"That's right, boy. You run and hide like that old man told you. You'n that other'n," Lute called. Hub disappeared around the cabin. "Old man!" Lute called again, searching down the cove bank. "You thinkin' to hide too?"

Back to the shallows . . . he's got to come across it there . . . got to make him though at the right spot. Once Uncle Ethel stopped and looked back at the burning tree. Lute was still there, just in the outer ring of light, but up and hobbling now, holding his side with one hand, his knife in his other, making his way along the bank.

Deliberately, the old man slapped the stumps as he moved through them threading his way to the saplings. Once there he examined the knotted lashings, testing the cords, touching carefully the drawn cane. They held firmly and he turned, moving swiftly, pumping toward his toolshed. After a moment he returned holding a hoe—one weapon more—in his hands. He crouched behind the saplings and waited.

"You there, old man?" Lute's voice issued from the thicket some yards across and down the cove. "I'm damned if you ain't a hard one to keep a eye on."

Closer . . . thisaway.

"I know you there. What you got? Nother jar a coal oil maybe? Huh?" Uncle Ethel felt about him in the darkness, found a twig, and snapped it. Silence.

Closer! And a second twig snapped crisply.

"You makin' a awful lot a noise, old man. I believe I could find you easy."

Yessir . . . find me.

And once more Lute advanced. He was close to the shallows now, ten feet away down the opposite bank, perhaps less, and the old man followed the sound of his movement through the palmettos and yucca clumps along the sandy edge of the cove. The length of trip wire was directly across from the old man. Freeman could be only a few feet from it now. *Jest a little bit on*, the old man thought. *Jest a little.* Then Lute's progress toward the shallows ceased, interrupted.

It began with a subtle shifting, the faintest alteration in the soft rhythm of the rain. Then there was an eruption of sparks, a rising trellis of white-hot particles exploding into the air at the mouth of the cove, drifting, a luminous veil across and down into the water like stars extinguished in a new dawn's light—the sycamore had given way, collapsing in a shivaree of steam and popping limbs as the last wood fibers incandesced, buckled, and the heavy trunk caved to the water's surface.

And in that instant they stared directly into each other's eyes—the old man's bent and stooped figure outlined beside the saplings, and across the shallows less than seven feet away now, the heavy, ragged gargoyle, his wide, round face puffed and his eyes, like the knife in his hand, rust-red.

Too far down, the old man realized. Lute was only a single step away from the trip wire. If he started across the shallows there he would miss the wire. The trap would fail. Uncle Ethel moved instantly, lifting the hoe like a spear and hurling it across the short distance between them. The blunt metal head struck Lute full in the chest, staggering him briefly. He stepped backward, his weakened ankle twisting, then he righted himself—

That's fine . . . there.

—staring down at the hoe, a look of surprised annoyance across his face. Then he bent forward and lifted it, stepping back along the bank and away from the trip wire. With both hands he brought the wooden handle down across his thigh and shattered it, dropping the splintered halves to one side.

"You didn't reckon to stop me with that little hoe, did you?" he said, still looking down, his voice oddly casual, toying. The last flickering light from the fallen sycamore was fading, and after a moment Lute turned his gaze up toward the old man. He was grinning—

Closer . . . take a step.

—loosely, his mouth twisted and open as he stared. He was enjoying the moment, unhurried now.

Then the old man moved quickly, stepping clearly away from the saplings. From his pocket he withdrew his bone-handled knife and raised it slowly, deliberately. He turned his shoulders slightly to the left, again slowly, deliberately—*Watch closelike, Mr. Freeman*—and threw the knife. The old man had so clearly indicated his purpose that Lute was already sidestepping to his left a single step—

Robert Herring

Yessir . . . that'll do.

—when the knife whipped harmlessly past. He stood now, closer to the neck, less than six feet in front of the old man waiting across it. Lute's shoulders bowed and his voice when he spoke was wet and whispered, like the sound of a snake through moist grass.

"Now, old man," he said, and swung out into the shallows, thrashing the water's surface, both arms raised now, the hooked fingers of one hand widespread and the knife poised in the other.

If his stride had not taken him two feet out into the cove and if his great weight had not plunged his brogan six inches beneath the mud bottom he might have missed the trip wire altogether. But even as he had swung out with one foot, mindless in that moment of his injured ankle, it had twisted, dragging down the bank's edge. Just with the toe of his shoe he caught the trip wire, and the cane pole, like something alien and many-fanged, whipped hissing through the air impacting, embedding, catching Lute full in his side even as he jerked his face toward it, his lips curled not in anger but in surprise as the blow sent him reeling, his body impaled, lifted briefly, gutted. He dropped the knife and clawed frenziedly at the cane shards, then pawed toward the old man only a few feet away. Twice his chest heaved, bloating, enlarging like a frog's throat, then he relaxed, slowly, his weight tearing the barbs from his body. His legs buckled and he slipped to his knees, grasped his side again, opened his mouth as if to speak, then coughed, choking.

In the last glow from the cove's entrance the old man watched a string of blood run down his chin. Lute turned his face side-ways, glanced at the bloodied cane stakes hanging limply, then back toward the old man. Still kneeling, hip-deep in the water, he stared, his face gone blank. Once his lips trembled, as if he tried to speak; then his eyes rolled upward and like someone settling down to sleep he toppled gently forward, face down upon the surface. The water was just deep enough, two and a half, perhaps three feet where he had fallen, and his body floated, rose and fell then lifted again, drifting with the slight current. The old man watched until the body reached the mouth of the cove, slipped beneath the fallen tree, and was swept out into the river.

Malcolm Glass

To The River

I   The light filtering through
the umbrella magnolia sent halos
of darkness across the sky
like thunderheads welling
on wind out of the east,

>One side of the bed
>was covered by a sheet, the starchy
>cloth so clean under his fingers
>he could smell soap
>and the hot iron.

and he woke to the rushing hiss
of the river below,
sudden from his nap on the flat rock—
sunlit, shaded, sun and cloud changing
places. He was sliding toward
the edge when a voice
rose out of the river,
out of the white water:

>"Dad. It's Dennis."
>Dennis. He must reach out,
>grab him by the arm and pull him
>back onto the bed,

back onto the rock, but his arm
was numb in the icy water. He would call
to him, but what was the word

Malcolm Glass

for *Dennis* when the water pulled you

        out of bed? He held tightly
        to the hand holding his, pulling him
        across the stiff linen, crisp as the breeze
        shuffling the leaves, pulling him back

onto the rock, into the sunlight
washing away the leaves of the magnolia,
all the clouds patching the sky blue again.

II The thick sky dropped
    into the palmettos, scrub
    sizzling, the gray sand
    pocked and cratered, then smoothed
    by the steady rain. Time
    to give it up, six crappie to the good.
    As he hauled in the jon boat, rocks
    slipped, and his ankle
    too, jammed under the boat
    every way wrong.

        A dagger of pain bore
        into his neck, not his ankle,
        like a hard bee-sting.

He drove back with his right leg
propped on the seat, braking
and clutching with his left,
leaning on the accelerator
with a stick. And every lurch
and twist of the road
from Sandy Fork

        He ran his fingers
        down the skin of his neck,
        searching for a welt, or cut.

shook his foot flopping
at the end of his leg, jolting
pain from ankle to neck.

    His neck. The pain stopped
    there. Stayed. He pressed
    his fingers into the tendons
    and veins, pushing back the pain.
    "Does it hurt? Your neck?"
    A white voice moving
    past the window.

And a face in the windshield, a grimace—
his face, rising like a pale moon.

    A hand slid between his fingers
    and his neck. "If it hurts,
    squeeze my hand." He gave
    the hand a squeeze.

III Rain had chattered against the sides
of the tent long after the sun
had faded and the sky had folded back,
and was pelting now in sheets against the tent,
against the draperies, against the window
behind the draperies. "Not quite
midnight," he heard a voice say.
But it was much later than that, he knew,
close to dawn now. And the rain
at the side of the tent. They hadn't seen
a buck all day. It was not quite midnight,
and long past it. Someone pulled back
the draperies. And the rain
faded to let the sunlight
spill in. He held the hand
holding him back, and felt it growing
colder. The door opened
onto a corridor of shade trees
leading to the sunlit river
a few hundred yards away, an easy walk
this early, in the cool air. He let go
of the hand, cold now, and got up,
his joints nimble and sweet.
The sun scattered the white
water, filling the sky as he ran.

John Osier

The Ritual

Granny flailed away out in the garden with her hoe. Even when there weren't any weeds, she went out and chopped them anyhow. She wore the sunbonnet and the same shapeless sack of a dress she wore every day since he had been back, Sundays excepted, and he could not persuade her either to stay out of the garden or to wait until evening cool. Every morning she was out there flailing in the hot sun, and he knew it was not just habit anymore, but a secret ritual. There was no way to stop it short of tying her to the bed.

Lee Guy pulled the rod out of the barrel and poured more oil on the swab. He thought of her shuffling through the old house like a lost child whistling under her breath, sometimes muttering to herself and talking to Mr. Jewett.

"Mr. Jewett," she said, "that Rhode Island Red ain't laying. I declare I don't know what's the matter with her. If she don't lay soon, she's going to find herself in the pot. That's right! That's just what's going to happen."

The other morning when Lee Guy had gone into the kitchen, she was talking with Mr. Jewett. He went up and tapped her shoulder.

"Granny," he said.

She turned, and he jumped back like he had been electrocuted. She had forgotten to put in her glass eye. For a second he had stared into the socket with a queer mixture of fascination and terror. Then he had stumbled out the screen door onto the porch, his eyes seeking the distant pines and his terror turning to rage. Now he approached her cautiously in the mornings, sidling around to peek at that side of her, before looking her full in the face.

From where he sat on the porch steps, her face was hidden by the sunbonnet. When she finished out there and fixed dinner, he would go into town, he thought. The car, a battered wreck minus two fenders, needed a valve job. The engine knocked so hard when he drove that any minute he expected a piston to explode. He knew there was no point in driving to town; there would be no work, but he was tired of hanging around the house. He looked out at the rotted stalks in the field from last year. When he had come back, that same day he told her he was going to plow them under. Now he looked abruptly away from them toward the pines. The second day back, he had gone to the shirt factory in town to see about a job, but they were only hiring women because they'd work the rest of their lives for next to nothing and never ask for any more. Except for the gin in the fall, the shirt factory was the only work in town, and the town was drying up like an August creek bed. Sometimes he thought about going to the city, but he knew she would never leave.

She was in the sweet potatoes now, next she would be in the watermelons. She always started with the cabbages and wound up with the turnip greens. He wished just once she would reverse the order, but she never did. He almost yelled at her to come out of the sun (it had become too hot for him to go out and replace the tin cans on the fence posts after knocking them off), but he knew it wouldn't do any good. She would ignore him, but he knew her secret. She felt *safe* out in the garden.

But how safe were you when you weren't going to make a crop this year, he thought. They had let him out too late to plant, and the man who was supposed to have done the planting had burned the bearings out of the old two-cylinder John Deere, then disappeared. Again his eyes moved to the rotted stalks bleak against the distant pines. Granny was right about one thing—even if he could have planted—there was not anybody to pick. All picking was done mechanically now except your nose and somebody would get around to that directly. He rammed the rod down the barrel and yanked it out again. Then he poured oil on the bolt and snapped it shut and aimed the empty rifle at a post where a can still gleamed in the sun.

He used to go hunting with the .22, rabbits and squirrels mostly. He had never hit a rabbit, but sometimes he would get a squirrel if it were motionless. The sun glinted off the tin can and hurt his eyes. Beyond, the pines shimmered in the heat. He lowered the rifle and wiped the sweat off his forehead. He was hungry now, but she was still in the sweet potatoes. If she had a heat stroke, it would serve her right, he thought.

"Granny," he shouted. But she didn't even look up. He felt his gut beginning to hurt, so he looked away from her and deliberately avoiding the rotted stalks, gazed at the distant pines where it would be cool. Beyond the pines was the river. He had been down there a few times since coming back, and every time he would think of C. T. and how he had almost killed him. Granny was sorry he hadn't. She hated C. T. and that is why he hadn't asked C. T. for a job. But lately he had been thinking more and more about going to C. T. He wouldn't tell her, but if she found out he could say to her, "I reckon you rather live in the city," or "If I don't get hold of some money, you ain't going to have that precious garden much longer." C. T. had said if he ever needed a favor, Lee Guy knew where to come.

Often as a boy, he had seen C. T. fishing from his boat. One day when he was thirteen, just a few days after the .22 had come from the mail order house, he had gone to check a trotline he had put out the night before. Crossing the railroad trestle, he had seen a man upstream in a boat, but too far away to be recognizable. He had gone on and checked the line. Coming back across the trestle again, he saw that the man in the boat was C. T. The boat had drifted down to within about forty yards of the trestle and was close to the bank under some overhanging willows. C. T.'s back was still to him, so he had decided not to holler and continued stepping on every other tie, gazing between them at the brown water. It had been a hot day then, too, and the stench of creosote had clogged his head, and the rails had shimmered and run together in a blinding haze. His eyes had sought relief in the green along the bank. Then he was standing on one foot, like a wind-up toy, as the other foot slowly ran down and settled on the sticky tie. Later he would ask himself, and be asked why he had not hollered, and it would never be clear in his mind, but he remembered first seeing the limb move, then suddenly dividing snake from limb and feeling astonishment at its size, thick as a man's leg and the color of dirty dishwater, slightly above and flowing steadily toward C. T.'s head. He never recalled hearing the shot.

Then he was staring at the empty boat rocking from side to side. He stood there it seemed a long time before he lowered the rifle and began to run and jumped ten feet off the trestle to the bank. He hit it running and all the time he kept repeating "God" over and over. He was running in wet sand and it seemed to him that he was outside himself watching himself flounder until at last he stood staring at C.T.'s hat and cane pole in the boat. His throat was still working, but no sound came now except the panting of his lungs. The hat and pole looked like objects he had never quite seen before. There was a quality of unrealness about them, and then he saw that it wasn't just about them, but about the sunlight and the way it struck the water and the trees.

As he stood there, C. T.'s head peered around the other side of the boat. His blue eyes protruded from his head as they recognized Lee Guy.

"You crazy bastard!" he said.

His eyes seemed to be popping from his head as Lee Guy raised the rifle; then they disappeared underwater. This time Lee Guy heard a click. The chamber was empty. He reached into his pocket and fished out a shell and fumbled it into the chamber and fired at the cottonmouth who was only a few feet away and whose tongue flicked in and out rapidly. Whether he hit the snake or it had had enough, it dropped off the limb with a heavy splash at the same time C. T. surfaced.

"Snake," Lee Guy warned.

C. T.'s eyes were still bulging, and he spit water out of his mouth. His thinning hair hung down in long strands over his ears revealing a shiny bald head, and Lee Guy realized that in all the times he had seen C. T. this was the first time he had ever seen him without his hat.

"You crazy bastard!" C. T. said again. He snatched his hat out of the boat and stuck it on his head. Then he had clambered toward the bank refusing Lee Guy's hand.

Granny was in the watermelons now. Each time she went out there it seemed she worked slower. And another thing Lee Guy had noticed, she only worked certain rows. She ignored the others until the weeds got so high they actually threatened her vegetables. Someday, he thought, she will only come out and work one row and not touch the others. And after that she will only work a certain spot in that one row. He watched her flailing now in the noon sun where she had been yesterday and the day before and the day before that. He knew her secret. Her world had shrunk to the garden, and it was still shrinking. She felt safe in the garden with her ritual. Safe from what?

"Granny," he shouted. "Come out of there."

He knew she heard him, but she was ignoring him. She wouldn't stop until she had finished the turnip greens. He stood up, and the sudden motion and the heat made him feel light-headed.

"There ain't any weeds. You got 'em all yesterday."

She paid him no nevermind. Stubborn old woman, once she got her mind set on something hell could freeze over before she changed it. She was that way in her hate for C. T., and he knew he couldn't change her mind. No use telling her again that if C. T. hadn't made and sold it, Mr. Jewett would simply have gone somewhere else. His grandfather had died of hemorrhage because he was an alcoholic, not because C. T. sold to him, but Granny's hard-shell Baptist upbringing could not admit that the man she married had died of alcoholism. So she believed instead that C. T. was Satan.

The Saturday after he had almost shot C. T., he had gone into town to the picture show. The incident had bothered him so much that he had told her about it after hesitating, because he had to get it off his chest and there was nobody else to tell. All she had said was, "You're a mighty poor shot, young man." So he had gone to the picture show hoping to escape, but he hadn't because he knew she was referring to his missing C. T. When he had come out of the picture show, he could not remember anything about the two westerns he was supposed to have seen. A voice hailed him from a car parked along the curb. He recognized it without looking up, and he had approached the car with a sensation that his feet were going to swivel around like weather vanes and spin him off in the opposite direction. When he reached the car, C. T. told him to get in. There were a lot of people coming out of the show, and he could have ducked into the crowd or just run, but he got into the car.

C. T. started the engine and drove through town. He was silent until they were on the highway. It was dusk and the highway ran gray beneath the hood.

"You know you damn near killed me the other day, don't you?"

Lee Guy could think of no reply. Doves mourned in the dark pines.

"I felt that bullet's breeze."

They drove another half-mile in silence. Lee Guy noticed C. T. was wearing the same hat that was in the boat. C. T. was not looking at him, his face was a rigid mask staring straight ahead, the eyes shadowed by the hat brim.

"What were you thinking boy, when you done it?"

"I reckon I wasn't."

"I reckon not! You're a queer one. I don't know if I'd let you run around with a gun if I was your Granny."

"You ain't."

"Naw, I'm not. Still" (Lee Guy thought C. T.'s eyes had flicked toward him for a moment), "I understand you were aiming for the snake. But couldn't you have just hollered?"

He had been thinking about that. At night his mind had carried him back to the trestle again and he would see the snake like dirty dishwater flowing toward C. T.'s head, and he was drawing a bead again, and sometimes he would think that there had been no time to holler; but he wasn't sure and even if there had not been, why, Lee Guy wondered, had he not hesitated on such a dangerous shot? Why hadn't he hesitated even a second? He could tell C. T. there had been no time, but instead he said nothing. C. T. slowed the car and turned up the clay rut that led to the house. He stopped the car a hundred feet away, and Lee Guy started to get out.

"Hold on," C. T. said. His face was entirely in shadow now, and he was staring out the windshield into the dusk. From the back of the house Lee Guy could see a light where Granny was working in the kitchen.

"I'd rather get snake bit than shot in the head any day," C. T. said.

"Yessir, I surely would."

For the first time since he had gotten in the car, C. T. looked directly at him. "You thinking I owe you something?"

The brim of C. T.'s hat almost hid his eyes, but Lee Guy could feel them studying him.

"Hah, you think I owe you something, boy?"

Lee Guy looked levelly at the darkness just below the hat brim. "You don't owe me nothing." He got out of the car, his hand trembling slightly on the door handle.

"Damn right!" C. T. said, and he started laughing. But there was a strained quality to the laughter, and suddenly Lee Guy understood. C. T. was afraid of him.

C. T. shifted the floorstick into reverse. "All right, boy. You're right, I don't owe you. But you need a favor you come see old C. T., hear?"

Lee Guy slammed the door and watched the car back down the clay rut, then turn on the highway and disappear between the dark pines. He started up the path to the house. A sliver of moon had risen above the bar. Granny met him at the front door; the hall was black and the light from the kitchen framed her.

"Who was it?" she said.

He could not see her features in the dark, only a faint gleam from the glass eye as her head jerked abruptly. "What were you doing?"

"C. T. give me a ride home."

"After you say you almost shot him?"

"Yes'm."

She was black against the distant light. They stood there in silence and he thought he heard a tick in the wall, and suddenly he was afraid of her, for the first time he was afraid of the woman who had been not grandmother but mother too, afraid of the silence and the darkness, but most of all afraid because he sensed something in her he never knew or suspected was there until this moment. It was as though she were no longer his grandmother, but someone else had taken possession of the familiar body. He heard her breathing then felt her breath dry and hot as she hissed, "He killed your grandfather."

"No," he said, surprised at the sound of his voice.

"The same as if he had poisoned him."

"No," he said. But he did not say anymore. She struck him across the face.

"Don't ever let me hear of you having anything to do with him. Never! He killed Mr. Jewett." Then she had gone into her bedroom, and he had not seen her again until the next day. He had gone into the kitchen where the food was still on the stove but had not been eaten that night. He knew then why C. T. had been afraid.

He stood in the heat aware now that she had at last moved into the turnip greens. He turned away, and the sun glinted off the tin can on the fence post hurting his eyes. Beyond was the field of rotted stalks, and he stared at them feeling the frustration rise from the ache in his belly until his face felt hot like it was breaking into a rash. He looked once again, and she was flailing steadily at the earth.

"You!" he shouted.

He knew she heard him, but the hoe rose and fell without slackening.

"You come out of there!"

The hoe rose and fell slowly, continuously.

"Dammit, there ain't any weeds!"

Her figure seemed black against the sun's glare, and he could not distinguish any features, just the shapeless smock and sunbonnet outlined against the glare and the hoe falling and rising.

"Why don't you come out?" he shouted. "Please come out!"

He stood there feeling strangely light-headed, his eyes slitted as the dark figure seemed to recede and blur for a moment, and he knew that wasn't anyone he knew out there centered in the rifle sight. He was sucking in breath, the stock pressed against his cheekbone. He did not hear the sound of a shot, just as he had not heard it eight years ago on the trestle, but he heard the empty click.

Afterward he felt like running toward the figure and dragging it out of the garden. But instead he stumbled up the porch steps and went into the kitchen. It was cool and musty-smelling inside, and he opened the refrigerator, and there was the smell of cucumbers, and he pulled out the half-gallon jug of ice water. He moved to the sink, set the water on the drainboard and reached for the metal dipper that hung from a nail on the wall. He poured ice water into the dipper and the water hurt his throat and chest as he gulped one dipper-full, then another. From the window he could see Granny as the hoe rose and fell among the turnip greens. He realized he was still holding the rifle clamped under his arm, and he let it clatter to the floor.

He watched the dark figure against the sun-glare. Every morning she would be out there flailing and it was not just habit anymore, but a secret ritual. She felt safe out there.

Ishmael Reed

Chattanooga

       1

Some say that Chattanooga is the
Old name for Lookout Mountain
To others it is an uncouth name
Used only by the uncivilised
Our a-historical period sees it
As merely a town in Tennessee
To old timers of the Volunteer State
Chattanooga is "The Pittsburgh of
The South"
According to the Cherokee
Chattanooga is a rock that
Comes to a point

They're all right
Chattanooga is something you
Can have anyway you want it
The summit of what you are
I've paid my fare on that
Mountain Incline #2, Chattanooga
I want my ride up
I want Chattanooga

       2

Like Nickajack a plucky Blood
I've escaped my battle near

From *Chattanooga*, by Ishmael Reed. Copyright © 1973 by Ishmael Reed. Reprinted by permission of Random House, Inc.

Clover Bottom, braved the
Jolly Roger raising pirates
Had my near miss at Moccasin Bend
To reach your summit so
Give into me Chattanooga
I've dodged the Grey Confederate sharpshooters
Escaped my brother's tomahawks with only
Some minor burns
Traversed a Chickamauga of my own
Making, so
You belong to me Chattanooga

      3

I take your East Ninth Street to my
Heart, pay court on your Market
Street of rubboard players and organ
Grinders of Haitian colors rioting
And old Zip Coon Dancers
I want to hear Bessie Smith belt out
I'm wild about that thing in
Your Ivory Theatre
Chattanooga
Coca-Cola's homebase
City on my mind

      4

My 6th grade teacher asked me to
Name the highest mountain in the world
I didn't even hesitate, "Lookout Mountain"
I shouted. They laughed
Eastern nitpickers, putting on the
Ritz laughed at my Chattanooga ways
Which means you're always up to it

To get to Chattanooga you must
Have your Tennessee
"She has as many lives as a
cat. As to killing her, even
the floods have failed
you may knock the breath out of

her that's all. She will refill her lungs and draw
a longer breath than ever"
From a Knoxville editorial—
1870s

                5

Chattanooga is a woman to me too
I want to run my hands through her
Hair of New Jersey tea and redroot
Aint no harm in that
Be caressed and showered in
Her Ruby Falls
That's only natural
Heal myself in her
Minnehaha Springs
58 degrees F. all year
Around. Climb all over her
Ridges and hills
I wear a sign on my chest
"Chattanooga or bust"

                6

"HOLD CHATTANOOGA AT ALL
HAZARDS"—Grant to Thomas

When I tasted your big juicy
Black berries ignoring the rattle-
Snakes they said came to Cameron
Hill after the rain, I knew I
Had to have you Chattanooga
When I swam in Lincoln Park
Listening to Fats Domino sing
I found my thrill on Blueberry
Hill on the loudspeaker
I knew you were mine Chattanooga
Chattanooga whose Howard Negro
School taught my mother Latin
Tennyson and Dunbar
Whose Miller Bros. Department
Store cheated my Uncle out of

Ishmael Reed

What was coming to him
A pension, he only had 6
Months to go
Chattanooooooooooooooooooga
Chattanooooooooooooooooooga

"WE WILL HOLD THE TOWN TILL
WE STARVE"—Thomas to Grant

7

To get to Chattanooga you must
Go through your Tennessee
I've taken all the scotsboros
One state can dish out
Made Dr. Shockley's "Monkey Trials"
The laughing stock of the Nation
Capt. Marvel Dr. Sylvanias shazam
Scientsts running from light-
ning, so
Open your borders. Tennessee
Hide your TVA
DeSota determined, this
Serpent handler is coming
Through
Are you ready Lookout Mountain?

"Give all of my Generals what he's
drinking," Lincoln said, when the
Potomac crowd called Grant a lush

8

I'm going to strut all over your
Point like Old Sam Grant did
My belly full of good Tennessee
Whiskey, puffing on
A .05 cigar
The campaign for Chattanooga
Behind me
Breathing a spell
Ponying up for
Appomattox!

217

Roy Neil Graves

Buffet Night at the Pizza House

Fat husbands usher in their fatter wives
to fill them up on Tuesdays, all-you-can eat.
The smock-topped women line up haunch to haunch,
ringed hands radiant under the warming lights,
piling up cavatini and spaghetti
and pizza wedges, some of every topping.
Their men outdo each other at the salad bar,
building their pyramids like pharaohs.
Such couples do not grace your corner booths,
your head-to-heads. Belly and bosom to table, rather,
head to spoon and plate, these pairs put distance
between themselves and all those stick children
everyone has seen, dusty and gut-swollen, sandwiched
in between Roger Mudd and R-O-L-A-I-D-S. These pairs
fill themselves as if in defense of all emptiness,
all famine, all times of hunger and desolation
endured, heard of, feared or dimly imagined.
Here under plastic shades of the Tiffany type,
twined so in latticed bowers,
spread Eden's children, calling into question
every sublime canvas, every fresco, every glory of the race
with each chomp of all their downturned faces.

"Buffet Night at the Pizza House," by Roy Neil Graves appeared in *Windmills*, Literary Magazine of the University of Tennessee-Martin. Copyright © 1982 by Roy Neil Graves. Reprinted by permission of the author.

Alan Cheuse

The Tennessee Waltz

1
MARTIN

I was dancing with my darling when the feeling hit, and I stopped dead on my feet, Sue Beth bumping up against me just as the laws of physics describe.

"Not again, honey," she said, her usually soft voice verging on annoyance. "Sugar, we got to do something for you."

We were clinging to each other, her arms about my neck, my hands on her hips, a rock formation in the middle of the great flow of dancers at Boots 'n Saddle, a favorite cowboy bar of hers. I liked it well enough, its Cotton-Eyed Joe and mournful country songs just about perfect for the kind of mood I found myself in on Saturday nights when Arlene went out to her "drama" club and the kids ran off with their friends.

"Would you like to go?" Sue Beth, arching up on tiptoe, spoke into my ear.

From the velocity of the dancers and the density of the smoke and musk and whiskey-fog, I could tell that the night was moving along and that if I could overcome my problem leaving might not be such a bad idea. For the past four Saturdays, while Arlene was at her "rehearsals" and Sue Beth's Andy (Andrew Jackson Goins) worked the night shift at the Telephone Company, we turned and strolled around the dance floor and then repaired to a nearby motel. My house in Oak Ridge was off limits. Even with Arlene away the kids were always in and out. The trailer that Sue Beth shared with her lineman, a tobacco chewing, salt-and-pepper bearded East Tennessean with a limp—and a smile, I guessed, that usually dared you to say I dare you to talk about something—that was forbidden

"The Tennessee Waltz," by Alan Cheuse appeared in *Quarterly West*, Fall/Winter 1984-85, No. 19. Copyright © 1985 by Alan Cheuse. Reprinted by permission of *Quarterly West*.

territory. Not that Sue Beth hadn't suggested we go there the first time. I told her that it was a law of courtesy that kept me from doing that—I wouldn't befoul another man's turf—but of course it was just plain fear. I read the *News-Sentinel* every night after the *Tennessean* and the *Wall Street Journal*. I knew what deep feeling creatures, prone as much to murder as suicide if pricked by self-doubt or a heart gone wrong, were the local caballeros. What if Andy came home from work unexpectedly and found us together?

"You're cute," Sue Beth had told me when I finally broke down and explained why I'd rather take a motel way out on Kingston Pike.

"Oh, I am, I am," I joked with her, mind whirling about from place to place in the universe, the lab, my house, the desert where I spent my adolescence, the warm but as yet undiscovered planet where I hoped to spend my old age. Last year I had tried running away from home and that hadn't done any good—but way led on to way and the fuss made by Security led to my session once a week with the Division psychoanalyst who had run into personnel problems one sunny morn and hired temporary help in the person of Sue Beth Reals.

If that's not fate, then I don't know Einstein.

"You look real nervous," she'd said when I showed up for that Saturday morning session.

"I am," I told her, "nervous like I never was at my senior prom."

And I talked about New Jersey, and she mentioned dancing, and the next thing you know I was asking her to show me one of those cowboy bars some evening if both of us could get free. One or two weekends later and just like tonight we were parking alongside one another in the big lot behind Boots 'n Saddle and lining up to get our hands stamped at the door. I hadn't figured out too well just what I was in for—not in the way of the spectacle, that is—and had arrived sporting a string tie that Arlene had bought me many years ago in Taos and a pair of boots I usually wore only when I was mowing the lawn. Sue Beth made my heart leap a little by the care she'd put into her own costume—not so much like the way a kid does on Halloween as a local shopkeeper or a barmaid or ticket taker must do at Carnival time in Rio, a change of habit that reveals rather than disguises the secret activities of the spirit. She'd combed out her medium-length honey-colored hair into a moderate version of the thing we used to call a duck-tail, buttoned herself into a shirt with frilly collar and cuffs so white it gave back every scintilla of light it passed beneath, and eased into jeans that boldly outlined her thighs high up.

I was more nervous about stepping out (single step or two-step, whatever the rhythm turned out to be) in my own town than I'd been about pulling a Gauguin and heading without so much as a word of notice for Hereheretue, belle isle of the tropics. Who could say why? It was much more of a scandal to take off the way I did than any rumors the sight of me and Sue Beth arm in arm prancing to "Waltz Across Texas" could inspire—and who that knew me frequented a place such as Boots 'n Saddle? The head of our company? The chief of security? The FBI, CIA, NBC, CBS? I'd never been good with other people. I'd backed into romance and a marriage and family with Arlene the way I used to find my way onto the subway cars at rush hour at Times Square, bumped and shoved and half-pushed by others. The desert years had been the happiest, blessed by air perfect for my adolescent's skin and a welcome absence of people. I lived and ate and slept the project and nobody could get through to me who didn't work with me, and they were for the most part odd ducks like myself, all of them older but all of them, like me, or at least the way I used to be, so cheerful when thinking about numbers, alone in a room or under the sky.

Sue Beth said she wanted to hear about what I used to do and I was willing to drink Irish coffee and talk as a way of calming myself down. So I told her about all that—I thought that I might as well have been describing the adolescence of a Martian as far as she was concerned, her own life was so different. But somehow she understood the problem it led up to, the sensation that I was an intern on call from another dimension. She'd learned about moments like that by growing up with her preacher "Daddy," as she called him in the familiar tone that we Yankees give up after our first hairs sprout on our chins and elsewhere. Reverend Reals was a man who had always claimed to have been in touch with the Ancient of Days. Though he had gone to his rest fairly early in her life, when Sue Beth was just budding in the chest and getting itchy around boys, hundreds of sinners had felt his touch as he brusquely shoved them beneath the sluggish waters of the Hiwassee. But for each one he'd baptized he'd apparently taken their sins on his shoulders, or in his liver, to be exact, tipping back a cup and then another and another of home-made corn liquor when they were first starting out. During the successful years, when boys in the Kinney community with bulging muscles and their hands in their coveralls sidled up to Sue Beth the preacher's daughter as though she might have been royalty, he switched to Jack Daniels.

At his funeral, a stringy-haired woman in a pale blue dress showed up and told the assembled family members that she was going to fight them for the possession of the estate.

"There weren't none," Sue Beth explained to me, "but he'd been keeping her all those years by telling her that he was investing money in stocks that was bound to build up and make him rich in his old age. Men! Oh, Lordy! I'm so glad I'm with you tonight, honey, instead of one of them go-rillas I growed up with."

"I'm still a man," I said, sweat pouring down my sides.

"I know, and I'm going to teach you the two-step."
And she did.

When it got to be that time on this one particular evening, multitudes sang along with the establishment's theme as it poured out of the loud speakers: " 'I got the boots'n you got the saddle . . . ' " The chill settled upon our sweating necks and arms and we shivered in the parking lot.

"There's another dance we're doing," I said as I opened the passenger door and watched her, slightly astonished, slide onto the seat.

"What's that, sugar?" Sue Beth, a smile on her narrow painted lips, walked spidery fingers along my shoulder.

"I used to hear it on the radio all the time when I was in New Mexico," I said. "I can't remember the name of the singer, but the song was called 'The Tennessee Waltz.' "

"Piggy Lee," she said.

"Who?" I said.

"Piggy Lee," she said.

"You mean *Peggy?*"

"That's what I said. Piggy. Piggy Lee."

"Here piggy piggy," I said, crooking my finger. "It was Patti Page."

"You making fun of me?" Her mouth opened into an almost perfect O.

"I'm *having* fun," I said. "And it's been so long I can hardly remember that it's not supposed to hurt."

The little death, the French call it, and it felt that way again this latest time. My heart was luffing like a hawk caught in a cross-wind. This was supposed to soothe me, I told myself as I drove Sue Beth back to the dance hall parking lot, so why does it throw me into such quantum despond?

"You know what?" Sue Beth said with a sigh, as though she somehow understood even after disengaging from me the deep sadness I felt at the awareness of my own particles, waltzing, whirling, in time to some music whistled by a God or cosmic band with flute and jews-harp, some country music combo of the cosmos ever mourning the impending divorce between every bit of matter in the universe.

"What's that?" I heard my voice as flat and uncaring as ever, the way I spoke to Arlene, the way that led me to catch myself when I spoke to the kids. "Sugar," I added. "Sugar, sugar."

"Sugar . . . " She snuggled close to me, the way my daughter did when she was very young and had not yet discovered the temporary fact of a permanent world outside the family. "Sugar, I'm craving one of them doughnuts."

Here was our famous local doughnut, its factory and coffee shop on the corner coming up. Here we stopped and dunked our Krispy Kremes into our coffees. Here we lingered, as was appropriate, animals dreamy if not sad in the wake of our coupling, seeking immediate replenishment of the sugar we had expended in our haste.

I drove the rest of the way to the parking lot without fear of coming apart. But as soon as we rolled over the lip of the entrance Sue Beth shrieked and grabbed the wheel.

"Don't stop!" she yelled—hollered might be more exact. "Keep goin', it's Andy, he's standing right there by that car over there, keep going'!"

"Was he armed?" I inquired as I turned and rolled us right out of the lot again.

"The ugly go-rilla was standing there talking to a little girl!"

"He'll get in trouble with the police that way," I said, steering us back up the street toward the doughnut shop.

"He's in trouble all right! We're all in trouble, oh, Lordy," and her voice cracked.

"I thought he was supposed to be working on Saturday nights," I said, feeling the wind without opening a window. My legs trembled, and my arms shook even as I held the wheel on a newly paved road.

"That's what he told me," Sue Beth said, "but looks like he's been out sneaking around with some teenage girl. And he always told me too he don't like to come to the dance hall because of his leg."

"His leg?"

"His limp. Pull up here," she said, and I turned into the Krispy Kreme parking lot once more.

"Would you like another doughnut?"

"At a time like this? When I just discovered the go-rilla I'm living with is a cheater?"

"Why not?"

"Would it do me good?"

"Nothing can hurt you any more," I said.

"Who you think I am? Piggy Lee?"

I hugged her right then and there.

"You made a pun, didn't you?"

"Did I? I guess I did."

A few minutes later I deposited Sue Beth back at the parking lot which was safe now, with her gorilla gone off with the girl. On the drive back to Oak Ridge, rolling past mile after mile of kudzu vine still growing in the dark despite the onset of autumn, I heard Simon and Garfunkel sing "Scarborough Fair" on the radio. And I wept because I couldn't go with them. I had a project in the lab that I had to finish—or it must finish me—and hungers that kept me rummaging about the town, and nothing Arlene or the kids, who were spending the night with friends, as it turned out, nothing they could still. One day the entire earth might be covered with nothing but water and desert and kudzu. Remember me to one who lives there.

2

ANDY

All the songs you hear as a boy out in the country they tell you there's nothing so lonesome as a train whistle blowing in the night. But I think that's got to change. I left work early—unusual, but my stomach was kicking hell out of me. Something I ate, maybe, but probably something I was chewing. It was a co-cola I drank along with a little pinch of Red Man and a dash of the good white powder my friend Dewey brung back from a roofing job he done for a rich kid out in Sequoyah. Supposed to clear out your head but what it did for me after the clearing, like somebody set a bomb under that roof, was everything caved in on top of me. My stomach started kicking like hell. So I come back. And like I was saying about lonesome, it used to be the train whistle in the night, but the new lonesome, lonesome for our time, like they say on the television, is walking into the trailer expecting to find the best gal you ever had sitting up in front of the television waiting for you, wearing nothing but one of her shortest nightgowns, a glass of whiskey in her hand, a smile on her face, that look in her eyes, and your own glass set right there on the table where she's got her pretty feet all propped up, waiting for you to pour yourself a taste—and, instead you find "Love Boat" showing on the screen with nobody watching, the sound way down, a half-filled cup of coffee on the kitchen table, a few ants enjoying themselves with a bit of crumbled Twinkies on the counter, smell of cigarettes and whiskey on the air.

I went right into the bedroom, and my heart sunk like a tire-iron in Loudon Lake. There was a depression at the end of the bed big enough for Sue Beth's sweet behind, the odor of her perfume, honeysuckle, and along with her gone is also her best cowgirl dancing clothes.

"Well, shee-it," a voice says in my ear. "Shee-it." I didn't know whether I was to kill her first or cry later, or cry first and kill her after.

"And your Wichita line-man, is still on the line," was going through my head while I was driving to the dance hall, don't know why, well, I do, because I'm a lineman and she likes Glen Campbell and I guess, well, I figure she's stringing me along and the way my heart feels, all swole up, I might as well be the fellow in the song. I pass motel after motel on the way down the Pike, and hamburger joints, and some movie theaters, and more motels, more motels, and Saturday night when I'm working overtime I never think about what the rest of the world is doing but tonight here I am driving past these places and I know that everybody is drinking and eating and making love while I'm just passing by, my stomach one hell of a party.

Who is she to be running off like that? Who is she? I give her what I do, help her make her car payments and fix up the trailer! She quit her job as ticket taker, I help her get through. She quit her job in the supermarket, I help her get through. She takes the job at the doctor's office and keeps on working and you think I never did help her when she needed me. The doctor's office. The doctor?

I know her. She's a sweet thing, but she also got a big pull for money. And I can't go up against no doctor and hold my own. Not when it comes to money.

BOOTS 'N SADDLE

There's the sign, and the parking lot as full as I ever seen it. Her car ain't nowhere in sight, but then I can't go looking through the whole lot when I got to go inside and find her in the flesh.

And her Daddy was a preacher.

Who knows what she wants? I'll bet she sure don't.

The way things has changed since I was a boy, and that wasn't all that long ago.

What's that there psychiatrist's name? Some Jewish name?

"Good evenin'."

"Howdy."

"That'll be two dollars. I need to stamp your hand."

I held out my paw to the gal with the ink stamp, trying to look past her into the dark insides of the hall.

"You seen a pretty blonde, hair all frizzed up, wearing probably a white cow-girl blouse or something and tight jeans? Oh, shee-it!" Bad enough I got this bum leg and I have to go put it in my mouth besides! There must to been a hundred and fifty two thousand of blondes dressed like that, and the gal with the ink stamp gives me a look that tells me I sure ought to know something as simple as that. So I didn't say nothing else and hurried inside and went right up to the bar.

"Stranger?" There's this big guy with glasses under a Stetson serving up the drinks.

I ordered him to pour me a Jack Black. The music started up real loud just then. Willie Nelson, "Bloody Mary Morning." "Willie!" people was yelling, "Willie!" like he was playing live in the place instead of just on a record. I drank up, and bought a few more, watching the crowd pouring round the dance floor, seeing nobody I knew, a lot of things out of the past flying through my mind like I was a drowning man, and wondering at the same time if these other sonsabitches at the bar looking so cool, if this bartender with his fancy eyeglasses and his Stetson trying to act city and cowboy at the same time, wondering if they could tell I was feeling low and lonesome? I had got Daddy in my mind, watching him waving goodbye or hello, picturing him in the door frame of the house on Crab Orchard Mountain. I never knew if he was coming in the door or leaving on his rig—and the train calling up from the valley, my stomach churning, remembering how many times he took me up on his knee and told me the story about how when he went west with his folks in the dust storms and got to California and ate the leavings from the fields and the garbage cans and how they must have fixed him up so bad that he got bad blood and he passed it along to me by way of my one leg shorter than the other.

"Stranger?"

"I had enough of these by now I should be your friend."

Now where was I? Daddy, I was remembering. And he's gone now, and how he'd whoop and holler if he could see me a lineman, regular check, my own little pickup. Of course this Mister Jack Daniels is helping me to forget for a second that because of my leg I'm not up and dancing like the rest of those hairy horny creatures out on the floor and that Sue Beth was fixing to leave me while I was heading out to work.

"Friend," the bartender says to me, "have one of these," and he slides his knuckles up to my glass and shows me the little red pill he's hiding underneath like the pea in a shell game.

"You know, buddy," I said, after I picked it up and popped it, "you're a lucky fellow, because something got into my head to take your glasses off and feed 'em to you lens by lens."

"Friend," he said, "why'd you want to go and do that?"

"Cause you're mule shit," I said, feeling this whooping ball of hate drive up out of my aching stomach into my chest and throat.

"On the house," the bartender said, without a crinkle in his cool way of talking, and he knuckled another red one over to me.

Everybody was singing, "I got the boots 'n you got the saddle . . . "

Next thing I know this little bitty woman—perfect body, hear this, just little, kind of like a doll-size female—comes right up to where I'm sitting. I acted real surprised, like nobody had ever done that before.

"Come on, you big hunk," she said, looking me straight between the eyes.

I didn't know whether it was me or Jack D. or the reds talking, but I heard someone using my voice say,

"Sure do 'preciate it, but I'd just like to take you home."

Usual I'm not so bold. When I first got to meet Sue Beth it took me about two times before I even tried to do more than kiss her, though once we got past that everything went real fast. So I didn't know what would happen next. She kept on staring and staring, like she wanted to recognize somebody inside of me—and a friend instead of a stranger—before she'd talk again.

"Well . . . awright," she said, like I was the second prize she won when she really wanted a big stuffed panda bear.

"Does your momma know you're out this late?" I said to her when we got to the parking lot. I was trying not to limp and be real charming and make her laugh, because I was flying high inside.

She swung quick and hard, leaving me with a stinging jaw. I pulled back and slapped her in the head—she was so low I missed her face—and she bumped up against a car and dropped her keys. We got down on our knees to look for them and she started laughing, laughing.

"What's the joke, sugar?" I said.

And she looked up at me from where she was kneeling shoulder-high alongside me and said,

"Looks like a dang prayer meeting, don't you think, Mr. Cool Hand Luke?"

3
SUE BETH

I was laying in the dark waiting for Andy to come on back, thinking about where I want to go, listening to the whistle of the L&N freight rumbling in from Nashville, and then I must have dreamed because the next thing I knew I was sitting up in bed, feeling around in the empty place where Andy should have been, and remembering that I had seen the woman in the blue dress rising up out of the waters of the Hiwassee, and she had a big grin on her face and I saw Daddy, his ugly big-nosed smile lighting up the world, and he anointed her a second time with the waters of the slow-flowing river, the same dream pretty much I had on and off for years now, and then Momma reaching out to me across the stream, and she's saying, "Little lamby, the Lord gave you feet to dance and Piggy Lee to sing with," and I blushed all over—this being a new part of the dream I just didn't know it was coming—and the woman in blue was standing there at my side, and she handed me a kerchief and I dabbed at little spots of blood on my knees and my ankles, all this talk about sinning in a dream of old timey washing away of sins, I was trying to ponder on it when the sun come bright smack through the window of the trailer and I got up real slow, wishing I'd a brought some of them Krispy Kremes home with me instead of eating two more while waiting for Andy to leave the parking lot. The handsomest preacher was on the TV, his hair all blown dry like Farrah Fawcett's and I was thinking what Daddy would have looked like if he'd a lived long enough, and the next thing I know Andy comes through the door, smelling like he spent the night in a barrel of fish and tobacco juice.

"Lordy," he said in a moan like a hurt dog.

"How you like 'em?" I heard myself asking him.

"Like what?" He held both hands to his head, like he was trying to keep it from falling into two pieces. His shirt was tore and he had a scratch like from a child or an animal along his right cheek.

"Your eggs," I said.

He looked at me like he was trying to decide whether to kill me or kiss me, and I gave him the same look back, figuring that if we both was to be true to what we said we believed in he would turn right around and walk out the door and I would pack and go my own way and the only thing left in this God-forsook trailer would be the eggs frying in the skillet alongside the curling bacon, and the preacher with movie star's hair working his mouth without sound, alone, all alone on the screen that you could hardly see now because of the angle of the light coming in the window. Sometimes it seems like our lives was made of trying to be music, but nobody was singing now.

Richard Tillinghast

Lost Cove & The Rose of San Antone

Evening comes on. I put on a clean white shirt
and feel how well it fits me. I pour bourbon,
with spring water from a plastic jug,
and look out sliding glass doors
at green suburban hills blurred with smog.
Two watches lie on the table before me:
one set for now, one telling time in 1938,
their glass faces reflecting the round California sky.

The man I see through the eye of the second watch
sits in a silence too deep for my nerves
and stares out at twilight
fading on trunks of pine and oak.
The black Model-A car rusts into the stream
that runs past his cabin in Lost Cove, Tennessee.
He reaches for the whiskey on the table,
and his sleeve clears a path through pine-needles and dust.

The coal that tumbles out of his hillside
soils the air and brick houses in Nashville.
Words burn in the rain there
from the power of water that runs past his door.
He looks at his watch and turns on the radio.
The music reaches him, all the way from Nashville.
He holds his glass of whiskey up to the light
that is almost gone. Its color suits his thoughts.

"Lost Cove & The Rose of San Antone" from *The Knife and Other Poems*, by Richard Tillinghast. Copyright © 1980 by Richard Tillinghast. Reprinted by permission of Wesleyan University Press.

The fiddles and autoharp fill up the dark room
and push out through paint-blackened screens
into black oaks that press against the house.
His face hurts me. It doesn't look right.
He goes against the grain
of whiskey he has made himself, and rides
the wire-song of a steel guitar through small towns,
through the bug-crowded air of farm-crossings late at night.

The disembodied, high guitar line swims in his nerves
like a salmon up a flint-rock stream,
falls like a hawk on blood.
The whiskey burns and soothes.
His tongue starts to move to the words of the song:
trains and big woods and bottomless rivers,
hard drinking, broken hearts, and death.
His blood knows whose song this is.

He's never swum in no bottomless river,
or rode that night train to Memphis,
or sat and stared at those thirteen unlucky bars.
But he sees the moon rise, with the Rose of San Antone
tattooed on it in blood.
A waitress in Denver glides toward him with drinks on a tray.
He stumbles, drunk, through strange woods by an airport
and walks out in San Francisco with a gun in his pocket . . .

The moon sets, over hills cold and unfamiliar.
I shut off the radio, and hear the sea-roar of the freeway.
Who is this man I have dreamed up?
I cork the bottle, and get up and lock the door.

Richard Tillinghast

Sewanee in Ruins

V.

In the 1850s the founders had envisioned
broad avenues, fountains, Jeffersonian symmetries.
In the 1890s
the Gothic battlements their survivors built
served their experience,
which told them there was something to fight against,
and something to fight for.

In those dilapidated, down-at-the-heels days,
when Sewanee had one tower,
still her loveliest—
a copy of Magdalen Tower, Oxford—
one that looked capable of repelling a proper siege
among the broadleaf trees,
complete with crossbows and catapulted stones,—
a genteel versifier,
seeing the real
through the ephemera of the actual,
called the University
A towered city set within a wood,
Far from the world, upon a mountain's crest:
There storms of life break not, nor cares intrude.
There learning dwells, and peace is wisdom's guest.

But why do I let these ghosts talk
and tire you with their names and histories,
their verses,
and stories of their houses,
so that the living faces of my students
blur before my eyes?

"Sewanee in Ruins," Part V, from *Our Flag Was Still There*, by Richard Tillinghast. Copyright © 1984 by Richard Tillinghast. Reprinted by permission of Wesleyan University Press.

Is it because *the present*
is a perpetual Never
and the past, detailed by memory,
pathetic because finished,
appealing to the imagination because half-imaginary,
lays its vanished, living hand on my hand
and demands to be articulated?

Or is there another reason?

My thoughts run from the past
to the future as I fear it will be—
to the bands of food-gathering nomads,
omnivorous bipeds bearing awful marks,
mouthing an eroded tongue,
who find their way through weirdly revitalized forests
to this mountaintop
looking for a stopping-place,
for water they can drink—,
when the freeways are lost to wild brambles
and New York and Atlanta are without power
forever—
when this Neo-Gothic library
has fallen into the ruins I strangely desire
(for the habit of rebellion dies hard)—
when this paper,
these many-layered words,
have ruined into grey dust that glows.

In these former buildings,
strangers out of the catastrophic future,
these traces that were roads,—
life was destroyed
and came back.
Literate people lived here,
whose sense of themselves as a nation drew breath
long after their armies disbanded;
whose pride was made homely by ruin;
who gave more than they got.

In their community the gifted and the gracious led;
but everyone had a place,
and no two people were the same;

Richard Tillinghast

and even fools were suffered, though never gladly,—
and laughter survived.

This was a place
where the sacraments were kept,
and people were kind—
though their fate and their times
might have made them otherwise—;
where the old names
for flowers
were remembered:
flags   heart's-ease   Confederate violets.

Two hundred yards to the west of here,
look for a limestone spring in a cave.

Henry Samples

Home Cooking

Cissy Farmer-Clevenger dusts her fingers lightly with White Lily flour and begins to attack the thin strips of dough salvaged from the plump apple pie now baking in the oven. She winces slightly as the moist dough presses under her sharply trimmed nails as she kneads it there on the sideboard. The sensation makes her think of earthworms, a slightly disgusting feeling, but not enough to make her quit baking in her grandmother's kitchen.

Cissy is making a Sugaroll, a concoction of brown sugar, butter, dough and pecans. Her mother made them for her when Cissy was a child, and now Cissy is making one for her eight-year-old daughter, Cassandra. It does not bother Cissy that Sugaroll is inconsistent with her policy of avoiding sugar. The Sugarolls are sinfully delicious, and she enjoys baking them.

As a matter of fact, Cissy admitted this morning to her closest friend, Janice Masters, baking is one of the few things she enjoys lately.

"Four generations under one roof is just too many," Cissy said as they shared a cup of tea in Janice's trailer.

Cissy and Cassandra are living with Cissy's mother, Celia, and Cissy's grandmother, Cordie. Sometimes Cissy likes to joke that they were named by the Chevrolet division of General Motors.

Cissy and Janice have resumed a high school friendship since Cissy and Cassandra moved back to Valley Forge in Carter County, Tennessee, Cissy separated from her husband, with intentions of divorce.

Cissy had discovered Janice's trailer one Saturday morning at the end of her daily jog. She had to ask Janice not to blow cigarette smoke in her face as they stood on the small stoop of the trailer, renewing a friendship now a decade old. The next day Janice had not smoked.

Cassandra thinks living on a farm with animals is a great experience. "It's like having your own zoo," she said. But Cissy worries about the coming fall, when Cassandra must attend the nearest county school.

Cassandra speaks with a distinct northern accent, and Cissy fears that television has not eradicated the mountain relish of poking fun at strangers. They'll probably call her a *Yankee*, Cissy thinks. She has read several paperback books on child rearing and does not want Cassandra to develop complexes.

Cissy and Janice often talk of child rearing as they have their morning tea, although Janice is divorced and childless.

"Bring 'em up right as a child and they'll not depart from their ways as an adult," Janice has said.

Which is fairly reflected in the admonitions of Cissy's grandmother, 74-year-old Cordie Jenkins, who holds that the Bible forbids the wearing of pants by women.

And Cordie finds it difficult to accept Cissy's name. "A married woman ort not to have two names," she likes to say, shaking her head.

Cissy and Cassandra have been living on her grandmother's farm for eleven weeks, following her breakup with her husband, Willard, an unemployed metals worker in Detroit, Michigan.

During their time on the farm, Cissy had resumed some of her grandmother's ways. She is dehydrating apples and peaches and has tried her hand at making butter and lye soap. In a few days they will make kraut, chopping cabbage by the pound and then packing it in small-mouthed Ball jars with scalding water and salt. "Just make sure the signs is in the Head," Cordie warns.

"I don't know why you all want to fool with that old-timey stuff," Janice said one morning while watching Richard Simmons. "You can get better stuff at the K-Mart, and cheaper, too."

Other irritants are emerging. Cissy has been assigned milking duty, a chore she has always hated. It has to be done twice daily, and she finds the manurey smell of the barn offensive.

"Even Tom's Natural Fennel Toothpaste won't cut through the taste of that cow shit," Cissy told Janice. "I can taste it for hours."

"You sure ought to smoke a cigarette," Janice said. "That's what I always did."

Other problems are developing.

One problem on her mind this July afternoon as she slides the Sugaroll onto a cookie sheet and into the shimmering heat of the oven is her husband, who has written that he intends to move to Tennessee and look for work.

"I miss you and Cassandra," his letter said. "We need to be together."

"I can't believe it," Cissy had told Janice. "For months he wouldn't look for work, and now he wants to move down here. I don't know why I married him anyway."

"Maybe there wasn't no work to be found up there," Janice said.

Janice has claimed to know all about the worthless nature of men. "A man is just about as trifling a thing that you're likely to find," she said.

This prompted her to drag out a pulp paperback extolling the virtues of cucumbers over men. The two had giggled like schoolgirls and then proceeded to evaluate the abilities of the local hairdressers.

But Cissy does not shy away from the company of men. Twice she has gone out — clandestinely — with Wayne Hopkins, a farmer and shade-tree mechanic from Braemer who is taking computer courses part-time at East Tennessee State University in Johnson City.

"Don't get the Data-Base Blues," he likes to say. His computer at school flashes "Waiting for the Data-Base" when the computer is at a heavy load.

Cissy and Wayne met one Saturday afternoon at the Elizabethton Bonanza Sirloin Pit when Cissy and Cassandra had stopped for a burger. He had been adroit at extracting an agreement for a date, quickly catching on that he needed to speak in code so Cassandra would not become interested in their conversation. He was a tall lean country boy with a shock of black hair. Cissy liked him, despite the fact that she guessed herself three years older. He had a solemn air about him, but he made Cassandra squeal when he bought her a bowl of orange Jello. Cassandra had thought Wayne was neat, although Cissy had to bribe her to keep her from telling her mother and grandmother about their luncheon guest.

On the second rendezvous, a glorious summer Saturday, they had ridden throughout the county in his Dodge. He pointed out the former tracks of the East Tennessee-Western North Carolina Railroad with the dignity of a historian.

"Feller used to could go all the way from Johnson City to Cranberry for 37 cents," he had said.

Even in the cool blue mountain shade they had driven with the air conditioning churning. It made her feel luxurious. They had ended up at the overlook at Watauga Dam, a massive earthen structure built in the 1940s which now restrained Watauga Lake.

Boldly, Wayne had produced a sweating six-pack of beer from the back seat. He didn't ask if she wanted one. He simply snapped two beers off the plastic ring and handed her a can. "I hope you don't mind drinking the real thing," he had said. "Light beer tastes watery to me."

They drank their beers in silence, save for the twilight sounds of the insects, watching the sunset. And then, wordlessly, Wayne made love to her there on the front seat. Alone later in her room, she had wept with joy, plotting other three-hour escapes from the aging farmhouse.

"It ain't fittin' for a married woman to be out at all hours of the night," Cordie had said in response to a mild inquiry from Cissy about going to a Friday night movie by herself.

So Cissy waits in the house, performing chores without aid of food processor or microwave oven, trying to ignore a growing dilemma.

She fears that her husband will arrive any day, presumably to look for work but more likely to resume residence with the family. And she wonders if Wayne will call again.

Sunday night services at the Full Bethel Independent Gospel Church had been her downfall with Wayne.

At first, Wayne coming for church had seemed like a good idea, a way to break the ice, a proper form of introduction. Her mother had not been overjoyed by the idea, but she had finally accepted the proposition that there are worse delights available to an estranged woman than going to church with a single man.

"It's not exactly a date," Cissy had said. "After all, we'll be going together."

But, after a whispered telephone call confirming the arrangements with Wayne, Celia had let the bombshell drop. "You know we're having footwashing services Sunday night," she had said.

Cissy had become terror-stricken, feeling her heart drop at the thought of Wayne watching the mountain ritual of foot-washing. The service consisted of each church member bringing a small wash basin, with the men pairing off with men, and women with women, for a little soapless foot bathing.

"You can't mean that church is still doing that," Cissy had said. "That's awful."

"It's in the thirteenth chapter of John," Celia had said. "That's in the New Testament, and we're required to follow the laws of the New Testament."

Later, when Cordie and Celia had gone to bed, Cissy had picked up the family Bible and turned to the authority on footwashing. She read: "He riseth from supper, and laid aside his garments; and took a towel, and girded himself. After that he poureth water into a basin and began to wash the disciples' feet, and to wipe them with the towel wherewith he was girded."

"I don't care," Cissy said the next day. "I don't want Wayne to come and see something like that, especially the first time meeting you and grandmother. I'm afraid he'll get the wrong idea about us."

"I think I'm getting the wrong idea about him," Celia had said with a firm jaw.

Cissy had prayed for a flat tire, even a minor accident, anything to prevent Wayne from keeping the date. But he arrived just as "60 Minutes" was ending. He was wearing a pale dotted tie and he smelled of Old Spice.

The five of them had bustled off to church, arriving midway through the second verse of the opening hymn. Cissy had felt every eye in the church swing to them as they made their entrance. The sermon moved quickly enough, a wild shouted litany about the evils of education. "They ain't but one book—the Good Book—a true Christian need have in his library," the minister said. Several men on the front row had shouted "Amen."

Wayne had watched stolidly as the congregation went about footwashing, the church grown silent save for the sound of sloshing water. He watched politely but curiously, as a sociologist might observe some ancient rite.

But Wayne's solitude was broken by a blue-haired spinster who came to inquire, "Are you saved, son?" Sweat glistened like oil on her prunelike face. The woman gripped the pew with gnarled fingers while Wayne pondered her question.

Wayne looked at the floor, "No, I don't reckon I am," he had said. Immediately, Cissy knew it was not the right answer.

"The Lord have mercy," the woman wailed. She turned to the congregation. "They's a sinner man right here, and he's a fine looking boy," she said. " I think it's the duty of every Christian person in this church to come and plead with him to fall on his knees and beg forgiveness of his sins."

Like cattle spooked by lightning, the Christians swarmed around them. One man jumped a pew to dash down their aisle. Cissy and Wayne stood surrounded by yelping Christians, each shouting his favorite exhortation. "He loves you, son, He loves you," a fat woman said. "Don't delay, don't delay," another said. So this is how Custer felt, Cissy thought.

Out of the corner of her eye she saw Wayne's color change, first a mild blush, then, quickly, a full beet red. He turned to her as if to speak, then collapsed, knees buckling. Two men caught him by the arms and lowered his head gently to the floor.

The church stood quiet, the plaintive cries suddenly calmed. Then, someone spoke: "He's under conviction, Brothers and Sisters. We've got to pray even harder for his soul now."

Like high school athletes the men and women quickly dropped to one knee, heads bowed, praying fervently, sending forth sounds akin to Babel. "He needs air," Cissy had yelled. "Don't any of you have enough sense to see that?" Her wails did nothing to diminish the praying, which had reached a pitch worthy of a mad auctioneer.

"The hell with all of you," Cissy had cried. She scrambled into her purse with a thin handkerchief and then dashed outside to the watertap where she soaked the cloth in cold Limestone water. Then she leaped the steps two at a time and ran back to Wayne's side.

The dampness of the cloth had brought him quickly around. "Well Glory," a toothless man cried as Wayne struggled to his feet. "The Lord has drained him of his sins," The minister quickly called for a song as the congregation slowly rose.

"Get me out of here," Wayne said.

Cissy drove Wayne's car back to her grandmother's house, leaving Celia and Cordie to bring themselves and Cassandra home as best they could. Twice Cissy asked, "Are you all right?" but Wayne said nothing. When they arrived at the house he had simply slid into the driver's seat when she got out, not bothering to answer when she asked. "Are you sure you can drive?"

That was three weeks ago and feelings have been tense among the four women. Even Cassandra has sensed a new direction in their living arrangement.

So Cissy stands watching the Sugaroll cool, thinking of her husband and of Wayne. Only one has a job, but which one has a future? She bites a nail and ponders her fate. She hears the telephone ringing in the hall. It rings clear and loud in the clapboard house. "It's for you," her mother says. Cissy takes a step toward the hall and pauses. She lacks the courage to speak to either her husband or to Wayne. Her mouth goes dry. She looks at the Sugaroll and remembers painless days of childhood. She takes a bite into the oozy sugar and pecan mixture. It tastes sinfully delicious. Time stands still.

Don Johnson

Grabbling

for Bob Higgs

Longer than any of us in air
or common light could not breathe
he would stay down, fishing
by braille in pools darker
than the skins of old bibles.

On the green bank, closing
my eyes, I would dizzy myself
holding my breath, trying
to picture him blind and unhearing,
while he probed under root knob

and rock. I would come back
always to the sheen of slow
current, an empty boat, birds
I made call, "rise up, rise up,"
till he boiled up sputtering

like a sinner the preacher
upstream had lost (it was always
Sunday). He would toss each
fish at his bucket, fling the occasional
snake at the bank without speaking,

then rest, wide-eyed at the gunwale.
I could not know what he did
when he ducked under, but squinted
trying to learn each surface gesture,
back-lighted move. And once

Don Johnson

I called out above the river's hum
to ask him, "How?" His answer,
"Get wet, boy." He didn't say
that each time down grows longer,
fish or no fish; that rivers

everywhere are one, never the same;
that when you finally let go
to float up clutching whatever
you can bring back, worldly light
explodes, barbed, uplifting, almost holy.

Jeff Daniel Marion

Touchstone

Here by the riverbank these rocks are braille
to our touch, a secret language of years
washing through fingertips into now: sift of a blue
February afternoon cupped in the open palms of mussel shells.

We spread our guilt on the grass near sycamores
& study swirls on the river's skin: what surfaces
we name—eddies, shoals & jags of lacy foam.
You laugh & say again your wish
that these rocks could talk.

Sun-baked & smooth as creek pebbles, these loaves
break water into voice: in this communion
what we hear are whispers
of our dreams drifting toward far shores
like a lone pair of Canadian geese winging down river,
past bends, field & coves,
safely home again before dark.

Love, I cup your face in my hands
& silence fills to the brim
wordless as stones in this river.

Jeff Daniel Marion

Ebbing & Flowing Spring

Coming back you almost
expect to find the dipper
gourd hung there by the latch.
Matilda always kept it hidden
inside the white-washed shed,
now a springhouse of the cool
darkness & two rusting milk cans.
"Dip and drink," she'd say,
"It's best when the water is rising."
A coldness slowly cradled
in the mottled gourd.
Hourly some secret clock
spilled its time in water,
rising momentarily only
to ebb back into trickle.
You waited while
Matilda's stories flowed back,
seeds & seasons, names & signs,
almanac of all her days.
How her great-great grandfather
claimed this land, gift
of a Cherokee chief
who called it "spring of many risings."
Moons & years & generations
& now Matilda alone.
You listen.
It's a quiet beginning
but before you know it
the water's up & around you
flowing by.
You reach for the dipper
that's gone, then
remember to use your hands
as a cup for the cold
that aches & lingers.
This is what you have come for.
Drink.

Judy Odom

Sole Owners of the Mountain

The rain is moving in. I sit at my desk and watch the mountains disappear. Shadows close over me, covering the papers in my hands. One flick of a switch and I could push the shadows back into their corners, but I don't have the energy. My interest in work has vanished with the sunlight, anyhow. I lean back in my chair and look out at the dark sky pressing itself against the land. The rain, when it comes, has a steady reassuring sound.

I wonder what you're doing—whether you're some place safe and dry. It's four o'clock; you could be anywhere—typing up your copy at the *Chronicle* or wandering without your raincoat in some open field.

Because the image pleases me, I seat you at your kitchen table. I make the steam rise hot and fragrant as you drink your tea. The mug you're holding has an earth-brown pattern, marked with an abstract blue design. You clasp it tight to warm your palms.

Once again, I admire the blunt strength in your fingers, the square sturdiness of your hands. When we first met, I thought the look of them was disconcerting; they seemed too powerful for any woman, especially a woman with your fine, sharp-angled features and small bones. But I've learned to see their beauty because I know their gentleness. I've watched them soothe a restless child and stroke the music from an old guitar, coax a withering plant to flower and calm a skittish horse. Your hands draw tension like a magnet; you comfort everything you touch.

I've never told you that I envy you your hands; you'd make a joke or get defensive if I tried. You're positive they're ugly. "Peasant hands," your father used to call them, laughing when you snatched them out of sight behind your back. Thanks to him, you won't buy skirts that don't have pockets. You're thirty-five years old and you still bite your fingernails.

That oversized blue cardigan you're wearing—it belongs to him. He left it at you house the last time he came to visit you. Ten years ago, it was, or more. I didn't know you then.

Your father lives in Asheville, eighty miles southeast—no great distance, even on a narrow Appalachian road. But you don't go there to see him, and he hasn't come to you again. Too many mountains lie between you, mountains you both refuse to cross. You don't talk about him very often, and you speak in past tense when you do.

Outside the rain drums harder. Except for me, the building's empty: the students and other teachers left an hour ago. There's nobody here to share the music of this late October storm. I trace your first name—Jessie—in the mist that clouds my window pane. The letters streak and blur. In seconds, they're unreadable.

I should go home to my kitchen—trust in my imagination and leave you by yourself to drink the tea I've put into your hands. Tim and the boys will want their dinner; it's time I changed into my wife-and-mother uniform. Tonight, I'll wrap up in my heavy flannel housecoat and hope it keeps out the cold.

My housecoat and your father's sweater—we do the best we can. But no matter what we decide to wear against the chill, the scientific truth remains: it's our own warmth we're giving to ourselves.

Such a simple fact, but such a revelation. I learned it in biology my sophomore year at West End High. All I have to do is close my eyes to see Miss Prescott's narrow face and hear her thin, shrill voice. "It's not the blanket stops your shivering in the night-time. That blanket—what it does is hold your heat around you so it won't be wasted on the air."

I wonder what my students learn from me and what they will remember.

I wonder if it's foolish, trying to claim you for a friend.

I rummage through the desk drawer until I find my cigarettes, hidden under last year's unused planbook and a stack of blank detention forms. My lighter sputters blue and yellow, its struggling flame reflected for an instant in the window glass.

The mist coils around me. Your red ski vest gleams like a bobbing lantern, ten or fifteen yards ahead. Guided by its brightness, I follow you up Ripshin Mountain with our kids.

You've got a special place you've just discovered. That's what you tell me early Sunday morning on the phone. It's so beautiful that you can't wait another day for me to see it. Half-asleep and yawning, I say yes. Of course I'll come. I always do.

So we leave our men at home to drowse in comfort while we take Christopher and little Tim and Sarah with us up a narrow unmarked trail into the clouds.

We're still on fairly level ground when Christopher pulls out his Boy Scout knife and hacks a low branch off a young ash tree. "For killing snakes," he informs us solemnly. "Copperheads—moccasins—you know.

Whatever kind of snakes we run into. No telling how many snakes I'll have to kill today."

A twelve-year-old general with a swagger stick, Christopher taps the skinny branch against his thigh. Timmy sidles closer to me. Sarah hugs your arm.

"Not today," you smile at Christopher. "You won't be killing any snakes up here. Snakes don't live on Ripshin—not poisonous snakes, anyway. It's the truth—I swear it is," you answer the unspoken skepticism in my grin. "Folks around here say there hasn't been a snake on Ripshin Mountain in a hundred years. Oh, a little ol' rat snake, maybe, but nothing dangerous. It's a friendly mountain, children. There's not a living creature on this mountain that would do you any harm."

Our caution vanquished by your confidence, we all relax. Christopher puts his knife back in his pocket and tosses the stick away. Timmy and Sarah scurry off together, and scramble happily over a rotting pine tree, blown down across the trail by some forgotten storm. I start to whistle "Woodstock" as the slope gets steeper and the mist begins to thicken into fog.

We force our way toward the summit of the mountain through a stubborn tangle of underbrush, past crimson staghorn sumac and dark green rhododendrons that shine like patent leather in the still, white air. Timmy cries out with pain when a blackberry vine rakes the back of his hand. The scratches are deep and red and neatly parallel, like furrows in a well-plowed field.

While you search your knapsack for the first-aid kit, I sit on the damp ground with Timmy in my lap. Kneeling beside us, you use one thumb to wipe a tear smudge off his cheek. Then you gently paint each scratch with iodine. He flinches at the sting, but wanting to look brave for Sarah, he doesn't cry again. In sympathy, she clamps her fingers tight around his shoulder; I notice for the first time—your Sarah has her mother's hands.

It's okay, hon," you murmur, ruffling Timmy's hair. "It's okay now." I catch your sidelong glance and know the words are meant for me.

Fully recovered, Timmy rockets away to show off his wounds to Christopher. I grasp the hand you offer and let you pull me to my feet.

With you in the lead, we continue our climb in single file. Somewhere to our right, we hear the rush of water. Chris wants to go exploring—he wants to leave the trail and make his own path to the creek and back. When I say no, he turns to you.

I read your opinion in the amused lift of your eyebrow. Let him, you prod me silently. Let him do it. Let him go.

Stubborn and defensive, I glare at you until you look away.

"Better not, Chris," you tell him with a shrug. "You might get lost.

It's easy to get lost in fog like this. Everything sounds funny. Your sense of direction—it gets all messed up. You can't trust it like you can when the weather's clear."

Christopher accepts your answer without question. He would have whined or pouted if the refusal had been mine alone. You'll probably make fun of my excessive caution later, but now—when it counts—you've lined up on my side. I know I should be grateful; instead, I'm irritated by your show of loyalty.

Deliberately, I slow my pace, examine a strange red lichen on a tree trunk, pick the cockleburrs and beggar-lice from my jeans. One quick wave in my direction, and you stride off with Sarah and the boys.

Like a bottle of white-out spilled by accident across an artist's careful drawing, the fog erases you and the children and the rhododendron and the ragged stand of oak trees just ahead.

I jam my hands into my pockets to still their trembling.

"Beth? Hey, Beth! Come on!" Absurdly relieved to hear you call me, I stumble toward the sound. Catching up with you seems impossible. If I stop to think about it, I'll be afraid to try. Your voice can't help me judge the distance or direction. In this fog, you might as well be shouting through a heavy woolen muffler. I might as well be listening with cotton in my ears.

Like a blind woman, both hands outstretched, I feel my way. Suddenly, you're there in front of me, and I see that you were always closer than I realized.

"Pretty soon, we'll be above this fog," you assure me. "I promise, you'll be glad we came." Improvising a quick dance step, you take your place in front of me. As usual, I plod along behind.

Twenty minutes later, we top a ridge and step out into sunlight. Below us lies a sheltered hollow, all meadow grass and goldenrod. The children tumble like excited puppies down the incline, while you and I stand quietly together in the shadow of a tall white pine. Everywhere around us, other mountains rise—the blue, sharp-crested waves of an ancient, undiscovered sea.

"Well?" you ask me finally. "What about it? Was it worth the climb?"

I feel like reciting Keats to you, or William Butler Yeats. But that would be a poor exchange, considering what you've done. You've brought me with you to this peak in Darien; you've given me the brightness of this noon at Innisfree. And I have nothing more to offer than somebody else's words I've memorized. So I try to thank you with an awkward stammer. You clasp your hands behind your back and mumble something about food.

Below us, Christopher has made himself the leader of a scouting party. He carries a stick on his shoulder for a gun. Holding shafts of goldenrod above their heads like torches, Sarah and Timmy follow him through the long grass into a grove of trees.

"Reckon they're hunting Indians?" you chuckle.

"Indians or Klingons, maybe. Depends on what galaxy Chris thinks he is in today. He just read *Treasure Island*, so I guess it could be pirates, too."

"Pirates. Indians. Whatever. I think we probably better feed them. Hunters're always hungry. It doesn't matter what they're hunting for. I think I'll be Nancy Drew, myself. Disguised as a cook for the wagon train." You put one finger to your lips. "Don't you tell, now. I'm trusting you."

"Okay. Right," I whisper, playing along with your new game. "You can trust me. The question is, can I trust you?"

"Cross my heart and hope to die." You bend down to pluck a blade of grass. "You can trust me. You can tell ol' Nancy who you are. You might as well. Ol' Nancy's such a great detective, she'll find out anyway." Hands cupped around your piece of grass, you try to whistle, but you don't know how.

"Here, let me show you. Give it to me." At least there's one thing I can teach you. There's one small skill you haven't learned.

Obediently, you hold out your open hand.

I take the sliver of grass, then pull it taut between my thumbs and blow. A shrill whistle slices through the air.

"It's easy. You can do it," I insist when you shake your head. "Hell, anybody can do it if Becky Thatcher can. Miss Becky—she's led a pretty sheltered life, you know."

"Jesus. Becky Thatcher!" You sag against the pine tree. "That's so perfect. I should've known that's—"

"Stop it, Jessie. Don't you laugh at me." Angrily, I pull at the grass blade it rip it apart. Instead, its sharp edge cuts my thumb. "Ouch! Damn!"

"Beth, I'm sorry." You shrug your knapsack off your shoulders. "Here, I'll get the iodine."

"Forget it." I wipe the blood on my jeans. "You're supposed to be Nancy Drew," I snarl, "not Florence Nightingale. You can't be everything to everybody all the time."

"Beth?"

"I said, forget it. Let's go find the kids." Without waiting for you, I begin the long descent into the hollow. Near the bottom of the slope, I trip over a hidden rock. You grab my arm and give me back my balance, and we wade out into knee-high meadow grass.

That grove of trees across the field turns out to be a ruined apple orchard, wild and scraggly now for want of care, its unclaimed harvest scattered on the ground. You stoop to choose two windfall apples—pale green, tinted with the faintest blush of red. Carefully, you wipe them on your shirt-sleeve and offer one to me. I like the cool heft of it against my palm. Each bite I take has a flavor crisp and satisfying as the smell of burning autumn leaves.

You finish your apple first and toss the core away. "The seeds will grow," you tell me softly. "We can come back once a year and see how much our trees have grown. Throw yours over there, too. Plant your tree over there by mine." When I've carried out your instructions, you pick up three more apples from the ground. "Hey, kids," you shout. "Where are you? Y'all come on—come plant an apple tree."

"Wait a minute, Mom, we're playing," Sarah calls, impatient at your interruption of the game.

"That's the younger generation for you, they don't give a damn about tradition," you complain. "Kids—what do they know? They don't know anything. This is important. A family needs its rituals."

I nod, remembering the reindeer cookie cutter that used to be my mother's and now belongs to me. "Like baking sugar cookies every Christmas."

"Yeah, that's right. Or planting apple trees." Suddenly, you seem embarrassed. You duck your head to examine the apples you're balancing so neatly in your hands. Before I can ask you what's the matter, Timmy and Chris and Sarah come racing toward us, clamoring to be fed. We sit in a circle on the grass and eat our peanut butter sandwiches and drink our orange Gatorade. You borrow Christopher's knife to cut an apple through the middle and show us all the star inside, but you don't mention planting trees again.

I have an apple on my desk now. We brought some with us down the mountain Sunday afternoon. This one is the last, and I think I'll save the core. With good soil and careful nurture, the seeds will sprout. If I keep them warm enough inside the house, they'll make it through the winter fine. I might have the beginning of an apple tree to give you in the spring.

The trouble is, I don't know whether you'll remember. I can't be sure you'll want it then. I don't know if I want to take the chance.

Savoring another apple, I watch the kids play hide-and-seek. Sarah's counting to a hundred while Chris and Timmy hurry off into the brush. Their home base is the gray fieldstone chimney that stands at the far side of the orchard where a cabin used to be. I think the chimney looks exposed and lonesome. It needs the rough embrace of cabin walls and the comfort of a fire on its hearth again.

The family that built the chimney and the cabin—they must have been the ones who cleared this ground and planted it with apple trees. Watching the game in progress around their chimney, I start to speculate out loud about their lives—what traditions they observed, what games they played. "Why d'you think they left?" I ask you. "A place this beautiful—

249

why would anybody leave?"

When you don't answer right away, I decide you haven't heard me. I glance at you and see your eyes are closed. I think you've gone to sleep here in the sunshine with your back against an apple tree. But then you clear your throat and shift your position slightly, and I realize that you've been listening all the time.

"They moved on west to better land, I guess." You pick up a dry leaf and twirl it by the stem. "Their great-great-grandchildren probably live in Oregon or somewhere. I doubt they know their family came from Tennessee. I doubt they give a damn." You crumble the leaf into a coarse brown powder, then dust your hands together, strewing bits of leaf between us on the ground.

"They might know," I try to pacify you. "Maybe their family history got passed on. These people"—I gesture toward the chimney—"when they left here, maybe they took some apple seed and planted it in Oregon. Maybe their great-great-great-grandchildren are sharing Ripshin apples with their friends."

"Jesus, Beth," you scowl at me. Angry tears are gathering in your eyes. Impatiently, you brush them away with the tips of your fingers. "What good's a handful of apple seeds?"

Snakes don't live on Ripshin Mountain. That's what you told Christopher this morning as we began our climb. There's no living creature on this mountain that wants to do us harm. But your unexpected bitter question slices deeper than any rattler's fangs.

All that talk before—that family ritual of planting trees together—I see now it didn't signify a goddamn thing. I thought I understood what you were saying, but it must have been the whisper of my own need I was listening to.

We grow up separated from our families—by distances too far to travel or differences too great to be resolved. It's a natural enough occurrence. Families scatter, bonds of kinship break apart. When that happens, we start searching for replacements. We try to forge new family connections with our friends. We repeat the pattern of the atom that searches for electrons to fill its outer shell. We form our human version of co-valent bonding to make ourselves complete again, to occupy our empty space.

Sometimes I want to say, "I choose you for my sister." I want to classify and label this special link we seem to share. But this compound we've formed will always be unstable. Change the temperature or pressure, and it will dissolve into its separate elements again.

So, fearing the consequences of your anger, I don't question you about the cause, although I'm curious.

A hundred years ago, one family trekked on westward from this mountain. You don't know their background or their destination or their names.

Why should you care if their descendants know the taste of Ripshin apples or the clean smell of sunlight on Appalachian pines? What difference should the outcome of that family's journey make to you?

Eventually, I hope, you'll tell me what their unrecorded travels say to you about your own. But I have to wait until you're ready. I have to let you choose the time.

"It'd be nice to own this place up here," I change the subject. "You know—rebuild the cabin and everything.."

"God. You are such a capitalist. What makes you think you have to own it? I can't see what you'd want to own it for." A small brown and yellow bee circles around you hopefully, but you ignore its tentative reconnaissance. It settles humming on your shoulder until you brush it back into the air.

"It'd be nice, that's all." I shrug and try to laugh.

Out of sight in a scrub oak thicket, Sarah shouts and claps her hands. She's discovered someone in his hiding place. Seconds later, she and Tim careen into the clearing, both of them galloping hard toward home. They reach the chimney together. Side by side, they lean against it to regain their breath.

I smile at you, but you're not watching—you're picking at one ragged fingernail. "Property's no good," you tell me with a stubborn frown. "Property doesn't count for anything. It didn't hold those people here. They didn't think about it—they went right off to Oregon and left it all behind."

"I wouldn't leave it, Jessie," I answer. "Not this place. I can't explain it, but—well, here lately I've been thinking I'd like to have a piece of land. Not much—not a whole big farm or anything like that. An acre or two. You know, with a deed and a title and everything, to prove it's mine."

"Mmmm hmmm." You rub at a splotch of dried mud on your jeans. "Listen Beth—suppose you owned it. Just suppose you did. What would you do then? What use would you put it to?"

"Use?" I raise my eyebrows. "Hell, I don't know."

"You have to use it some way—you know, like raise a couple head of cattle or make apple cider. Maybe you could plant a little corn. You have to use it. That's tradition, that's the mountain way. If you don't use it, you'll just be an intruder on the land."

"I swear to God, sometimes I think you're crazy. People do start new traditions. It's not some kind of sin to start your own. I'll watch the sunrise every day, all right? If I get hungry, I'll eat an apple. Is that useful enough to suit you? Will that do?"

Refusing to look at me, you hunch forward and lock your hands together around your knees. "It's my land, anyhow," you mutter, "I'm the one who found it in the first place. I brought you up here. You wouldn't be here now except for me. You'd be reading the Sunday funnies in your breakfast room."

As the silence settles like another fog between us, I curse my blundering. Alone without a compass on unfamiliar ground, I've stumbled into barbed wire fences and NO TRESPASSING signs. "You're right," I admit awkwardly, trying to wriggle free with a minimum of cuts and scratches on my pride. "I'm sorry, Jessie. You can have it back, the whole damn mountain, it's all yours."

"Lord, listen to this woman!" Your laughter dances bright as sun on water, and your eyes are clear again as any mountain spring. "You think I want to hog it, don't you? I didn't mean you couldn't share it with me. It's no fun up here by myself—at least not all the time. Honey, what you think I went to so much trouble dragging you up this mountain for?"

Both arms stretched wide in a formal gesture of bestowal, you cede me half your claim to your discovery. For three days every week, you grant me sole possession of this mountain; the other three, it will belong to you. With ceremonial formality, we agree to joint entitlement on Sundays and on holidays.

We're laughing when the children come to join us. "Y'all sure are silly, Mother," Timmy chides me. "Y'all sit around and laugh at nothing all the time."

"Kids!" we exclaim together. You fill your knapsack full of apples, and we start the long hike down.

I pick up my apple core and wrap it in a piece of notebook paper, then put it in my raincoat pocket so I won't forget to take it home. There's a farm-and-garden store on Market Street where I can buy some potting soil. The traffic should be lighter now, and I like driving in the rain.

Ripshin Mountain or a clay pot in my kitchen—it shouldn't matter where the seeds are planted, so long as they have light and air and water, and enough free space to grow. But I realize that any planting anywhere will always carry its uncertainties; sometimes the seeds refuse to germinate, even in the richest ground. Considering the promise of the harvest, I can accept the risk of cultivation. Any woman who's co-owner of a mountain can afford to take a chance on planting apple trees.

Elizabeth Cox

The Minister's Daughter

They tell me
the minister's daughter
is beautiful. Men call to her
from the road. She answers
back, pinned to her chair,
fluffing her hair in the light,
her dress undone at the waist.
She will not walk in her sleep,
or in her own lifetime.

She stares down the long valley
and admits to herself, she wants
to do the most outrageous thing,
in the number of years she has left,
to lift one heavy foot and put it
like a fist into the ground.
She wants to stop the old couples
from coming to the house,
stop them from bringing loaves,

handing them like small
birds about to be crushed.
When she goes in to dinner,
her body is carried, her legs
hang over her father's arm,
not like a lover,
not with the promise of something,
but proper, like an ant
carrying another ant's head.

The Wish for Sea-Birds

You wish for a flock of white sea-birds
to be born in your mouth, you wish
for them to gather in a dark tree
near your house, for anything different

to keep from thinking you have failed.
Indifference in this night air
can count itself lucky, not roused
like beasts by beastly sounds,

but resting firm like wall.
It rises up to the holiest bead,
higher than the plumage of youth,
higher than the moon scanning the earth,

and you wish for a thousand trumpets,
or one proud man to believe he is right
when the last light breaks through.
And when the birds return from the sea,

when they sprout over the wall,
you wish for them to rise up
like fat white pulpits, tell you things
that will bring you to your knees.

They will sound like a few dry leaves
moving across your lawn, their wings
when you lean to rake them up,
will be hollow-boned and going south.

Nikki Giovanni

400 Mulvaney Street

I was going to Knoxville, Tennessee, to speak. I was going other places first but mostly to me I was going home. And I, running late as usual, hurried to the airport just in time.

The runway is like an aircraft carrier—sticking out in the bay—and you always get the feeling of drunken fly-boys in green airplane hats chomping wads and wads of gum going "Whooooopie!" as they bring the 747 in from Hackensack to La Guardia. It had been snowing for two days in New York and the runway was frozen. They never say to you that the runway is frozen and therefore dangerous to take off from, and in fact you'd never notice it because all the New York airports have tremendous backups—even on clear days. So sitting there waiting was not unusual but I did notice this tendency to slide to the side with every strong wind, and I peeked out my window and noticed we were in the tracks of the previous jet and I thought: death has to eat too. And I went to sleep.

The whole thing about going to Knoxville appealed to my vanity. I had gotten a call from Harvey Glover about coming down and had said yes and had thought no more of it. Mostly, as you probably notice, artists very rarely have the chance to go back home and say, "I think I've done you proud." People are so insecure and in some cases jealous and in some cases think so little of themselves in general that they seldom think you'd be really honored to speak in your home town or at your old high school. And other people are sometimes so contemptuous of home that they in fact don't want to come back. This has set up a negative

"400 Mulvaney Street" from *Gemini*, by Nikki Giovanni. Copyright © 1971 by Nikki Giovanni. Reprinted by permission of Macmillan Publishing Company.

equation between the artist and home.

I was excited about going to Knoxville but I didn't want to get my hopes up. What if it fell through? What if they didn't like me? Oh, my God! What if nobody came to hear me? Maybe we'd better forget about it. And I did. I flew on out to Cleveland to make enough money to be able to go to Knoxville. And Cleveland was beautiful. A girl named Pat and her policeman friend couldn't have been any nicer. And he was an intelligent cop. I got the feeling I was going to have a good weekend. Then my mother met me at the Cincinnati airport, where I had to change over, and had coffee with me and had liked my last television appearance. Then they called my flight, and on to Knoxville.

When we were growing up Knoxville didn't have television, let alone an airport. It finally got TV but the airport is in Alcoa. And is now called Tyson Field. Right? Small towns are funny. Knoxville even has a zip code and seven-digit phone numbers. All of which seems strange to me since I mostly remember Mrs. Flora Ford's white cake with white icing and Miss Delaney's blue furs and Armetine Picket's being the sharpest woman in town—she attended our church—and Miss Brooks wearing tight sweaters and Carter-Roberts Drug Store sending out Modern Jazz Quartet sounds of "Fontessa" and my introduction to Nina Simone by David Cherry, dropping a nickel in the jukebox and "Porgy" coming out. I mostly remember Vine Street, which I was not allowed to walk to get to school, though Grandmother didn't want me to take Paine Street either because Jay Manning lived on it and he was home from the army and very beautiful with his Black face and two dimples. Not that I was going to do anything, because I didn't do anything enough even to think in terms of not doing anything, but according to small-town logic "It looks bad."

The Gem Theatre was on the corner of Vine and a street that runs parallel to the creek, and for 10 cents you could sit all day and see a double feature, five cartoons and two serials plus previews for the next two weeks. And I remember Frankie Lennon would come in with her gang and sit behind me and I wanted to say, "Hi. Can I sit with you?" but thought they were too snooty, and they, I found out later, thought I was too Northern and stuck-up. All of that is gone now. Something called progress killed my grandmother.

Mulvaney Street looked like a camel's back with both humps bulging—up and down—and we lived in the down part. At the top of the left hill a lady made ice balls and would mix the flavors for you for just a nickel. Across the street from her was the Negro center, where the guys played indoor basketball and the little kids went for stories and nap time. Down in the valley part were the tennis courts, the creek, the bulk of the park and the beginning of the right hill. To enter or leave the street you went either up or down. I used to think of it as a fort, especially when it snowed, and the enemy would always try to sneak through the underbrush nurtured by the creek and through the park trees, but we always spotted strangers and dealt. As you came down the left hill the houses were up on its side; then people got regular flat front yards; then the right hill started and ran all the way into Vine and Mulvaney was gone and the big apartment building didn't have a yard at all.

Grandmother and Grandpapa had lived at 400 since they'd left Georgia. And Mommy had been a baby there and Anto and Aunt Agnes were born there. And dated there and sat on the swing on the front porch and fussed there, and our good and our bad were recorded there. That little frame house duplicated twice more which overlooked the soft-voiced people passing by with "Evening, 'Fessor Watson, Miz Watson," and the grass wouldn't grow between our house and Edith and Clarence White's house. It was said that he had something to do with numbers. When the man tried to get between the two houses and the cinder crunched a warning to us, both houses lit up and the man was caught between Mr. White's shotgun and Grandfather's revolver, trying to explain he was lost. Grandpapa would never pull a gun unless he intended to shoot and would only shoot to kill. I think when he reached Knoxville he was just tired of running. I brought his gun to New York with me after he died but the forces that be don't want anyone to keep her history, even if it's just a clogged twenty-two that no one in her right mind would even load.

Mr. and Mrs. Ector's rounded the trio of houses off. He always wore a stocking cap till he got tied back and would emerge very dapper. He was in love with the various automobiles he owned and had been seen by Grandmother and me on more than one occasion sweeping the snow from in front of his garage before he would back the car into the street. All summer he parked his car at the bottom of the hill and polished it twice a day and delighted in it. Grandmother would call across the porches to him, "Ector, you a fool 'bout that car, ain't cha?" And he would smile back. "Yes, ma'am." We were always polite with the Ectors because they had neither children nor grandchildren so there were no grounds for familiarity. I never knew Nellie Ector very well at all. It was rumored that she was a divorcee who had latched on to him, and to me she became all the tragic heroines I had read about, like *Forever Amber* or the *All This and Heaven Too* chick, and I was awed but kept my distance. He was laughs, though. I don't know when it happened to the Ectors but Mr. White was the first to die. I considered myself a hot-shot canasta player and I would play three-hand with Grandmother and Mrs. White and beat them. But I would drag the game on and on because it seemed so lonely next door when I could look through my bedroom window and see Mrs. White dressing for bed and not having to pull the shade anymore.

You always think the ones you love will always be there to love you. I went on to my grandfather's alma mater and got kicked out and would have disgraced the family but I had enough style for it not to be considered disgraceful. I could not/did not adjust to the Fisk social life and it could not/did not adjust to my intellect, so Thanksgiving I rushed home to Grandmother's without the bitchy dean of women's permission and that dean put me on social probation. Which would have worked but I was very much in love and not about to consider her punishment as anything real I should deal with. And the funny thing about that Thanksgiving was that I knew everything would go down just as it did. But I still wouldn't have changed it because Grandmother and Grandpapa would have had dinner alone and I would have had dinner alone and the next Thanksgiving we wouldn't even have him and Grandmother and I would both be alone by ourselves, and the only change would have been that Fisk considered me an ideal student, which means little on a life scale. My grandparents were surprised to see me in my brown slacks and beige sweater nervously chain-smoking and being so glad to touch base again. And she, who knew everything, never once asked me about school. And he was old so I lied to him. And I went to Mount Zion Baptist with them that Sunday and saw he was going to die. He just had to. And I didn't want that. Because I didn't know what to do about Louvenia, who had never been alone in her life.

I left Sunday night and saw the dean Monday morning. She asked where I had been. I said home. She asked if I had permission. I said I didn't need her permission to go home. She said, "Miss Giovanni," in a way I've been hearing all my life, in a way I've heard so long I know I'm on the right track when I hear it, and shook her head. I was "released from the school" February 1 because my "attitudes did not fit those of a Fisk woman." Grandpapa died in April and I was glad it was warm because he hated the cold so badly. Mommy and I drove to Knoxville to the funeral with Chris—Gary's, my sister's, son—and I was brave and didn't cry and made decisions. And finally the time came and Anto left and Aunt Agnes left. And Mommy and Chris and I stayed on till finally Mommy had to go back to work. And Grandmother never once asked me about Fisk. We got up early Saturday morning and Grandmother made fried chicken for us. Nobody said we were leaving but we were. And we all walked down the hill to the car. And kissed. And I looked at her standing there so bravely trying not to think what I was trying not to feel. And I got in on the driver's side and looked at her standing there with her plaid apron and her hair in a bun, her feet hanging loosely out of her mules, sixty-three years old, waving good-bye to us, and for the first time having to go into 400 Mulvaney without John Brown Watson. I felt like an impotent dog. If I couldn't protect this magnificent woman, my grandmother, from loneliness, what could I ever do? I have always hated death. It is unacceptable to kill the young and distasteful to watch the old expire. And those in between our link commit the little murders all the time. There must be a better way. So Knoxville decided to become a model city and a new mall was built to replace the old marketplace and they were talking about convention centers and expressways. And Mulvaney Street was a part of it all. This progress.

And I looked out from a drugged sleep and saw the Smoky Mountains looming ahead. The Smokies are so called because the clouds hang low. We used to camp in them. And the bears would come into camp but if you didn't feed them they would go away. It's still a fact. And we prepared for the landing and I closed my eyes as I always do because landings and takeoffs are the most vulnerable times for a plane, and if I'm going to die I don't have to watch it coming. It is very hard to give up your body completely. But the older I get the more dependent I am on other people for my safety, so I closed my eyes and placed myself in harmony with the plane.

Tyson Field turned out to be Alcoa. Progress again. And the Alcoa Highway had been widened because the new governor was a football fan and had gotten stuck on the old highway while trying to make a University of Tennessee football game and had missed the kickoff. The next day they began widening the road. We were going to the University of Tennessee for the first speaking of the day. I would have preferred Knoxville College, which had graduated three Watsons and two Watson progeny. It was too funny being at U. T. speaking of Blackness because I remember when Joe Mack and I integrated the theater here to see *L'il Abner*. And here an Afro Liberation Society was set up. Suddenly my body remembered we hadn't eaten in a couple of days and Harvey got me a quart of milk and the speaking went on. Then we left U. T. and headed for Black Knoxville.

Gay Street is to Knoxville what Fifth Avenue is to New York. Something special, yes? And it looked the same. But Vine Street where I would sneak to the drugstone to buy *Screen Stories* and watch the men drink wine and play pool—all gone. A wide, clean military-looking highway has taken its place. Austin Homes is cordoned off. It looked like a big prison. The Gem Theatre is now some sort of nightclub and Mulvaney Street is gone. Completely wiped out. Assassinated along with the old people who made it live. I looked over and saw that the lady who used to cry "Hot Fish! Good Hot Fish!" no longer had a Cal Johnson Park to come to and set up her stove in. Grandmother would not say, "Edith White! I think I'll send Gary for a sandwich. You want one?" Mrs. Abrum and her reverend husband from rural Tennessee wouldn't bring us any more goose eggs from across the street. And Leroy wouldn't chase his mother's boyfriend on Saturday night down the back alley anymore. All gone, not even to a major highway but to a cutoff of a cutoff. All the old people who died from lack of adjustment died for a cutoff of a cutoff.

And I remember our finding Grandmother the house on Linden Avenue and constantly reminding her it was every bit as good as if not better than the little ole house. A bigger back yard and no steps to climb. But I knew what Grandmother knew, what we all knew. There was no familiar smell in that house. No coal ashes from the fireplaces. Nowhere that you could touch and say, "Yolande threw her doll against this wall," or "Agnes fell down these steps." No smell or taste of biscuits Grandpapa had eaten with the Alaga syrup he loved so much. No Sunday chicken. No sound of "Lord, you children don't care a thing 'bout me after all I done for you," because Grandmother always had the need to feel mistreated. No spot in the back hall weighted down with lodge books and no corner where the old record player sat playing Billy Eckstine crooning, "What's My Name?" till Grandmother said, "Lord! Any fool know his name!" No breeze on dreamy nights when Mommy would listen over and over again to "I Don't See Me in Your Eyes Anymore." No pain in my knuckles where Grandmother had rapped them because she was determined I would play the piano, and when that absolutely failed, no effort on Linden for us to learn the flowers. No echo of me being the only person in the history of the family to curse Grandmother out and no Grandpapa saying, "Oh, my," which was serious from him, "we can't have this." Linden Avenue was pretty but it had no life.

And I took Grandmother one summer to Lookout Mountain in Chattanooga and she would say I was the only grandchild who would take her riding. And that was the summer I noticed her left leg was shriveling. And she said I didn't have to hold her hand and I said I liked to. And I made ice cream the way Grandpapa used to do almost every Sunday. And I churned butter in the hand churner. And I knew and she knew that there was nothing I could do. "I just want to see you graduate," she said, and I didn't know she meant it. I graduated February 4. She died March 8.

And I went to Knoxville looking for Frankie and the Gem and Carter-Roberts or something and they were all gone. And 400 Mulvaney Street, like a majestic king dethroned, put naked in the streets to beg, stood there just a mere skeleton of itself. The cellar that had been so mysterious was now exposed. The fireplaces stood. And I saw the kitchen light hanging and the peach butter put up on the back porch and I wondered why they were still there. She was dead. And I heard the daily soap operas from the radio we had given her one birthday and saw the string beans cooking in the deep well and thought how odd, since there was no stove, and I wanted to ask how Babbi was doing since I hadn't heard or seen "Brighter Day" in so long but no one would show himself. The roses in the front yard were blooming and it seemed a disgrace. Probably the tomatoes came up that year. She always had fantastic luck with tomatoes. But I was just too tired to walk up the front steps to see. Edith White had died. Mr. Ector had died, I heard. Grandmother had died. The park was not yet gone but the trees looked naked and scared. The wind sang to them but they wouldn't smile. The playground where I had swung. The courts where I played my first game of tennis. The creek where our balls were lost, "Hot Fish! Good Hot Fish!" The hill where the car speeding down almost hit me. Walking barefoot up the hill to the center to hear stories and my feet burning. All gone. Because progress is so necessary. General Electric says, "Our most important product." And I thought Ronald Reagan was cute.

I was sick throughout the funeral. I left Cincinnati driving Mommy, Gary, and Chris to Knoxville. From the moment my father had called my apartment I had been sick because I knew before they told me that she was dead. And she had promised to visit me on the tenth. Chris and I were going to drive down to get her since she didn't feel she could fly. And here it was the eighth. I had a letter from her at my house when I got back reaffirming our plans for her visit. I had a cold. And I ran the heat the entire trip despite the sun coming directly down on us. I couldn't get warm. And we stopped in Kentucky for country ham and I remembered how she used to hoard it from us and I couldn't eat. And I drove on. Gary was supposed to relieve me but she was crying too much. And the car was too hot and it was all so unnecessary. She died because she didn't know where she was and didn't like it. And there was no one there to give a touch or smell or feel and I think I should have been there. And at her funeral they said, "It is well," and I knew she knew it was. And it was so peaceful in Mount Zion Baptist Church that afternoon. And I hope when I die that it can be said of me all is well with my soul.

So they took me up what would have been Vine Street past what would have been Mulvaney and I thought there may be a reason we lack a collective historical memory. And I was taken out to the beautiful homes on Brooks Road where we considered the folks "so swell, don't cha know." And I was exhausted but feeling quite high from being once again in a place where no matter what I belong. And Knoxville belongs to me. I was born there in Old Knoxville General and I am buried there with Louvenia.

And as the time neared for me to speak I had no idea where I would start. I was nervous and afraid because I just wanted to quote Gwen Brooks and say, "This is the urgency—Live!" And they gave me a standing ovation and I wanted to say, "Thank you," but that was hardly sufficient. Mommy's old bridge club, Les Pas Si Betes, gave me beads, and that's the kind of thing that happens in small towns where people aren't afraid to be warm. And I looked out and saw Miss Delaney in her blue furs. And was reminded life continues. And I saw the young brothers and sisters who never even knew me or my family and I saw my grandmother's friends who shouldn't even have been out that late at night. And they had come to say *Welcome Home*. And I thought Tommy, my son, must know about this. He must know we come from somewhere. That we belong.

Nikki Giovanni

Her Cruising Car

A Portrait of Two Small Town Girls

There is nothing . . . that can be said . . . that can frighten me . . . anymore . . . Sadden me . . . perhaps . . . disgust me . . . certainly . . . but not make me afraid . . . It has been said . . . Learn What You Fear . . . Then Make Love To It . . . dance with it . . . put it on your dresser . . . and kiss it good . . . night . . . Say it . . . over and over . . . until in the darkest hour . . . from the deepest sleep . . . you can be awakened . . . to say Yes . . .

She never learned . . . no matter how often people tried . . . that it was hers . . . the fear and the Life . . . the glory of the gamble . . . It was her quarter . . . she had to pick the machine . . . She never understood . . . simply duty . . . knowing only to give all of herself . . . or none . . . There was no balance . . . to her triangle . . . though three points . . . are the strongest mathematical figures . . . no tingle . . . when struck . . . no joy . . . in her song . . . no comfort in her chair . . . war/always war . . . with whom she was . . . who she wanted to be . . . and what they wanted . . . of her . . .

One reason I think . . . I am qualified . . . to run the world . . . though my appointment is not imminent . . . is when I get . . . what I want . . . I am happy . . . It is surprising to me . . . how few people are . . . When they win . . . like Richard Nixon or John McEnroe . . . they are unhappy . . . when they lose . . . impossible . . . One reason I think . . . I have neither ulcers nor nail biting habits . . . is I know to be careful . . . of what I want . . . I just may get it . . .

She was never taught . . . that everything is earned . . . that Newton was right . . . for every action there is an equal and opposite reaction . . . Interest is obtained . . . only on Savings . . . Personality is developed . . . only on risk . . . What is sought . . . must be given . . . We please others . . . by only allowing them access . . . to that part of ourselves which is public . . . If familiarity breeds contempt . . . use breeds hatred . . .

"Her Cruising Car: A Portrait of Two Small Town Girls" from *Those Who Ride the Night Winds*, by Nikki Giovanni. Copyright © 1983 by Nikki Giovanni. Reprinted by permission of William Morrow & Company.

Turtles . . . the kind you find in pet stores . . . the kind Darwin met on Galapaloupus . . . grow to fit the environment . . . There are . . . probably . . . some genetic limits . . . but a small turtle . . . in a small bowl . . . will not outgrow . . . her home . . . Flowers . . . will rise . . . proportionate more to the size . . . of the pot . . . than the relationship of sun . . . to rain . . . Humans seldom deviate . . . If she hadn't been a small town girl . . . with a mind and heart molded absolutely . . . to fit the environment . . . she might have developed . . . a real skill . . . a real desire . . . to discover herself . . . and her gifts . . . As it was . . . as it is . . . she simply got used . . . and used to using . . .

She was never a loner . . . never made . . . to understand that life . . . in fact . . . is a solitary journey . . . that only *one* . . . was going to St. Ives . . . that no one held her bag . . . while the old woman traveled to Skookum . . . that the Little Red Hen and the Engine That Could . . . did it themselves . . . She was . . . let's face it . . . the leader of the pack . . . the top of the heap . . . cheerleader extraordinaire . . . She was very popular . . . sought after by all the right people . . . for her jokes . . . her parties . . . her parents' car . . . The telephone was invented . . . just for her . . . She set up the friendships . . . the going steadys . . . the class officers . . . yearbook staff . . . Who's-In-Who's-Out . . . through the witch wire . . . Nothing could happen . . . without her input . . . She actually thought . . . it was important . . . who went with whom . . . to the junior prom . . . But somebody had to pick up the fallen streamers . . . sweep the now scarred dance floor . . . turn out the lights before they could go home . . .

We were born . . . in the same year . . . our mothers delivered . . . by the same doctor . . . of the same city . . . in the same hospital . . . We were little chubby girls in pink . . . passing cigarettes at the lawn parties . . . My mother made me play . . . with her . . . and hers . . . with me . . . We didn't really mind . . . we shared the same friends . . . hers . . . and the same ideas . . . mine . . . Maybe I became . . . too accustomed . . . to the sameness . . . It was certainly easier . . . for me to shed . . . her friends . . . than she to shed . . . my notions . . . Our mothers belonged . . . to the same clubs . . . Our fathers tracked . . . the same night devils . . . They all had the same expectations . . . from . . . of . . . at . . . or to . . . us . . . I liked to brood . . . she didn't . . . She liked to laugh . . . I didn't . . . I thought I was ugly . . . she didn't . . .

Pots are taught not to call kettles Black . . . people who live in glass houses . . . don't throw stones . . . small town girls learn early . . . or not at all . . . that they can make a life . . . or abort the promise . . . One of us tried . . . one of us didn't have to . . . To each . . . according to her birth . . . from each according to her ability . . . Which is bastardized Marx . . . but legitimate bourgeoisie . . . She was never caring . . . She never learned to see . . . beyond her own windshield . . . that there were other people on the sidewalk . . . other cars . . . on the road . . . She drank . . . too much . . . for too long . . . Maybe in the back of her mind . . . or heart . . . or closet . . . there was a sign saying: There-Is-More-Than-This . . . but she wouldn't pull it out . . . put it up . . . or even acknowledge that some things . . . many things . . . were missing . . . I accept . . . if not embrace . . . the pain . . . the sign on my car says: I Brake For Gnomes . . . the one in my heart reads: Error in Process—Please Send Chocolate . . .

Into the rising sun . . . or setting years . . . accustomed to the scattered friends littering the road . . . she drives on . . . with the confidence of small town drivers who know every wayfall . . . toward the smaller minds . . . around the once hopeful lovers . . . into the illusion of what it is . . . to be a woman . . . through the delusion that trip necessitates . . . never once slowing . . . to ask Did I Hurt You . . . May I Love You . . . Can I/May I Please Give . . . You A Lift . . . With the surety . . . of one who never had to walk . . . she accelerates . . . toward boredom . . . secure in the understanding . . . that everybody knows her . . . and would be unlikely to ticket . . . her cruising car . . . She was my friend . . . more than a sister . . . really . . . a part of the mirror . . . against which I adjust . . . my makeup . . . I have no directions . . . but here is a sign . . . Thomas Wolfe was wrong . . . Maybe it will be read . . .

Robert Michie

Naming the Trees

for Steve Killebrew

On this July Sunday after
the fireworks of national independence,
we walk tangled trails in Tiger country,
assessing the trees.
You are Teacher asking again and again
"What tree is this?"
Often I guess and miss.
When I identify oak, magnolia, even ginkgo,
you spur me into specifics:
pin oak, water oak, sweet bay.
You urge me to look closer
at blooms, colors, the elm shaped like a vase.
You ask if I know the ginkgo is
one of the world's oldest trees.
I think of the Redwood Forest caught
in the music of "This Land Is Your Land."
I think of sandy steps on Long Island Sound
and trimming the arborvitae
at the Madison Beach Hotel
where I earned summer wages toward higher learning.
Now, Memphis green leaves sing through sizzling breeze.
We walk and talk, remember and forget.
I wonder what Great Arms shade the trees
that shade us from necessary sun.
I wonder where the Computer is
that holds all the generations of trees.
I wonder Who the Programmer is—
and if He could walk the Tiger campus,
would He name the trees to us.

Robert Michie

Sunset Rock

(in White County, Tennessee)

At the right time of afternoon
you climb breathing up
away from the rush of civilization,
climb this altar to Time's Marker
that is older than the movement of clocks,
climb this survivor of the whims of weather
and the mean marks of Man.
Your hands become paws in crevices,
stretch out to friend,
sift fine white sand and collected pebbles.
You stand above the sprayed on names
of lovers and clowns and years,
and litter of the careless,
and the scars of rappelers
who practice for the Big Rescue.
You circle the edge and gather perspective
on the old journey which always awes,
then face the valley
whispering dreams into the wind
that will carry them beyond your Spartan home.
You question the geography that grows
valleys, mountains, springs;
wait for sun to shed its skin
like a snake that crawls the clouds;
and watch the sky slow-motion cartwheel
its magic into shadow.
You taste the elixir that brings men
with music and laughter.
You descend into the "leaves of night,"
banking trust in the sun's eternal light.

Lisa Alther

Termites

I hate to be the one to mention it, being her only child and sole support and all. But Mother's getting senile. No doubt about it, to my mind. First signs are last month, just before spring up and decides to break over here at Beulah. I could tell it was coming—spring, I mean—because the termites had started to swarm. Don't know what it is about that front porch, but you wouldn't believe how those termites flock to it. Why, last spring they gnawed right through one of those front columns. I mean to tell you, onct they started in, sawdust was just a'flying ever which way. Well, the porch roof fell in. Mother had me out there that very night hammering board splints on the pillar till we could discuss what to do. She wanted to replace it, but I thought that was real silly myself. Well, we know whose is the hand that feeds her, and I don't need to tell you that those splints are still there this spring. Well lord, you can't keep a termite from wood. So course this year they start in on the splints. I don't know what we'll use to prop up the splints with.

Anyhow, it was a lovely early spring afternoon, irregardless of them all over the porch and lawn. I'd come home early. I work over at the Beulah Basin Hospital for Dr. Bradford Allen. Been with him twenty-five year now, I reckon. Ever since I come back after that month in Knoxville. I'm selling tickets over at the Rebel Theater there at Knoxville when she catches up with me. Having me a big old time. Rented me one of them tourist cabins out on 11-W, with a screened-in front porch. Free entrance to the theater on my time off, plus all the free popcorn I could care for. When she calls up to say that Daddy is passing away and would I please get myself home and what do I want to go live in a city for anyhow. Well, Beulah, Knoxville, they's all pretty much the same to me, so course I go on home. And then's when I start working over at Dr. Allen's.

I was going to say that this particular day I'm speaking of turns out to be an exceptionally busy one down at the office. I brew Dr. Allen's coffee. Then Ida Faye from over at Dr. Malcolm Standish's comes in bringing some of her sea foam divinity and we sit around eating that till we're almost sick. Then I order me some of them red plastic gladiolas out of this discount catalogue to kindly decorate up the office with. Then I type up that week's *Beulah Basin Bulletin*. That was my idea—a sheet ever week for all the patients that come in, announcing births and deaths and whatnot. So's people can know to send flowers and cards and all like that. Dr. Allen says he's got such a degree of good faith in me that he'll just leave the en-tire thing to my doing.

Who prisses in then but the little Renfro girl (the one marrying the Sturgiss boy next month) demanding can she see Dr. Allen. Course I leave the door open a crack so's he can call me if he wants. I happen to be working in a file cabinet by the door, so I overhear him talking to her on the subject of the marriage bed, and her acting like it's all news to her. Like everybody in town didn't know about her. If you ask me, instruction probably should've been passed out in the opposite direction. I used to wonder didn't Mrs. Allen have cause to fret over him and me being together all day, till I come to see that's the least of her worries with him. It's no normal man can look at naked women all day and not never pay no mind to his secretary. Anyway, I'm working so hard I don't hear Dr. Allen get up. He like to knocks me over with the door when he opens it. He says, "Felicity, I don't have anything further for you today, so why don't you just go on home?" So I thank him and pick up my hat and gloves.

When I get home, I close my eyes and run past the swarm fast as I can with my eyes closed. Inside Mother has the shades down like always. Keeps it cool, she says. I don't know about that, but I do know that's what kills her plants, and not me like she claims. Well, it's been so bright out that I don't see a thing, except the plants turning yellow, but I'm sure she's setting around somewheres talking to herself in the dark. So I call for her, but she doesn't answer. The house just kindly creaks and echoes. So I figure she must be out to tea somewheres. I decide wouldn't anything be nicer than to sip a little something up in my room till she gets home. Nothing more pleasant that I can see than setting up there sipping and looking through the *National Enquirer*. "My Husband Doesn't Know I'm Really a Man," that kind of thing. So I go out the kitchen door and around to the cellar where Mother's been saving this here champagne for long as I can remember. Used to say all the time how it was for my wedding. Well, that's all her fault and not mine anyhow. I had a boy one time was real sweet on me. We used to sit in the parlor after Mother got Daddy quiet for the night. I'd let him kiss on me, and I'd generally let him feel me some. But Mother found out all his daddy did was run Mr. Claiborne's farm up at Big Lick, and that was the end of that. I said at least his daddy worked, unlike some I could name. And she said like always, "Hush, child. Your daddy comes from family." Like the rest of us had been hatched in incubators or something.

Law, I remember the girl that boy finally married. Ugly little tow-headed thing from somewheres up North. New Jersey or somewhere like that, I reckon. Mrs. Claiborne had a tea for her when they first come to Beulah, and she turned out to be real nice. I told her so. I says, "Why honey, you're a real nice little thing. But why do you reckon Ned, Jr., had to go all the way up there to find him a wife?" I didn't bear him no grudge on the subject. Next time I seen him on the street I says, "Lord, Ned, she's not real attractive, but she's surely a charming little thing. Just charming. Don't even sound too much like a yankee." And he seemed real appreciative that I'd forgave him like that, and he just grinned at me like a panting dog. I always was one that gave credit where it was due and didn't nurture no spite.

Well anyway, I figure they's no sense letting all that champagne go to waste. I have long since made my decision not to marry. I don't aim to spend my life waiting on some man, like Mother did. So I take a bottle of it ever now and then when she's not around. Just dirty, moldy old bottles anyhow. Then I toss the empties down the laundry chute up in my room. Works out real well. Ends up over in some corner of the cellar nobody's seen in years. Or is likely to see in that many more years.

Poor Daddy. I remember one night after I'd come home from Knoxville. It was shortly before he went to his reward. His room was right smack under mine. He'd just stuck his hand into the chute with one of his empties when one of mine crashed into it from up above. He must'ev thought the hand of God had dashed it from him. (Course his stuff was a good deal stronger than mine. I just sip a little something to refresh myself after a hard day.) Anyhow, I hear him go stumbling cross his room just hollering for Mother: "Pristine honey, my time has arrived! I have received the summons to judgment for my transgressions!" Then there's this crash, and I don't hear anything further from him. The only summons he ever got was all them times for drunk driving. Turns out he just tripped over his own feet and decided he'd as soon lie on the floor a while as get up.

Like I was saying, this particular afternoon I just get around to the cellar door when I hear Mother's voice out back by the cemetery. She like to haunts that place, cleaning up the graves and growing ground covers and all like that. And she sets up dis-plays with Greatuncle Travis' medals and swords. Sometimes she hangs up what's left of his uniform, so's it looks more like a scarecrow than anything else. Though course when I told her that, she took on like when I slap her cross the face. And on pretty days she generally raises his raggy regimental flag. She says he sacrificed his life for the South and deserves this much from his own. Personally I find it real curious that she considers succumbing to measles at Lookout Mountain a holy act.

She normally asks me to help—like I don't have enough to do as it is. Besides which, I don't care none about those folks. I didn't even know them.

This particular afternoon I can't imagine who she's talking to out there. I wonder is she sure enough gone batty this time? So I head on back out there. I see her standing there shaking her pruning shears in the air. She has her red baseball cap pulled real low so her frizzy hair is sticking out straight on all sides. And she keeps stamping her plaid tennis shoes like stepping on termites. I can tell she's in a rage. I get near enough so's I can see two little boys almost hid behind Greatuncle Travis' tombstone. The bigger boy is holding one of the swords in one hand and the other little boy in the other hand. Their eyes and mouths are open about equal. Turn out to be those little boys who've just moved in down the street. Their daddy is down from New York with that hose mill that's going up on all sides of our house. Law, they offered Mother the moon for that house. Said up at New York they tear down tenements like ours quick as they can, factory or no factory. That's what they said—tenements. After that Mother just absolutely refused to even talk to them. Carpetbaggers, she calls them. So I reckon they're just gonna let her see how she likes living smack in the middle of the worker's recreation area. Just to the left of the baseball diamond, so I'm told.

Mother's voice is grating like somebody after an operation on their voice box: " . . . and don't you all think you can come in here trampling and pillaging our very graves. We're not beaten down here. We're just resting." She shakes those shears like a tomahawk, and the little boy waves Greatuncle Travis' sword at her like a lion tamer's chair. Then she just plops down on her granddaddy's marker and starts bawling to beat the band. The little boys drop the sword and shoot through the hedge and down the street. I lead her towards the house and then, to beat all, she turns and stares me up and down like I'm some freak in a sideshow. And I have to ask myself if some of them termites haven't started in on her brain. Because when you start pitching fits for no reason at all, that pretty well shows you're getting screwy. So that's why I'm being forced to consider putting her in the county home. Though I just hate the idea, you understand.

Jean Guerrero Gore

Drowning at Radnor Lake

Up through the dark, deep water come
Ice-bent edges of headlights
Shining the souls of the dead
To the surface of tranquil
Green, thin-layered life,
Supporter of duck flocks,
Fish and snakes.

Casting shadows on skeletal trees,
The bright beams rise and curl,
Hover among the fingering twigs,
Pace their change into color,
Gold and wing, bill and song,
Become birds of flight, alive
To cycles, to seasons, to the sanction
Radnor gives the tenants
Of its still, watery world.

Richard Jackson

Greenwood

What I wanted to say to her
was the prayer the deer turn into
as they step deeper towards those woods
grazing on darkness, or the silence that is
the thistle light of their eyes staring back
for whatever we say means something more.
In whatever language this was before
it was the snap of greenwood on coals
there is a work I have never spoken
that calls out to the hurt it belongs to
the way a flock of swallows, at dusk,
makes visible a turn of wind
and the night unhinges on that simple gesture.
Or her touch, say, across a table,
a woman so beautiful the deer abandon
whatever words I have invented for them
and turn to graze in a meadow or marsh
for herbs, salt grass, greenwood,
sometimes springing suddenly, whistling,
as they will, in a language of fear or surprise.

"Greenwood," by Richard Jackson appeared in *Georgia Review*, Vol. 37, no. 1, Spring 1983 and in *Part of the Story*, by Richard Jackson. Copyright © 1983 by Richard Jackson. Reprinted by permission of Grove Press.

Someone Is Always Saying Something

Even if you were here, you wouldn't spend
the last few minutes as I have peering
into the flower of the delicate pitcher plant
that has bloomed in the shadow of a cannon.
Just west of here, someone would tell you,
the Confederate lines faltered, and no one
turned back. Time was the stone someone kicked up
under his feet. But this pitcher plant—I have
been watching how, filled with water, it curls,
dissolving a spider. He must have
entered the space between two dark moments
where we peer into the history that always fails.
Sometimes we walk so deeply into that past
someone begins to remember us. The wind doesn't have
to come from anyplace. There's nothing
the wind wants to be. That's when someone tells us
that desire is the backwards journey into ourselves.
I can't tell. But I know that entering that past
I enter you again, hearing, in the abandoned air,
someone calling my name, as if I were
leaving a place I never lived, as if the light
were rescuing a little truth from the shadows.

"Someone Is Always Saying Something," by Richard Jackson appeared in *The Sonora Review*, no. 5, Fall 1983. Copyright © 1983 by Richard Jackson. Reprinted by permission of the publisher.

Melissa Cannon

The Dark of Eyes
for Jim Clark

You follow the dark of eyes
like a tunnel
travelling back
through the past of our bones

you hear shadows
signalling in old voices

barn owl striking night air
coyote calling to stars

hammer wind
drops a fist

at the end is a blank
the veins numb
as shell-shocked veterans

This dark is not animal

whose fears are red
the leg left at the trap
hawk wings nailed to barn doors

the bright pains of dying

our eyes darken with other losses

"The Dark of Eyes," by Melissa Cannon appeared in *The Greensboro Review*, Spring 1978 (Number 24). Reprinted by permission of *The Greensboro Review*.

the sight of ourselves
in bloody eyes
bullets
nails in palms

the erased animals
"here for our use"

each blinked out
like an only fire

*bison and crane
whale indian*

The knowledge of these tribes
is gone from the gene
forever

you cannot ask them *why*
this dark of eye

this black breath
spreading like flag shadow
over cave eye

gutted can staring up
out of a gold moon's dusty
cup

Jeanette Blair

Child Abuse

The child is dead, the one whose mother's
boyfriend squeezed her head until
it cracked, because she told a lie.

Children make convenient truths,
their motives, purest, self-defense.
We lie along subtler themes.

The child's face, barbed with pain, blurs,
as they rush her to sterile quiet, but
the question remains and must be answered.

I'm anxious to leave this news, to find
my own child sleeping loudly upstairs.
Restless, she mumbles out her dreams.

Do I hear only nightmares? She's a tangle
of golden arms and gilded hair,
a Byzantine reposing on Disney sheets.

She survives my dogmatic insistence of lamb
before peach, my shrill impatience wrapped
like rags around her innocence.

Wrung from the blood of my heart, she rests
now, still as the little girl whose mother's
boyfriend sits in jail, waiting.

My daughter's porcelain breathing hums
domestically around the air.
I stroke her forehead, an anxious touch,

Distressed that behind the web of small
blood in her lids, I might have left
livid welts of love, that somewhere

in the hems of my soul, a brown recluse hides.

Background

If we were Japanese, I would make you
a ceremony; in a room as bare
as infants' eyes, I would place two pillows,
silver on black. I would slide the doors
aside and let a brook's sibilance
tiptoe into our silence. All the rocks
in the garden are arranged. Beside
me is a candle, round with light, glowing
off my silken gown. I read a love
poem, my best, the only copy; the words
brush your eyes like small birds flying into
the past. The poem surrounds the quiet, then an
edge to the flame and onto a tray lacquered
hard as rocks. The paper surrenders to fire,
twists briefly, chars. We watch until
the ash completes. I have honored you,
and myself. My ancestors were English,
except for one dusky Cherokee.
Faint as smoke in the family
memory, she knew about gifts;
if I were she, I'd sew moccasins,
warm against the ground's growing rigid,
but better than warm, a poem in beadwork, some
gentle thought dreamed into pattern
with needles. By firelight in a drafty cabin
you would hold them, wondering at the colored
chips of love. The scraps are thrown
in the fire. Nothing is wasted. The wind

Jeanette Blair

howls like wolves, sounding a new thought
for moccasins. But the Cherokee
floats around me in cells. My eyes
are grey as gunsmoke. And when I start to sew,
I stick myself and bleed. I could invite
you into my parlour where crochet doilies hang
in abandon and violets are painted
on all the lamps and the settee is velvet, and red.
We English drink tea with milk. Our porcelain
cups click as we chat, the candles glow
against the alabaster. I offer you
a sweet from a silver cake tray, draw
a hush like curtains around us, unveil a poem
copied on scented paper, read it softly,
careful of inflection, catch the edge
to the flame, rapt at its burning, awed
at the smudgings it wriggles on the silver.
It is the only copy of the poem,
but I have memorized it. It writes itself
repeatedly just behind my eyelids.
We are heavy as oak, which is perhaps
a strength. The rain slides down the windows on the
other side of the curtains, and the sky
is the color of tea and eyes. Raindrops burst
on the roof; I try to forget that poem.

James Summerville

Paper Fires

Twice a week between October and May, a volunteer from the Community Chest of Nashville drove up the driveway to the back door of the house and left a stack of newspapers. In the coldest weeks of January, she piled the trunk full, and unloading it took several trips up and down the crumbling steps.

A number of times that first autumn, she knocked at the sprung door. When there was no answer, she pushed the papers next to the siding, away from rain or snow. On top of the pile she set a chunk of concrete that she found among the weeds in the yard so that the wind would not blow the papers away.

The neighborhood meat and produce market, when it was sold and changed over to an A & P, stopped delivering to the house, until the manager received a call from the attorney who managed the Albrecht estate. After that, the same order was brought, also to the back door, every Monday morning, when customer traffic in the store was slowest. A generation of sackboys, thinking about inaccessible thighs they had glimpsed in the housewares aisle, trundled the loads onto the listing porch while the radio rattled in the dash of the truck.

One summer the city sent a notice that cited penalties in the code against keeping unkempt property and lots. The rusted mailbox overflowed with circulars and boxholders from the local Congressman, but since the city's letter was sent first class, the postman slipped it between the peeling door and the jamb.

After dark, Leisl Albrecht, leaning on her cane, trudged through the hallway. The passage was bare except for a rock that someone had thrown through a sidelight, the glistening trail of glass, and the dust that her slippers raised. The door opened on the night air; the envelope clattered to the floor. Bending, she picked it up and was gone again, tugging shut the bolt behind her.

Some weeks after the order to clean up the property came, a car with official plates turned into the drive, the frothy heads of the Queen Anne's Lace thumping against its grill. For several minutes it sat with the motor running. Then it backed slowly out into the traffic, which was beginning to swell with the rush hour. No more notices came, and in the third week of October, when the first cold blew across Nashville, the old woman used the original notice to kindle her paper fire.

Sometimes the wind, ringing and tapping the windows in their frames, roused her in her sleep. Then she would dream, until the chill brought her fully awake, that the sound was Father's boots on the stairway to the rooms where they had lived when they first came to the city.

Every year until the war began, a new pair arrived from Father's cobbler in the town not far from the Ruhr where Leisl had been born. The firm heels, fixed by fine iron nails, shook the steps as Papa climbed, crossed the landing, and flung open the door.

His shadow, cast by the lamp in the hallway, covered Leisl. In an undertow not to be resisted, he gathered her up from among the alphabet blocks. Her face was pressed against his starched collar, and she heard his voice through the bones of her head.

"My little girl, she has been good?"

"Yes, Papa."

"Maman will not tell me that she has disobeyed?"

"No, Papa."

"She has learned the letters that I gave to her?"

"Of course, Papa."

When she grew too tall to be lifted into his arms, she learned to curtsy. In time, he offered his cheek for her to kiss, with its day's growth of sharp whiskers. His questions scarcely changed as the years passed, and her answers remained as unvarying as a nun's.

There had been no doctor in the immigrant community until they arrived in 1910. Father was honored with a banquet that the millwrights gave in their hall.

In their third year in Nashville, his success purchased Maman a piano. One day at lunchtime he brought home some sheets of music bundled tightly in a roll. Sweeping his hand above the keyboard, he gathered up the scores by Wagner and Liszt and set out the new pieces. On the cover of one of them, a young man and woman rowed on a moon-streaked lake. The tinny notes, when he played them on the ivory, hung light and cool in the midday air.

For Leisl, Maman was able to buy mail-order dresses from New York. The childhood frocks brought across the ocean she packed away in a leather-strapped trunk. The bright new things she lay in the deep, scented drawers of the dresser.

One Sunday as they walked toward the buggy after church, the wife of Hoefner, the mercantilist, stopped Maman and asked her her reasons for never appearing in their store. "Fine good from home we have," Frau Hoefner said, "and not dear."

Maman had replied politely, acknowledging old ties. But alone later with her daughter, she said that it was strictly necessary for Leisl to present herself as other little girls did. When the first day of school was over, she asked about the dresses and blouses and shoes that Leisl's classmates wore and only then about the beginning lesson in sums. Under the green lamp they turned through the catalog from New York. "Like this?" Maman asked. "Were they dressed as is this little girl?"

A dozen years later—after they moved to the never-finished house on the edge of town, after the dinner party that was never held—all Leisl's clothes that Maman had bought by mail were taken from the dresser and thrust deep into the old trunk stored in the attic. Its straps were cinched tightly shut.

Parts of the roof, when it began to give way, lay open to the air for years, and in winter the frost drew the heat upward from Leisl Albrecht's paper fires. Once a starling fluttered through one of the gaps in a mindless search for food and, unable to find its way out again, screeched itself to exhaustion and died. The bones and the dust moiling around them lay next to the rusting trunk.

The house was the great boon from Father's practice. In the spring of 1914 he bought the land in Belmont Heights and commissioned the builders to begin.

To move from the old community was daring. But Nashville's future, Papa declared to Leisl and Maman, lay along the streetcar lines that went past the towers of the Vanderbilt, nearly to the corn that grew on the old battlefields of the Civil War.

"You will like the house, little one, I am sure of it," Papa said to Leisl as the buggy raised the hot dust from the road and twirled it behind them.

From beneath the canopy's quivering fringe, she stared at the tower of the university's main building. It came into view each time there was a space among the maples that were covered with amber dust.

The unfinished house in the rude neighborhood was quite acceptable to Leisl once she discovered that she would be able to see the tower's parapets from the window of her room.

Young women not much older than she matriculated at the university. Some of them, it was said, even went abroad unchaperoned. She glimpsed one of them, not long after they moved to the new house that summer. "Coeds," they were called. She wondered how it would be to wear her hair according to the coed fashion.

In the morning Leisl sat at her dressing table, pulling a brush through its heat-tangled length and pausing now and then to let her hands rest in her lap.

At every quarter hour the couple who lived in the cupola of the clock on the mantel took a turn along their unvarying path. She looked up to watch them until they disappeared through the tiny wooden doors. Then the single tone faded, the hammers and wheels sank into silence, and the cicada was the only sound in the vast room.

It made her giddy to contemplate the patterns and contrivances that were deliberately made to seem matters of choice. Where was caprice in the marriages that, at the moment of the figurines' stroll, sank into speechlessness on the other side of town? And the errors posted by countless clerks in the last hurried transactions of the day that would multiply into ruin? And where was the play of life in the artifice and will of others, by which she had been raised? How was she different from the objects in the house?

Her father's purposes in building their new home were not corrupt, she knew. Through the house, life was revealed to have been not turns taken blindly but an orderly progress, begun with a passage to America.

Nonetheless, when she could, she would divest herself of all its empty, leaden weight. She was willing to have nothing if she could have pure, clear discernment about life. She longed for perfect clarity and understanding, devoid of things and undiluted by certainties. Such a house hid all private disquiet; such safety stopped life.

As she rose from the dressing table and walked to the window to see the tower of the Vanderbilt in the falling sun, the hammering on the west lawn ceased. Leisl watched as the Negroes dropped their tools into a cloth satchel and flung it onto the worm-gnawed buckboard. Roused from sleep, the mule flinched and shimmied as the men climbed into the seat. The animal turned a wide, lazy circle and sauntered off, the three of them bobbing on the spavined springs.

Maman postponed the paying of calls while their new neighbors in the settlement were away at Monteagle or Beersheba Springs for the hottest days of summer. One evening in September, at dinner, she mentioned her felt obligations. Papa gazed at the ceiling high above.

"For an evening," he said, "we will invite them all. It will not be necessary, absolute, that everything be finished first."

It required many tasks, nonetheless, to ready the house for the guests. Maman and Leisl dipped their table linens in the foul-smelling starch and shaped them with their hands. They raised the new floor to a high gloss. The face of the clock was hidden behind the sheen they put on its convex face. The air of the house smelled of the rosewood polish that Leisl applied to the banister of the stairs.

Maman wrote the invitations by hand and from house to house in the neighborhood they halted the buggy, on an afternoon when thunderheads piled high on the horizon. The reins grew slick in Leisl's palms.

At each gate Maman took an envelope and, lifting her hem out of the burning dust of the road, strode to the door.

A house servant curtsied and took the proffered envelope, studying the queerly formed letters. Over the sound of the insects that dipped against the blooming vines, Maman made her practiced speech. Then smiling at the blank face, she turned to the steps, her mesh purse swinging from her wrist. In the cool, dim interior the servant passed and shut the door against the heat.

Papa helped with preparations on the day of the dinner. While Leisl and Maman broke open the cabbages and sliced the potatoes for dumplings, he pounded the schnitzel into tenderness with the blunt face of the cleaver.

It was not yet four o'clock when he declared that it was time for the table to be set. Carrying the felt-lined box, Maman paused at each place around the table while Leisl took out spoons, forks, cutlery. Then they stood the napkins stiff as sentries and, opposite each, set a sparkling goblet.

Following Maman as she set the plates, Leisl aligned each glass so that from the head of the table the points of light that sparkled from them inscribed a rigid stellar line.

It was, of course, a trick. The long table required the slightest asymmetry from glass to glass if to Papa's view they were to appear perfectly ordered.

Without glancing to the side, Leisl went and stood at his place. Dropping her face and shutting her eyes, she let go the knowledge that the order before her was an illusion; and when she opened them again, she saw the table as Papa would.

When in the evening would it come, his vision for her, the first glimmer of his intent to send her to the university? Amid the tableaux in front of her, she placed herself as Papa would see her. She imagined the professor of chemistry as, halfway to his mustache, he halted his napkin and reflected on the remark Leisl had just made. And there was the Latinist who would select a dried fruit that Leisl proffered and chew it gravely while pondering her respectful query. For the first time Papa would see her in the setting where she belonged. He would smile thinly and nod slightly to himself at the next confirming bestowal of the new world, that his daughter should become a "coed."

She stood over the last simmering kettle while her parents went upstairs to prepare for the company. In her turn, in the last afternoon light from the window, she dried her hair. The maples, mountainous and stolid in the motionless air, waited for a breeze to sift the light of the shortening days through them. Then at her mirror she drew the tiny compact from the drawer where she had concealed it since a secret purchase.

When she came down to the parlor, Papa was turning the pages of the new *Collier's*, and Maman had taken up her needlepoint. For the cool of the evening, she had opened the curtains.

Between the house and the city a mile away, the haze was deepening. In the mist the fireflies made their gentle waves in the slate-gray air. Through the trees the streetlights in town flickered. The spires of the churches that sunlight seemed to diffuse into the hot metallic sky receded into their simplest lines and blocks and angles. Above the lavender clouds in the west the first star rose, faint and red.

Soon, at any moment the cooling gravel in the road would fly from beneath the shunting hooves, and the horses, whinnying in their traces and shaking sweat from themselves, would draw up before the gate. A petticoat would faintly rasp on the boards of the porch and then would come the *rap, rap, rap* of the knuckles from which the traces of chalk had been scrubbed or the scent of money washed over by cologne.

As daylight seeped out of the foyer, the hands of the clock emerged to view. The moon rising over the plateau far to the east played on the heights of the new house. It trespassed against the tower that vaulted over the university. Between the two, the woods, the old inviolable wilderness, deepened into darkness.

A rain crow called out of that dark place, and the clock struck eight notes. On her stool by the cupboard, Leisl marked time with heel and toe as on the table the cooling broth began to leaven.

Papa had sheared slices from the cheese with a paring knife. For a long time she watched the faintly darkening edge, humming a song that Papa favored them with one noon at the piano. Then she reached across to the silver tray and pinched a morsel from the tepid yellow mound. Slowly she bit into it, still bright on its nether side. Listening for the hooves, she chewed quietly. She was eating a third crumb when the pure crystal tone of the half hour rang through the house. The taste turned sharp and sour on her tongue.

She raised her eyes slowly over the table, where all things that they had arrayed there had been rising toward some new composition. After the dinner party, all these objects, and the house, were to be some memory of the past, made acceptable through her future in the shadow of the tower that rose above the cornfields.

In the silence that followed the chime, each one began to reclaim its relentless true proportion. From the bosom of the creamer a rivulet of water rolled and spread on the starched tablecloth.

No dreamed-of thought, no thought-of thought had prepared her for such refusal as this. A cup with gilt rim answered her stare.

No one? she thought. *No one at all?*

That meant, of course, that the dreamers would talk without her on the cobblestone walks amid the magnolias. Behind garret windows they would compose their books, written against time. If any of it was of use in clearing new spaces to the west, she was not likely now to learn. All that was possible to foresee was that the hammer blows of the hammers wielded by the laborers would carry the city on beyond them. As the crickets rose in the thistles, the mule was even now carrying the workmen on their worm-gnawed buggy down into the bottoms in the old town. The buggy would stand until after midnight, the mule sleeping a blind, dumb sleep as the music blared from a dim dance parlor.

Father stood in the doorway of the dining room. He had set his heavy jaw, and his face was the color of one who had walked a long distance on a cold day.

For the first time since they had come to America, he spoke the language that Maman had screamed when the girl was born. She could wash her face, he said, and put on her clothes. Then she might clear the table.

At the gate at daylight Papa met the workmen. There would be no need after all to hang the gutters on the eaves, he told them, and he paid them for the work they had done through the day before on the gazebo. Before the end of September, the relentless grass sprung up in the unfinished well of it.

The autumn was unusually wet, and the water pouring from the roof of the house faintly streaked the new wood and carved small pits at each corner. The multicolored sand from the shingles of the roof collected there. That winter the puddles froze and began to push against the new foundation.

Ten years passed before the first tiny cracks showed in the piers that supported the roofline. By that time a score of new houses was being raised along the road from the city, which passed the Vanderbilt and traveled toward the south. A councilman lived on the crowded length, nearest the cottages of machinists and clerks. A vice-president of the Louisville and Nashville line built on the lot next door.

The same year that the crest of the chimney toppled among the weeds in the side yard, the chancellor of the university moved into the West End. When he read the news in the social column of the *Banner*, Father laughed out loud, behind the door that was shut against the benches of his waiting room. He kept his office in the old precinct, too, where most of their countrymen had once lived before their names were changed or lost as the children of their children moved out into the town. In time he sold the horses and purchased a sedan, which he drove two miles each day, to town and home again. They ceased to attend church, reading aloud to each other from the Bible on Sunday morning instead.

The interior of the house remained comfortable as the thorns overtook the porch steps. But in 1938 it became necessary to close the second floor as sections of plaster began to sag.

Father died in his bed on the eve of the Second World War. The letter signed by their neighbors asking him to attend to his property for the good of the community marked his place in the poems of Heinrich Heine, which lay on the bedside table. The estate would be adequate, the lawyer implied, and he promised to see to whatever they needed.

Maman grew old, busying herself in steaming labels from empty jars or nodding in her chair. The round face that Father had once thought beautiful was no more, as gaps appeared among her teeth. Still, she could whistle the notes that her own mother had used to greet the peddlers, which she had not heard for half a century. Sometimes she would forget what year it was.

One day Leisl hurried into the room where she heard her mother quietly murmuring. Pointing to the empty rocker by the draughty window, the old woman introduced her to the sister who had died when both were children. In her last illness she talked about the son that she had wanted to bear.

The goods that Leisl cared to save she pushed and pulled, one at a time, into the middle room. Fall, the first after her mother's death, was coming in earnest. The frost had already wrinkled the fluted flowers of the creeper vine. The horn blasts of the train that left the city at dawn carried from the depot in town through the molting trees. Cold weather had come upon the city when the relief volunteer called for the first time with the newspapers.

They might have brought Leisl Albrecht the news, but she did not read them before she twisted them into logs and kindled them with loose pages and boxholders.

In the winter the charity women piled the papers as high as the hem of her coat. On a visit one February, when ice crunched under her tires in the driveway, she came twice with a new load to find the rock on top of the pile had not been moved. A red and yellow comic page was flattened over it by the wind.

Without unloading the car, she drove to the gas station in the next block and telephoned the attorney. By the time he arrived, it was the nameless hour of late afternoon. The sun made bright red flecks in the dirty snow along the shoulders of the boulevard. He told the dispatcher at the general hospital that there would be no need for the lights or the siren.

The ambulance nonetheless came roaring down the street, twisting in and out of the traffic, and bounced, blaring and flashing, up the rutted driveway. The two mustached attendants rolled the stretcher to the front door and locked the wheels.

On the return trip toward the ambulance they stepped carefully as the boards sagged under their feet and the awful weight under the sheet swung between them.

Wyatt Prunty

The Distance into Place

Dolls in gallery along her walls,
she'd broken one so, bending down,
opened a sewing box then knelt,
the needle's eye narrowing her gaze
to fractions in a room where clothes
and broken doll cluttered the floor.

Already forty-three and gray,
She focused on a wilderness
of close particulars, a bird
imagining a cage, her eyes
turned like an animal's caught by
a car's headlights, reflecting blind
and lost inside the light they saw.
Later, the family away at church,
she used a butcher knife to carve
initials in the dining room table.

On Sundays, we drove to Memphis
where each visit I waited in the car,
studying the windows I was told
were hers, my talented aunt,
playing the piano as soon as she
could stand, homely, proud, and silent.
No photograph could get a smile.
The term I heard was that she was
afflicted. My parents spoke in fragments

"The Distance into Place" from *What Women Know, What Men Believe*, by Wyatt Prunty. Copyright © 1986 by Wyatt Prunty. Reprinted by permission of Johns Hopkins University Press.

as riding home I strained to catch
a phrase that held the syntax to her name.
Those trips, made thirty years ago,
we stepped out of our upright cars,
mother and grandmother in hats and gloves,
my father smoking, fedora cocked
ironically but eyes measuring
the distance out ahead as though
he walked into some fixed perspective.

Cold nights the house contracts
to the tightness of its carpenter's
precise intent, leveled and squared
again as if to match his mind.
A car's headlights scroll across the wall
as a figure deepens where curtains bell.
It bends and waves, ushering me
beyond the place it disappears
dark into dark and soft, a thing
coagulate as guilt in memory,
as my aunt, childishly petulant yet old
and fluttering like an antique doll,
a miniature of iced velocities.

Broad day, I kneel to gather scrub
grown up along the barbed-wire fence
that frames our farm. The fields
are frozen hard, resistant as
the locust posts punctuating each fence.
The stream is skimmed with ice and makes
a fixed division of the land.
But night, when I wake to a figure
idling across my wall, dissolving
dark, the surface of that stream
cuts to a slower, colder path.

One name becomes the secret to another,
blue into gray, like rain, and gray
to deeper blue, till all the down-rush
we anticipate, the waking sleep of things,
turns to a clarity like pain.
I see my aunt, alone and still,

Wyatt Prunty

her room cluttered with the objects of
intentions neither she nor her doctors knew
because mutation made its own way
through her life, carving its initials
as the code that waits inside a seed,
its rope-like strands curling into thought,
and that thought, in turn, a distance we contrive.

Steve Stern

Shimmele Fly-By-Night

Everyone ran away from my father. My mama ran away from him into the scrawny arms of Mr. Blen the hatter, who was so frightened of my father that he fled the Pinch with my mama at his coattails. My sister Fagie ran away from him to the sanctuary of the Green Owl Cafe, managed by her fiancé, the bootlegger Nutty Iskowitz. The neighborhood kids ran away from him, afraid of his fiery beard, its edges ragged from the tufts he pulled out of it in his wrath. They were scared of his voice and his bloodstained apron, his colossal hands, the shredded left thumb on which he tests the sharpness of his knives, his furious eyes in the shadow of the black homburg he never took off.

The kids along North Main Street ran away from him to their mothers, who told them, "Read your lessons, eat your whitefish, don't wet the bed, or Red Dubrovner will get you."

They ran away from me too, though you couldn't exactly call it running. But they walked away. They turned their backs and whispered whenever they saw me, like I might be my father's spy. This I was used to since I was little. Then—running from behind my sister's skirts as we crossed through the Market Square Park—I used to chase after them. But eventually I got the idea that they weren't playing games with me, that for them the son of my father was something to beware of. So I got used to being lonely, and sometimes I thought that it wasn't the butcher but me that they feared. Then I was able to enjoy their silent treatment a little. What bothered me was when they broke their silence and dared each other to make cracks about my family. What bothered me was when some wise guy got the nerve up to ask: "Hey Shimmie, why don't you run away?"

It was Papa's theory that our neighborhood was haunted. He believed that the gamblers and fancy women, the river rats and drunken Indians who used to live here were now dybbuks. They were taking possession of the Jewish shopkeepers and their children one by one.

"It's the truth, cholileh!" he would declare in his borsht-thick accent, kissing his mezuzah and spitting against the evil eye. And if someone who didn't know about his rotten disposition should say otherwise, suggesting that the Pinch wasn't so bad—if they said that it wasn't Russia after all, my father would insist it was worse.

"Some golden land!" he would groan, slapping his barrel chest. Then he would count on his fingers the ways that we were persecuted: by the infernal heat and the crooked politicians, the high water at Pesach, the diseases that followed the floods, the yokels in their white sheets that they bought wholesale at Zimmerman's Emporium . . .

It was the peculiar quality of my father's voice that it could grumble and bark and whine all at once. And coming as it did out of his flame-red beard, it was as good as if delivered from a burning bush. He was at his best when he was laying into his own kind.

"This North Main Street, I'm telling you, it's a regular circus parade . . . and bingo bango bongo," hopping from one foot to the other, pounding the cash register keys, "here comes the Jews! They are shaving off their beards and peddling corsets on Shabbos, they are stuffing themselves with chazzerai. They are running away to join the vaudeville. They are forgetting their mameloshen, which ends up where? In the mouths of the schwartzes is where. The schwartzes have stolen our tongue!"

It was true that the local colored porters and maids seemed to have an especially good ear for Yiddish. There was even a street musician who sang "Oif'n Pripechuk" to his own accompaniment on washboard and jug.

"Pretty soon they pick up all the Jewishness that the Jews are throwing away. Then nu? what will the Jews have left? Cold cuts and dry goods is what."

But as bad as the Pinch was, the South outside its boundaries (according to my father) was even worse. The river was awash with dead men and snakes. Beyond our neighborhood the poor people married their own mothers and had two-headed children. For sport they wrestled pigs and cut the private parts off of Negroes, which they framed and hung up in the barber shops. The South beyond the Pinch was gehinnom, it was sitra achra, the other side; and it was seeping into Jewish homes the way the creepers poked through the tenement walls.

I had no reason not to believe my father. When had I ever been further from home than the Market Square School? After school I went for my Hebrew lesson to Mr. Notowitz the melammed in his rooms across from Blockman's junkyard. An ancient mildewed gentleman with breath like a toilet, he would prod me with his walking stick through my alefbais;

this until—convinced of my ineptitude—he sat down at the table and fell asleep. From Mr. Notowitz I went straight home to work in the shop. On Saturdays my father took me with him to shul, on Sundays to the Auction Street stockyard. During the rare unsupervised moments when I was out of his sight, I didn't know what to do with myself. Then, like my miserable mama, I tended to sit in an upstairs window and look out onto the tumel of North Main Street.

If he hadn't been the only ordained ritual slaughterer in the Pinch, my father with his temper would have chased away what business he had. But as it was the women had to come to Dubrovner's for their kosher meats. They came to him by the dozens on Shabbos eve, carrying live chickens from the market by the trussed up feet. As they approached the shop, the cackling would swell to an unholy pitch, reminding my father of one of his pet complaints.

"Gevalt, the noise!" he would cry, clapping his hands over his ears. He was forever at odds with the pandemonium of the streets: with the bell from the Chickasaw Ironworks, the calliopes from the excursion boats on the river, the shouts of the newsboys, the songs of the cantor at the Anshei Sphard shul—though none of them gave his own bellowing any serious competition.

In any event, when the ladies had gathered in the shop with their chickens, my father would roll his sleeves above his ham-sized forearms. He would take up his blade and, muttering a benediction that sounded more like a curse, shut the birds up for good and all. Then he would call me: "Shimmele Goylem, pipsqueak, shlemiel!"

It was my job to hang up the chickens in the stinking rear of the shop. I hung them upside-down on a row of hooks so they could finish twitching and leaking blood onto the sawdusted floor. The women would look on with a kind of reverence, like the chickens had been justly punished for daring to squawk in the face of Red Dubrovner.

Then they took their seats in a half-circle of folding chairs near the open back door. In faded kerchiefs and dowdy dresses ringed in sweat under the arms, they sat with their knees apart, waiting for me to drop a dead bird into their laps. After that they proceeded to flick the feathers, tossing them by the fistful into the air. In this way, in the sweltering rear of Dubrovner's, the wives of North Main Street became the engineers of a blizzard.

Feathers would swirl and spiral around the dangling lightbulb, flurrying down from the ceiling and settling in drifts over the filthy floor. Then we were no longer in the back of the butcher shop, but in the snowy woods of Byelorussia. Or so I imagined. I imagined it not because I'd ever been in any such woods, but because my papa, resting after one of his outbursts would sometimes recall them.

"You had the mud and the drek but what's new?" he would shrug, brushing chicken guts and toenails from his apron. "Then comes the snow—kadosh kadosh . . ." Here he closed his eyes, his fingers wriggling an imitation of falling snowflakes. "Kadosh kadosh and everything's kosher again."

It was the same snow, I once heard him suppose, that had covered the bodies of his family, murdered by Cossacks in a village pogrom. The pogrom had occurred after my father, fleeing military conscription and chasing rumors of freedom, had already run away to America. This he'd let out before he knew what he was saying. Then angry with himself for his moment of weakness, he clenched a fist to shout: "Here it only pishes dirty rain!"

That's how it was with the storm of feathers. They lulled my father into thoughtfulness just long enough to make him mad all over again. Then he would come from behind his butcher's block, swatting blowflies away from his beard, and accuse the women of everything under the sun. He blamed them for bad weather, bank panics, arson, for binding their husbands to their steam presses and lasts by the cords of their own phylacteries. And sometimes he accused them of cutting the cords. He accused them of putting ideas in my mama's head.

"Yentes!" he bawled at the wives, who had the good sense to keep their heads bent over their laps. "Where is your gossip? Y-t-t y-t-t, why don't you! Shmoose!" Then he would sway in front of them, pressing his palms together and fluttering his eyelids, a housewife expressing concern. " 'Poor maidele, how she suffers; on a dog I wouldn't wish it . . .' "

He always turned around to make sure that none of his antics were lost on Mama. Usually she was standing behind the marble counter preparing to dress the chickens. Thin as a candle, she was often caught gazing wistfully at a naked bird, like maybe she recognized it from better days.

"What do you think, that's your cousin Chaim on his deathbed?" my father would growl—making me think of the Lord goading Abraham to butcher his son. "It's a chicken, cut out his kishkes!" And later on, when he caught her hesitating, he began to say: "What do you think, that's your precious Mr. Blen?"

How Papa hit on the notion of a romance between my mama and the little hatter, I'll never know. Mr. Blen—with his nervous stammer and banjo eyes, his yarmelke riding his wavy hair like a buoy—was the least likely candidate for anyone's suitor. Never mind the wife of the terrible Dubrovner. But it was like my father to expect miracles at his own expense.

"I know what you tell my Rosie," he hounded the women, always in my mama's hearing. "You tell her run away from your momzer husband.

You tell her go to the shmendrick Blen, that he's pining away in his shop for you. You tell her—" raising his voice in a rasping falsetto, " 'He needs you—which is more than we can say for the crazy butcher, not to mention your floozy of a daughter and your nebbish son . . . ' "

On her own, I don't think it would have occurred to my long-suffering mama that there was anywhere else to go. So maybe, without any faculties of resistance, she finally gave in to the power of my father's suggestion. Maybe his constant kvetching browbeat her into a glimpse of another life. Because one day, between the meat scales and the butcher paper, I saw her blush. Then the first blush must have awakened others, spreading like a rash, until the whole length and breadth of my mousy mama became enflamed.

That's how it started, the itch of her late-blooming passion. It kept her from sleep and drove her to highlight her tired eyes. She marcelled her stringy hair and swapped her drab gaberdine for a taffeta shirtwaist with lavender trim. It probably wasn't as complete a shedding of her old worn-out skin as she must have hoped for: Not quite a butterfly, she was more of a caterpillar with wings. Still, it was enough to give her the nerve to throw her couple of dresses, along with her mother's candlesticks, into a carpet bag, and walk out of the apartment above the butcher shop forever.

Never much of a match for my ferocious father, it seemed to me that my mama and the hatter had been paired in heaven. Where neither of them made much of an impression when they were around, now they were gone they were legendary. Though everyone naturally fell silent when they saw my father coming, the story was in the air. Who didn't know how Mama, with baggage in hand, had entered Blen's Custom Millinery in the early morning? Who but my papa hadn't heard the women in the gallery at the synagogue, or the old kuckers on their bench in front of Petrofsky's fruitstand, repeating my mama's words: "Wolfie, mein basherter, my destined one. God help us, I belong to you."

After that it's unclear whether Mr. Blen was fleeing Mama (who pursued him) or whether they were burning their bridges together. In any case, they were last seen boarding a streetcar amid a spray of sparks.

To be honest, neither my sister nor I missed our mama very much. What was there to miss in her day-long sighs, her taking to bed with a headache, her staring dumbly at dead chickens, dumbly out the window at North Main? Papa, of course, made up for our lack of concern. He howled his shame and rifled the pages of his grease-stained Shulchan Aruk, looking to brand himself the male equivalent of aguneh, abandoned wife.

"Am I the only one who doesn't run away from this farkokte place?" he cried, though only Mama was gone. But that was his favorite refrain. In his tantrums he always talked like he was completely alone, betrayed by one and all. Still, I could tell that some of the heart had gone out of his hysterics. It wasn't the same complaining about Mama's leaving him, now that her desertion was fact.

Nevertheless he went through the paces he was famous for. He caterwauled and butted the doorposts with his head until he'd ruined the crown of his homburg. He bloodied his own nose, blackened his eyes, carrying on in the way that kept alive the tall tales of Red Dubrovner's mishegoss. But to me the whole thing lacked conviction, like he was performing through force of habit. I'd seen worse when he had no reason at all to be mad.

At one point during his demonstration he tore off his lapels; he went down to the meat locker and brought up a case of his home-brewed kiddush wine. With every bottle he swilled, his roaring diminished a little, until finally he had drunk himself into silence. Then the sounds of North Main Street—the shmeikel-ing shopkeepers, the delivery wagons, the bells—had their turn. They took up the roaring where my father left off. And that's when I got the willies: not from the butcher's ranting, which was the familiar music of my days, but from the thunderous noise which the world made when he stopped. I was scared when all I could hear was the world, and my father's small voice—when he'd pulled his tallis from under his apron to cover his head—saying a kaddish for Mama.

In the shop downstairs, however, it was business as usual. Papa continued haranguing the women, who continued flicking their chickens with heads bowed. But upstairs was another story. Abandoned by Mama the apartment over the shop was even worse off than before.

Nobody would have accused my poor footsore mama of being a housekeeper, but at least she had swept up the wreckage in the wake of my father's wrath. Now she was gone the place was a shameful dump. Glass dropped out of a crack in the skylight and the kitchen table listed from a broken leg. The pan under the icebox had overflowed, warping the floorboards. As I watched my father sniffing around in the debris, I saw it coming.

"Faigele!" he bawled. "Where is my shikse daughter?"

That was when he must have realized that my sister Fagie was seldom at home. Afterwards, whenever she stopped by for a bite to eat or to wind her victrola in the bedroom we shared, Papa would start in on her.

"Vildeh moid!" he wailed, with or without his audience of women. "She got to run, you know, she got to skidoo. They are missing her already in the speakeasies of Babylon . . . " Then he would lift alternate feet in a grotesque black bottom, slapping the soles of his shoes.

But Fagie could take the hint without all of Papa's displays. Nobody needed to put ideas in her head. Hadn't she been gallivanting, chasing boys and making scandal, for a couple of years?

She was a pip, my sister—a flashy dresser, always with bracelets and beads, high-heeled pumps and seamed stockings rolled below the knee. Her short pleated skirts swished as she walked, the necklines plunging toward the bosom she didn't have. Her carroty spitcurls dangled like burlesque sidelocks, and her cheeks—feverish anyway—were heavily rouged.

"I can't do anything with her," our mama used to grieve before she went away—which was no news, as what was there that Mama could do anything with? Meanwhile Papa might call her nafkeleh on principle; he might, finding part of a barbecue sandwich she'd brought home from the Pig 'n Whistle, bellow until blood vessels burst. But mostly, too busy with his general ravings, he took small notice of my sister's shenanigans until after Mama was gone.

Then all it took was his declaring that she would depart soon for the Unterworld, that already she smelled of sulphur and deep-fried sin, to send Fagie straight into the arms of Nutty Iskowitz.

He was the local bootlegger, owner of the notorious Green Owl Cafe and of the largest piece of the broken-down middleweight boxer, Eddie Kid Katz. He wore padded suits and two-tone shoes, and pomaded his hair until it looked like record grooves. On any day you could see him driving his Studebaker down Main Street, unaware that half the neighborhood kids were hanging onto the fenders and running boards. For all the shadiness of his reputation, nobody seemed to take him very seriously, least of all Fagie.

"The Czar of Market Square he calls himself," she would sigh to me with a ha. "He's a czar all right: he fortzes Mrs. Rosen's meatballs and it's a pogrom." She would joke about his pitted weasel features, his jaw always snapping gum. "A face he ain't got, only a pair of profiles."

But she liked him all the same. I could tell by the way that she squirmed when she spoke of him, toying with the gaudy jewelry he bought her. She bragged about his connections with ward-heelers and the celebrities of Beale Street, whose gambling houses he claimed to supply with his bathtub gin. She described for me with affection the rooms above the cafe where Nutty held court—the green felt crap tables overhung with blue muggle smoke.

It made me nervous to hear about her life, all of it so foreign to the butcher shop. But I was glad, on the other hand, that Fagie had finally found herself a sweetheart. The others had always run away from her on account of her meshuggener father, and because, frankly, Fagie was no prize. Only it seemed like what was discouraging to everyone else was what attracted Nutty, which was maybe how he got his name.

"He thinks it makes him some kind of a macher to be seen with Red

Dubrovner's daughter," Fagie told me once while buffing her nails. "It's his idea of living dangerously." And later on she mentioned off-handedly that he had asked her to stand under the canopy with him.

"So I says to him: 'What do you think, it's going to rain?' " Then she left off plucking an eybrow to squeeze my hand. "Oh Shimmie," she said, "it looks like I found my ticket out of this bughouse."

I thought of pointing out that, as big noises went, Nutty was second only to our father in the Pinch, but it didn't seem like my place to say so.

Anyway Papa, for all his prophesying the worst, was the last to know that my sister and Nutty had become an item. This was owing partially to me. While secrets tend to make me nauseous, I had helped to keep my father in the dark. I covered for Fagie in her absences, straightening up the apartment and cooking the briskets, everything short of which my father considered trayf. (He liked to eat them almost raw with the juice running into his beard.) So—except for Papa's appetite, which had fallen off lately—everything was going along as usual. Then Fagie had to spoil it all by coming into the shop with her boyfriend on her arm.

They strolled in—Fagie swinging her beads, Nutty under a fedora with a thumb in his lapel—looking like this must be how the other half lives. Behind them loomed an individual whose chest and biceps strained the seams of his pin-stripe suit. I guessed that this was Eddie Kid Katz, Nutty's partial property and bodyguard, in whose puffy eyes there shone not a speck of light. With his lantern jaw working its gum in time to his boss's, he took up his post by the open front doors—while Fagie and Nutty browsed the meat cases, casually approaching the butcher.

He stood in his sleeveless undershirt behind his chopping block. The sweat poured off of him, beads of it glistening the hair on his shoulders like raindrops in birds' nests. Busy trimming the flanks of salted beef that I was shlepping in from the locker, he didn't even bother to look up.

"Papa," said Fagie, tightening her grip on Nutty's arm, "I want you to meet my fiancé."

Still he didn't look up, though his slicing became more vigorous, and I could tell that he was biting his tongue. But though she knew better, Fagie continued to needle him: "Papa, maybe you didn't hear . . . "

I don't know what she was up to, asking for trouble that way. It was like they were sightseeing and she'd brought Nutty to show him the most celebrated temper in the Pinch. So it must have disappointed them when Papa, who looked like he was going to explode, only fizzled.

"Lilith," he hissed, calling on the Lord to witness what a brazen thing was his daughter, that she should soak in a mikveh for ninety years—and that was it. He went back to his trimming and chopping.

Nutty looked over his shoulder at Eddie Kid Katz, as if to say: So this is the big wind? I wanted to shout over the counter that he hadn't seen anything yet, just wait until Papa got hot . . .

Meanwhile Nutty was making motions as if he were taking control. Giving Fagie back her arm, he shoved her politely to one side. Then squaring his shoulders, checking his shirt cuffs, he planted himself directly in front of the butcher.

"No Papa," he began, patronizing and familiar, rocking back and forth on his heels. "We come here in good faith, didn't we, to ask for your blessing. So please, spare us the 'Vey is mir,' just 'Mazel tov' and we're on our way." Evidently pleased with his speech, he glanced over his shoulder again.

He turned back around in time to see the vein at my father's temple pulse like blue lightning. Impaling a loin roast with his cleaver, Papa started to tremble, taking hold of the underside of his chopping block to steady himself. But the huge wooden block, despite its weight, wasn't anchor enough for his rage. As his temper rose, so did the chopping block, coming away from the floor with all four legs.

From the way that the bootlegger's jaw dropped, the gum rolling out of his mouth, you'd have thought that Papa was lifting the block by magic, and not just by dint of his awful strength. Mr. Iskowitz, I imagined myself saying, meet Red Dubrovner.

With the tendons like roots in his neck, his teeth clenched about the tip of his tongue, Papa bent his knees to hoist the chopping block over his head. But for Eddie Kid Katz, who went on noisily chewing his gum, nobody breathed. We were spellbound watching the way that the block was suspended above my papa—like Moses about to smash the tablets of the law. In a minute, I knew, he would let loose his tongue and spit out whole plagues of abuse. He would froth into his beard.

But Nutty Iskowitz, snapping out of his stupor, wasn't hanging around for that. Taking cautious steps backwards, he grabbed my sister (whose eyes were still glued to the block) and dragged her behind him out the front doors. Not so impressed, the stone-faced palooka turned and strutted slowly after them.

No sooner had they gone than my father dropped his chopping block. He let it fall on top of his head, rattling his teeth which bit off the tip of his tongue. It plopped like a little strawberry onto his apron bib. Then Papa folded under the weight of the block, his thick body crumpling like the crown of his homburg. The building shuddered and the floorboards splintered beneath him.

Later that evening he sat motionless in the kitchen upstairs. On the crippled table in front of him was his open Shulchan Aruk and three empty bottles of his kiddush wine. In his mouth was a piece of melting ice, and an ice-pack was perched atop his bald and swollen head, fastened there by his blue-striped tallis. Standing beside him in the coppery light, I saw a mouse crawl unnoticed over his shoulder. The Saturday night hullaballoo started up outside the window, nearly drowning out the voice of my father, lisping a kaddish for his daughter Fagie.

In the weeks that followed he never took eyes off me. He must have thought, now that Mama and Fagie were gone, that I too would soon be running away. The worst of it was that he watched me without ever speaking his mind. True, he still let off steam from time to time in the shop, parading his anger in front of the women on Shabbos eve. But he would trip now over his hobbled tongue before he got very far, and fall silent. And upstairs in the apartment, which I was still taking pains to keep straight, he seldom spoke a word.

What's more he was losing weight. Brooding at the kitchen table like he was sitting shivah, he refused his bloody briskets—though he might occasionally pick at the tripes he brought home from the slaughterhouse. His shoulders had begun to droop and his beard was getting sparse and lusterless. Bags like bruises appeared beneath his eyes.

Meanwhile business, such as it was, had fallen off. The wives, no longer so shy about gossiping in his presence, still brought him their chickens of course. But in Mama's absence they carried the carcasses across to Makowsky, my father's non-reverend competitor, who dressed them out for a dime. Cradling dead birds with lolling necks, they would file a little smugly past Red Dubrovner, as if there was maybe a better show over the road.

I wanted to tell him don't worry on my account, I'm not going anywhere; but I didn't even like to mention the possibility. I didn't like to think about leaving my father's sight. What was there, anyway, outside of our neighborhood? Swamps and vicious three-legged dogs and yokels who hitched Jewish boys up to their plows—as my papa had always assured us. And now that he wasn't shouting about it, I was more fearful than ever—now that the sounds in the distance were coming so clear: the whistles of the packet boats, the singing of the roustabouts on the levee . . .

But one afternoon I didn't wait, as I usually did, for my Hebrew teacher Mr. Notowitz to wake up and dismiss me. Instead, leaving him asleep at the table, I picked my way through his fishbones and stacks of books, and slipped quietly out of his apartment.

Following my feet I found myself headed up Main Street toward the Green Owl Cafe. I was drawn there by my fondness for Fagie. Though she'd never hung around much, now that I knew she wasn't coming back, I missed her. I missed her dirty mouth and the reek of her cheap perfume. hadn't she always been more of a mama to me than Mama? What harm would it do, I wondered, if I paid her a visit? I would drop by briefly on the way home from cheder—it was that simple. So why did my heart hammer my chest like it wanted out?

Then I was standing on the curb at Poplar Avenue—which I'd never in my life been across—looking for any excuse to turn around. But the avenue didn't appear to be different from any other street; it was no Red Sea. The other side was still Main Street, still shops and offices, and there was the Green Owl less than a block away. So I hitched up my shorts and crossed over.

The curtained door of the dingy cafe was the only one on the street that was closed against the muggy sunlight. I was shuffling in front of it, having second thoughts, when the door suddenly opened and a customer came out. I expected raucous noise to tumble down on top of me, saw myself bolting away. But as I heard nothing, only the knocking of what I guessed were billiard balls, I took a deep breath and sidled in.

The men sat at tables under harsh lights, in the sluggish air stirred by ceiling fans. They were drinking from porcelain mugs which they took under the tables to refill, spitting dolefully into dented cuspidors. From my father's ravings I'd imagined that they would be brawling and sinning openly. So I was relieved, if a little disappointed, by their silence. All things considered, the Anshei Sphard shul, with its reeling and chattering daveners, was more like I'd expected the cafe to be.

Then I realized that the quiet was due in part to the fact that everyone was looking at me. Accustomed to being practically invisible, I was that close to backing out the door—when the man behind the counter, wiping a spoon in his apron, asked me: "What can we do for you, small change?

I swallowed and told him I was looking for Fagie Dubrovner.

"Sorry, sweatpea," he replied, turning his head aside to wink. "She's already spoken for."

Everyone chuckled over the way I was blushing. "But I'm her brother," I explained.

"Ohhh," nodded the man behind the counter. "In that case . . .," and he jerked his thumb toward some stairs in back of the pool table.

Upstairs it was even harder to breathe than down. The smoke hung so thick I had to wave it aside like cobwebs in order to see. Then everything was pretty much as Fagie had described, only faded. The draperies were threadbare, the windowpanes painted an ugly red. The men in vests and gartered shirtsleeves, standing over the dice table, looked grim, like they were peering into somebody's open casket.

Fagie saw me before I saw her.

"Shimmie!" she hailed from a table in the back. At the table, which was littered with amber bottles, a group of men sat playing cards. Nutty Iskowitz was among them in striped suspenders, a cigar stuck in his mouth, and behind him in his too-tight suit stood Eddie Kid Katz. With his arms folded the boxer made me think of a genie popped out of one of the cuspidors downstairs.

"Look everybody," said Fagie, risen from Nutty's side, her tassels swishing as she crossed the room to hug me. "It's my longlost baby brother." But nobody even bothered to turn around.

"Hello, brother-in-law," Nutty Isowitz called out to me, leaning back in his chair to study his hand of cards. "I'll buy you a pair of long pants for the wedding."

"You're coming, ain't you kiddo?" asked Fagie, breathing toilet water and whiskey in my face. "Every gonif in town will be there."

Somehow it hadn't entered my mind that Fagie would be having a wedding. On the Other Side, where Papa claimed she had gone, who had weddings? Now that I knew hers was coming, I was excited for Fagie's sake. But I was sorry for myself, knowing that the butcher would never let me attend.

"That's right," said Nutty, laying down his cards, locking his fingers behind his head in an attitude more suited to blowing his horn. "Nothin's too good for my angel drawers . . ."

Fagie beamed through her make-up as she told me how they were renting the banquet hall of the Cochran Hotel. She practically crooned the words: "catered affair," waving her hankerchief la-de-da over the elegance of it all. But all I could think of, as she carried on, was that it was past the time when I should have been home from Mr. Notowitz's.

Meanwhile Nutty was still putting on the dog.

"Shapiro's got his whole sweatshop working on her gown" he was saying. "The train's so long we can use it for a chupeh. And wait till she gets a load of the ring." Here he crossed his legs on top of the table and shut his eyes. "We'll bring down a wonder rabbi from Chicago, and Eddie here can jump out of the cake, and to close the show, we'll set a flock of chickens free . . ."

At this Fagie's face suddenly clouded. "No chickens!" she snapped, turning hotly toward Nutty. "I want real birds—pigeons and doves."

"Awright awright," protested Nutty, "whatever my little knish . . ." Then his eyes went wide as he righted his chair, hopping abruptly to his feet. "Nail down the furniture, boys," he exclaimed, showing the empty palm of one hand, tugging at Eddie's coat sleeve with the other. "It's him again!"

At the head of the stairs stood my father in his homburg and apron. Stoop-shouldered and pale, he was resting his chin against his sinking chest, so that his beard resembled a shirtfront. He was moving his lips, trying

I suppose to tell me that he'd come to take me home. But no sounds emerged from his mouth.

The whole room, distracted from gambling, was braced for some kind of eruption. Then Fagie, having sized up our papa's condition, took the liberty of putting words on his tongue.

"I come," she said, making her voice sound Russian and gruff, "to give a blessing on my daughter's marriage." After which the gamblers relaxed into horse laughter and guffaws. Encouraged by their response and Papa's continued speechlessness, Fagie went on.

"I will slaughter a bull in her honor, kaynahoreh, with my bare hands."

Everyone was howling over her impersonation. Stepping from behind Eddie, Nutty sauntered over to put an arm around her shoulder. "What a gal!" he grinned, while his other arm he put around me.

Then I wished I could enter into the spirit of it all. But when I tried to laugh with them, my Papa's downcast presence reminded me of my place. His lips were no longer moving and he appeared to be shrinking, the general hilarity affecting him like salt on a snail. So I broke away and hurried to his side.

As I began to lead him out Fagie gave me a look like so long, it's been nice to know you.

When we were back across the avenue, my father's hangdog silence was even more of a spectacle. Everyone noticed how he trudged in front of their shops, his eyes fixed on his feet. Seated in a folding chair outside his dry goods store, Mr. Bluestein was the first to say it.

"Whaddayaknow, Dubrovner's lost his temper."

That was his joke, and he liked it so much that he shouted it to his wife in her upstairs window, resting her bosom in a flower box. She passed it on to Mrs. Ridblatt in a neighboring window, who called down to Mr. Sacharin rolling a herring barrel into his market. He shared the information with a couple of firemen outside the No. 4 station, who dispatched their idiot mascot Arthur to Mrs. Rosen's next door. In a little while the newsboys would get wind of it. Pretty soon the whole street, when they got over the shock, would maybe turn out to give the butcher back some of his own.

It was up to me to do something.

"Papa," I said, clearing my throat to speak a little louder. "Papa, I don't think that the Green Owl is so bad."

Don't ask me how but it worked. I heard a rumbling in his belly as his chest began to swell. His beard bristled and the blue vein flashed at his temple.

"Then go back!" he cried, miraculously overcoming the handicap of his lisp. "Go to the goyim, why don't you! Gey in drerd arayn! Run away!"

I was trotting to keep up with him now, staying out of the way of his flailing arms, his fingers squeezing air.

"Or maybe you want to wait for the dark. You burn your skullcap and black your face with the ashes, you hide in a schwartze's wagon and roll away. Or sail away, that's good. You wait for the floods, you put a washtub in the bayou—you're a regular Hucklebee Dubrovner. You hop on the ice truck, you hop on the freight train that is crossing over the bridge. You tie your tallis to a stick—Shimmele Luftmensch; you sprinkle salt on the Pinch, you don't turn around . . ."

He was himself again, sounding off to spite the whole neighborhood. Mothers grabbed their children and merchants pulled down the shades inside their shops—while Papa continued his rampage, suggesting so many colorful ways of departing that you might have thought he'd considered them for himself.

But by the time we got back to the shop, he was spent. Gloomy again and short of breath, he slogged up the stairs to our stuffy apartment. In the kitchen he slumped into a chair and lay his head across the sticky tabletop. Seeing him like that, dead silent in the failing light, I thought I knew what he was feeling: that he was all alone in a deserted house.

"Papa, get up!" I pleaded, trying to shake him by the hairy shoulders. "Tell me I'm a no-good, I'm running away! Say, 'Shimmele Shnorrer, you take up with gypsies . . .' "

Unable to move him, I was shaking myself over what might come next. In a little while, I thought, he would lift his head slowly. He would pick himself up, go down to the meat locker, and return with his ritual wine. He would drink two or three bottles, cover his head, and say the kaddish for me.

But since he was behaving anyway like I'd already left him, I left him, creeping stealthily out of the room. I went down to the locker in the rear of the shop and pulled open the thick wooden door. I hauled out a case of wine from under the hanging flanks of beef, dragging it through sawdust to the screen door in back, then down some clattering steps into the yard. Then I returned to the locker for the remaining case.

With chattering teeth I uncorked a bottle of wine. I poured it—so it shouldn't be a total loss—into an empty birdbath, which stood choked by rotten vines in the center of the yard. I did the same with another and then another, asking my father's forgiveness for every bottle that I poured. Soon the wine was slopping over the bowl, spilling onto the broken stones, sending up steam in the setting sun.

Down to the last bottle, I suddenly realized how thirsty my labor had made me. It was Friday evening so I said the blessing before I drank. The first sip, which set off a pleasant tingling inside me, called for another deeper swallow. Refreshed but a little dizzy, I went over to the low brick wall that surrounded the yard, squatting there with my back against the bricks as I continued to drink. It was then that the birds began to come.

They were pigeons—some blue and gray, some mottled albino. Swooping down into the birdbath, they fluttered and splashed and preened, battling for space in the crowded bowl. Edged out, they glided to the ground and wobbled about. Some keeled over as if they were stalled; some came to rest within inches of my feet. Watching them, I worried that the wine had gone bad; they were poisoned and so was I. Then a hiccup brought home to me my own condition, and I understood the birds were drunk.

This got me tickled. The more they stumbled and capsized—making trilling sounds that might have been snores—the more amused I became. In the end I had to laugh out loud, clapping a hand over my mouth. I tried to get hold of myself. After all my father might appear at any moment—and what would he find? Me sitting in the mud made from his own spilled wine, a flock of shikkered pigeons at my feet. It was disgraceful all right . . . but it was funny, and I was laughing fit to be tied.

And in the midst of it—remembering my sister's request for pigeons, pigeons and doves to set loose at her wedding—I had an idea.

Wiping tears from my eyes, I fumbled back into the shop, snatched a spool of shaggy twine from a counter and returned to the yard. I unraveled a length and bit it off, then stooped to tie the end around the leg of a snoozing pigeon. As the bird only twitched a little and moaned, I was encouraged to try another. Then, by the time I had run out of twine, there were strings attached to nearly all of the birds in the yard.

I dried my sweaty hands on my shorts and, taking up all the loose ends, went back to the wall and sat down. Now I had only to wait for the birds to sober up and begin to stir. And when they rose into the air, I would carry them like a bunch of balloons to my sister Fagie.

I took one last swallow of wine and tied my fistful of string through a belt loop. Then I closed my eyes to imagine how they would greet me: "Hurray for Shimmele Badchan, the wedding jester!"

I was waked by a tugging that jerked me forward and up. Fuddled from my nap, I knew before my eyes were open that it was my father. I could feel the wind from his wrath in my hair.

But when I looked, I saw it wasn't Papa but the birds who were carrying me aloft. Already I was as high as our kitchen window, through which I glimpsed a dark and empty room. I was dangling by the seat of my pants, swinging just above my father as he came out onto the steps behind his shop.

He might have reached up then and grabbed me, and pulled me back into his arms. He might at least have called my name.

"Shout, Papa!" I cried, still hoping he would scare the birds into letting me down. "Say, 'Cruel boychik, you give me a this, you break my that!' "

But he only stood there looking helpless and small, the feathers falling into his upturned face.

So maybe he took the grubby pigeons for angels, I don't know. By then I was over the rooftops, the neighborhood diminishing to a huddle of tenements below me. And what with all the commotion of the birds, their pitching and diving and beating their wings above my head; what with the breezes flapping in my baggy shorts, I had enough trouble just trying to stay horizontal. I had my hands full with pawing the evening air— which was smoldering red in the west, beyond the river over Arkansas. I had my own problems now with learning to dip and soar, never mind worrying about the butcher.

David Spicer

The Back Row
for E. M.

The line of chairs against the wall
has appealed to me and my kind,
for those who know truth know each other.
We've always laughed together;
wherever the place, we had the world
before us: in a theatre,
with darkness valid the moment just before
the lady holding the torch appeared,
or the lion roared like a million men.
And on a bus, joining those
who love the black taste of exhaust.
The first time we were the same spirits
in different bodies
was the morning Vita Sico, Cindy Lane,
and I heckled the teacher and blew spitballs
at every punk in class,
even the pinup pet.
Expelled for that one,
we went to any event we could
to look at everybody in the crowd.
In *The World's Religions*
I sat in the back row with two women
listening to a stand-up comic
discuss the Tao with a frown
that made us pass love notes.
We swore to find those like us
who favored seats serving
as their own protection—whether
at the Liberty Bowl or in the Shell,

David Spicer

we'd seek the slouches knowing
that sane people had no charm,
the slouches wanting the hardest benches,
the loneliest cushions,
the worst seats in the house.

Leaving Things Behind

We piled into an old black coupe,
peered through the back window,
my five sisters and I crying
about the pink house twenty feet
from the prairie highway,
hoping somebody would send us
the brand new washing machine.

Our father laughed at innocence
of children with Einstein's hair,
but we didn't know why until
three hundred miles later,
when the car chugged and collapsed
near a wheat farm in Iowa,
and he hitchhiked to Sioux City,
pawning our mother's rings.

In the car we honked the horn
as though it were a new toy
until the woman by a silo
invited us to her home,
fed us puffed rice and strawberries.

Her family asked us questions
and we giggled, nagged our mother
for the curios in the lady's cases.
We couldn't understand why
she owned so many dolls and trains,
didn't know people kept objects
in place of daughters who always left.

When our father returned
we remembered the woman saying
*Here, keep these, you'll remember
what the clouds looked like today.*

We stayed in Sioux City a month
before my father bought a junker,
pulled us out of school,
and drove to Tennessee
without a restaurant stop,
angry he forgot his tools,
too disgusted to turn around.

Every year after that
we abandoned countless things:
a brown puppy on the side of a road,
a bicycle bought with paper route money,
a St. Christopher medal bordered
by turquoise and sterling silver,
too many mementos that are gone
or belong to a person in another city.

I always wondered why
leaving things behind
didn't bother my father
and I never discovered the reason.
I'd look at his troubled face
to see that he felt loss
is the only wound that doesn't bleed,
and he'd had enough baseball bat beatings,
August jail visits, stolen guitars.

As I grew older I acquired the habit
of not keeping a lucky cat-eye marble,
an autographed copy of *Lonesome Traveller,*
or an emerald fish hanging from a chain,
and finally saw that I lost
a piece of my spirit in those places,
that I was a jigsaw puzzle falling apart.

Then I knew the items bestowed us
by the grace of chemistry have a meaning
only the smallest tokens enjoy:

David Spicer

they, too, have souls because they live
in our hearts, and when we no longer
desire them, they whisper *Keep us*.
So we turn back and hold them,
looking up at the clouds to remember.

Daniel Foltz-Gray

Departed Coming Back

People kept asking how he felt, how he was doing; but Waters didn't know how he felt. He'd been getting through the weeks okay, so he guessed he was okay. Sometimes he went whole afternoons without thinking about what had happened. But sometimes he found himself terrified, imagining, as he got on the elevated: we're going to crash, I'll be pinned screaming; or at work, answering the phone: it's Lil, or Charles—drowned, butchered. Once in the middle of conversation he had a terrible vision, and he excused himself, and called home.

Then, other times, he felt happier than he'd ever felt. He drove to a stream near Elkhorn, just over the Wisconsin line, and wept with joy at the clear water, the bright fish, the stillness broken only by his whispered words to Peter. He thought: this is where my friend is, this is where I'll be. He stripped and swam. Death didn't frighten him.

Then later, fishing, crossing the stream on a steep log, he remembered it was gravity that killed him; and he froze, and fell on sharp rocks in a strong current, and struggled out bleeding.

He thought: he falls down steps and dies; I fall onto rocks, from a log, and live. There was no logic. But he knew now that life was short—or maybe long—but never secure.

After a time, the event of that first week distilled into moments burnt into his memory. Whole conversations, whole hours he had forgotten; but some things were burnt in. And so he had only to think about it to see again Mrs. Koskin's face like a varicose leg at the door, to hear again her voice which he had heard all his life but hardly knew, which he would never again not know—less a voice than a transcription of voice, so that he had seemed to see rather than hear the words.

But life had compensations, if you looked for them. The good moments were as tenacious as the bad, though fewer. In a trough of bitterness, remembering Peter's lifeless pale hands, he remembered too his friends' strong hands circling him, holding him up when his own limbs would not bear—Paul Kovik, Shorty Zido, Steven Huber: friends he hadn't seen in years, who came each day, who kept him going. He had lost one friend and found three more: compensation, life being what it was.

But not compensation enough. Faces of friends from decades past haunted him, woke him at night. His lips opened with a name—or not a name, only a smile, a soft word, a way of walking to bring them back— or less than that: the memory of his own affection, the peculiar joy they inspired in him.

The night before the funeral, he and Huber had gone out for coffee and pie. Across the street they could see the long canopy, the mortuary steps beneath it, shoes and pantscuffs on the high porch.

"You know, I hadn't seen him in . . . ten, fifteen years," Huber said. "I don't know how many nights I almost called him up. But you wonder, you know, maybe he's doing bad, maybe he's doing too good."

"He was doing bad," Waters said simply.

"What?"

He looked up into Huber's piercing gaze.

"He wasn't doing so bad," he said.

"Oh yes he was. You said he was doing bad." He sat back suddenly. "Well I guess I was a real asshole then, a real fucking prick."

"No more than anybody else. I was just thinking I should get in touch with Craig Nedz. I should get in touch with—"

"Do it," Huber said. "Or you'll be sorry like me."

All the way back to Chicago, in a haze of sleep and waking, the faces haunted him: Greg Pack, Arleen Ditka, Lou DiNardi. The wheels of the train seemed to call them out: Karen Toia, Steven Huber, Peter Waters, Peter Waters.

After a month the faces dimmed—or came back plainly, with faults he had forgotten. But some only brightened. In dreams they stood with Peter, eyes shining, gazing at him from a cloud of light.

But these departed he could bring back.

He wrote his high school. In October he received a letter from the reunion committee. Most of the names they couldn't track down; but Lou DiNardi had died in Little Leaf, of cancer, just weeks before; Fandozzen was a cook at Poole's, in Pittsburgh; and Karen Toia, now Karen Merman, lived on Ridge Road, Evanston, Illinois.

Evanston! He looked up from his desk near the top of the house. The grey-green lake swept north toward the Loop, and beyond. Evanston!

He had never hoped to find anyone so near. He wrote to her at once:

Karen,

> I've been thinking about you recently and learned that you're living in Evanston, not twenty miles from me here in Hyde Park. I've been thinking a lot about old friends, how important it is to keep them. What a long time it's been since we've talked to each other!
>
> Peter, my nephew, died this summer . . .

Two days later, he answered the phone in his office on Randolph Street and heard her voice.

"It was so good to hear from you," she said. He remembered at once the huskiness, the languor, as if she were always just waking, that had drawn him to her first. "But I'm so sorry to hear about Peter."

"I wasn't sure you'd remember him. He was a few years—"

"Of course I remember. How could you think I wouldn't remember? I'm so sorry you lost him. I wish I'd known sooner. Are you . . . how are you doing?"

He shrugged. Then he said, "Better."

"Your family?"

"They're fine."

"I know they've been a comfort to you. Your brothers—"

"I was lucky," he said.

"And your old friends? Steve Huber?"

"He never left my side." He laughed. "Can you believe I hadn't seen him in twenty, twenty-five years?"

In the silence he heard her breath like a wave breaking far away.

"My God, Herman. Has it been so long?"

"It doesn't seem like it."

"How did we let it happen?"

"I don't know," he said. "We just got lazy."

She was coming into town next day to do some shopping. Could they meet for lunch?

"At the Berghoff," Waters said. "Do you know it?"

She was already seated when he arrived, dressed—as he knew she would be dressed—darkly, richly, seeming to melt into the dark walls, or melt out of them. Her black hair swept about itself like the grain in the lacquered wood behind her. And as she stood, embracing him, with what looked like tears in her eyes, he thought: this is a face I knew so well and know still.

"Oh God it's good to see you, Herman," she said.

"You look good," he said. "You look wonderful."

They ordered drinks.

"I was thinking," she said, "after I talked to you: what a lot he's been through! And I was afraid you'd seem . . . you'll laugh, but I was afraid I wouldn't know you."

"I lost some weight."

"But I do know you."

"Of course you wouldn't know if it was from . . . from the years or—"

"Really I knew you right away. It's funny."

"You look good," he said. He studied her face, smiling. She smiled back and did not lower her eyes.

"But how are you, Herman? How are you doing now?"

She asked it so intently, with such concern in her black eyes, that he could hardly answer.

"Really I don't know. I'm pretty good—better than I was." More than anything he wanted to be frank with her.

"I'm so sorry." She looked away. "It must be so hard to—well, of course it's never easy, no matter how much . . . how much warning you have, I don't mean it's ever . . . easy, but I think—"

"Surprises are hell," he said. "You're right."

"How awful that phone call must have been for you."

"I wish it had been a phone call," he said. "But I was there, or on my way there. I'd gone down all night and day on the train."

"To see him?"

"Yes, to see him." He gazed at her. Then he shrugged. "He was supposed to pick me up. And he hadn't bothered to tell anybody I was coming." He watched her. Then he glanced away. "He just—you know, it just slipped his mind, I guess."

She frowned, unbelieving, but did not speak for several moments. "So when no one met you, that's when you . . . you began to have an inkling that—"

"Oh no. I wasn't worried. I was mad. I was pissed-off. I figured he was in a bar somewhere. In fact I walked out to a couple places where we used to hang out. But . . . ," he opened his hand swiftly, like a boy pitching cards. "I couldn't raise anybody at home. So I took a cab. I had to go next door to get the key from Mrs. Koskin—and there they all were in the living room—his wife Evelyn, their kids, my brother Sam, everybody. Sam rushes up and throws his arms around me and starts to cry. 'You came,' he says. 'You knew!' They thought it was a miracle.

"So he'd been dead five hours and they hadn't called me. She couldn't make one stinking phone call to Chicago to tell me my best friend was dead."

She reached over to take his hand, then hesitated, touched his wrist lightly, and sat back with a sigh.

"But you shouldn't let that upset you," she said. "She couldn't have been thinking all that clearly. Maybe she—"

'Well . . . that's right. That's fair. But even if she *could* she wouldn't have called. But, you know, when I walked in that door and she looked up at me like I was some messenger of God, you know, like her pathetic Christ had whispered in my ear, I could see she was thinking—God help me, Herman, I was wrong about you. You're not such a louse after all." He smiled wryly. "It passed. She's back to hating me."

"But why?"

"God knows," he said. "She thinks I was a bad influence." He allowed his smile to dissipate slowly. "For all those twenty hours he was the sole reason I was doing what I was doing. And then to get there, pissed-off . . . " He felt the bitter longing rising in his throat. He looked at her and shrugged again.

"Just one wrong step," she said, disbelieving. "Just inches."

He said, "I've driven myself crazy thinking that."

While they ate, she talked about Peter. She remembered more about him than Waters would have guessed. In fact her memory was astonishing.

"Your son," she said, "I'll bet he's like him. Yes? Quiet, a little . . . moody?"

"Not moody. Not really much like him."

"No? I'm surprised."

"Well, he's quiet. But . . . well with Peter you were, in a way you were just as glad sometimes he didn't talk. I mean, sometimes you just didn't want to hear it." He looked off into the aisleway that led downstairs. "I mean, the man was a pessimist. If there ever was a pessimist, it was him. But Charles is just preoccupied. He's too busy thinking."

"He's . . . what? A teenager?"

"Fourteen," he said. "Eighth grade."

"And I suppose he's become quite a ladies' man."

"I don't think he's that far along yet."

"You mean . . . sexually? You don't think he's interested?"

He shrugged.

"Well that's not unusual. I didn't know a thing about sex in eighth grade."

After a pause, thinking, almost not saying it, thinking—isn't this the point after all?—Waters said: "Well you learned fast."

She gasped, then let her mouth fall into laughter.

"I almost didn't say that," he said. "But I thought, the whole idea—"

"Well I did," she said.

"I mean, when a thing like this happens, you want to look back and say, in other words, to people you cared about, care about, who care about you—this is what I was really feeling, this is—"

"You're right," she said. "We can share so much."

"Exactly. There's not time enough for . . . for pretense and . . . ." He gazed at her. "Tell me something. Do I look old? Do I seem . . . sad to you?"

"You look wonderful," she said.

She invited him to bring his wife and son to dinner in a week. She wanted them to meet her husband and two girls. But as they were eating Black Forest cake she remembered a commitment. And things in fact were crazy at home—Berty changing jobs, pool being built.

"Why don't let's meet for lunch next week?" she said. "This has been so good for me."

That night in bed, waking in cool sheets, hearing the slow moan of a ship well out, hearing his wife's slow breath, he thought: she's Peter's way of saying—you're doing just right, you're doing right. He opened his eyes. The fog-bound moon drenched his feet in violet light. God knew he needed a friend. But an old friend was a miracle.

The second time, he arrived first. He watched her come in the door and pass through the crowd, moving sinuously as shadow, though she was—he had forgotten—a full-bodied woman, with breasts large and comfortable-seeming as couches, with a couch's-leg waist—a spindle. Then the hips that were perhaps too lavish though so well draped in navy wool. Then the strong calves like turned wood.

"I wish I could see you the way I saw you in high school," he said, when they had ordered. "I keep wanting to tell you what I thought of you."

"So tell," she said.

"But I can't remember."

She frowned at him.

"I don't mean I've forgotten it, for God's sake."

"Right. You just can't remember."

"I just wish I could see it more clearly."

"It's a blessing in life. You can't look back and see how silly you were."

"But I wish I could see you, you could see me, the way we were then with the eyes we had then."

"I wouldn't go back," she said, "even if I could."

"But I was thinking we really haven't changed. Maybe—well of course we've changed, I don't mean we haven't changed, but maybe we've changed in the same way. And I thought, maybe I saw you last week the same way I saw you in eleventh grade."

"What?"

"Well, I think—"

"Okay," she laughed, "I follow. So what did you see? I mean last week."
"A very attractive woman."
She smiled indulgently.
"What? That's bad?"
"You could be more specific," she said.
He nodded. "That's right. Of course. I was just . . . I was a little . . . ," he frowned, "shy about—"
"That's no good."
"I know," he said. "I think you . . . I thought you had very attractive breasts." He bit back a smile. But then, seeing her own lips trembling, feeling the swell of laughter in his chest and throat, he surrendered to it and grinned unabashedly. He laughed out loud. She was laughing too. When he could speak again, he said, "And lovely legs, nice legs. You're a terrific dresser."
"And my hips?"
"Well—"
"I know," she said. "You don't have to say."
"But even in high school you were a little—"
"All right," she said smiling. "I thought you forgot all that, I thought you couldn't remember."
In fact he was certain she liked her hips perfectly well.
"But what about me? I never really knew what you liked."
"Can you guess?"
Grimacing, he cupped one hand gently over the dome of his belly.
"Oh stop," she said. "You have a nice comfortable body, a little bear's body. Don't you know that? And a wonderful sweet smile and a . . . a boy's innocence, in a way. I don't mean you're naive, God knows. And your sense of humor was always very . . . very appealing. And that's gotten better. I think because you're a happy man. Do you know? I think you're a happy man."
"I'm not *un*happy, usually."
"But you like your work. You seem . . . I think you like yourself. You have a nice family. You've suffered, God knows. You've been through a bad time. But what really could you want that you haven't got? I don't mean a yacht or something."
He said, "A friend."
She touched his hand. "Please don't take offense—but I'm not Peter. Peter was—"
"I know that," Waters said gently.
"I just don't want you to be disappointed."
"You couldn't disappoint me," he said.

They met the next week as usual; but the following week she disappointed him. Still he went to the Berghoff for lunch that Thursday. And afterward he walked by the lake. It was a dark day, threatening rain, but mild for December, and perfectly still. Even the sounds from the Loop seemed to hush. On the water a light haze shrouded the big ships that squeezed the horizon like islands, that moved like the drift of islands. He gauged the passage of one ship against the fixed point of the Planetarium; but after three minutes he could not tell whether it had moved toward him or away.

He found himself reciting again silently the litany of times they had had together, the three of them. It was a recitation as natural to him now as breathing. And just as naturally, he remembered best the last of those times, the worst of them. On a damp afternoon that turned cold, too cold to swim, they had gone up to the mountains east of Pittsburgh. It was a day or two before he was to leave for college. Peter, a ninth-grader, had been forced on them.

His plan had been to use the day to take back his ring—not to break off, really, but to take back his ring. He didn't like her any less; but he had begun to trust her less. In fact she had never embarrassed him, but never had they been separated by four hundred miles, by the three months till Christmas. He did not want to be made a fool of at home. Without the ring she wasn't really his, unless of course she wanted to be. He was counting on her wanting to be. But more than anything he did not want to be made a fool of at home.

And yet all the sleepless night before, all morning as they drove out country roads by sodden lots piled high with gleaming coal—now in the empty littered park that smelled of cedarwood and ash—his logic had begun to weaken under the press of something he had never known, a nameless unease that made him feel as if he had been inflated with cold air. Every word he spoke was an effort; and he could tell from Karen's attention to Peter, to his eating, to his constant questions, that she had noticed. She was taking it personally. But he hadn't the strength of will to explain it to her. He could not even have explained it to himself.

Then from the treetops he heard a shriek, the strong boating of wings . . . silence. A single leaf fell. And then a large bird with something in its talons broke swiftly straight away from him into the mists above the deepest part of the lake.

He thought: in another day the life I know will be gone like that.

When they had eaten, he sent Peter off fishing and led her up a rocky slope. All around them lay the vast cold levelness of water.

"Well," he said. Maybe he'd been foolish. He put his arm around her. But she stiffened.

"Maybe we shouldn't go together anymore," she said. "I think we ought to . . . see other people."

It was the last time he had seen her. He mentioned it at lunch the week before, and she said:

"But you were the one leaving."

She called the office next Thursday morning, breathless.

"The pool's finished!" she said. "I never thought they'd finish so soon. They're cleaning now. And I . . . well I thought, why don't you come here for lunch—and a swim? You can be first in the pool."

"Don't you think it's a little cold for swimming?"

"It's heated of course, you foolish man. Can you come?"

He took a cab up. He sat in the front, as he had done those summers when Peter drove a cab in Chicago, though he had first to convince the driver, a young Greek with stiff mustaches, that he was no thug, no homosexual. Sunlight splashed the storefronts of Michigan Avenue, and he thought: how wonderful to be zooming out with Peter on this day for swimming.

"I don't know Evanston good," the driver said. But they found it finally, a house of stuccoed cubes, flat roofs, wrought iron. He walked up terra-cotta steps and remembered he had brought no trunks.

She answered his knock in a one-piece burgundy swim suit, and slippers, with heels. She smiled brightly, if a little shyly, muttered that her legs were pale, and, instead of embracing him, led him by the hand through sliding doors into an atrium, a forest of ferns and trees in clay pots, with a circular pool at its center.

"*He* wanted square," she said. "Do you like it?"

"I love it." Outside, a community of marble nudes, brilliant in the sun, knelt under the brown vines of the arbor.

"Do you really?"

"Oh yes." He smiled at her, a little sarcastically, to hide the truth. "I'm just afraid you'll find my house . . . boring."

"I'd be happy to find it anything."

They ate lunch at a glass table under a catalpa tree. Behind them two workmen fussed at joints, faucets—"finishing up," Karen said; but Waters knew why they had stayed. Every time he looked at them, their eyes moved.

"They're not very subtle," he said. She only smiled. "You don't mind?"

"They've been waiting a long time to see me like this." She was eating a tangerine. He couldn't help but notice how lovely her lips were—full, well-defined, with hardly a crease, with twin peaks and, between them, at the base of the furrow, a pillow. How many times he had laid his head—lips first—against that pillow!

And gazing at her lips, wondering—Did I feel then what I feel now? Did I see what I saw?—he thought: they're a part of me as much as her, thinking: if I could touch them once, maybe I could go back . . .

She was watching him. He felt the blood rise to his face. Yet it seemed to him, just for an instant, that she ate with more drama, with more pout.

"Well if *you* don't mind . . . " he said. He wanted to say: take me back there, let me go back.

"It's only looking," she said.

Later, floating on his back in her husband's shorts near the side of the pool, his ears underwater, the workmen gone, he saw her lean down to him, her lips moving, no sound coming, with his second—his third—margarita, smiling the smile he had seen in his memory all those years and which he saw now as in a picture or a dream—a smile squeezed against giggling, a girl's smile. He did not raise his hand as she leaned slowly lower, so low that her breasts touched his arm, and placed the glass on his chest—and leaned again, smiling, with no apparent strain, and drank.

He closed his eyes. Through the glass he felt the touch of her lips. And in his throat and behind his eyes he heard the murmur of his blood as he had heard it twenty-five years before. He felt again the blistering heat of the shingled roof where they had lain that first time and saw her lips shining with liquor. Sharply as flame, he felt her mouth on his chest.

And if that could be so alive to him now, why not Peter? Waters spoke his name softly, a whisper—and for an instant saw clearly the thin mouth and high lined forehead, the green eyes that met him, as they used to meet him, with a woeful humor, as if to say, you wouldn't believe what's happened now—as if to say, as he used to say—lifting his dark brows, his eyes more pale than before, as though each time it surprised him: things are getting crazy, Herman.

A disturbance of his balance made Waters open his eyes. Karen had slipped into the pool and stood close above him. She bent forward and kissed him—a long gentle kiss. But he splashed to his feet.

"*Oh* I'm sorry!" she said. "I didn't mean to drown you. Are you all right? Can you breathe?" She put her hands behind his shoulders and drew herself closer. She touched his lips again—and drew back.

"This is what you wanted," she said, "isn't it? This is what you meant."

But it was not what he meant, not what he had meant at all. He told himself that it was not what he had meant. And yet from her kiss, the touch of her hand, from the face which looked at him with no whisper of doubt or fear, he understood that she knew him better than he knew himself. And she knew, she must have known, that he could not resist her now.

Dorothy Foltz-Gray

The Lucky Roofers

All night the men hang by their hammers;
the roof is slick.
They call to each other across the tiles.
"Hey boy you quitting?"
Long after I have gone to bed, I waken.
Sleepless, I stand at a window
and watch the abandoned world.
Tonight shadows creep across the shingles.
Squatted on its slanted side,
the roofers' knees draw up like repeating roofs.
I wonder what the owner pays them
to stay so long, to eat dinner on his roof.
I guess they hate his job
and work all night to be through,
their wives and children waiting like cold supper.
But then I think they love it
and stay because no one can get them off.
Like new lovers, they talk until dawn, skins glistening.
I return to bed. In the morning,
I hear hammers, and half the roof has shingles.
I imagine the roofers are friends laughing.
One has a belly like Buddha.
Together they read a map of what they are doing.

Dorothy Foltz-Gray

The Chasing Heart

"Today, while we were running, we saw a pregnant woman searching for, then chasing, two men, one the father of her child."

June 7, 1981

Chasing her breath,
her breath is all she hears.
Not river water,
not leaves she steps on,
not snakes she surprises.
And the parting of dark-faced men
who pass broken-fisted in black shirts,
whose slurred bodies bend
jagged as open cans,
does not really sink in,
not like the fear, or the leather bracelets on their wrists,
or the scared mean look they give her.
Her feet keep pounding, and they are no more
than a black breathing train,
or the headlights of a truck
or a pack of dogs out of the new clay sewer.
The steamy earth still takes her,
her legs stretched past them and their place
to a place she doesn't notice.
But the long terrible crying,
much worse than the last train blast,
governs her skin.
Her cries like a light sheet rise,
and it's the two men she's after,
loping toward them on the tracks
like an endangered deer able to attack.
Bent at the hip,
folded at the shoulder,
her arms cradle her bursting stomach like a fruit,
a group of bitches with her from the sewers howling,
this mother forcing the forest to be right.
Through the graveled clearing she sees them,
black spurs spitting mud,
dark ivy spreading faster than stains;

they turn and, seeing her,
run into a forest of yells scissored as a dogfight.
"Dwayne" her scream splits gravel,
the train's wide whistle,
the storm's black air.
And there, on that pitch driveway,
two swirl round like the meanest pack of tunnel dogs.
Her heart still in her hands,
she springs after them light as a web
(as if her stomach swings and holds her too)
and those light long hands
grab out for steaming leathered wrists
like some wild trapeze swinger over gravel pits,
she swings and hooks
whatever fluttering thing she can:
the sucking noise the catch makes,
the hand he rakes across her beating heart.

Sandra Moore

Dove Shooting

Even before I pulled off the street I could see the weeds growing through cracks in the service island, and under the front door sill. The first thing I thought was that he must have died and nobody told me. I couldn't believe how rundown the place looked. Six months ago when I'd stood here saying good-bye to him, it had looked clean and prosperous like always.

I got out of my car, stepping over broken glass from a shattered coke bottle. I was ten years old the first time my father brought our '65 Plymouth here, with a first-class knock under its hood. We'd just moved to town, and somebody at the bank recommended the Esso at 6th and Main. Mr. Carlson had come out to meet us, a solid and competent-looking man with the biggest pair of hands I'd ever seen. My father was tall, a skinny bank officer who wore glasses and had a pencil callus on his middle finger. I was a pudgy fifth grader.

That day while he listened to my father explain about the car, he'd nod occasionally, the whole time watching me squirm and toe the gravel. My father knew doodly-squat about cars; I was embarrassed for us—him pointing to the fuel pump and calling it the carburetor. I wanted to tell this guy in the Esso shirt how smart my father was with money, nevermind about cars.

I learned later that Mr. Carlson usually didn't work on Plymouths, but for some reason, that day he made an exception. And for some reason, he and my father seemed to hit it off, though two more opposite men I don't think you could find. Different as they were, the only thing I ever heard them disagree about seriously was dove shooting.

Albert and Kate Carlson didn't have any children. I don't think it was because they didn't want some. Their house sat directly behind the station, with a stand of yellow pines on one side and a sage brush field on the other. Back of the house was the garden and grape arbor. It was a kid's paradise, and they seemed to like having me around.

Over the years, Mr. Carlson worked on whatever car my father was driving, and my father did Mr. Carlson's taxes and helped him make some shrewd investments. And every fall, they'd have their annual argument over dove shooting.

Hunting birds is the one blood sport my father takes an avid interest in, especially doves. But every year when the season rolled around, Mr. Carlson would insist it was a sin to kill a dove. For any reason, and especially for sport. He said bringing the olive branch to Noah made the dove a sacred bird, and it was a sin to kill something sacred. My father laughed at him and said it was no different than butchering a pig or a cow. "It's a sin," Mr. Carlson would say, "and the wages of sin is death."

I was just back from six months in Germany. I was driving in from New York in my new Mercedes, and I'd been looking forward to showing it to Mr. Carlson. The condition of the station put a lump in my chest.

I left the car where it was and walked up the hill to the house. Miss Kate opened the door immediately as if she'd been waiting for someone. It took her a minute to register who I was.

"David!" she said, pushing open the screen. I held her while she cried on my chest. "Lord, it's David!" I patted her back, and wondered when it had happened.

She inspected me at arms length. "When did you get back?" she said. She dabbed at her eyes, then linked her elbow through mine and said, "Albert's going to be so glad to see you!"

I let her lead me through the living room, relief washing over me. I was thinking that he'd decided to retire. Had I expected him to work forever? He was probably on the backporch tying bass lures.

At the end of the hall she stopped by their bedroom door. She turned and looked up at me, her blue eyes red and watery. She pressed her lips into a thin line. She said, "David, Albert has had a stroke."

A stroke, I thought.

"He's much better, now that I've got him home."

A stroke, I thought.

"Actually, it was a series of strokes. The first one wasn't so bad."

"Why didn't you tell me?" I said.

She turned her face away for a minute. "He didn't want to worry you. After the first one, the doctors thought he was going to be fine." She looked up at me again, struggling for control. "But then he had others."

She had meant to prepare me, but there's no way she could have. The last time I saw him, he'd weighed close to 200 pounds. Now he lay on his back in a hopsital bed, birdlike, wasted, those wonderful hands curled into talons. "Hey," I said, swallowed. "Mr. Carlson?"

His eyes, which had been tracking back and forth, quit their lateral movement and fixed on me like a scanner on something alien to the room. I stood beside the hospital bed, my hands clenching the guardrail, and surveyed the wreckage. He'd never been sick a day in his life. "Mr. Carlson," I said, "it's David."

During the summers, when I was growing up, I'd spent most of my time at the service station. There'd be me and Mr. Carlson, and Solly and Bubba, two old farts that lived on social security and disability checks. They spent most of their time arguing over things like which checker at the A & P had the biggest pair of jugs.

Solly had a blind eye that wandered around in its socket. He was always asking about my dipstick, wanting to know if I'd stuck it in anything interesting lately.

"Mr. Carlson," I said. He was looking at me, his eyes huge in their bony terrain, but there was no indication that he recognized me. He started moving his mouth like he was chewing.

"He's hungry," she said. "I have his lunch ready, but Louise doesn't seem to be coming."

Louise Bates is Solly's third wife and good household help when she's sober. Every now and then, Louise ties one on.

"I can help you," I said. "Just tell me what to do."

She had me put him in a wheelchair. I couldn't get over how much weight he'd lost. It was like picking up a child.

"That hospital food," she said. "Albert wouldn't eat it."

She brought in a serving cart with his plate, and coffee for me. She had me pull up the rocker, and she took the straight back chair.

I watched her cut a pork chop into tiny pieces, and there were mashed potatoes and mashed green peas. She spooned a small bite of potato and meat into his shrunken mouth and waited for him to swallow it. "His teeth don't fit anymore," she said.

He was smaller than lifesize, shriveled. He had aged years in the six months I'd been away. The vacant stare. It was hard. It was very hard.

"You should have let me know," I said. "I'd have come home."

She spooned up another bite. "He was afraid of that, afraid you'd cut your trip short on account of him. I'm going to have to get a grinder for this meat," she said. "He was planning on being well by the time you got back. You *are* getting better, aren't you, Albert?"

It was only then, when she spoke directly to him, that I realized we'd been talking about him as if he weren't there. How much, if anything, did he understand? His eyes moved to her when she spoke, to me when I did.

"You're getting stronger, aren't you?" she said. "By spring you and David can go fishing."

How much of the man I knew was left inside this ruined version of himself, sitting there placidly gumming his food? It was so very hard for me, I wondered how it must be for her. She was intent on getting him fed, and I sat there watching, sipping my coffee and remembering.

He'd always made time to take me fishing. As soon as the weather was fit, he'd get Solly to watch the station, and I'd sleep over the night before, and we'd be up and on the road before dawn. We'd stop at a bait shop for some worms and a couple dozen minnows for me to drown, then drive to the Lockhart Memorial Bridge and park at the base of the levee. Carrying all our stuff, we'd have to climb to get to the sloughs on the other side. Mr. Carlson carried the heavy things, the five hp Johnson and the tackle box. I carried my cane pole, his rod and reel and fly rod, the net, and the sack of food Miss Kate had packed.

If his jon boat wasn't there, we'd borrow someone else's; boats were selected on a first-come-first-served basis. He'd use the motor to get us where we were going, then switch to the shorthandled paddle for sculling. I baited my own hook, threading on the worms to leave the end part wiggling attractively for cat. I hooked the minnows in the cartilage below the dorsal fin, the way he had showed me, being careful to miss the guts. A minnow can live a long time snagged like that, with enough action to lure the crappie. The minnows, worms, and cane pole were for me, and I was supposed to take care of business at my end of the boat. Mr. Carlson was after bass.

On one particular morning, we were having no luck at all. Maybe it was too hot. It was almost noon, and I was sunburned and plagued by gnats and mosquitoes. Mr. Carlson was still hard at it; it looked to me like he planned to try every lure in the box. I'd drunk too many RC's, and I needed to take another leak, but I'd peed three times already, and I could just hear him if I let go again over the side of the boat. "Shit, boy!" he'd say. Come to think of it, I needed to do that, too.

He was sculling carefully through stumps and bushes, teasing the still water with his dry fly, and I got to thinking what his face would look like if I hung my butt over and floated a big turd his way. I was choking back the giggles when suddenly he dropped the paddle and grabbed my pole before it got away, more than half of it already sunk under the water.

He gave me a look and handed it to me.

I was so embarrassed to be caught short like that, I almost broke it in half setting the hook.

"Take it easy," he said. "Don't you remember *anything* I taught you?"

"I'm sorry," I said.

"Sorry don't help. Go at it that way, you'll lose him, if it's a fish. Maybe you've caught yourself a stump."

I felt a firm tug and the line started moving sideways, slicing toward the boat. It was no stump.

"Lead him away," Mr. Carlson said. "Can't you see he's heading under it. Lead him away!"

Sweat popped out on my face. I almost wished he'd take the pole and land the fish for me. I was afraid I'd lose it. Finally, I got the fish to surface at the side of the boat.

"Don't try to lift him, he's too heavy for your line." Mr. Carlson slipped the dip net under him and brought my fish flopping and fighting into the boat.

"Son-of-a-bitch," he said. "It's a gar."

I didn't know but what that was good. I'd never seen a gar before, and this one was big, at least an eight pounder, and it was weird. It was the strangest-looking fish I'd ever seen. It had a long silvery body, sort of snaky, and a beaklike snout full of sharp teeth.

Mr. Carlson held it down with his foot while he got it untangled from the net and tried to work the hook out of its jaw, being careful of the teeth. Between spells of lying still and gasping, my fish would thrash its head and tail wildly about, and Mr. Carlson would say "sumbitch" through his gritted teeth. I wondered why he didn't whack it across the head with the paddle to stun it like I'd seen him do with catfish, but he didn't, just kept working the hook back and forth till he had it loose.

Still holding my fish down with his boot, he reached in his pants pocket and brought out his Case knife. He opened the larger blade, and while he kept his boot on the tail part of the gar, he grasped its head behind the jaws with his left hand and dug out its eyes with the knife.

It took a while for my brain to accept what I was seeing. I stood there with my mouth hanging open, watching the knife move around and around, like he was coring an apple, until he had the eyeballs gouged out and floating in the bilge at the bottom of the boat. "Goddam scavenger," he said through his teeth.

He laid the knife aside, and picked my fish up head and tail and put it back in the water. It lay on its side a while, one empty bloody socket staring up, and then it dived.

I turned on him, Mr. Carlson with his lips skinned back off his teeth, watching it go.

"What'd you do that for?" I said.

He was chuckling, an awful sound. "Scaly bastard," he said.

"That was *my* fish," I said.

He looked at me then. I was shaking.

"David, it was a *gar*," he said, as if that explained everything. He picked up the eyeballs and flicked them into the bushes. "It's a goddam fresh water *shark*, boy."

"It was mine," I said. "I caught it."

He threw up his hands. His mouth got hard at the corners. "All right," he said, "it was your fish."

"It won't die, will it?" I said. "Not for a long time. Not till it starves."

"David," he said. He talked slow, with exaggerated patience, like I was some kind of dummy. "It was a gar."

"I don't care," I'd said. "I don't give a damn what it was."

She had asked me if I wanted more coffee. I think she'd had to repeat it before I heard her.

"No, thanks," I said. "I'm fine." He'd cranked up the motor, and we'd gone home. We never mentioned the gar again.

She was putting the last bite in his mouth now; he had cleaned his plate.

"Would you mind sitting here with him while I wash these up?" she said. "And maybe I ought to change the bed, in case Louise doesn't come."

"I'd be glad to," I said. "Is it all right if I smoke?" I knew she wasn't going to like it, but I needed a cigarette.

"David! You're not smoking!" she said.

"I'm trying to quit."

"Oh, David," she said, and went to get me an ashtray. I could hear her rummaging in the kitchen, opening and closing drawers. When she handed it to me, she said, "Do you remember the time Albert made you smoke?"

"I didn't think you knew about that," I said.

She smiled, and reached to touch the thinning strands of his hair. "Oh, he told me."

I had a Winston in my mouth and was bending over the lighter.

"He meant for it to teach you a lesson."

"I don't smoke much," I lied. Not over three packs a day. "I'm cutting down." I hadn't yet, but I meant to.

"You know, I can't imagine what's become of Louise," she said. "I hope it's nothing bad."

I didn't know what to say to that. I wasn't even sure Miss Kate knew Louise drank.

"Solly's not been well either, you know."

"No, I said, "I didn't."

"I'm afraid it'll turn out to be cancer. Well," she said, a little too brightly, "I'll just do these up, won't take me a minute."

When she was gone, I lit another cigarette. It's a filthy habit. Mr. Carlson watched me, or his eyes watched me; I don't know if he was seeing anything. Maybe he was dying for a cigarette and couldn't tell me. "You want a cigarette?" I said and held it up. "You want a drag?"

He had smoked Chesterfield Kings till the cancer scare switched him to Kents. He put a lot of stock in the Lorillard Company and their micronite filter. Solly dipped. I don't know how many hundred times I'd watched him pull his bottom lip out and tap a can of Brutons over it, with me always hoping this would be the time he'd dump the whole thing in his face. He never did. I'd hang around the station, watching them enjoy their tobacco habit, willing to try cigarettes or snuff, either one, if they'd just offer me some.

The day Miss Kate was talking about, I'd gone out the front door of the station, antsy, looking for something to do, and scuffling through the gravel in the driveway, I'd kicked up a couple of butts. They were pretty long butts; they looked like very smokable butts. I glanced over my shoulder to see if anybody was noticing before I picked them up. Cupping the cigarettes in my sweaty palm, I moseyed toward the house.

I knew Miss Kate was at her sister's for the afternoon, and I didn't think Mr. Carlson would miss me. I went down the back steps to the basement where Miss Kate kept her canned goods, and her laundry detergent, and a big box of Diamond matches for starting trash fires.

I had straightened out one of the butts and was trying to light it without setting my nose on fire when I felt his hand lock on my shoulder like a pair of vise-grips. "Whatcha doin'?" he said.

I dropped the match and the smoldering butt on the cement floor, and Mr. Carlson twisted a shoe on it. "You figuring on taking up smoking?" he said.

I told him I'd like to give it a try.

"Two things, then," he said. "Don't bum and don't sneak. If you're going to do it, do it like a man."

He took me upstairs and had me sit in his chair with the smoking stand beside it. He offered me the pack and I took a Kent between my thumb and forefinger like I'd seen him hold them. He lit me up with his Zippo, and I pulled in as much smoke as my mouth would hold, then blew it out in a cloud.

"Naw, naw," he said. "Lemme show you."

He lit his own cigarette, took a pull that left a half-inch glowing coal on the tip of it, and inhaled the smoke down to his toenails. He blew a stream of it out his nostrils, and the rest came up while he explained to me how to inhale like he did.

I coughed and got strangled the first couple of tries, but eventually, I could inhale to his satisfaction and blow smoke out my nose, too. Then he told me if I held on to it long enough, the smoke would begin to leak out around my eyeballs. I thought that sounded neat, so I tried it. It didn't work.

It was along about then that I couldn't ignore any longer how wimpy I was feeling. But I smoked my Kent down to the filter, like he was doing. He offered me another, but I declined, saying I might lie back and relax after such a good smoke.

That's how Miss Kate found me when she got home from her sister's.

She knew immediately that something was wrong, since my face wasn't normally green. "What in the world's happened to you?" she said.

"Now, Kate, don't get excited," he said. He'd looked pretty guilty, so I must have looked awful. "The boy's just . . . "

"I think it was something I ate," I said.

I wasn't about to rat on him. I might not be able to smoke like a man, but I sure as hell could die like one.

While she changed his bed, I held his hand, wrapping it around mine in a semblance of the handshake that had always been a ritual between us. Once or twice I thought I saw a flicker of something in his eyes. But I couldn't be sure what it was.

Dove season opened the next Saturday at noon. I was buying shotgun shells at WonderMart, and I ran into Louise Bates leaving the pharmacy section. She had a little vial of pills that she said was some Elavil Doc Patterson had prescribed for Miss Kate. "I hear you was over to see Albert the other day," she said.

I told her I was.

"Looks like hell, don't he?" she said, her voice louder than I would have liked.

"He looks bad," I said. "But Miss Kate says he's improving."

She barked. You couldn't call it a laugh, and several heads turned our way. "She's always saying that. She thinks she gets him to eat a bite or two, he's better." She held the prescription for me to read the label. "Happy pills."

"Maybe," I said. "I don't know."

"Well, I do," she said. "He won't never get no better. He'll get bedsores next, you wait and see."

I switched hands with the shotgun shells, wanting to get away.

"I hope he dies," she said, pushing a finger at my chest. "I do, I hope he dies today. Best thing for him. And her, too."

"How's Solly?" I asked her, wanting to change the subject.

Her face completely fell. It crumbled. "What'd you hear about Solly?" she said.

"Miss Kate told me he'd been a little under the weather."

"Yeah," she said. "That's right. A little under the weather." She stared off into space for a minute; I was getting set to excuse myself, tell her I had to get along to my dove hunt.

She said, "Them two, they was as proud of how you turned out as if you'd been their own. Sit around crowing over how good you was doing, how much money you was making."

She laid a rusty, knuckly hand on my arm. I think she knew how much I wanted to get away before she told me any more. "Not to have children," she said. "That's the worst part."

My father was excited to have me home for opening day, and we were going to a private field owned and operated by the Rod and Gun Club. It was as close to being baited as they could make it and still be legal. There was a bracing sting in the air and an overcast sky so that the sun in our eyes wouldn't be a problem. It was the perfect afternoon for a dove hunt.

As we walked the edge of the field looking for places to set up, my father introduced me to a business acquaintance of his and they talked about the job I'd done in Germany, and about Reaganomics and the strength of the dollar. My father pointed out my new Mercedes, proud of me and proud of the machine, not for the way it worked, but what it stood for.

As soon as I could, I told them I was going to move to the other side, so as not to crowd them and spoil their chances of getting the limit. They laughed a little at that, and I ignored the questioning look on my father's face as I raised a hand and walked toward the other side of the field.

I worked my way to the opposite corner and set my camp stool in front of a small stand of scrub oak. It was a good spot, it was a perfect day, and mid-afternoon, hundreds and hundreds of doves flew in to feed on the cut milo. The hunters ringing the edges of the huge field kept the birds ricocheting back and forth across it.

As a wave of doves flew toward me, I'd raise my 16 gauge and pull the trigger. I did that all afternoon, using most of a box of shells turning them back when they'd head my way. But I managed not to hit anything.

Bob Millard

Giles

    Giles getting tall,
really tall, standing angled,
slumped, slouched, leaned up
against high school brick walls
caging Camels, laughing,
staccato finger popping . . .

    Giles hunkered down
in twilight green '53 Ford,
long legs speed clutching,
gear jamming, scowling, head cocked
to one side, left hand fastened
around chin, zipping
through neon lit wild sides
of Saturday night howling
"dog dick," "dog ass,"
"dog breast," at old drunks
in paint trucks, red lights,
fire plugs, pedestrians,
colored girls hooking on Jefferson Street.

    Giles floating on
Center Hill inner tube islands,
sharing beer sneaked from the old man's Frigidaire,
overhauling trolling motors, making them whine
across the lake, jumping off 20-foot sheer bluffs
screaming skeins of "dog breasts," laughing
wildly, catching glimpses of angels
out of eye corners on the way down,
landing can openers.

Bob Millard

    Giles reading Catcher
In The Rye seven times and leaving home,
note under windshield wipers
half a block from my parents' house,
hitching illicit rides on mail trucks
and semis, change of socks, pack of Camels,
leather hump strap unloading freight,
moving vans from Houston to Las Vegas,
getting street wise, sullen, gambling
intuition against the odds, sleeping
with one eye open.

    Giles coming back,
arriving bit by bit like post cards
mailed from truck stop restaurants, constant
slipping out back doors to six pac recollections
of 12-year-old chippies, hungry, hanging out
cold and crazy on dust tumbled
late night freight docks, shivering smart-assed
come-ons, bumming smokes with Cagney sneers.

    Giles in and out
of college, eluding draft boards,
trailing reefer giggles and raving letters
through my room, screaming at me, Uncle Warren,
the old man, the old man's light bulb business,
"you prick, you sonofabitch," swilling rum,
fluxing through psilocybin hallucinations with
amazing deftness, punctuating conversations
with stiletto finger flexes.

    Giles drifting back
out on the road, catching buses, working odd jobs,
stuffing parachutes,
jumping from airplanes outside Denver,
Phoenix, L. A., Seattle, with other sky mad
derelicts, streaking through air like back doors
to hundreds of Saturday nights, dancing in clouds,
laughing all the way down still screaming
"dog breast," "oh you mother."

Levi Frazier, Jr.

In the Presence of Mine Enemies

Big Six had been at The Wall for 10 years, but he still hadn't quite gotten the hang of it. Freeworld and inmate alike all knew that Six didn't have the heart to be in the worst prison in Tennessee.

"I ain't got use to it yet, don't reckon I ever will," Six said to the shoes of Warden Clark, who stood exactly two feet shorter and at least a foot wider than Six.

"Well, just maybe this prison ain't the place for you to be Big Six. Hell, after a while, The Wall'll get to ya. Shit! Look at me!" The warden shot out his pudgy pink hands from his side, resembling a miniature Christ on the cross.

"I could give you a transfer this week and you'd be in Memphis by Monday."

"I appreciate it Warden, but a prison is a prison, and work is work. I hate to see any man, anywhere locked up 'bout as much as I hate being cooped up in a place. So if it's all the same to you, I'd just as soon stay put."

Six had just returned to The Wall after a two week hiatus for recuperation at Mercy Hospital. He had seen two inmates fighting, but he did not see the homemade shank they were fighting over. As a matter of fact, he didn't remember getting stuck at all. What he did recall though, was his solid bright blood sprouting three feet into the air from his side as he lay staring at ankles and cuffs staring at him.

"If I had'a knowed either one of 'em was strapped, I wouldn't have gone in there by myself," Six told officers Brandon and Crabtree, who stood on either side of his hospital bed, nodding their head "yes" to an obvious lie. They knew that shank or no shank, Six would have taken his two hundred and seventy-five pounds into the trouble, even if there was a gun. It had happened before.

But Six was back on his job, walking the yard like he owned it, showing off his iron-on looking scar to whoever wanted a peek.

"Almost got your big ass killed, didn't you Six?" jived Bobby, sliding a joint back into his pocket as Six strolled up. "I bet the next time your jolly butt's gon run the other way when you see somebody thump'n."

"Yea, but I bet if Six was running this joint, wouldn't be no fuck'n, fight'n, steal'n, or squeal'n," Frog said with a toothless grin.

"Damn right, and church services three times a day."

Six tucked in his shirt.

"If you'd a' had your behinds in Church, maybe you wouldn't be in here now. That goes for you too Frog." Six stood staring at the young armed robber whose daddy was a minister.

"Your ass was in church," Bobby responded, "and still is to this very day. Now look where you at. You ain't got a damn thang!"

Big Six knew by Bobby's deliberate manner that this speech had been planned, if not rehearsed for many nights by the twenty-six year old lifer. Six wanted to walk away but he was afraid that one step would cause Bobby to finish in grand fashion just what he had started.

Out of nervousness, Six batted his eyes.

Bobby took his cue.

"You know something Six . . . ain't no difference between your time and my time, except for your little extended furloughs and that's all they are. Tell me Six, what more you got that I ain't got?"

The unruffled young triple murderer grabbed his crotch, leaned back against the barbed wire fence and cocked his head to the side.

"What is it? You get a chance to watch a few more hours of TV. You can keep your lights on a little longer? I know what it is!" Bobby snapped his fingers, springing off the fence. "If you've been a real good boy, you might, just might, get a chance to sit next to the warden at lunch time . . . Get wise Six. You just as institutionalized as I am. We both behind bars, see?" Bobby said, pointing at the tall gray spikes guarding the corridor's entrance to the units.

Six stared at the bars hoping they would unlock themselves so he could escape this punishment for a crime he had not committed.

"Remember how you was gon always start your own business or help your son get one started for himself? I just don't hear it no more Six! Now, your eyes and my eyes see the same thang."

Bobby walked over and stood between him and the bars.

"If you live in a man's house long enough, Six, whether you like it or not, it becomes your home."

Unspoken, jumbled phrases lay heavy on the old man's tongue as a mixture of fear and confusion swirled in his head.

"And in so far as all that church bullshit is concerned," Bobby started up again, "Frog got his charge because of church."

"Stop lying on the church, boy!" Six shouted, feeling a bolt of lightning doing a two step above his shoulder.

"Lying, who's lying?" Bobby continued. "He held up his own daddy's church the first Sunday he come back from De-troit."

They slapped, clapped, and laughed until tears ran down their faces and hid their wire beards.

Six shook his head and guided his huge carcass toward the staff dining hall on the other side of the yard.

"Why bother?" he thought. "For every one that sees the light, one hundred go astray. Why bother?"

"Ask your son why he didn't stay in church, Six. Ask him." Rising on the tip of his toes, Bobby yelled his words like javelins across the void between them.

Given a choice, Six would have welcomed the shank repetitiously into his side, rather than feel the dull fangs of Bobby's words rip into his chest like a committee of rabid dogs.

Barry or Lil' Six, as he was known on the streets, was nothing like his father. He was small, mean, quick-tempered, and a thief.

"Boy, you can steal anything but somebody's heart," Six schooled Barry before he got locked up the last time.

"Why steal something that's worth so little and breaks so easy," Barry replied.

That was the last time Six had seen his son. He had sent him letters but Six never received a reply.

"He got hisself in this trouble, let him get hisself out!" Six said to himself, not feeling at all what he was thinking. If he didn't act and look so much like his mother, Six possibly could have blotted him out, or at least his faults, but like his mother, Six loved the bitter and sweet or in this case, the thief and the child.

About a month after Six had gotten out of the hospital, he started talking about how he was going to leave The Wall and never come back, maybe even go out of state and change his name. Every conversation he had with the guards and the inmates had something to do with how "ti'ed" he was of doing nothing with his life for a bunch of nobodies who didn't give a damn one way or the other. Many days he would saunter up the tall fence budding barbed wire at the top, look up and smile, then walk away, shaking his steel gray head, while mumbling aloud to himself.

"Think'n 'bout escaping," Bobby laughed one day.

"What's it to you!" Six snapped, his wrinkled uniform in much need of ironing.

"Well, it just seems to me that these walls kinda tall for an old gray ass fool like you Six. Better go out the front door. It'll be a lot easier."

"Tall walls don't hold nothing but short minds," Six replied, turning away, reciting the Twenty-third Psalm to himself over and over again.

The next day Frog caught Bobby coming out of the mess hall and handed him a newspaper he had found lying on the yard. Bobby took the toothpick he had in his mouth out, and folded the paper like it was a program from the racetrack.

"Damn!"

"Happened two days ago." Frog stared at Bobby.

"No wonder, he's been acting so fuck'n crazy."

Word slowly sanked through The Wall that there had been a suicide at Fort Pillow. Lil' Six was found in his room, hands tied behind his back and hanging from sheets knotted over the waterpipe above his bed.

For the next fews days, The Wall was like a monastery. And though no one said anything to Six, everyone knew that Six knew why the silence scraped the walls in hushed tones.

"I'm leaving goddammit, I tell you! I'm leaving." Six mumbled to himself, no longer reciting the Twenty-third Psalm.

This went on for two days and on the third day, it happened.

It was during yard call.

Six was watching a basketball game between E North Upper and F West Lower.

The dark horse-muscled tight bodies dipped and angled for the seminetted rim attached to a pole flung into concrete. As Six watched and mumbled to himself, he thought of Barry and the many games of twenty-one they had played before Barry lost his mother and many of his interests.

F West Lower was leading by three points needing only two more points to win the game. Lucky had the ball and the crowd as he climbed an invisible ladder and escorted the brand new orange ball into the nets. But before the ball could disengage itself from the cloth, Six was on the fence, inches away from the barbed wire.

The game stopped.

The inmates said nothing as one guard yelled, "Six, Six, where the hell do you think you're going?"

"Man on the fence! Man on the fence!" blared Tower One over the walky-talky.

"I'm going to blast him to hell if he doesn't halt," Tower One continued.

"Blast my ass," said the Warden over his radio.

"How the hell you gon' explain shooting a damn guard. Just wait for him on the other side."

Wendell Carl Murray

Desire, and Other Topics

His name is Paul, but he lacks conviction about it. Indeed, his last girlfriend called him nothing at all. To attract his attention, she spoke loudly. One night after making love, he cupped her face in his hands, kissed her eyelids, and said, "You never use my name."

"I know."

"Why?"

She sat up in bed and considered. Her eyes lowered, she watched her hands, her fingers which absently kneaded the hem of the blanket.

Paul lit a cigarette. Its coal traced a bright arc across the mirror. Again he asked, quietly, "Why?"

She surrendered: "Paul, Paul, Paul, Paul, Paul," she said, then lay on her side, turned away from him for the night.

Paul laughed. He didn't know what else to do.

Pinned to the wall above Paul's desk is a sheet of plain white paper. On it he writes words or phrases he wishes to remember, names such as Inoshiro Honda and Ahasuerus; references for future study on such topics as the seventeen-year locusts; and obscure dialogue from forgotten movies: "Mr. Freud," Van Heflin says in *Johnny Eager*, "take a letter."

One evening, a TV newsman interviews a Pentagon general, questioning him about the effects of nerve gas on civilian populations should it ever be used in Europe. Paul writes on the paper in large letters, "COLLATERAL DAMAGE!"

Paul sits in a new restaurant with his new girlfriend. Over stuffed flounder, they speak of the Victorians.

"But the poets," Paul says, "understood well the dilemma of the modern age. The Romantics lost God and drank to their freedom. The Victorians just drank. They lost God and understood what that meant."

"I found a bone," Ginger says.

"Looks like it," Paul says, watching her pull the bone from the fish with her fingers and drop it on the edge of the plate.

"You would think," Ginger says, "you could go into a place these days without having to worry about things like that."

"You would think so," Paul agrees.

Coffee started, Paul opens the kitchen curtains. The ascending and cantilevered spars of the bridge which spans the river are a dark graphic against the morning sky. During the first of what seems to him sometimes his excessive number of years in college, Paul had studied piano. "To build a bridge," his teacher had said, "takes great skill . . . but not art." A man in his sixties, Venetian by birth, Mr. Bruno had come to the States in the thirties. His history included suffering the invasion of Austrian troops during the Great War and an American wife born in Denver.

Ginger stands in the doorway, her hair still rumpled from bed. She smiles, "Bye," she says.

"Coffee?"

"Thanks, but I'm late."

When she is gone, Paul pours his coffee and sits at his desk. Opening his notebook, he writes, confident one sentence will lead to another. "Sometimes you can't help it. You sit at your desk, bent over your work, and your muscles tighten. You draw yourself up straight in your chair and, after some moments, find you have been staring into the glass of the window before you, into the moon of your lamp reflected there . . . ."

He continues: "Or you are on the highway, driving your car under the real moon, which is perhaps gibbous, the landscape washed in quicksilver, the air through your open windows cool, made odorous by pines, and for miles you don't realize you've missed your turn, not until the next town which is named Bolivar or Bunkey where you wheel around in the gravel lot of a Bar-B-Q joint, its neon sign singing, glaring in the clear night air . . . ."

His coffee is cold. Paul warms it from the pot. Mr. Bruno had died during the second month of his sixty-fourth year. A lung hemorrhage. On his stone was engraved

> AND AS THE ARTIST MADE HIS MIRACLES
> THE ARTLESS BOY WAS OFTEN IN HIS WAY.

Paul takes his pencil and tries again: "You're distracted," he writes simply, "and you don't know why."

That is better, Paul decides. Much better.

Baldwin, an acquaintance of Paul's, discusses over beers one night the advantages of an open marriage. As an anniversary gift for his wife, Baldwin plans a surprise. The gift is to be a night in a motel with a man she will enjoy.

Paul declines.

"There'll be champagne," Baldwin says.

Paul shakes his head.

"Why not?"

Paul considers. "The whole idea is repulsive," he says.

Baldwin is offended. "You don't like girls or what?"

"She's very pretty," Paul says. "That's not the point."

"Jesus," Baldwin says. He leaves the money for his two beers and moves to another table.

On an overcast January morning Paul turns thirty-two. His body revolts. His doctor tells him it is nothing more than the stomach virus that is going around. Paul is skeptical, decides to quit smoking, to get more exercise. "It wouldn't hurt," the doctor says.

For his birthday, Ginger buys him a coffee mug to take to work. Painted on it are caricatures, three barely recognizable birds perched on a prostrate elephant. "Don't Let The Turkeys Get You Down," the legend reads. Along with this came a card. "Thanks for being you." Paul considers the gift thoughtful, affecting. By evening he feels a little better. He and Ginger go to a movie: a science-fiction film which the media claims is a phenomenon. For nearly two hours the screen suffers flashes of multicolored light. An arcade game, Paul believes.

"You don't know how to have fun," Ginger says afterwards in the cafe where they have stopped for hamburgers.

Paul is still a bit dizzy from the virus. "Maybe not," he says. Not yet as ready to eat as he had supposed, he pushes away his food.

"You need to loosen up," Ginger says.

Paul curves the thumb and index finger of one hand into a circle and presents it to Ginger for her inspection, moving his hand so that she might see all sides. With his other hand he repeats the performance. "Now," he says, "watch. I shall amaze." He hides both hands behind his head. "Poof!" he says, then reveals his magic. These circles made by his fingers are now interlocked.

Ginger is amused. "You're crazy," she says. "I'd suspected it before, but now I'm sure."

"You're on to me?"

"Afraid so," Ginger says.

"Ah, well . . . better you should know." Paul orders a Coke. The carbonation will settle his stomach. "I once had a mind," he says. "Years ago, it was . . . I've forgotten how many."

Paul is very tired. He decides he would rather spend the night alone.

In the afternoon paper, Paul reads that a woman has drowned herself in the river. A simple affair: during the night she stopped her car, a rented car, on the bridge and climbed over the rail. This morning, downriver, in a cul-de-sac bounded by sand and overgrowth, two men fishing for cat found her. Strangely enough, the car hadn't been rented to the woman but to a man named Jarvis whom the police are now trying to locate.

Paul writes in his notebook: "She had gone for a drive, stopped on the bridge, perhaps, at first, only to look. She considered her life. It by now had become only a matter of heartbeats . . . ."

He is alone and drinking whiskey. He wonders about Linda. It has been four years since their divorce.

She *was* lovely, Paul admits. And intelligent. Her recent book—*Martin Heidegger: The Failure of Sensibilities*—was acclaimed. Paul read the reviews. "Long overdue," one had said. Another: "The author describes the failure of our civilization as a whole, and she does so brilliantly, objectively and with grit . . . ."

Paul doesn't understand how one can be objective about the failure of civilization. With his pencil he draws a line across the page beneath his last passage. They were in school too long, he and Linda. No money, no time for each other. He is pleased by her success. "But you so admired the orderly mind," he writes. "Always you preferred counterpoint to chords, roses to orchids . . . fish to crustaceans . . . monoliths to me."

Paul's work disturbs him. He is a typographer. Part of his job consists of setting type for the newspaper ads of a national discount drug chain. Some of the items advertised are quite personal. Paul is weary of being assaulted daily by these reminders of the bodily functions of strangers.

Over lunch, he argues with his supervisor. "And besides that, they take advantage of people," Paul says. "Sure, the prices are cheap, but their merchandise is worthless."

Elizabeth, his supervisor, is proud of her Irish descent. On Saint Patrick's Day she wore a jumpsuit of green satin accented with sequins arranged into the shapes of shamrocks. During the time he has worked under her, Paul has become her friend. She is now on her third marriage, and, though this husband excites her, as she explains it there is in the marriage no warm spot into which she can curl herself up. She misses this warm spot, she has confided to Paul. It's more important than she had imagined.

"I wish my name were Mercedes," Elizabeth says, ignoring Paul's complaint, and, indeed, Paul is not really serious about it. The drug chain is a major account, their prompt payments responsible for the monthly unsticking of an otherwise hopelessly mired cash flow.

Paul laughs. Elizabeth's fingers are studded with rings: all three wedding sets, a turquoise, a star sapphire, a cameo, a plain gold signet. Too, she wears earrings, necklaces, bracelets, an anklet. Linda would be appalled.

"The name doesn't matter," Paul says.

Elizabeth smiles. "Still straight out of a dime novel, am I?"

"Something like that."

Elizabeth's eyes are suddenly those of the wounded. "I know," she says, the words soft, barely voiced.

For supper Paul cooks spaghetti. The garlic and onions must fry in oil and butter for five minutes. Paul switches on the TV. The police have found Jarvis. He is a journalist, it turns out, in town to cover the concert of a popular musician for a popular magazine. He explained when questioned that he had just met the woman, that she had taken the car while he slept. "She was confused," Jarvis is reported to have said. "She wanted to know why things happen the way they do." The police, the broadcaster teases, have not ruled out the possibility of foul play.

Ginger arrives with the wine. The sauce must simmer yet another thirty minutes. Paul recounts for Ginger the broadcast.

"He should've known," Ginger says, speaking of Jarvis. "He should've done something."

"What could he have done?"

"I don't know. He could've talked to her."

"He probably did."

"Not about the right things," Ginger says.

"What are they?"

"What?"

"The right things?"

"Something besides body talk," Ginger says, apparently disgusted with the lascivious natures of men. "Oh, baby," she mocks, affecting a male voice, "that feels so good . . . oh . . . oh . . . oh . . . ."

"Beautiful," Paul says.

"Men are such dorks."

"All pecker and feet," Paul tells her. "Christ, she should've gone to a priest."

Ginger sets her glass of wine on the TV and picks up her purse from the floor. "Call me when you're in a better mood," she says.

Paul watches the taillights of her car until they disappear around the corner, hidden now by the house at the end of the block. "Christ," he says to no one. "Jesus Christ."

Desiring to revive the soliloquy, Paul has started a play. At one point, the principal defends to the audience his unpredictability:

GEORGE

> Must there be a reason? In these times when the *non sequitur* has become our escape, our watchword, our *modus vivendi*, must there be . . . a point? Illogic—it ranges the earth as welcome in our hearts as a warm day in March.

Alone in his apartment, Paul recites the speech. He is pleased with it, but he wishes for an actor's voice. It is early in the evening when Paul does this; it is much later when he wonders if he should have stayed in the sciences. Having left the notes and typescript of his play to clutter his desk, he has discovered while reading a physics text what appears to be a paradox: in the case of mass approaching the speed of light many changes occur to that mass; it doesn't seem to Paul that energy is properly conserved. The laws of thermodynamics are explicit, Paul believes. The answer, he decides, must lie in some quirk with which he is unfamiliar. He pulls from his shelf Einstein's *The Meaning of Relativity* and, though his calculus is poor, resolves to work his way through it.

Paul considers calling Ginger to tell her good night. She has been busy lately—her job, she has repeatedly explained. Ginger works for an advertising agency. Paul isn't sure what she does there. She never wants to talk about it. "People *make* time for what they want to do," Paul told her. "I can't help it," Ginger answered. Paul dials her number but hangs up before her phone begins to ring. It is very late by now, and he is afraid to know that she isn't yet home.

He is less pleased with the play than he was. George's speech, after all, is not a proper soliloquy. It is alienation, a deliberate destruction of the audience's suspension of disbelief. Before going to bed, Paul sets Einstein's book on the nightstand on top of Proust and his Italian edition of Dante.

By summer Ginger has gone. "It's not fair to you," she tells Paul. He is spending the night with his play when Arnie stops by with bourbon. Arnie is a big man of Norwegian descent. His family has a nickname for him which Paul has never learned to pronounce.

Paul and Arnie drink the bourbon and talk for some time. They joke about Baldwin and his accommodating wife. They speak of *Moby Dick*, of the power of Joyce, of baseball and obscure players they had admired when they were boys. Paul remembers reading in the paper of the death of Ron "The Suitcase" Steinberg.

"So, 'The Suitcase' packed it in," Arnie says.

Paul smiles. For a moment he and Arnie are quiet together. "The

Suitcase" was at one time or another on the team rosters of most of the franchises in both leagues. He was famous for his travels. It hardly mattered whether he could play ball.

The bourbon is nearly gone before Arnie brings up the subject of Catherine.

Arnie feels used by her. Having made during the past weeks all sorts of excuses for not seeing him, last night during a thunderstorm she called him on the phone. She was in tears.

"What's wrong?" Arnie asked.

She was breathless. "I can't talk . . . " she said, "don't want to . . . . There's nothing to say . . . ."

Silence. Her tears might have stopped—perhaps, not. But Arnie heard no more sounds of her crying. He listened to the hum of the wire. Finally, in a low voice, "I want to die," Catherine said.

Arnie has no car. Some months ago he was arrested again for driving while drunk. His license was revoked, his car impounded. He had to run to Catherine's apartment. It was several blocks through the rain. Wet and cold, he stood at her door and knocked.

There was no answer.

"Catherine," he called, now knocking louder, but, still, the house was quiet.

Arnie put his shoulder into the door, and the jamb splintered. Catherine sat naked in the lotus position on her living room rug. Her eyes were closed in meditation.

"Catherine," Arnie said, and she held up her hand, a signal for him to wait. It was after a minute or so that she stood, took him in her arms. "Thank you for coming," she said.

Catherine stroked Arnie's wet hair, held him tightly against her body. She kissed his cheek and looked into his eyes. "I need to be by myself," she said.

"What's the matter?"

"I don't know what to tell you."

Arnie carried her to bed, undressed, and slept all night with her in his arms. When they woke, she told him she didn't want to see him again.

He doesn't understand.

"It's not fair to you," Paul explains.

"What does that mean?"

Paul shrugs. He thinks of telling Arnie about how a fisherman returns his catch to the water, how he holds the fish until the water expands its gills and then lets it go, watching it slip away beneath the light.

"I don't know," Paul says.

"I'm worried about her."

"I can see." Paul divides what is left of the bourbon between them. "I would be too," he says.

Paul has lost heart. His play is too strident. Page one is laughable, no way to begin a play.

He turns his notebook to a clean page.

To my descendants, or whomever—An Indulgence:
I am thirty-two and already fearing death. This notebook is no record of a life. It cannot show you my shape, my gestures, my curly hair, my dark eyes. All it can do is show you my mind, such as it is, during these moments I choose to write.

Amazing, really, that I'm here, speaking to you, my fingers hurting from the pressure of the pen, my eyes burning from cigarette smoke and glare, my watch ticking. The ink slides onto the page as the fan in the doorway pulls the August night into my room. Cicadas chirr in the shrubs outside my window, their shared song quite different from that of the tree frogs down the street.

I would tell you that I've tasted sea water, seen the halo of the moon, and felt the warmth which is not purely physical of a wood fire on a cold night. I've loved and hurt. I've laughed. I've done all this before you. It is what we have in common.

Look at my words. I scream at you. My chest rises and falls as I breathe deep draughts of air. Listen. You can almost hear me.

Paul closes his notebook. "I knew him, Horatio," he says aloud. Paul begins to laugh. It is a nervous laugh, self-conscious—the laugh one politely manufactures at the end of a tired joke.

Linda is to give a lecture at the university. The philosophy department is bringing her from New York where she now lives and teaches. Her topic is to be German existentialism.

The chairman of the philosophy department introduces her, citing a review of her book as proof of her expertise. Paul has arrived late and stands in the back.

"Much critical ink has been spilled . . . " Linda begins. She once started a paper that way. After Paul had laughed, she had crossed it out.

The audience is small but rapt. Linda has gained weight. Paul waits for her diction to lapse. She will add s's to her words and speak baby talk, joking as she used to when testing a paper on Paul. But her diction doesn't lapse this time. Her eyes meet his, and she smiles a hello.

To illustrate a point, Linda relates an anecdote concerning her husband, who is an administrator of some sort for the government. The story has something to do with a trip to Greece, but Paul doesn't really listen. It presumably is a funny story, for the audience laughs. Some people clap.

There is a reception afterwards, held in the home of the chairman. Paul smokes a cigarette before going inside. It is nearly Halloween. The air is crisp, the moon egg-shaped and yellow. Firewood is burning somewhere. Paul finishes his cigarette and goes inside to the hors d'oeuvres and wine.

It is some time before he can talk to Linda. She and the host are discussing points raised during the lecture. The chairman looks like Francis Drake, Paul decides. Finally, Linda is left alone.

"Congratulations," Paul tells her.

She nods her head in acknowledgment. "Good to see you," she says.

"You too," Paul says.

They drink their wine.

"So," Linda says, "what are you doing now?"

"The same," Paul says.

"Any writing?"

"Not very good."

"I'm sorry."

"Right," Paul says. He pauses for a moment. "I couldn't read your book," he says.

"You didn't like it?"

"I didn't say I didn't like it," Paul says, suddenly angry. "I said I couldn't read it."

"Oh," Linda says.

"I'm sorry." Paul dips a celery stick into some kind of curry. "Tell me about this husband of yours," he says.

"What do you want to know?"

"Are you happy?"

Linda considers. "Yes," she says.

"I mean, do you gargle the same mouthwash? Lick trading stamps on Saturday afternoons after shopping? Rub feet under the covers?"

"Don't be stupid," Linda says.

Paul shakes his head. "Again," he says, "I'm sorry."

"Why do you hate me?"

"I don't," Paul says. He takes her hand. "I really am sorry."

While driving home, Paul is careful. He doesn't understand what it is that keeps someone on his own side of the road. What is this control? How did we all come to agree that it is necessary?

The play abandoned, Paul listens to Brahms. He has decided that records are a miracle. "To be able to hear Brahms any time you want," he explains to a friend at work, "it's like having the 'Mona Lisa' hanging in your living room."

His friend, a pressman, unwraps a sandwich, his hands black with ink. "I suppose it is," the pressman says, "but what amazes me are airplanes.

It's hard to imagine that something made out of all that steel can fly."
"Yes," Paul says, "it's hard to imagine."
"Of course, sometimes they fall."
"Yes, sometimes they do."

Don Keck DuPree

Gross Anatomy: September 7, 1983
for Cissy

    Synergists also are important
    when a Prime Mover crosses
        several joints

    Friday bombed Med/CATs twice :
Friday Tutweiler, dean's child. Boy from Gaffney
    Like tress.   Battery girl, a tad precise.
     They're fine. And good to me.
    Secure the wrapping : Tuck my sheet.
   Our formalin friendship deep as gneiss.
    No son or lover had me this way :
     Palmar aponeurosis cut free :
Never to wander; however bed clothes might lay.

     Movers now are three :
Hefting scalpel; flexing : *Abductor pollicis brevis*
   Draws a thumb forward : phalanges meet.
   That last day; neither considered this :
I touched his tie, and turned, needless of premise
    Or future : And now three of us.
   Forester louder than other two :
Friday and girl work hard; don't say much :
We've no time for gossip, these afternoons.

     Friday's my chuck
Now. Perfect symphysis : muscle, organ, and bone :
 I grow less that he grow great : his surgeon's touch
  Raw; but one day fine : he'll toughen and hone :
    I be scattered about the brome,

Don Keck DuPree

Backfield, family home   :
Friday forget, save this   : cheshire ring   :
Orbicularis oris, seat of a kiss, exposed, known   :
Wake one day   me inside growing

Perspectives in the Dark

with Blanton and Max

Coves bleed from the Mountain
The moon burns upon the dark
The valley is a cutwork plane
And we stand safe on this scarp
Of bluff above the town.

Three of us keep the house
This winter firing hearths
Measure of the time from zero
Center when the fiery dwarf
Turns again from the south.

It is the precise chill
Which refines the light
And counts each tree in rank
On rank down the dry
Tiered slope as the cove spills

To the plain. Her movement
In green nephrite is tabled
Among plants which escape
Their seasonal due by craft.
And what is the sense

Of this moment in the dark
Watching? The cold defines
Our blood; we stand
Mute keeping fire behind
Glass, where man charted

Toward silence stops to hear
And see, straining after
The searing reverberance
Of that first moment before
The edges began to blur.

We will do what we can
When the reel begins again:
The river goddess, lotus
Along arm, will remind.
And she but stone by man.

Alison T. Reed

Red-Bellied Woodpecker
for Robert Penn Warren

I 9:30 A.M.

His head was on fire with the blood
Of the midmorning sun. He shone
Like a copy from a coloring book, a painted beauty.

An eternal moment he sat, fluffing out
His black and white zigzag. He stared
With a cold and blank impiety.

Without an eyeblink he left in the glory
Of a red charge,
A child's mighty rocket, squawking.

II

Above Kentucky Lake the hawks
Fishtail. In downtown Cadiz, in Trigg County,
A man sells red mullet and laughs like a boy.

The southeast view from Barkley Inn,
Miraculous Orion and Aldebaran,
Clears the head, starts haunting.

Along a tension cable blackbirds
Settle into place. A man with carroty hair
Watches and jots something in a book.

The wind moves in their feathers
And the marshals of the field
Show their red and yellow wings.

• • •

Light thins gradually along the Hickman Bottoms
Like an evaporating stream
Or the slow loss of goldenrod from the air.

Two finches in their summer yellow
Lift their wings in the ashes of Claudette's,
The fish place that caught fire last winter.

On the long table a man had put a note:
Do not try to rouse me. You'll find me rather dull,
Flying out of the candle-colored air.

His eyes were flaggy gray, but always reddened with thinking.
Once when an owl looked in the window he turned crimson
And stared through the glass like a mother into a nursery.

• • •

Leaves curl to the green spine
Roll to the crisp edge and sweat lightly
In the shadow of their branch.

The migrating warblers, particularly cerulean
And myrtle in the fall of the light, ripple like a deep breeze
The understory of dogwoods in the climax forest.

This is the day. There is Wordsworthian stone
And the violet by the winding trail.
The dark trees protect the tunneling clear space.

• • •

Above the ridge the birds fly in a great black scarf.
The pass through low clouds, and light,
Folding the wings of a thousand collapsing tents.

For a moment the one red brow of sun
Is over the cliff-hanging congeries. The eyes catch fire
And then the ragged profiles are backlit by gray.

Alison T. Reed

At the edge of Birnam Forest, someone is awake with the owls.
It is barely a man's shadow,
But a slight irregularity in the air.

III   9:31 A.M.

A moment later he came back,
Midmorning sun breaking cover,
Sudden arrowshine shot through clouds.

He stopped his stiff tartan body
In a magic focus
And cocked his overbearing eyes

Before he clawed skyward in a clear, thought-free pattern,
Cool and utterly content,
Like a great-winged child.

Leigh Allison Wilson

The Snipe Hunters

On a map the state of Tennessee is a rough parallelogram. At a glance, though, you can tell that the east and west sides are neither parallel nor equal. For instance, when I was a little girl, a governor by the name of Dunn changed all the interstate highway signs to read "Welcome to the Three States of Tennessee." He meant to point out to tourists the fact that not only were they crossing into a different state, but they were also in one of three separate places: East Tennessee, Middle Tennessee, or West Tennessee. In a strong sense this is true. However, in 1976 another governor changed the signs to read "Welcome to the Great State of Tennessee," and now tourists glide on through our state and are not privy to its secret.

My people are East Tennesseans, have been since James Patrick McGuire took a wild hair in 1783 and moved from Fermanagh County, Ireland, to White Pine in Jefferson County, Tennessee. According to the family rumor, he was a short and ugly one-legged man with a short, ugly temper, given to spurts of *dementia praecox* and, at times, to beating his wife. Otherwise, he is an unknown factor. But there we were, blossoming into Ashmores and Dinwiddies and Hitchings at each successive decade, branching from a one-legged man throughout the heart of East Tennessee.

Few of us ever leave home, or ever want to, save for those men who fight our country's battles overseas and who become lieutenants or heroes, or else become dead. We like it here; we like it fine, thank you. In fact, my Grandfather Ashmore, a very wise man in his way, once pointed out that if you took the state on its easternmost edge and lifted it, like a rug so to speak, everything and everyone in Middle and West Tennessee would go tumbling off into the Mississippi, but East Tennesseans would be caught by the mountains, would just burrow deeper into the hills. Of course,

---

"The Snipe Hunters" from *From the Bottom Up*, by Leigh Allison Wilson. Copyright © 1983 by Leigh Allison Wilson. Reprinted by permission of The University of Georgia Press.

it would greatly facilitate our state's commerce, which is known for its cotton and other goods, to have everything bleed out naturally and quickly onto the Mississippi where large, empty boats are always waiting.

My grandfather has many such good ideas. When he really gets going they tumble from his mouth like watermelon seed. Sometimes they even clog up, due to a faulty gum plate that slips onto his tongue along with two front teeth. He is an eighty-nine-year-old man with none of his faculties impaired, unless, of course, teeth are a faculty. Just on general principles, I believe he will never die.

The thing is, I go to see him today. This morning Timothy came around my office with a note from Grandfather inviting me over for supper. He is an odd one, this Timothy, partially because he blew half his head off in a Russian roulette game twenty years ago, and therefore scattered most of his wits into random pockets throughout his brain. But every once in a while a circuit will connect and then Timothy will have the uncanny sense of a terrestrial demon. For example, this morning he hung around my desk after giving me Grandfather's note, just to make sure no money would change hands. I send my grandfather fifty dollars every week like clockwork, a fact of which Timothy is vaguely aware and is driven to investigate. Sometimes I give him five dollars and he says, "Direc'ly," meaning he'll take it straight to Grandfather, then he goes and buys soda pop and picture postcards. He is a collector of sorts, and the walls of his room in Grandfather's house are covered with ten-cent scenic views.

"Thank you, Timothy," I say, when he hands me the note. His black head has a bell-shaped aspect since pieces of it have been forfeited by bullet, and he holds his chin in the loose support of one black hand.

"Mmm," he says and shuffles forward until his thighs rest against the desktop. "Mmm."

"*Thank* you." He nods and grins and stands there, cupping his chin with a quizzical-keen expression. At times I believe he is more sane than anyone I have ever met. For a fact, my grandfather enjoys his company.

"You better get back to the house, Timothy, it's almost lunchtime." He nods seriously, suddenly aware that his mission is accomplished and he must leave empty-handed. Instantly he assumes his dead expression, vacant eyes and slack mouth, an expression that effectively wards off all outside communication.

"Night," he says, meaning "goodbye," and away he shuffles, chin in hand.

I look at Grandfather's note again. It can mean only one thing: he has broken a code of some sort. This is a game we have played for years, twenty to be exact, and we are quite serious about it—dead serious, in fact. My grandfather and I are snipe hunters.

I experienced my first snipe hunt when I was eight years old, and after

I told Grandfather about it we developed the game. This is what happened. Some friends of mine from the grade school invited me on a hayride through Dumplin Valley, located in the northeast corner of Jefferson County. A little past sunset they came by and picked me up and off we went in the bed of the haywagon. They were giggling and whispering and shutting flashlights on and off at the dirt road that oozed by ever so slowly behind the wagon. Something was up. When we got to Dumplin Valley, a place out in the middle of nowhere with stiff pine forests that jut out like fangs into the sky, when we got there, the wagon pulled off at the side of the road and stopped. Everyone clambered out. Except for the flicker of flashlight, the night was as thick and dark as bear's fur. Over by the wagon cab, Ernest, somebody's big brother, lit a cigarette and his face shown pale and bored. The company of eight-year-olds was probably beneath his dignity.

"We're going to hunt snipes, Elizabeth!" someone shouted and everyone cheered. There was an excitement in the air, an excitement akin to the smell of roasted meat right before dinner. With the flashlights bobbing and weaving, we set off in a pack into the forest. We walked and walked and occasionally somebody would yell, "I see one!" Then the excitement would mount. I couldn't see a thing, but, of course, I didn't have a flashlight. At last someone found a hole in the middle of a mat of pine needles. Everyone grew almost hysterical over this hole; that was a snipe hole, they said. It was agreed that I would stand guard over the hole while they looked for more holes. So I sat down on the needles and stared, armed with a big stick to beat to death anything that stuck its head out. I stared and stared.

For a few minutes I could make out the glimmer of flashlights and the snap of twigs, but after a while—nothing. It was awfully lonely, the loneliest I've ever been. No moon was out, no stars, no east or west, only this small black hole in the ground out in the middle of nowhere. I was profoundly lost, lost to death, Grandfather would say, meaning "utterly." I grew very familiar with the hole; it seemed to center the strangeness of the entire forest.

Suffice to say, by daybreak I found my way home, hitched a ride into Jefferson City on a tractor. Later I discovered from Grandfather that snipes, a kind of woodcock, have not existed in East Tennessee since the days of the primordial swamp lizards. Then we developed the game. The point of our snipe hunt is the hunt itself. Though snipes do not exist, still you must hunt, you must hunt and hunt or else you are utterly lost, lost to death, without the familiarity of even a small black hole.

So we, Grandfather and I, that is, are always on the lookout for codes, hints, and messages to facilitate the hunt. For instance, just the other day I found an interesting article in the *Jefferson Standard*, our local newspaper which, by the way, has won many state awards for its Republican editorials. Such a newspaper is full of useful hints. This article said: "Due to the frequency of his hoarse and inarticulate elephant cries, the original movie Tarzan has been moved from his double-occupancy room to a private suite in the Oakdale Nursing Home." The point, of course, is not just *what* was said, which may or may not be misleading, but *how* it was said, which is rarely misleading. This, then, is the nature of an undecoded hint. My grandfather loves this particular hint.

I place Grandfather's note in the upper right hand drawer of my desk, filing it carefully under "A." As secretary for a prominent law firm in town—Hale and Hale Associates—I pride myself on the efficient disposal of all information. Both Mr. Hap and Mr. Hap, Jr., as well as several other professional people, have spoken highly of my efficiency. The two years I spent at a prestigious state university left me fairly well-educated and certainly more efficient. In fact, I was once engaged to a fraternity boy there. During the course of an activity known as "rush," however, three of his friends pushed him out a window on the fourth floor of their fraternity house, and his neck snapped like a twig on the pavement below. It was an accident; they were drunk and having a good time. I left the university and went home soon thereafter.

It is a quarter to five. In a few minutes Mr. Hap, Jr. will come into my office and shoot the breeze until five o'clock, then we can all go home. On my desk all papers and folders are neatly aligned at the edges, all pens and pencils tucked away in their respective drawers. The dust cover is snug over the typewriter to my right, warding off the grit that is deadly to a well-oiled machine. I take great pleasure in following the factory instructions to the letter, and consequently this IBM is practically factory-fresh. Other secretaries I know, who will remain unnamed, are inattentive with their machines and therefore constantly wrestle with a hiccupping return button here or a stubborn tab-set there, wasting precious minutes.

Mr. Hap, Jr.'s head suddenly bobs just inside my office door. Suspended in the air, his head reminds me of those carnival kewpie dolls—gleaming bald head, pudgy cheeks, a pinkish smile that won't come unstuck no matter what the wear and tear. He is quite a character, never misses a trick. It is common knowledge that his father forced him into the law practice, but because of his flexible nature, he has made a good show of it. Unfortunately, he shows no knack for making money, a bone of contention between him and his father.

"Ding-dong," he says and the pink lips part slightly. "The world ends in six and a half minutes." He is in his silly-serious mood, smiling and smiling, entering the office with his arms flung over his head like a grown Chicken Little. As if to assess the state of affairs, his eyes dart back and forth across the top of my desk until, apparently satisfied, he edges closer and swings a hip onto the lip of the typewriter stand. Though half-sitting, he appears to be in perpetual motion. He never misses a trick and everything is a trick not to be missed. For the life of me, after every conversation with Mr. Hap, Jr., I can never remember a word that was said.

"What a day," he says, expelling some air, juggling his vision between me, the desktop, and the window to our left. I wait for something more to go on.

"That Devotie case is going to blow up any day now. Judge Hanson's fit to be tied and me running my legs off between the courthouse and city hall. I tell you what, it's been a real day." He sucks in some breath that whistles hollowly inside his cheek; his eyes rove the room and come to rest on his wristwatch. In a flash his body is back in motion, standing upright, moving off toward the door.

"Let's go home," he says and is gone.

The smell of his after-shave lingers in the office, then succumbs to the more pervasive scent of metal and ink. In seconds there is no trace whatsoever left of Mr. Hap, Jr. Grandfather would say that he is one of the lost people, hasn't a clue and doesn't even know it. I pick up my handbag, cross through the office, through the anteroom and on outside the office building. Mr. Hap will lock up later this evening, after the sessions court closes. Interestingly enough, all thefts in Jefferson County occur after a lock has been forced; an unlocked door in this county is as good as four large policemen armed to the teeth. As my grandfather says, there is always the taint of an unknown behind unlocked doors, while a locked door merely presents a duty in the course of a criminal job description.

O, but it is a fine day, a snipe hunt kind of day. Great pregnant-looking clouds are swelled to bursting over the southwest horizon, and the sharp point of a flock of geese pricks the outermost cloud, disappears inside, heading farther south. The streets are full now with people off work and going home. I know most everyone and receive businesslike nods from the men, flickering smiles from the women. But I am busily hunting among them. The danger is that, by becoming too familiar with one's surroundings, things recede into invisibility—they do not exist and, by extension, neither do you. So I keep a sharp lookout, not a moment's lapse of attention for me, thank you.

To get to Grandfather's house I need only walk down Main Street, then take a right onto Dogwood. All the storefronts on Main boast bulky-knit sweaters and heavy galoshes, anticipating winter by two months; it is all a person can do to hold tight with the present. I notice Miss Ruby Lee Prigmore eyeing the winter lingerie in the Belk department store window, sizing up, testing seams with her discriminating shopper's glance. All small towns have their local gossips, and Miss Ruby is ours. She has known my family since the days of Grandfather's youth, and occasionally she corners me to pump for more up-to-date information. However, at the moment she is engrossed in lingerie, but—no—she shifts her field of vision in my direction, her radar as keen as any bat's.

"Elizabeth, dear," she says, eyes sizing me up though her mind has shifted gears from lingerie to information.

"I was just telling Sarah the other day, I said, 'Sarah, it's been ages since I saw that Elizabeth Ashmore, and I wonder what she's up to.' I said those very words. And here you are, big as life."

"Yes'm."

"And where are you off to, young lady, some gentleman no doubt, some dark, handsome stranger?"

Miss Ruby would like to see me get married although she and her sister remain unmarried with a vengeance. A story floats around town that Miss Ruby was once engaged to a man from Knoxville, a Fuller brush man, who during the course of an intimate dinner asked Miss Ruby whether or not her eyelashes were fake or real. Affronted, Miss Ruby said, "Pull one of the damn things and see," and the man was never seen in town again. Possibly he changed his sales route. Nevertheless, Miss Ruby and Miss Sarah love a big wedding and are present at all but spur-of-the-moment elopements.

"No'm, I'm going to supper at Grandfather's."

"O yes, fine man your grandfather, a fine man. His health . . ."

"Fine," I say, but this is not what she wants to hear, having a keen interest in minor ailments, malignant cancers, and hardening arteries. "Fit as a fiddle," I say.

"Yes, of course, no doubt." She is gathering momentum, building up a relentless pressure that will expend itself in the next question. The minute you begin to squirm, however, she pounces, and so one must keep one's demeanor wholly intact.

"And your mother, poor thing, is there any . . ."

"The same, no change at all, Miss Ruby."

I do not know my mother, and therefore this question is not squirming material, although it is indeed of great interest to the nitty-gritty of Miss Ruby's world. Exactly three months after I was born, my mother suffered a near-fatal automobile accident that left her a complete vegetable in the Cumberland Mental Hospital. I visit her twice a year even though she does not know me and never will; I do not exist for her and, in essence, she does not exist for me. During my visits, I have noticed that she is steadily turning yellow over the years, yellow as summer squash.

"It's tragic is what it is, truly tragic. I was telling Sarah this morning just how tragic your mother really is. Your whole family is probably Jefferson City's one unwritten tragedy."

She is referring to my father now. We have run the gamut of possible information leaks, and soon Miss Ruby will dismiss me for larger game. I barely remember my father. He was a short man with large, capable hands that he often put to use on my bottom for the least domestic infraction. We lived together out in the country and my father used to ropewalk every day across a ramshackle railroad trestle in order to get to the post office more quickly. One day he fell thirty feet onto a slab of Tennessee marble. It was billed a fluke accident, but even at six I knew the real story. I grew up in Grandfather's house on Dogwood Street.

"Well good to see you, dear. Looking well, very well, considering." Miss Ruby places a finger beside her nose and stands and considers me.

"Yes, quite well. Do stop in on Sarah and me, Elizabeth, we're just two lonely old women in need of company. Stop in anytime between six and eight on Mondays or Fridays. We'd love it."

"Good afternoon, Miss Ruby," I say, but she is stalking away, legs pumping up and down, making a beeline for Ramona Stewart, the local beauty school operator, who is crossing the street in her honey-yellow raincoat. Ramona, like Miss Ruby, is chock-full of tragic insights into our town and they barter them, slyly, between them. Grandfather asserts that the two of them have one foot in the grave, so lost that they exist on sheer determination, and a certain tenacity to which they adhere their pieces of information.

I turn onto Dogwood Street, suddenly rich with the crisply-cool smell of maple trees and dying purple rhododendron. The white front porches grin and grin from out of the dusk, the grasses of lawns bristle with a deep green promise. The light itself writhes in the sky against the horizon, then falls to earth in beckoning tendrils. Lord! it makes a body feel alive—this is my home. Yet even here or, rather, especially here, one must keep one's wits about; danger is everywhere. As a matter of fact, across the street is the house where my kindergarten teacher, Miss Nancy—a nice lady, by the way, who would giggle at our jokes even without the punch line—where Miss Nancy took a shotgun and blew her brains out right in her own front yard while half the neighborhood strolled to church on a Sunday morning. The story goes that she left a note which explained to the county medical examiner, and to the county, she just couldn't keep her kitchen floor clean anymore and so bedamned with it.

Suicide is popular in this county and is second only to automobile accidents as a vehicle for unnatural death. It is a clue that neither I nor my grandfather have overlooked, I assure you, though indeed it is more than a clue: It is the very reason we are snipe hunters. Not to be a snipe hunter is to throttle your own throat day after day, is to be, in a word, a suicide. For if you don't at least hunt for the snipes, you can never know that the hole is profoundly empty. You are already dead by your own hand, you do not exist. The point is to hunt on for *dear life*. All else is a deadly prank. All others dead pranksters. Grandfather has pointed out, and I agree, that we two are perhaps the only living adults in the entire county.

There sits Grandfather's house, encased in a line of poplars that stand like proud sentinels over a treasure. Timothy will open the door and Grandfather will step over, peck a kiss on my forehead, his eyes wide and surprised, and he will pretend that I'm the last person he ever expected to see, as well as the most welcome. Last week I found him on his knees in the study, oiling an ancient, broken rocking chair, a madman with flying rags and linseed oil. His eyes watered and he seemed to caress the chair in his haste: the chair was a message. This was his father's chair, he said, eyes sweating great rounded water, found it at the Salvation Army. I happen to know that Grandfather's father chased him at gunpoint from their home in Dandridge, when my grandfather was fifteen, and they never spoke nor saw each other again.

As soon as I cross the front yard, I can smell it, something gone wrong wafting from the house through the night air. On the porch I can see it, parked inside the garage (where no car is supposed to be) and wedged into the shadows, ticking strangely, like a clock. It is the fat man's Buick.

My Uncle Ashmore is notable for two reasons: he is my father's brother and he is a short and ugly fat man, so fat that his eyes and eyelashes are approximately the same things on his face. After my grandmother's funeral, when I was eight years old, Grandfather stalked home, swallowed a bottle of aspirin, then lay down on my grandmother's bed to die. Uncle Ashmore and Aunt Mildred conducted a series of skirmishes downstairs among the in-laws, everyone laying claim to the land, the house, the kitchen utensils when, finally, Grandfather jumped out of bed, ran downstairs brandishing a piece of firewood, shouting: "I'll break your knave's pate you fatherless son-of-a-saint!" and then Uncle Ashmore retreated, troops in tow, out of the house. Soon thereafter we became snipe hunters by mutual consent.

Timothy answers the door and, immediately, I can see a crisis at hand. With both palms cupping his chin, like a terrified child, he minces back and forth across the threshold. "Lord Lordy!" he says, meaning "trouble." The last time Timothy said "Lord Lordy!" there was three feet of water in the basement and he held a drowned rat in both hands. He stops mincing and comes closer, mouth to my ear.

"Lord Lordy!" he whispers confidentially, then grabs the back of his pants for a steadier stance.

"It's all right, Timothy," I whisper, but he moves quickly up the stairs and disappears. They are in the library down the hall, the fat man's drone welling out from inside. Framed by the library doorway is a ceiling-to-floor case of books that appears to lean uncomfortably against the wall.

I have not noticed this before and will certainly attend to it shortly. It would not do to have such a bulk of books collapse upon some innocent passerby.

"Lizzie! I'll be damned"—it is Uncle Ashmore, smiling profusely, his face so swelled I envision his lash-eyes bursting apart to reveal two empty sockets—"Look Mildred, it's Lizzie herself."

"Good evening, Uncle Ashmore, Aunt Mildred." They perch as best they can on a sofa, Tweedledee and Tweedledum grown to mammoth proportion. The sofa visibly sags, and Uncle Ashmore is making quick, furtive glances toward the fireplace. Grandfather sits in his father's chair, rocking it lazily with a thin-lipped smile on his face. In three steps I am beside him, kiss his cheek, then I move off to an easy chair, settling into it.

"Looking real good, gal," Uncle Ashmore says, "just real good. Mildred, just look at our Lizzie, grown right up is what she's done."

"Right up," Aunt Mildred says and studies some difficulty in the hem of her skirt.

"That's just what I say," says Uncle Ashmore. "Lord how time flies," he says, glancing toward the fireplace.

"Time flies," I tell Grandfather and he nods and smiles, thinly.

"What was that?" Uncle Ashmore says. He looks quickly at me and then at Grandfather. "I missed that one," he says.

"I said: 'Time flies.'"

"O yes, it do, indeed it do." The atmosphere is strangely akin to a high-pressure salesroom, Uncle Ashmore looks fit to explode out of his fat-stretched skin, and I notice that this easy chair is much more unyielding than I remember. Aunt Mildred is busy picking strings from her cotton hem.

"Elizabeth," Grandfather says, rocking. "James here has spent the day discussing, what *was* your word, James?—a proposition?—discussing a proposition he and Mildred have come up with."

"O, and what is it?" I ask and turn to look at Uncle Ashmore, who becomes quite red and appears to contemplate assisting Aunt Mildred with her hem.

"It ain't a proposition, never said it was. I'd say it's more like a necessity, practical, I'd say." Amazingly enough, Uncle Ashmore has of a sudden become deeply engrossed in my aunt's hem.

"We're practical people," Aunt Mildred says quickly, not looking up.

"Well, what is it?" I ask.

"Well." He rears back and places his hands palm up on his knees in imitation of an honest man from the movies. "You're a smart girl, Lizzie, only person what can talk sense into this old rascal." He pauses, looks shyly in Grandfather's direction, then carefully studies the fingernails of his right hand. Then, as if he can't keep it in any longer, might burst with it, he leans forward: "Sell the house, I say, sell it and let this man rest at last." That said, Uncle Ashmore slaps his knee and returns to his perching position with the facial expression of a man who's just made good sense.

"James wants me to rest at last, Elizabeth, and he wants you to talk sense into me and Mildred, I believe, agrees with James." He keeps rocking, back and up, his smile a tight, thin curve.

"Mildred and me've got it all figured out," Uncle Ashmore says, excitement like the pox all over his face. "We'll do all the organizing for the auction. Get a good price, too, in this neighborhood. Then we'll take this man to a place Mildred and me found in Memphis this summer, most beautiful place you ever saw, weather always fine, 'mongst people with the common interests. You should see the care they take with their people, doctors and checkers and dancing every weekend. Damn near made *my* mouth water. It's what he deserves, too, and about time he got it." Uncle Ashmore has become downright angry with the rush of his own train of thought, and then immediately he becomes bashful, hanging his head, as if such a show of emotion were unbecoming to a grown man. I realize that my hands are somehow driven deeply into the cushions of the easy chair.

"Is that it?" I ask.

"Yes," he says, "except a course the details come later. Now don't it make sense, Lizzie, him here all alone in a house too big for him, you out on your own, and him all alone in this great big house? Don't it make sense?"

"Practical, I'd say," Aunt Mildred says. They both stare at me with whatever lies behind their lashes. Grandfather just rocks, eyes closed and smiling, thinly and tightly smiling.

"Get out of here, please," I say, quite calmly. "Will you both please leave this house, please?"

"Hold on now, Lizzie," Uncle Ashmore says. "This is new and all, think it out, try it on for size."

"Timothy!" I shout and, miraculously, he appears in seconds. I point toward Uncle Ashmore and Aunt Mildred, then toward the library door. "Show my uncle and aunt to the front door, would you."

"Mmm," he says and grins and points a bent arm toward the library door, shuffling up to within inches of Uncle Ashmore's feet.

"Sure," Uncle Ashmore says, loudly. "O sure, we can take a hint." Already Aunt Mildred has teetered to her feet with a sniff and is waddling in the direction indicated by Timothy's finger. "Get one thing straight you, you cash register." Uncle Ashmore flings a hand toward Grandfather, shouting now: "This man's old and incompetent and he's taking that trip west, O yes, law's on my side this time. Talked to a lawyer and I got the court in my pocket. You're all goddamned crazy and the whole town knows it. Hell! that idiot standing there with his arm crooked and his head half gone is enough to prove it."

"Thoroughly enjoyed your visit, James," Grandfather says. "Always remember that my home is your home and do come see us again soon." He stops rocking.

Uncle Ashmore rises to his feet, his breathing harsh, and pushes Timothy roughly aside, apparently digging out from the room a space for himself to breathe.

"Crazy sonsabitches," he says and is gone.

The three of us remain motionless until the sound of the fat man's Buick ticks out of hearing, then Timothy breaks out into an elaborate frown. "Night Lord Lordy," he says and then abruptly we are all laughing, slapping our thighs, hooting an unbroken tattoo of simpleminded hoots. But after a while, we hush.

"Grandfather," I say.

"Elizabeth?" he says.

"I believe I'll fix that bookcase, it looks a trifle unsteady."

"You're right, by God," he says, looking. "It's warped around the edges."

"Grandfather," I say.

"Yes," he says.

"Let's leave it be."

"Yes, of course, we won't touch it. We won't even think it."

And then my grandfather, who will never die, not so long as I live, not so long as the mountains and valleys of East Tennessee live, commences to rock. For we, my grandfather and I, are snipe hunters.

David Daniel

December Portrait
for Staŕenka

There are wet blades of grass bending
over her feet, old feet,
hard and beaten

like veined yellow stones
placed sometime beneath
our blossoming branches.

It is May there, and no traces
of winter cling
to our conversation

which now, I think, is forgotten
or hushed
beneath an inch or two of snow.

Fallen beside us, my grandmother's
gloves are still
curled and brown and strong.

But by this time of year, those weeds she missed
have surely died as she did
despite the interruption of this photograph

"December Portrait," by David Daniel appeared in *The Cumberland Poetry Review*, Vol. III, no. 1, Fall 1983. Copyright © 1983 by *Cumberland Poetry Review*. Reprinted by permission of the publisher.

and the coming on of evening
to the west
which shadows her face

with grey streaks of poplar
that confuse her
and the landscape

which cracks with my weight
as I walk out, warm and discreet,
into a December evening.

Kiernan Davis

Roach Bait

She is my blood. I mean blood, as in relation. Sister. Bone and flesh as my own. But we are not the same.

I watch out the kitchen window as she moves, a rolling walk, bubble fleshed curves, across the gallery to the porch post. White skinned, red hair a hot lick along her bare neck.

I can see my husband, Bennie, watching her, sucking her up whole and sticky as a marshmallow gone soft in the sun. Inhaling her with open eyes onto his brain. Turning her over and over with his staring.

I paw the sweat off my temple with the back of my wrist, plow the bread dough forward with my palms. It caves in and rolls towards the windowsill like a boneless thigh, pale, and fleshy smooth.

Bennie halts his glider, glances through the window at me. He crosses his legs and scatters his attention towards the lumps of furry hills to the east, beyond the porch.

They don't love on each other like human folk, but like insects do. Shuffling. Stifled Hunkered up in mindless wanton on the pantry floor. Roaches.

I heard it and I saw it. Two roaches in my pantry, under a naked light bulb. The door kicked ajar by a straining, pumping leg. A mistake, in the silent dark kitchen. What God's little ugly critters, his low crawling things do, when his human souls go to bed for the night, and the crawlies come out to get what's been left over. To take what's forgotten, what hasn't been sealed tight against them. Crumbs, on the floor. Flour, in a can.

They had stole away. Him, slipping from my bed. Her, from the guest room. And had joined with the skittery low beings that hide in daylight and creep and grapple with one another in the night.

"Roach Bait," by Kiernan Davis appeared in *Passages North*, December 1985. Copyright © 1985 by Kiernan Davis. Reprinted by permission of the publisher.

I could no longer see Bennie as I had known him, when he was a tall man, standing upright. I could no longer count her equal to me. Her blood, not mine, had metamorphosed from red to black. Shiny. Beetle-backed. Clicking winged.

The sunlight fooled us all, casting illusions of man and woman, full-bodied, soul-filled, grown large in daylight upon the porch. If a cloud should pass over, an eclipse of the sun, their antennae would appear, wiggle with insect smelling, searching out one another across the distance. Bug-eyed.

I flatten the dough, rolling it, turn it over, roll it again. Bennie loves my breakfast rolls. Before she came, he would stand in our kitchen and run his finger along the bread board gathering gummy residue, butter and cinnamon flecked, on the tip of his nail and slip it off into his mouth. Eat them warm from the oven. Hardly could spare enough for tomorrow's breakfast.

He stands, and again, looks at me through the window. I pour the warm butter on the thin skin of dough, carefully guiding it to the edge. I keep a clean board, a clean house. He crosses the porch, standing behind her, rubbing his hand along the rail, speaking to the back of my sister's ear. I see his lips move. Filthy talk. They will meet again when night comes and they assume their shapes.

I scatter the cinnamon heavy, loaded down with sugar to hide the taste. You have to be smarter than a bug.

Bake them, set them out on a plate with the plastic cover just loose enough to let the sweet scent fill the pantry. I will put them on the floor where they can get at them.

David Huntley

Gerald at the Fair

The summer air rolls
with scuffed field dust, with breeze
from a slow storm approaching
the second night of the fair.
Gerald walks the boardwalk
as if drunk, a slow weaving.
Winding past the cotton candy stand
he belches at high school girls
older than him, and prettier,
who deign to whisper "asshole"
as he passes. He pretends his role,
is not drunk, never was. Why,
Gerald couldn't ask to buy
a bottle without nervous gutterals.
When he is alone in the dairy tent
he senses the hour and knows
his mother will worry, yet he pats
the belly of a Guernsey, whisks
his lips past the fine hair
of the cow's ears and is happy.
Leaving the fair he will pause again
by the live dancing girls tent
set against the parking lot's edge,
where neon bulbs flash
to the beat of his racing heart,
where white tee-shirted teenagers
laugh and will want to
hit him hard all over
in the dark lot that reaches
beyond the fair's noise.

The Making of Voice

I listen to the rising
of Grandfather's voice
while he talks of the first
of the family to understand how seasons
fall together this side of the Atlantic.
They never planned on coming;
too young, with child coming, they fled
to marry on this rolling shoreline.
The way he tells it we needed such
beginnings to people the land with us.
I stand, unnoticed, and watch my father
hold Grandfather's every turn of breath
in memory, taking in the quivering words
before the talking quiets to sleep,
before Grandfather grows unable to form
the long cadences moving his story's length,
before his joining of story to story ends
in a last pause from which my father
will pick the tale up and tell on. Later,
lights out, touching the wide doors
central to the house, I wait to hear
the stories my father will bring to me,
know that even now he is sleepless
in the next room, folding words together
with his round lined mouth that opens
to the air as if in imitation
of his father's voice.

Madison Smartt Bell

The Day I Shot My Dog

The dog was suffering, mainly from old age. She was twelve, thirteen maybe? I couldn't remember for sure. She was a Doberman, black and tan but going gray now, a brush of white hair running the ridge of her back, which was mounded with knots of muscle and some new lumps which were tumors. My dog had cancer. She was also blind in one eye, and had little taste for life left in her. A vigorous fighter and hunter in her prime, she now lay day-long on the pad I'd made for her in front of the stove, unable to drag herself up and out, uninterested in doing that.

Once a day I could coax her out for a walk. We'd take a turn around the place, the dog limping badly from a tumor behind her left shoulder, but wanting to go. The place had gone to seed too. All the fences were down, almost, but that didn't matter so much, since there was hardly anything to keep in. No more horses, that barn stood empty. In or around the second barn, about a half mile from the house down a little lane and through a couple of broken gates, I still had a few sheep and I'd take the dog with me in the evening to put out a little molasses for them, though they were half wild anyway and didn't particularly care if I showed up or not.

On one of these little outings I was in the feed room dipping a coffee can into the molasses bin, and there was a rat in there, a fat gray one—I stabbed down with the edge of the can without thinking, broke its back but didn't kill it. Now I had a paraplegic rat in the molasses bin, and I couldn't quite bring myself to hit again, finish it off. This is what I have a dog for, I thought then. I tipped the bin and the rat fell out in the trampled mud in front of the feed room and began trying to drag itself up under the barn, using its front legs only. The dog crippled after the rat,

"The Day I Shot My Dog," in slightly different form, is part of the forthcoming novel, *Available Light*, by Madison Smartt Bell. Copyright © 1986 by Madison Smartt Bell. Reprinted with permission of John Farquharson Ltd., N.Y.

did catch it, did kill it. Then she took it off somewhere to maul it and bury it. Probably that was the most fun she'd had in a year, but a broken-down dog catching a broken-down rat was too much for me to contemplate, and I knew I had to do something.

There were plenty of guns in the house; my father had left them there. When I got back I dug out a rifle and cleaned it and found a box of shells. The dog had stayed out with her rat and sometime after dark I heard her dragging herself up the porch steps, one step at a time. I let her in and she limped over to her pad. I built a fire in the stove for her; it was May and we didn't need it, but she liked a fire.

Do it and get it over with, was what I told myself the next morning. I called the dog and she stood up shakily, looking at me and then at the rifle. Her blind eye, the left one, had swelled and turned a light marble blue, and it always seemed to be looking at something, the next world, perhaps, or something else I couldn't see. The sighted eye, a soft gold brown, looked at the gun and said no to it. The dog lay back down and wouldn't get up again, not even when I took the gun and went a little way into the yard, hoping to fool her out of the house that way.

There went another day, and the day after I got a leash on her and got her in the car and drove her off to the vet, something she hated. I parked outside the place and led her into the waiting room, where she skittered around a minute or two on the slick linoleum, legs slipping out from under her right and left, before I persuaded her to sit down. There were a couple of other dogs there with their owners, and it's a measure of her misery that she didn't offer to fight any of them. She just crouched there, trying to sit down and not touch the floor at the same time. I was glad we didn't have to wait very long.

The vet knew me and knew my dog; he'd been treating her for years, and dogs I'd had before, and dogs my family'd had. So when we took her back he didn't even bother putting her up on the table.

"You want her put down," was what he said, a statement not a question. My dog was squatting on the floor against my leg and I could feel her trembling.

"I was going to shoot her myself yesterday," I said. "She saw me pick up the gun and she wouldn't come out with me."

"Gun shy?"

"Didn't use to be," I said. The vet looked at me for a long time. I'd known him most of my life and now he was getting older too, fifty or fifty-five he must have been. His hair was running back at the sides and a big blue vein had popped out of his forehead and forked over the bridge of his nose.

"This is not something I'm supposed to do," he said finally. "I could lose my license. You know that."

"Oh, that's all right," I said. "I'll figure out something," I flicked the leash and the dog got up, looking a little happier than she had been, thinking she might get out of there without anything horrible happening.

"Wait a minute," the vet said, and he left the room and shut the door behind him. It was a very average little cubicle, not much different from a doctor's examining room, with a sink and table but no chairs. There were a couple of tin cabinets on the wall and next to them a faintly humorous print featuring cats. I was looking at that when the vet came back. He had a heavy-duty syringe in his hand with what looked like about ten cc of some lethal mauve-colored liquid.

"A big muscle's best," he said. "The hip or the shoulder."

"You sure it's okay?" I said. He looked at me; he wasn't going to answer that. I picked up the syringe, which was capped.

"Wait," the vet said. He handed me a little paper sack to carry the syringe out of the office with.

"I appreciate it," I said, and it was true. It had been a long time, I realized in the car, since I'd had a disinterested favor from anyone, though of course that might well have been my own fault.

Back at the house the dog and I went our separate ways till late in the afternoon. Then I went out to the shed beside the house and got a shovel. The dog fell in with me as I started toward the back of the place. She was moving a little better, I thought, stiff but steady, a sort of marching pace. From the lane to the sheep barn I could see the sun dropping down behind the far end of my biggest field, the field green and turgid with spring rain. In her younger days the dog had spent hours running that field, trying in splendidly idiotic wonderment to catch meadowlarks on the wing. My pleasure in the grace of her movement had been almost as great as her own, though of course that wasn't something to think about now.

I threw out the molasses for the sheep, with the dog sitting down to watch and panting rather heavily, though it wasn't really very hot. There was a new lamb that day, I just barely noticed. It looked like it would make it without being put up. I went through a gate at the back of the lot and into a sort of thicket that ran up the edge of the hill field. The dog followed along at her workmanlike trot. We broke into the open again just above the sheep lot fence and the pond, above the first of the three terraces too. The hill was steep and it had been terraced years before to keep it from washing out altogether. By the time I reached the second terrace the dog had fallen behind. At the third terrace I had to stop myself. I dropped the shovel and leaned on my knees, panting like the dog. Here in the upper reach of the pasture there were more buckbushes than grass this year. My family had reclaimed this land, and I was letting it go to ruin, but there we are. I climbed more slowly to the brow of the hill, and stopped where the ground leveled off. A few yards further was another fence and woods ran back from it to the crest of the hill and down the other side. I stopped where I was and began to dig.

The dog was coming up more slowly, stopping now and then to rest and zigzagging across the slope to make the grade easier. She reached me before I was half-done with my hole, walked past without interest, and flopped down on her side, a position which made the tumor under her shoulder more prominent. I remembered in spite of myself how fresh-turned earth had once affected her as vividly as a drug.

There'd been a lot of rain so it wasn't hard digging, and I wasn't asking a big hole of myself, just one deep enough to discourage the buzzards. It wasn't long, not really long enough, before I got it three feet deep, and I put down the shovel. The dog was sitting up now and I went and sat crosslegged on the grass beside her. After a moment I drew her head down into my lap and began to rub her ears at the base, which she loved. At the same time, with my other hand, I slipped the big vicious syringe out of my shirtfront where it had been riding and jabbed it into her shoulder. The dog shivered a little and looked up at me with her live brown eye and that other-worldly blue one, but she didn't match me with the pain. I was the person that was rubbing her ears, after all. I pushed in the plunger and two seconds later I had a dead dog on my hands.

I sat there for quite some time with the dog sprawled over my lap, and while I was sitting there it got dark. There was an excellent view from the hilltop. Scrub was creeping into the pasture from both sides of the cleared field, and on the southern side the woods ran back out of sight, hiding the road which was my border there. But I was looking down to the west, over the pond with sheep gathered around it no bigger than toys, past the road that bordered two sides of the big front field. There were lights starting to come on in the new tract houses on the other side of the road, creeping toward me, it almost seemed. I looked to the north, over the abandoned horse barn to my own house, an old saltbox, dark. There was a hook of crescent moon up above it and as it got darker there were stars emerging too, out of the fading chalk-blue of the sky.

You get over your old dog by getting a new dog, but I understood, sitting there on the hilltop, that I wouldn't have the heart for that this time. I was too washed out, too numb, inert. In eight months I'd be forty, not old, certainly, but not precisely young anymore either. Thinking of that I shifted the soles of my feet together and pressed my knees all the way out to the ground. Light karate workouts I'd kept up over the years made me still able to do little tricks like that, and it was some comfort when I thought of my age, which I seemed to do more and more often these days. On the other hand my left elbow was permanently wrecked with tendonitis. There'd be no cure for that or for other tribulations the years would be careful to bring my way. Also, my wife had left me five months before, though that was neither unexpected nor catastrophic; the marriage had been a bit on the technical side anyway. What was bothering me, I suppose, was the notion that not soon, but eventually, I'd be as dead as my dog was now. Then I got up and buried her and went back down the hill.

Contributors

LISA ALTHER, a native of Kingsport, now resides in Vermont. Her previous books include *Kinflicks* (1976), *Original Sins* (1981), and *Other Women* (1984).

MARILOU AWIAKTA (Bonham-Thompson) is a native of Oak Ridge, a graduate of the University of Tennessee-Knoxville, and now a resident of Memphis. Her books *Abiding Appalachia* and *Rising Fawn and the Fire Mystery* were included in the USIA 1985-86 global tour "Women in the Contemporary World," and "Motheroot" was picked by Alice Walker to head a section of *In Search of Our Mothers' Gardens*.

MADISON SMARTT BELL grew up around Nashville, was educated at Princeton and Hollins, and after a time in New York City now lives in Baltimore. He has published three novels: *The Washington Square Ensemble, Waiting for the End of the World*, and, most recently, *Available Light*; his story "The Naked Lady" was chosen by John Updike for *Best American Short Stories 1984*.

JEANETTE BLAIR was born in Milan, grew up in Humboldt, studied English and journalism at Memphis State, and now resides in Mt. Juliet. She has published poems in the *South Carolina Review*, the *Cumberland Poetry Review*, and elsewhere and is currently completing a novel.

JOHN BOWERS grew up in East Tennessee and has most recently settled in Manhattan, where he is currently teaching at Columbia University and working on a "narrative on Stonewall Jackson" in addition to new fiction. His most recent book *In the Land of Nyx* was published in 1984.

Contributors

MELISSA CANNON is a poet and playwright who was born in New Hampshire and raised in Tennessee. Her work has appeared in various periodicals and anthologies, and her chap-book of poems, *Sister Fly Goes to Market*, was published by Truedog Press in 1980. From 1980-1984 she edited the poetry journal *Cat's Eye*.

ALAN CHEUSE has lived since the late 1970s in Knoxville and has taught writing at the University of Tennessee-Knoxville, Sewanee, and most recently at the University of Michigan. He has published a book of short fiction, *Candace & Other Stories*, and two novels, *The Bohemians* (1983) and *The Grandmother's Club* (1986). Cheuse regularly reviews books for several national publications and for National Public Radio.

ELIZABETH COX is from Chattanooga and now resides in Durham, N.C. Her novel *Familiar Ground*, set in Sweetwater, was published by Atheneum in 1984; her poems have appeared in several regional journals, and her short stories have been cited for excellence by selectors for both *Best American Short Stories* and the *Pushcart Prize* anthology.

DAVID DANIEL calls Murfreesboro his home town. A graduate of Vanderbilt, he is presently a Hoyns Fellow at the University of Virginia, completing an M.F.A. in writing. Daniel has published poems in the *Cumberland Poetry Review* and other journals.

KIERNAN DAVIS resides on Lookout Mountain and was a student at the University of Tennessee-Chattanooga, where her teacher for fiction writing was Luke Wallin. "Roach Bait" was awarded 3rd place in the Associated Writing Programs' Short Fiction Contest for 1985 and was published with the other winners in *Passages North*.

ROBERT DRAKE is a native of Ripley, a graduate of Vanderbilt and Yale, and professor of English at the University of Tennessee-Knoxville. His fiction collections include *Amazing Grace*, *The Single Heart*, and *The Burning Bush*; and his memoir *The Home Place*, subtitled "A Memory and a Celebration," vividly evokes life in rural West Tennessee during the first half of the century.

DON KECK DUPREE holds graduate degrees in English from Vanderbilt and Bread Loaf and has recently had poems published in such prominent journals as *Grand Street* and the *Southern Review*. Now resident in Sewanee, he is putting together a collection of his poems.

WILMA DYKEMAN was born in Asheville, N.C., but has for many years made her home in Newport. She has written notable fiction (*The Tall Woman, The Far Family*) as well as studies of Tennessee rivers and *Tennessee: A Bicentennial History*; a collection of her occasional pieces, *Explorations*, was published in 1984.

JOHN EGERTON, though a Kentucky native, has lived in Nashville for over twenty years, producing in that time five major books (including *The Americanization of Dixie, Visions of Utopia*, and *Nashville: The Face of Two Centuries*), the latest of which, *Generations*, won both the Weatherford Award (1983) and the Lillian Smith Award (1984). He has written numerous feature articles for national journals.

JACK FARRIS, novelist and screen-writer, has recently retired after teaching Romantic poetry at Rhodes College in Memphis for many years. Recipient of The Nissan Motor Manufacturing Corp. USA Tennessee Arts Commission Literary Fellowship for 1986, Farris' most recent books are *Me and Gallagher* (1982) and *From Here to Sundown* (1986).

DANIEL FOLTZ-GRAY, graduate of the University of Pennsylvania and the writing program at the University of Chicago, has taught at Roane State Community College in Harriman since 1977. "Easygoing," a story from the collection that includes "Departed Coming Back," was published in 1985 by the *Minnesota Review*.

DOROTHY FOLTZ-GRAY is a past recipient of the Tennessee Arts Commission Literary fellowship in poetry. Her poems have appeared in such magazines as the *Chicago Review, College English*, and the *Mississippi Review*. She is currently the managing director of Sidewalk Dance Theatre, a modern dance company based in Knoxville.

SHELBY FOOTE is native to Greenville, Mississippi, but has lived for many years in Memphis and written extensively about Tennessee, in fiction as well as history. His three volume *The Civil War* is widely acknowledged as the best narrative account of the conflict, and his six novels (most recently *September, September*) have earned him a high and distinctive place among Southern writers.

JESSE HILL FORD, Alabama native and graduate of Vanderbilt, has set almost all of his fiction in West Tennessee, including *The Conversion of Buster Drumwright, The Liberation of Lord Byron Jones*, and *The Raider*, as well as the much acclaimed short story collection, *Fishes, Birds and Sons of Men*.

Contributors

LEVI FRAZIER, JR., playwright and poet as well as writer of fiction, is writer-in-residence at the Blues City Cultural Center for the Performing and Visual Arts in Memphis, where he has contributed to various local publications and been active in the city's—as well as the state's—literary community.

NIKKI GIOVANNI was born in Knoxville and graduated from Fisk University in Nashville. Although best known as a poet—the most recent of her numerous collections being the highly original *Those Who Ride the Night Winds*—Giovanni's autobiographical study *Gemini*, nominated for a National Book Award in 1973, and her *Conversations* with other black writers such as Margaret Walker have received wide attention.

MALCOLM GLASS is a Floridian who did his graduate study at Vanderbilt and has lived for many years in Clarksville, where he teaches writing at Austin Peay State University. Glass has published poetry and short fiction in a number of national journals; among his several books are *Grab Me a Bus* and *Bone Love*.

ELEANOR GLAZE, a well-known Memphis novelist and screen-writer, is the recipient of a Tennessee Arts Commission Literary Fellowship for 1981; her latest book *Under a Green Moon* joins *The Embrace and Stories* and *Fear and Tenderness*. More than thirty of her stories have appeared in such magazines as the *New Yorker*, the *Atlantic*, and *Redbook*.

JEANNE GUERRERO GORE is a Nashville poet and English teacher who has given numerous local readings and been published in several regional journals, including the *Cumberland Poetry Review*. Her "Poems for Post-War Babies" earned honorable mention in *The Poet's* chapbook competition for 1985.

ROY NEIL GRAVES grew up in Medina and attended Union University in Jackson before earning degrees at Princeton, Duke, and Ole Miss. He has published poems in some thirty different journals and anthologies, and a chapbook *Medina and Other Poems* appeared in 1976. A scholar and critic as well as poet, he teaches English at the University of Tennessee-Martin.

ALEX HALEY grew up in Henning, the West Tennessee hamlet that provides the title for his forthcoming memoir. Haley's first book was his *Autobiography of Malcolm X* (1965); his second book *Roots* not only became a household name but gave crucial impetus to the nation-wide movement to recover and preserve family history.

TOM T. HALL, musician and songwriter, author and raconteur, philanthropist, civic leader, and wit, resides in Nashville but is truly "at home" almost anywhere. Among his uncountable creative projects is putting together a collection of short fiction.

ROBERT HERRING was born in Mississippi but has been settled for a number of years in Murfreesboro where he teaches writing at Middle Tennessee State University. A Tennessee Arts Commission Literary Fellowship winner for 1983, Herring began to receive wide national attention with the novel *Hub* (1981). A new novel, also published by Viking, is appearing in 1986.

DAVID HUNTLEY resides in Nashville where he works as television director for an independent production company. He was named the *Appalachia Journal* Poetry Prize Winner for 1984 and has published poems in the *Cumberland Poetry Review* among other regional journals.

RICHARD JACKSON, editor of *The Poetry Miscellany*, has taught literature and writing at the University of Tennessee-Chattanooga since 1976. A collection of poems, *Part of the Story*, was published by Grove Press in 1983, the same year Alabama brought out his *Acts of Mind: Conversations with Contemporary Poets*. Holder of a National Endowment for the Arts Fellowship among other prizes, he has published poems in *Prairie Schooner*, the *Georgia Review*, *Poetry*, and other national journals.

DON JOHNSON is a widely-published poet who lives in Johnson City and teaches English at East Tennessee State University. "Grabbling" has appeared in *Coroebus Triumphs: The Alliance of Sports and the Humanities* (1985). He has recently published a new collection of poems, *The Importance of Visible Scars*.

MADISON JONES was born in Nashville and studied at Vanderbilt as well as with Andrew Lytle at the University of Florida. His fiction includes several novels (most notably *A Cry of Absence*, 1971) and a collection of short stories, most of which, like his current novel-in-progress, make striking use of Tennessee settings. Jones is writer-in-residence at Auburn University.

H. T. KIRBY-SMITH grew up on the Cumberland Plateau and was educated at Sewanee and Harvard. Formerly editor of *The Greensboro Review*, he has published poems in the *Hudson Review*, *Southern Review*, *Poetry*, *Virginia Quarterly*, *Sewanee Review*, and numerous other journals. He continues to teach at UNC-Greensboro.

Contributors

ETHERIDGE KNIGHT, author of *Poems from Prison*, *Belly Song and Other Poems*, and *Born of a Woman*, has also compiled a significant collection of prison writings, *Black Voices from Prison*, published in 1971. Mississippi-born, Knight was one of five Tennessee writers featured in the Memphis Public Library's *Talking Leaves* video series.

ANDREW LYTLE, Murfreesboro native now living in Monteagle, is author of four novels, a biography of Bedford Forrest, a chronicle-memoir called *A Wake for the Living*, and a collection of critical essays. His novel *The Velvet Horn* and *Stories: Alchemy and Others* have been reprinted by the University of the South, where Lytle was editor of *The Sewanee Review* from 1961 to 1973, and a new collection of his essays is forthcoming from Louisiana State University Press.

CORMAC MCCARTHY was brought to Tennessee as an infant and was reared around Knoxville; he studied at the University of Tennessee. All of his fiction but his latest novel, *Blood Meridian* (1985), is set in East Tennessee, including *The Orchard Keeper* (1965), *Outer Dark* (1968), *Child of God* (1974), and *Suttree* (1979). McCarthy is presently living and writing in the Southwest.

JEANNE P. MCDONALD lives in Knoxville, where she works as a managing editor for publications of the Center for Business and Economic Research at the University of Tennessee. She won First Prize in the short story competition sponsored by the 1983 Cumberland Valley Writers' Conference and has been published in the *River City Review*.

DAVID MADDEN was born and grew up in Knoxville, the setting for his early novel *Bijou* as well as for his latest, *Sharpshooter*. Author of five other novels, a collection of short stories (*The Shadow Knows*), and, among other criticism, A *Primer of the Novel*, Madden has also edited *Remembering James Agee* and *Re-Discoveries*, and continues to teach writing at Louisiana State University.

JEFF DANIEL MARION grew up in Rogersville and now lives by the Holston River near Jefferson City where he teaches writing at Carson-Newman College. A recipient of a Tennessee Arts Commission Literary Fellowship in 1978, Marion has published four collections of poems, most recently *Tight Lines* in 1981.

ROBERT MICHIE, a native of Jackson now living in Sparta, is widely known as "Tennessee's Performing Poet," having traveled throughout the state since 1980 as a regular in the Tennessee Arts Commission's Arts-in-Education Program, and having appeared in numerous festivals and conferences. A collection entitled *The Addie Poems* was published in 1978.

BOB MILLARD works and writes in Nashville, where he has been conspicuously active among writers and literary events for several years, having appeared in the *Nashville Poets' Anthology* of 1978 and having given numerous readings from his work.

SANDRA MOORE, who lives in Paris (Tennessee) with her husband and two daughters, has just completed a collection of short stories while also continuing work on a novel. Her story "Caesar" was published in *Crazyhorse* in 1984.

WENDELL CARL MURRAY was recipient of the Tennessee Arts Commission Literary Fellowship for 1985. He studied writing at the University of Arksansas and has had fiction published in such national journals as the *Yale Review*. He lives and writes in Memphis.

JUDY ODOM is native to Birmingham, a graduate of Birmingham-Southern and Emory, and presently a teacher of English in Johnson City, where she has lived since 1971. Two of Odom's stories appeared in *The Crescent Review* in 1984 and another in a recent Appalachian Consortium anthology called *Footprints on the Mountain*.

JOHN OSIER grew up in West Tennessee, worked as a newspaper reporter for the now defunct *Memphis Press-Scimitar*, and has taught English at various Southern colleges. His first novel *Covenant at Coldwater* was published in 1984, and a second novel *Enemy of the State* is appearing in 1986. He lives with his family in Horn Lake, Mississippi.

GORDON OSING, who has taught poetry and creative writing for more than a decade at Memphis State, has published two volumes of poems: *From the Boundary Waters* (1982), winner of the Walter R. Smith Distinguished Book Award at MSU for that year, and *Town Down-River*, published by St. Luke's Press in 1985.

WYATT PRUNTY, a native of Gibson County, spent much of his childhood in West Tennessee. Now a teacher of writing at Virginia Polytechnic Institute at Blacksburg, Prunty has published two highly-praised volumes of poetry, *The Times Between* (1982) and *What Women Know, What Men Believe* (1986), and has had individual poems in a number of distinguished publications: the *New Yorker, Poetry,* the *New Republic, Ploughshares,* the *Southern Review,* and others.

Contributors

PAUL RAMSEY studied at the University of Chattanooga (now UTC) before taking degrees at Chapel Hill and Minnesota. He has published more than 400 poems (including seven collections) and the latest of his four major critical books is *The Truth of Value* (1985). Spoken Arts of New York has released a recording of Ramsey's accomplished reading of some fifty of his poems. Since 1966 he has been poet-in-residence and professor of English at UTC.

ALISON REED has published poems in more than seventy journals in the U.S., England, and Canada, won several prizes (including an Academy of American Poets prize). and issued two strong collections: *The First Movement* (1976) and *Bid Me Welcome* (1978). A member of the editorial board of the *Cumberland Poetry Review*, Reed has also been active in workshops and readings in the Nashville area.

ISHMAEL REED, who was born and spent his early childhood in Chattanooga, now resides in Berkeley, California. He is the author of six novels (including *Flight To Canada* and *Terrible Twos*), four books of poems, and two books of non-fiction. Among his many awards and recognitions have been a Guggenheim Fellowship and a National Endowment for the Arts Fellowship.

HENRY SAMPLES is a native of Greeneville and a graduate of East Tennessee State. Formerly a statehouse correspondent, now columnist, for the *Johnson City Press*, Samples has been published in *Appalachian Heritage* and is at work on two novels.

GEORGE SCARBROUGH was born in Patty in Polk County, studied in three Tennessee institutions (Lincoln Memorial, UTK, and Sewanee), and as farmer, librarian, and teacher has lived his entire life in East Tennessee, for many years now in Oak Ridge. Scarbrough's *New and Selected Poems*, published by Iris Press of New York State in 1977, collected verse from three earlier volumes.

DAVID SPICER lives in Memphis, where he is publisher of raccoon Books, Inc., *raccoon*, and *Outlaw*. He is also the editor of five chapbooks of poetry: *The Beasts Remembered* (1976), *Paula and the Lions* (1980), *Beautiful Strangers* (1984), *Cowboy* (1985), and *Flying Underwear* (1985).

STEVE STERN is the author of a collection of stories *Isaac and the Undertaker's Daughter*, the title story of which won an O. Henry Award, and a novel, *The Moon & Ruben Shein*, published in 1984. A new collection of stories is forthcoming from Viking Press. Stern lives with his wife, Violet, in Memphis.

Homewords: A Book of Tennessee Writers

JAMES SUMMERVILLE was born and continues to live and work in Nashville, having so far published more of his historical writing (in such places as *Harper's Weekly*) than his short stories, though "Paper Fires" is part of a growing collection.

PETER TAYLOR grew up in Gibson County and in Memphis, though his extensive family connections in both Middle and East Tennessee have helped make him familiar with the whole state. Frequently lauded as the nation's most accomplished writer of short fiction, Taylor continues after retirement from the University of Virginia to reside in Charlottesville. His best-known collections of stories are *The Old Forest and Other Stories* (1985), *In the Miro District* (1977), and *Collected Stories* (1969).

PHYLLIS TICKLE, who grew up in Johnson City and is now editor and publisher of St. Luke's Press in Memphis, received a Tennessee Arts Commission Literary Fellowship for 1984. Widely published as a poet, both in journals and in collections, Tickle has pioneered poetry workshops for children and young people, as well as working in conferences and programs for adults. She and her husband, Sam, are raising a large family on a farm near Millington.

RICHARD TILLINGHAST grew up in Memphis, attended college at Sewanee, and earned his Ph.D. at Harvard, where he studied writing with Robert Lowell. Currently co-director of the writing program at the University of Michigan, he has published three collections of poems: *Sleep Watch, The Knife and Other Poems,* and *Our Flag Was Still There* (which incorporates the long poem "Sewanee in Ruins").

EVA TOUSTER, professor of English emerita of Vanderbilt University, is an editor of the *Cumberland Poetry Review*. Founder of the oldest poetry group in Nashville, which has been meeting twice a month for more than ten years, she has taught poetry writing and given readings at various locations in Middle Tennessee.

ROBERT PENN WARREN, though born and reared in Kentucky a hundred yards north of the state line, has said that he "always felt myself more a Tennessean than a Kentuckian." He attended school in Clarksville and college at Vanderbilt before taking degrees at Berkeley and Oxford. Author of some forty books, three times winner of the Pulitzer Prize, Warren is indisputably Tennessee's most significant man of letters. His latest collection is *New and Selected Poems 1923-1985*.

Contributors

LEIGH ALLISON WILSON was born in Rogersville and has recently been a teaching-writing fellow in the Writers' Workshop at the University of Iowa. *From the Bottom Up*, her first book, published by Georgia in 1983, won the Flannery O'Connor Award for Short Fiction and was subsequently published in paperback in the Penguin Contemporary American Fiction Series (1984).

CHARLES WRIGHT was born in Pickwick and grew up mostly in East Tennessee around Kingsport. His seven major collections of poems to date include *Country Music* (co-winner of the American Book Award for Poetry in 1983) and *The Other Side of the River* (1984). Wright has been awarded numerous prizes and fellowships, including a Guggenheim, and has established himself as our best translator of Italian Nobel laureate, Montale. He currently teaches writing at the University of Virginia.

Homewords has been composed into type on the Compugraphics MCS 100 digital phototypesetter in ten point Sabon with two points of spacing between the lines. Sabon was also selected for display. The book was designed by Cameron Poulter, typeset by BGA Graphics, printed offset by Thomson-Shore, Inc., and bound by John H. Dekker & Sons. The paper on which the book is printed embodies acid-free characteristics for an effective life of at least three hundred years.

THE UNIVERSITY OF TENNESSEE PRESS : KNOXVILLE